L. S. BOURNE is a member of the Department of Geography and Director of the Centre for Urban and Community Studies at the University of Toronto.

J. HITCHCOCK is a member of the Department of Urban and Regional Planning and Associate Director of the Centre for Urban and Community Studies at the University of Toronto.

The Conference on Urban Housing Markets sponsored by the Centre for Urban and Community Studies in October 1977 was the first major conference on housing to be held in Canada since the First Canadian Housing Conference sponsored by the Canadian Welfare Council in 1968.

This volume is at once a record of the Conference and a review of important recent research on urban housing markets and related public policy issues. The book captures the flavour of a lively debate between academics and policy analysts, and the commentaries and discussion sections provide, in non-technical language, a statement of some major questions confronting government policy on housing.

In addition to its use as a record of an important Canadian conference, the book is a valuable collection of recent housing research. The ten papers cover a wide variety of topics ranging from conceptual and methodological issues on the one hand to critiques of Canadian housing policies on the other. They indicate the range of issues which must be taken into account in assessing housing policy. Taken together with the discussion material which helps to focus attention on strategic issues in both Canada and the United States, they provide a useful introduction to current debates over housing policy.

Edited by Larry S. Bourne
John R. Hitchcock

With the assistance of Judith M. Kjellberg

Urban Housing Markets: Recent Directions in Research and Policy

Proceedings of a Conference
held at the University of Toronto
October 27–29, 1977

UNIVERSITY OF TORONTO PRESS
Toronto   Buffalo   London

© University of Toronto Press 1978
Toronto   Buffalo   London
Reprinted 2014
ISBN 978-0-8020-2339-1 (paper)

Canadian Cataloguing in Publication Data

Main entry under title:

Urban housing markets

Conference organized by the University of Toronto
Centre for Urban and Community Studies.
ISBN 978-0-8020-2339-1 (pbk.)
1. Housing – Canada – Congresses. 2. Housing policy – Canada – Congresses.
3. Housing research – Canada – Congresses. 4. Housing – Canada – Finance –
Congresses. I. Bourne, Larry S. II. Hitchcock, John R. III. Kjellberg, Judith
M. IV. University of Toronto. Centre for Urban and Community Studies.
HD7305.A3U73   301.5'4'0971   C78-001600-9

Contents

Urban Housing Markets: Recent Directions in Research and Policy

Introduction

Larry S. Bourne and John R. Hitchcock, Editors

Housing remains a persistent problem for all modern societies. Even in those societies which now seem to have solved the problem of an absolute housing shortage, there appears to be literally no end to the difficulties of rising housing costs, as well as of unequal allocation of new housing and conservation of the old. Now, in Canada at least, a central issue is affordability, that is the ability of society and consumers to pay for the amount and kind of housing which they can or would like to consume. In good times as well as bad, housing persists as an issue of widespread social concern and as a focus for government policy. Moreover, at all times housing absorbs an enormous proportion of our national wealth and its allocation to members of society carries with it substantial implications for the distribution of wealth.

Unfortunately, in Canada, public interest in housing has not been accompanied by a corresponding tradition of research. Although there is now a voluminous list of academic papers, government reports and policy documents on housing, most of the housing research undertaken in Canada has been either highly specific to a given sector or problem, or overly generalized. Moreover, of the valuable research which has been done most has not been widely disseminated, nor has it played a large part in the policy-making process. Often members of the research community, particularly in the universities, are unaware of the questions which the policy sector is asking, and vice versa.

Background to the Conference

With these concerns as background the University of Toronto's Centre for Urban and Community Studies organized a conference on recent developments in research and policy on urban housing markets. The conference was held on October 27-29th, 1977 under the joint sponsorship of the Connaught Fund and Varsity Fund of the University of Toronto. The topical emphasis of the conference was on housing issues and research problems, particularly those of interest to Canada. Participants were drawn from across the country and also included a number of speakers who had recently been involved in policy-oriented research in the U.S.

It was the intention of the organizers to bring together researchers from different academic disciplines and representatives from the private sector, from institutions and from all three levels of government, in an interdisciplinary forum. These diverse groups very rarely meet in Canada, at least in the context of debating housing policy issues and research priorities. Even less frequently do they have an opportunity to exchange ideas and debate differences in research methods and in the interpretation of recent trends. They often act as if they dwell in "separate worlds", to use the phrase of one participant in the conference which became part of the vocabulary of subsequent debates. Yet housing is simply too broad and complex to be the sole province of any one perspective or discipline, or of a single theoretical or analytical approach, government agency or specific interest group.

This mix of background provided opportunities for a substantial and often animated exchange of information, ideas and viewpoints. These exchanges revealed some sharp differences of opinion on what our urban housing problems are, on how these problems have arisen and on the setting of priorities for both research and policy. For most participants the breadth and diversity of the debate represented a unique experience. For some it was an environment not duplicated in Canada since the "First Canadian Housing Conference" held in 1968 under the sponsorship of the Canadian Welfare Council. The proceedings of that conference were subsequently published under the title *The Right to Housing* (edited by Michael Wheeler, Harvest House, 1969).

In part, difficulties of communication arose because of understandable differences in the perspectives of each participant group, but they also derived from simple misunderstandings and confusion in terms and concepts. We hope that the publication of these proceedings may assist in reducing these misunderstandings and in clarifying which differences of opinion are attributable to a confusion in concepts, as well as misinformation, and which reflect the legitimate but often contrasting priorities of each group. We certainly did not expect to see the emergence of a total uniformity of perspective, but some convergence in attitudes and a broadening in awareness of the complexity of housing issues did take place.

The Interrelationship of Housing Issues
The emphasis on the housing markets of urban areas was intended to reflect the

fact that urban housing is part of a complex social environment. It is not meant to imply that the housing problems of rural areas, small towns or of native peoples are unimportant. Indeed these problems are often more critical in relative terms. Instead, the purpose here was to focus attention not solely on housing but on the interrelationships between housing and other phenomena which are generally associated with living in urban areas. These include high land costs, speculation and population densities, as well as highly differentiated systems of transportation, water supply and job location. Urban housing problems and policies cannot be divorced from planning directed at these issues. Even within this broad context, however, neither the discussions at the conference nor the papers in this volume pretend to be comprehensive.

Organization of the Volume

The papers in this volume are arranged in seven sections. In an introductory paper the editors undertake to provide a brief overview of alternative concepts and definitions of urban housing markets, the diversity of local housing markets, and of some of the gaps between research and policy formulation. Section II summarizes the results of the opening session of the conference. John Quigley's lead-off paper is an attempt to document what we have learned about housing markets over the last decade, with particular emphasis on studies of the demand for housing. Following this paper, detailed comments, criticisms and suggestions for further research are given in three commentaries by experts drawn from different disciplines: Larry Smith (economics), William Grigsby (planning) and Jeffrey Patterson (social policy). Each of these comments represents a significant statement on housing research in its own right.

Sections III through VI contain the bulk of the papers submitted to the Conference. In the first paper in Section III, David Scheffman discusses the various factors which produced the boom in land and housing prices in Canadian cities during the early 1970s and compares these trends with the experience of Britain, Australia and the U.S. He attempts to demonstrate that a rapid increase in demand, stimulated by financial incentives, was the principal factor in pushing prices upward. In the second paper, John Bossons examines empirical evidence on the relationship between the demand for housing and household wealth. He argues that wealth is a much more relevant predictor of housing demand than is income.

Section IV is concerned with studies of aggregate housing supply and the dynamics of price changes. In the first paper Larry Ozanne and Raymond Struyk undertake to estimate the price elasticity of supply changes emanating from within the existing housing stock, drawing on research based on U.S. data. This is an extremely complex but important area in which very little research has been done in Canada. As pressures for the conservation of older housing increase, the role of the existing stock in the supply of housing will also increase. Gordon Davies then summarizes the literature on filtering in housing markets. Filtering — the process by which households adjust their housing needs — is an implicit assumption underlying housing policies in North America. Stuart McFadyen and Robert Hobart examine the effect of inflation on the relative financial advantages of owning rather than renting housing.

Sections V and VI take a rather different direction and scale of analysis. In the former, Michael Goldberg outlines the results of a detailed study of developer behaviour in the residential construction industry in Vancouver. This study represents one component of an ongoing experiment in developing a large-scale simulation model of urban development in the greater Vancouver area (the IIPS model). This study is one of the few attempts to introduce behavioural data into large-scale urban models. The IIPS model itself is one of the most ambitious modelling efforts undertaken in Canada.

In the second paper, Eric Moore and Stewart Clatworthy focus on an extremely fine grained level of analysis. They argue the need for data which follow the actual movements of individual households through the housing stock on a year-to-year basis. They then demonstrate the utility of the approach with results deriving from analyses based on an annual population enumeration of Wichita, Kansas. Specifically they are able to document how the prices paid for housing, and indices such as rates of overcrowding, change as households move through the housing stock. They show that substantial variation exists in the housing experience of different types of households, differences which are largely obscured by aggregate data.

In Section VI discussion turns to the social dimension of housing policy. First, Albert Rose examines some recent changes in housing policies in Ontario and their implications for the provision of social housing for particular groups. Rose argues that there has been a major shift in government policy away from subsidies for family and rental housing towards the home ownership market and housing for specific groups such as the aged, who are considered to be administratively more convenient. The escalating operating costs of government-run housing are also beginning to frighten housing authorities and thus to discourage the construction of public housing. Jeffrey Patterson then looks at examples of some of the social and distributional impacts of housing policies more generally in Canada. These two papers pose the question, in explicit form, of how public intervention in housing markets is to be related, in both conceptual and political terms, to the economic or market processes discussed in the first four sections of this book. This question remains largely unresolved to this point, although some progress has been made in identifying areas of common concern.

The final section presents a cross-section of views on the general themes of the conference. Here the editors have drawn on the transcripts from the final session of the conference — which was primarily concerned with current and future research needs and policy problems — in an attempt to illustrate the wide-ranging nature of the debates which took place and to highlight the issues which permeated those debates. The raw transcripts of this session provide a wealth of material but unfortunately their length and often inconsistent quality prohibited their full inclusion here. As a result, we have taken considerable editorial license in selecting and then rearranging the material to bring together discussions on these themes. As anyone who has been through this kind of editing process knows, it presents a frustrating dilemma: how best to strengthen the logical flow of ideas without losing the sense of presence and timing of the key exchanges.

ACKNOWLEDGEMENTS

We wish to thank all those individuals and institutions who helped to produce a very successful conference and thus contributed to the production of this volume. There are too many to thank individually here but we will express our appreciation in other ways. Specifically we should acknowledge the support of the University of Toronto's Connaught Fund, through their grant to the Urban Housing Markets Program, and the Varsity Fund which provided assistance for the expenses of visiting speakers. We also wish to acknowledge the assistance of Blain Berdan, who typeset the volume under difficult time constraints.

I

Concepts and Context

1.1 HOUSING RESEARCH AND POLICY DEVELOPMENT: THEMES FROM THE CONFERENCE

Larry S. Bourne and John R. Hitchcock

The debate on urban housing issues which took place at the Conference reflects a much wider, though not clearly articulated, debate in our society concerning the goals of housing policy. An integral part of this debate is the potential contribution of housing research to the development of housing policy. In both cases there are almost as many perspectives on the issues as there are commentators.

In this introductory paper we do not undertake to catalogue these points of view in detail. Rather, our purpose is to provide a brief overview of the themes which emerged from the conference and thus, hopefully, to provide an organizational framework within which the following papers and discussions can be interpreted. A central feature of the overview is an examination of the value, and limitations, of the concept of urban housing markets as a point of departure for the research and policy debate. We also attempt to document the diversity of local housing markets in Canada and to raise questions on the possibilities for closing the gap between research activity and housing policy formulation. The paper concludes with some speculations on future directions of enquiry.

Themes from the Conference

The principal focus of the papers given at the conference was to be on housing research. Initially we posed a number of broad questions for discussion: What do we know about urban housing markets and what do we need to know? How should we go about finding answers, and what research methods and paradigms are most appropriate? To whom should the results of this research be directed?

Policy concerns were to be given a higher profile than might be expected in a research forum. In fact, and perhaps expectedly so, policy issues increasingly dominated the discussions and debates as the conference progressed. The reasons for this emphasis are obvious: policy priorities clearly shape the development of research, both directly, through the provision of research funds, and indirectly, through an increased awareness of those specific problems which are of social and political concern. Moreover, most researchers have a goal, however long term, that their research should somehow help to clarify policy alternatives. The result, demonstrated in the following pages, is that despite the wide gulf remaining between the research and policy communities, we are considerably closer to understanding the differences in the questions asked by researchers and policy-makers.

Although a large number of basic issues ran through the discussions at the conference and are reflected in the papers in this volume, four dominant themes stand out:

1. What do we mean by urban housing markets and how do different groups view such markets?

2. Are these markets working effectively? Who benefits and who loses?

3. To what extent do housing markets differ between cities (or regions) and how significant is this variation in terms of selecting among policy alternatives, such as housing allowances or construction subsidies?

4. How can communication between the research and policy communities be improved? What kinds of research are most relevant to housing policy?

The Concept of Housing Markets

The term "housing market" itself produced very different responses among the participants. Some took the term literally and strictly, concentrating almost exclusively on research which fell under that label. Others saw housing markets basically as an economic approach to housing research which had considerable shortcomings. Still other participants essentially ignored the term and the focus it was intended to provide. Nevertheless, throughout the conference essentially the same questions — relating to the nature, efficiency and effectiveness of the housing market — kept reappearing. For this reason it is useful here to elaborate on the concept and on the divergent interpretations expressed by participants in this conference.

The concept of an urban housing market was employed as the starting point with three purposes in mind. First, it was to serve as a conceptual framework within which contributions to the conference could be organized. Second, it was to serve as a methodological and analytical focus for the policy issues debated and the research results reported. Third, it served to emphasize the numerous interrelationships between housing and other components of urban development and planning. The utility of the concept is that it forces us to attempt to view the complex systems or processes by which housing is produced and consumed in their entirety. Moreover, the concept of a market is dynamic: it stresses the evolving structure of housing opportunities and transactions in any urban area and the ever changing needs of households. The fact is that the relationships of most interest to us are primarily evident, not at one point in time, but in the way demand (consumers) and supply (building industry and financial institutions) respond to changing conditions over time.

By employing the concept of the housing market as an organizing device we are not, however, asserting that the market works efficiently nor that this market is the only or necessarily the most effective method by which society can allocate housing. These are in fact the subjects of debate. Nevertheless, we are cognizant of the obvious fact that, in our society at least, housing is primarily an economic good which is for the most part transacted through the private market mechanism even though substantial government subsidies are provided.

What is a housing market? An economic market, as most readers know, is a set of procedures for the buying and selling or exchange of goods and services. A housing market, like most other economic markets, represents the interaction of the supply of goods and services and the demand for those goods and services. An urban housing market then specifically focuses this interaction on specific locations and types of environments. How any market actually works is defined by the *terms of trade*, that is the schedules by which supply and demand co-vary, the characteristics of the goods exchanged and the rights or privileges conveyed in the transaction.

It is primarily in reference to the terms of trade that housing markets differ from most other economic markets. For one thing most housing is locationally immobile and thus the consumers must move to the goods rather than the reverse. In the conventional sense there is no market-place. Not only is housing immobile, it is also highly durable. Although there is a finite life expectancy for most housing structures, that life span can be very long. Housing is also expensive, so much so that the purchase of housing is the major investment   decision for most households. At the same time most owners do not sell their houses frequently. Hence the common impression of rapid turnover and high mobility rates in North America requires considerable qualification.

Given physical durability and stability of occupancy, housing markets tend to be dominated by the character of the existing stock of housing. Only a small proportion of this stock enters into the market for exchange over short periods of time. Thus there is always a much greater potential for a disequilibrium to develop between housing supply and demand relative to other more fluid markets. Moreover, because of immobility, the housing markets of geographically distant regions can demonstrate substantial independence, again at least in the short term.

Analytical Perspectives

Although we all tend to talk of "the housing market" there are, if not many different markets, at least many different ways of looking at this market. Perhaps the principal distinction which should be made in defining housing markets is between macro-level and micro-level perspectives. In the former, housing is a sector of the national (or provincial) economy or an element in tables of national investment and social accounts. Research at this scale of analysis has been primarily concerned with accounting for investment levels in housing compared to other sectors (capital markets), the volume of construction activity (housing starts), and the responsiveness (elasticities) of supply and demand to changes in price, income, credit availability, tax provisions, cash subsidies and the like. Several contributors to this volume direct their attention to these kinds of questions.

The second basic type of approach, that dealing with the micro-level, usually refers to the market of a particular region or urban area. Here interest focuses not only on the issues outlined above but on the spatial pattern of housing consumption and on the behaviour of local institutions and social groups. Given the geographic immobility of the stock noted earlier, these localized markets often tend to function in quite distinct ways. Later in this introduction we undertake to document just how diverse such local markets are in Canada. For the moment, however, we should note that this independence does not apply to all factors of housing production and consumption, such as interest rates, economic growth and aggregate levels of demand, which tend to be determined largely at the national level. Independence among local housing markets seems to come primarily from inherited differences in the housing stock, the effect of local policies and political institutions and regional differences in income and demographic structure.

Even if the concept of an aggregate housing market is in theory straightforward, the empirical delimitation of a local market in space and time is not. What are the appropriate criteria for delimiting a local housing market? How far do the boundaries of a large urban housing market extend? Do we simply use the equivalent census definitions for census metropolitan areas and urban agglomerations, concepts which derive primarily from the notion of an integrated labour market? Or do we pick a particular index, such as house prices, and examine the area over which price changes seem to be closely related? Or do we make use of political boundaries, thus recognizing the importance of local public institutions?

Further complicating the issue is the extent to which one can treat an urban area as one single integrated market for research and policy purposes. Is it necessary to disaggregate that area, and the housing units and households which occupy it, into distinct classes or submarkets? If so, how should these classes or submarkets be defined? Are they essentially neighbourhoods or areas of homogeneity in housing type? Must they be spatially contiguous? These kinds of definitional questions are for the most part not addressed directly by the contributors in the volume but, as we argue in the final section, they are central to a number of policy concerns.

An additional component which emerges frequently in the discussions to follow is the extent to which we are primarily concerned with the housing market strictly as a set of *transactions* or processes, primarily defined in economic terms, or with the *outcomes* of those processes. This distinction between process and outcome in turn raises the issue of the efficiency of the market and its effectiveness in achieving certain social goods. The transcripts of the final session of the conference, reprinted here in edited form in Section VII, demonstrate just how different our views are on those questions. Some observers view efficiency in terms of whether changes in transactions in the housing market are responding to given stimuli in what are deemed to be expected directions. For instance, an increase in the tax advantage of home ownership should produce a corresponding shift in demand and thus in the price of owner-occupied housing. Others view efficiency in terms of social effectiveness: that is, who benefits and who loses from changes in the market. These views are not necessarily in conflict; they simply have different problems in mind.

The Diversity of Local Housing Markets

The previous section recognized the relative uniqueness and independence of the housing markets of each urban area. In Canada there is an immense diversity among urban areas in terms of the character of the housing stock, in the basic properties of demand and thus in the definition of housing problems. As one example, table 1 provides selected indices on the size, age, composition, price, quality and rate of change in the stock, and on differences in the levels of household income and population growth which determine demand, for the twenty-two metropolitan areas in Canada as defined in 1971.

One initial difference between local housing markets is of course their size. The total number of dwelling units in these local markets in 1971 varied from over 805,000 units in Montreal and 774,000 in Toronto to under 29,000 in Saint John. The number of additions to the housing stock (completions) also varies: for example, from 30,000 units annually in Toronto and Montreal (in 1976) to just over 800 in Chicoutimi-Jonquière and Thunder Bay. Other indices do not vary as widely, but the differences are still considerable. The average age of the stock, measured in terms of the number of units built before 1920, varied from nearly 38 per cent in Saint John to just over 6 per cent in Edmonton and 9 per cent in Sudbury. The proportion of the stock in single-detached units varied from 23 per

TABLE 1 Regional Diversity in Urban Housing Markets in Canada

Census Metropolitan Area	Size: No. of Occupied Dwellings	Age: % Built 1920 or before	Income: % of Canadian Average	Type of Units: % Single Detached	Price[1]: Median Value (000's$)	Quality[1]: % Units in poor Condition	Growth: % Pop. Change 1961-71	Additions to Stock: Completions, 1976
Calgary	121,100	9.4	114	60.3	38.0	5.0	44.5	6,817
Chicoutimi-Jonquière	29,700	11.9	95	45.8	24.4	16.5	4.8	830
Edmonton	144,505	6.2	111	62.2	39.3	5.2	37.8	8,495
Halifax	59,505	17.5	106	47.7	36.5	8.5	15.1	3,662
Hamilton	146,255	20.3	112	63.6	38.5	6.3	24.3	6,578
Kitchener	66,570	19.3	111	58.2	42.3	2.7	46.5	3,296
London	87,160	25.1	112	60.9	39.8	3.2	26.2	2,081
Montreal	805,435	14.9	107	23.7	27.1	14.6	23.8	26,932
Ottawa-Hull	170,015	15.0	125	46.4	45.2	5.8	31.8	6,556
Québec	127,240	18.9	106	35.3	28.2	7.5	26.8	4,976
Regina	42,585	10.7	100	68.5	28.7	10.8	23.7	2,665
St. Catharines-Niagara	88,885	20.5	104	73.6	32.7	4.9	17.7	2,900
St. John's	29,635	18.4	88	53.4	32.8	7.5	23.6	1,672
Saint John	28,645	37.9	92	44.8	23.2	18.2	8.8	1,866
Saskatoon	38,610	9.5	99	66.2	28.0	10.8	32.3	2,575
Sudbury	39,415	9.1	122	60.2	31.2	10.9	22.0	980
Thunder Bay	32,345	18.0	106	76.1	31.2	7.3	9.8	846
Toronto	773,830	14.2	123	45.9	61.7	4.7	36.9	29,521
Vancouver	345,870	9.4	111	62.6	52.5	5.9	30.9	13,662
Victoria	66,255	16.2	103	64.6	45.4	4.2	25.7	4,345
Windsor	74,090	18.5	118	71.3	31.9	7.2	8.5	1,985
Winnipeg	166,220	20.1	104	63.4	26.1	12.9	6.2	6,340
Metropolitan Canada	3,843,770	15.0	112	48.2	–	–	27.8	139,580
Canada Total	6,030,805	19.9	100	61.2	–	–	18.3	236,249

SOURCES: 1971 Census of Canada; F.I. Hill, *Canadian Urban Trends: Metropolitan Perpectives*, Vol. 2, Copp Clark, 1976; CMHC, *Canadian Housing Statistics*, 1976.

1 CMHC, *Survey of Housing Units*, 1974

cent in Montreal to 73 per cent in St. Catharines-Niagara and 76 per cent in Thunder Bay. The proportion classed as in poor condition varied from 18 per cent in Saint John and 16 per cent in Chicoutimi to less than 3 per cent in Calgary and just over 3 per cent in London. Average price levels (in 1974) varied from $23,000 in Saint John to over $52,000 in Vancouver and nearly $62,000 in Toronto. Average incomes, on the other hand, varied considerably less: from 88 per cent of the national average in St. John's and 92 in Saint John to 122 per cent in Sudbury, 123 in Toronto and 125 per cent in Ottawa-Hull. The growth rates of these metropolitan areas also varied, over the 1961-71 decade, from under 6 per cent for Chicoutimi to over 44 per cent in Calgary.

This diversity suggests that we must study local as well as national and provincial housing markets, and that housing policies must be sensitive to these regional differences. Given the variable character of the housing stock, and of the demands placed on it, a uniformly applied national or provincial policy could, and very likely would, produce very different market responses in different cities and in different parts of the country. This is not to say that we should not have national housing policies, or provincial policies for that matter, but that they have to be applied with a differing combination of elements in different areas. As several of the contributors point out in the last section of this volume, policies which are effective in an urban housing market with a high vacancy rate may be completely inappropriate where the vacancy rate is very low. Nor can the same policies be applied both to an urban area where the major problem is one of cost or the affordability of housing and to an area where the problem is one of quality, without producing negative effects in one or both areas.

On The Interface Between Research and Policy

Given the divergent views on what constitutes an urban housing market, particularly between the research and political communities, it is not surprising that research often seems to have had little impact on the formulation of housing policies. In part this is attributable to the relative lack of thorough, well-documented and clearly presented research results, and in part to the inability or unwillingness of policy-makers to make effective use of available information. But it is also a reflection of differing attitudes. This problem was apparent in the discussions between participants with different research and policy interests, and is reflected in part in the final section of this volume.

One additional difficulty in linking research and policy appears to lie in differing views of the role of government, and the public sector generally, in urban housing markets. To many researchers the housing market is an efficient mechanism for allocating scarce social resources, but a mechanism which is constrained by government actions and policies. Their analytical models often ignore the role of government or treat it only peripherally. By contrast, others, notably politicians, see the market itself as a constraint on the political decision-making process and on the attainment of social policy objectives. These differences obviously reflect contrasting assumptions concerning what part of the housing problem is given and what may be changed directly through policy decisions.

A further difficulty is that the style of research undertaken in universities and in government is often different. Each group has its own goals and time frames, often its own terminology and language, and each is subject to unique constraints and reward systems. To the extent that research is directed toward specific operational problems in the housing field, these differences are generally minimized. However, in those instances where the definition of the problem of interest is much broader and more complex, the difference in perspectives becomes fundamental. The academic or basic researcher may be concerned primarily with understanding the market interdependencies, and perhaps with making the market work more efficiently, while the politician is more aware of the individual actors involved in the debate and the practical and political restrictions on undertaking any kind of initiative. In the latter context basic research may be largely irrelevant. Overlying these differences of emphasis are varying ideological positions on the role of housing in our social structure. Is housing a commodity? Is it a social privilege or a social obligation? Even if these differences are not resolved in the process of debate, as reflected in the papers in this volume, that debate should serve as an important learning experience for all parties.

Future Directions

As with most conferences the questions which remain unanswered at the end of the discussions are invariably more numerous than those resolved. Nevertheless this conference did serve as a forum for a relatively unique assembly of persons and perspectives, all with an interest in housing research and policy. It is the feeling of the editors, and many of the participants, that this forum should be continued.

Although we do not have a formal agenda for future directions in policy-directed research, there are a number of critical areas where more effort is clearly warranted. We need to know more, for example, about how local housing markets in individual urban areas may vary in their response to changes in the national economy, in demographic structure and income, as well as to the introduction of new policies. The final session of the conference highlighted the fact that, for example, a national consumer-oriented subsidy in the form of a housing allowance may not be equally appropriate in different regions of the country. At the same time financial institutions and political forces tend to lead toward one national rather than a variety of provincial or regional policies in this area. Thus, market differences and political forces seem to impose conflicting demands on policy. We were also struck by the need to re-examine the governmental decision-making structures within which housing policies are established and implemented. A number of participants commented specifically on the lack of open debate on policy alternatives before decisions were made.

There is certainly room for an expanded effort on the part of researchers from different disciplines in seeking common frames of reference for the policy debate. While in many respects the housing problem continues to be like the proverbial elephant, which the blind man could not comprehend as a whole, there are parts of the problem which could be more carefully identified given the conceptual frameworks we now have at our command. It would appear for example that the apparent diversity of views on whether the housing market is or is not working well can be partially reconciled by the simple expedient of defining precisely what is meant by the term market in each particular context. It should also be made clear on what criteria the evaluation of market efficiency is being made. We do not suggest that these clarifications would remove disagreement, but hopefully they might relocate the debate to a more constructive arena.

In a similar vein one suspects that disagreements between those concerned with national economic mechanisms and those concerned with the social outcomes of national policies might also be partially reconciled if the latter made clear the economic costs of socially preferred outcomes while the former made a greater effort to include assessments of the differential social impact in their analytical paradigms. William Grigsby, for example, noted in his remarks following John Quigley's paper that while there had been numerous attempts to estimate demand elasticities for housing, few had disaggregated the estimates by income group, despite the fact that there is every reason to believe these groups differ in ways which are important for policy purposes. The analytical complexities are real, of course, but not insuperable. Additional research along such lines could serve to move these   two perspectives closer towards a debate within the same plane.

There is a gap, however, which cannot be easily bridged without resort to a larger (or at least different) frame of reference. The bulk of the standard housing literature is not well suited to addressing the desirability of a particular pattern of distributional effects. Nor does it appear to be well suited to an examination of the ways in which economic and financial institutions and policy-making bodies could be changed in order to produce different social outcomes.

One cannot for long consider the extent to which economic and policy structures can be changed without consideration of political power. What are the political forces supporting current housing policy? How strong are they? How accurate have they in fact been in assessing their own interests? Given the political and economic forces which exist, how much "room for manoeuvre" is there in policy approaches? These are the kinds of questions we would like to know more about in order to assess the desirability of changing (or attempting to change) our current arrangements for establishing housing policies and delivering housing services. There were allusions to these issues throughout the conference and the reader may find some explicit comments on this point by Lloyd Axworthy, Michael Dear and John Burkus in the final session. In the main, however, this particular perspective on national housing issues is relatively undeveloped. This may in part represent an omission on the part of the conference organizers. We suspect, however, that it also reflects the fact that the political economy or politics of housing are not as thoroughly studied and reported on as are other issues of national concern. There would appear to be room for substantial further development in this field which in turn may pose new questions for those studying housing market processes and outcomes at the national as well as local scales.

Improvements in our ability to deal broadly with housing issues thus could be brought about by a redirection of efforts using standard research "technologies". This is not to say that conceptual and methodological advances are not needed. Such needs become particularly evident at the scale of local housing markets. Although not explicitly discussed at the conference, projections of demographic change in Ontario and other regions in Canada over the next decade or two suggest that there will be a substantial drop in the number of new housing units needed to meet anticipated rates of household formation. One effect of this decline, as noted earlier, may be to bring into prominence qualitative questions about the flexibility of the existing stock and its ability to adapt to changing demands for alternative types of accommodation and for different levels of housing quality. Questions concerning the measurement of housing quality, broadly considered, have been largely submerged by our preoccupation with rapid urban growth. The ability to measure the need for and the net benefits of housing, measures which capture the flow of services from as well as the quantity of the existing stock, is largely missing at the present time.

We need to develop conceptual frameworks which are more useful than those currently available for simultaneously considering activities within the public and private sectors of the market. As the paper by Albert Rose, for instance, suggests, it is extremely difficult at the moment to deal with the social housing sector, particularly public housing, except as a separate and isolated phenomenon. Site choice and tenant selection policies in public housing, for example, obviously have ramifications throughout the region, but these are difficult to trace and evaluate. Moreover, the boundary between public and private markets has become increasingly blurred as both the range and level of government subsidies increase.

A central aspect of housing quality is its location. This is often cited, as it has been earlier in this paper, as one of the attributes which makes housing a different commodity from those in most other kinds of markets. In spite of the obviousness of this difference, the significance of location is still not well understood. Recent research at the Centre for Urban and Community Studies, as well as that research reported in John Quigley's review paper in the following section, indicates how difficult it is to measure and analyze the importance of location within an urban area by means of economic indices.

In our view this problem is part and parcel of the more general question of the extent to which different sub-regions or neighbourhoods constitute distinct sub-markets. Jeffrey Patterson, in the last part of his paper in this volume, alludes to qualitative deficiencies in the social and physical environment provided for newer suburban housing, particularly that designed for moderate income families. On the other hand, studies supporting a "one-big-market" hypothesis, suggest that in economic terms, and over the longer run, no one group defined by location is paying more (in terms of a location premium) for a given set of housing attributes than any other. We do not know to what extent these contrasting views are valid descriptions of how the market performs. We also do not know whether such locational premiums exist and, if they do, how they arise and who pays them.

The extent to which the housing market of an urban area is spatially integrated, in the sense that all locations respond in essentially similar ways to the same forces, is not just a theoretical problem. At a minimum, the degree of interdependence within local markets is suggestive of the extent to which housing policy can and should be sector and location specific. That is, if the housing market of an urban area is weakly integrated, i.e. if submarkets exist, then policies must be directed to the specific problem area which is of concern. We cannot really comment more fully on this issue here except to say that it is not clear what analytical paradigm should be used to clarify the nature of locational interdependencies. Nor is it obvious what kind of empirical evidence whould be most useful to those with policy obligations. Nevertheless, it is clear that further research in this direction represents a challenging theoretical exercise and a fruitful contribution to policy.

We might close with a brief mention of the enormous difficulties imposed on those attempting to analyze the dynamics of housing at the scale of the metro-politan region or some smaller area. Part of the problem is the existence of com-plex interdependencies as noted above, but part is also simply a lack of appro-priate information. It is even difficult to determine with any confidence how many housing units of a particular type have been added to or removed from the stock in a given period of time, let alone measure more complex phenomena such as changes in housing quality and needs. These conceptual and definitional issues may seem mundane but, if the research community is to provide informed opin-ions to the policy community within an acceptable time horizon, it has to have reasonable raw material to work with.

The research agenda, then, is a substantial one. It extends from broad theoreti-cal and policy issues to hard slugging over numbers. From our perspective each step in this process should be taken with periodic debates among those with dif-ferent interests at stake.

II

Overview of Housing Market Research

2.1 HOUSING MARKETS AND HOUSING DEMAND: ANALYTIC APPROACHES

John M. Quigley

During the past decade, social scientists have devoted increasing attention to describing, understanding and to modelling the process by which households choose among alternative dwelling units in an urban area. In part, the increasing attention to this behavioural question has arisen from one or another of the "crises" of urban policy of the painful period beginning in the mid-1960s. It became increasingly clear that neither policy makers nor urban scholars possessed the theoretical knowledge or the forecasting ability to devise efficient programs for improving urban life in general, much less to "insure a decent home and a suitable living environment" for all citizens. In part, however, the increasing attention to this behavioural question by geographers, economists and sociologists, as well as by traditional planners, has resulted from the embarrassment of information, that is, from the increasing availability of detailed bodies of information describing the characteristics of individual households and their housing choices.

In the United States, for example, the Bureau of Public Roads began, for the first time, to gather information about the characteristics of households and their housing as well as their transport choices. This kind of information has been gathered for large samples of individual households in a number of metropolitan areas. In addition, a number of Community Renewal Programs and other social action programs gathered and made available specialized bodies of information. In a sense, the simple availability of data has challenged social scientists to develop models of the housing choice process with richer implications for empirical testing.

This paper reviews, somewhat selectively to be sure, the progress of research on the determinants of housing demand during the past decade or so. It concentrates on the ways in which economists have approached the relationship between the pattern of housing occupancy observed in the world and the characteristics of the consumers. The process by which households choose housing units is a transaction in what appears to be a highly competitive atomistic market. Nevertheless, the analysis of consumer demand is somewhat more complex in this market than in most. As discussed below, this results from several distinctive features of the housing market and of its transactional institutions.

It is worth noting the limits of this discussion. First, the paper presents no new research findings (although it does discuss a number of papers not yet published). Second, this review is confined for the most part to analyses of the *economics* of household choice. At several points, however, a cursory link is made to recent developments in economic geography and sociology. Third, the paper is not "policy oriented". It makes a serious attempt to synthesize the body of scientific knowledge which has accumulated so rapidly, but does not draw out their implications for public policy in a systematic way.

The plan of the paper is as follows: in the section below we characterize the housing commodity; we outline the distinctive features of the market for this commodity and indicate how this complicates the analysis of consumer demand. In the third section we review developments by economists of the long-run equilibrium position of the market and note some limitations to these analyses. In the fourth section we review recent aggregate analyses of housing demand, analyses which have reduced our uncertainty about the parameters of the aggregate demand relationship. Then we return to the microeconomic question of housing choice by individual consumers. We review several developments in characterizing housing services empirically and the resulting strategies for analyzing housing demand. The paper concludes with some remarks and observations on future research.

HOUSING AS AN ECONOMIC COMMODITY

The principal features of the housing commodity which distinguish it from most goods traded in the economy are its relatively high cost of supply, its durability, its heterogeneity and its locational fixity. Many commodities exhibit one of these features; however, it is the interaction of these distinguishing characteristics which complicates theoretical and empirical analysis of the housing market.

The high costs of constructing housing imply that housing is expensive, that a large rental market exists, and that mortgage repayment makes owner-occupied housing an attractive instrument of wealth accumulation. In addition, it makes the level of new construction of dwelling units and the occupancy costs for prospective purchasers quite sensitive to macroeconomic policy.

The durability of housing implies that there are fairly narrow bounds to the rate of disinvestment in existing structures. Housing lasts a long time; older structures may become "obsolete" but they do not necessarily lose substantial market value because of their vintage. Housing services (the flows of consumption) are "emitted" by a configuration of residential housing (the stock) over an extended period of time.

Together, durability and supply cost indicate that it is typically fairly expensive to convert a unit in the existing stock from one configuration to another, suggesting that the supply curve for housing services is inelastic, even over relatively extended periods, and even if the elasticity of supply of newly constructed units is rather large. Substantial quasi-rents may accrue to particular units in any market run, and the long run is very long indeed.

The heterogeneity of housing indicates that housing units differ in a number of important dimensions, quantitatively and qualitatively, and thus that units commanding the same market price may be viewed as substantially different by both suppliers and demanders.

Locational fixity implies that the spatial characteristics of housing units — their location with respect to other dwelling units, with respect to employment, shopping centres and neighbourhood amenities — are purchased jointly with structural characteristics. The close proximity of housing units in urban areas indicates that there may be important physical or social externalities inherent in the location chosen for housing consumption. Locational fixity also suggests that dwelling units may differ greatly in their accessibility to sites of production or consumption activities, a factor which has been greatly emphasized in the urban economics literature. Finally, in most of the United States and Canada, the spatial location chosen for housing consumption is the admission ticket for those goods and services provided by local government — the choice of a dwelling unit *is* the choice of a school district and a "mill rate". Thus, given the fragmented structure of local government in most metropolitan areas in North America, the market for housing is intimately connected to the financing of the local public sector.

Together durability, heterogeneity and fixity indicate that "the" housing market is really a collection of closely related, but segmented, markets for particular packages of underlying commodities, differentiated by size, physical arrangement etc., and location. These submarkets are connected in a complex way. At neighbouring locations, differences in prices between submarkets cannot exceed the short-run cost of converting a housing unit from one submarket to another. If there were no locational-specific component of the housing commodity, then at different sites differences in prices within any submarket could not exceed transport cost differentials for the marginal consumer. However, a price inelastic demand for some of the attributes jointly purchased, combined with inelastic supply in the short run may make the structure of housing prices even more complex, even in a market in temporary equilibrium. In the extreme, if the demand for some locational aspect of housing services is relatively price inelastic and if the supply of dwellings is fixed, the equilibrating forces of substitution in demand will not equate prices over space to marginal transport differentials. The equilibrating competition of demanders may permit significant segmentation of the market over locations (that is, high quasi-rents accruing to particular locations); the equilibrating competition of suppliers may permit significant segmentation of the market over types of housing accomodations (that is, high quasi-rents). The "equilibrium" set of housing prices in an urban area may be quite complicated indeed.

LOCATIONAL FIXITY AND ACCESSIBILITY: THE "OLD" AND THE "NEW" URBAN ECONOMICS

A point of departure for the state of housing market research a decade ago is the observation by Muth in 1967 that:

> Until quite recently, most writings on urban residential land and housing markets tended to neglect accessibility. They emphasized instead the dynamic effects of a city's past development upon current conditions, and preferences of different households for housing in different locations . . . (cited in Perloff and Wingo, 1968: 300).

Many of the seminal insights about the operation of housing markets were derived in the mid-sixties from the observation that housing and employment accessibility are jointly purchased. This insight, plus the assumptions that there exists a single urban workplace and that housing is produced competitively from land and "non-land" by a constant returns technology, led to a number of important propositions about the form of urban areas in long-run equilibrium, the intra-metropolitan distribution of housing and the location patterns of urban households. These propositions, that residential densities decline with distance from the central place; that densities decline at a decreasing rate; that housing prices decline with distance, also at a decreasing rate; that the land price gradient is steeper than the housing price gradient; and that households with higher incomes locate further from the central place,[1] were based upon the ingenious model developed initially by Alonso (1961) and Wingo (1961), generalized by Mills (1967) and synthesized by Muth (1969). These conceptual results, derived from what is, in the late 1970s, the "standard model" (to use Solow's terminology) of the urban area (Richardson, *et al.*, 1973), were not well known at all within the economics profession at large a decade ago.

More recently, a number of scholars have tested the qualitative implications of this model of the spatial distribution of housing services within metropolitan areas, expanding upon the original contribution of Colin Clark. These tests have typically involved the estimation of relationships between the distance from the city centre and the density of economic activity, for example, population density. These studies, usually involving the estimation of density gradients (regressions relating distance to log-density) for various urban areas and time periods (Mills, 1970 and 1972; Muth, 1964), generally fail to reject the hypothesis of a convex density relationship. In addition, due to the ingenious method contrived by Mills, it has been possible to estimate population density gradients[2] historically for some cities beginning in 1880 using census data. These historical analyses suggest a systematic decline in central densities and in gradients across time periods. At a descriptive level, these results indicate strikingly that the post-war decentralization of workplaces and the suburbanization of households has been no more pronounced than the decentralization which occurred a generation earlier; central densities of population and employment have regularly declined, as have their gradients, for as far back in time as we have data.

It has been sometimes argued that the convexity (or even the log-linearity) of population density functions provides something of a "test" of the "standard model", at least as it applies to housing markets (White, 1977). At best, this is quite a weak test of this class of model. Empirically, it has been shown that estimates of density-distance relationships are highly sensitive to the partitioning of geographical units (Kemper and Schmenner, 1974). More important, as noted by Harrison and Kain (1974), it is possible to derive plausible density gradients from assumptions about the nature of the housing stock (in particular its durability) that are diametrically opposed to those of the "standard theory".

Among economists a great deal of professional energy has been devoted to extensions of this basic conceptual model, for example, to make congestion costs to the workplace endogenous (Solow, 1972) and to include economies of scale in the production of goods (Dixit, 1973). Indeed, there have been at least two collections of papers devoted to these extensions (termed somewhat unfortunately the "new" urban economics) in major journals.[3] It is not hard to account for the interest in these extensions; mathematical puzzles have always been intriguing.

It is somewhat harder to account for the fact that they were taken at all seriously for any policy purposes. The applicability of these sophisticated "new" urban economics models to the study of housing markets is tenuous at best and the potential research benefit to housing analysis of further extensions is likely to be small. Of course, this is not the only instance where mathematical ingenuity has been economically uninteresting.[4]

This judgment reflects, in part at least, the importance of the features of fixity and durability in real housing markets. These features are typically ignored completely in the "new" urban economics literature; mathematical tractability virtually requires that the assumption of "long-run" (as opposed to "temporary") equilibrium be maintained. This, in turn, forces these models to assume that the distribution of housing over space conforms to that distribution which would be observed if the urban area were built anew. In North America it is not unusual to find residential structures that are a century old; in Europe, three centuries. For many purposes, the dictates of mathematical tractability may focus attention on non-problems.

THE DEMAND FOR THE COMPOSITE COMMODITY: "HOUSING SERVICES"

Assume, contrary to the discussion in the second section, the existence of a single valued measure of "housing services". It should then be a simple matter to estimate the price and income elasticities of demand from market data on housing, just as demand curves have been estimated for countless other goods. Measuring the importance of price and income in housing demand has not proved to be a simple matter however. In part, the dispersion of price and income elasticity estimates results from traditional measurement problems — sample selectivity, econometric specification and the like (see de Leeuw, 1971, for a review of these measurement problems and the empirical evidence as of 1971). In part, however, the interpretation of empirical evidence depends upon the peculiar characteristics of the housing commodity.

Consider the costliness and durability of housing; housing expenditures represent a large fraction of income and it is costly for any household to change the configuration of housing services received (by modifying its current dwelling unit or by searching and moving to another unit). Thus, the appropriate concept of income is less clear cut than in the study of most commodities. Housing durability and high transactions cost imply that the relevant notion of income for analyzing consumer choice is some "normal" or "long-run" income as opposed to annual income. This by itself suggests that the estimates of income elasticity obtained from observations on consumers grouped randomly by income will be larger than those obtained using individual households as units of observation,[5] a finding consistent with the empirical evidence assembled over the past few years (Aaron, 1975; Maisel, 1971). Since de Leeuw's review of the cross-sectional evidence on income elasticities in 1971, several studies which use individual households as units of observation and which also employ some measure of permanent income have been reported (Carliner, 1973; Kain and Quigley, 1975). These studies typically report statistically significant elasticities with respect to *both* annual and permanent income, with a higher elasticity estimate computed for permanent income.

In addition, the permanent income elasticities reported in these microeconomic studies are generally smaller than those derived from grouped data. The review of this evidence presented by Kain and Quigley (1975) provides several possible rationalizations of these findings. One appealing explanation is not based upon economic theory but rather on loose sociological reasoning. It is certainly possible that decisions about how much housing to consume, though made individually by isolated households, are not made completely independently. A significant peer group effect may exist if households' consumption is influenced by the housing choices of their reference group as well as by their own incomes. If this is so, then the average peer group effect is included (by construction) in the coefficient of "permanent income" in these recent microeconomic studies.

The conceptual and empirical problems in estimating the price elasticity of housing demand arise from the peculiar nature of this commodity. In the market for housing, "prices" are never directly observed at all. Market transactions produce monthly rents for flows of housing service or market values for stocks of housing capital. Neither of these is a price. They are expressed in units of price-times-quantity (see below).

Thus, in regressions relating housing consumption to incomes and prices, price is usually approximated by inter-urban (or inter-temporal) variation in construction cost indices (Muth, 1960) or, more recently, by the average costs for an arbitrarily specified dwelling unit gathered by the Bureau of Labor Statistics (BLS) for different cities (the BLS indices are described and criticized by Gillingham, 1975). Estimates of the price elasticity of housing demand based upon these indices have ranged from about −.3 to −.9 (Carliner, 1973; de Leeuw, 1971; Maisel, et al., 1971).

The recent paper by Polinsky (1977) attempts to reconcile these differences in price elasticity estimates as well as the differences in long-run income elasticities estimated from grouped and ungrouped data. Part of the reconciliation reflects "standard" econometric problems, the particular specification and measurement of housing prices relative to the prices of other goods employed in various studies. In part, however, the reconciliation emphasizes theoretical issues in housing markets — the inherent jointness in the housing consumption and location decision and the meaning of housing "prices", between as well as within markets. Polinsky's analysis considers the effect of specification errors upon price and income elasticity estimates arising: (a) from samples of individual households within a housing market; (b) from samples of individual households drawn from several housing markets; and (c) from averaged data drawn from several housing markets. The theory of residential location suggests that higher-income households will consume more housing and will locate where housing prices are lower within a housing market (see Note1). On the other hand, higher-income households are more likely to live in cities with higher average incomes and housing prices. Thus:

1. If housing demand is price inelastic, estimates of income elasticities ob-

tained from the bivariate regression of housing expenditure on income in sample "a" will be biased downwards (since housing expenditures will fall as price decreases with distance and higher-income households will choose more distant locations).

2. Estimates of income elasticity obtained from the bivariate regression on sample "b" will also be biased, the intra-city residential location pattern imparting a downward bias, but this time reduced by the magnitude of the inter-market effect (i.e., the positive bias imparted, assuming price inelasticity, by neglecting the positive relationship, on average, between income and housing prices across cities).

3. Similarly, if a regression is estimated for sample "b" between housing expenditures, income and some average metropolitan price index (e.g., from BLS budget data), the downward bias in the estimated income elasticity is larger (since the average price term holds the inter-market effect constant to the extent that, across cities, incomes and prices are correlated). Of course, if prices and incomes are perfectly correlated (completely uncorrelated) the bias is equivalent to case 1 (case 2).

4. Finally, in the case 3 regression above, the estimated price elasticity based upon the average prices is, in general, biased upwards.[6]

This taxonomy proves very useful in narrowing the range of empirical estimates of "the " income elasticity of demand;[7] overall the reconciliation suggests a slightly inelastic demand of about .7 to .9 for housing with respect to income.

With regard to estimates of the price elasticity of demand, there is less empirical evidence available and only a few studies have measured housing prices, other than as a market-wide average in samples gathered across cities (i.e., case 4 above which leads to an upward bias). Two analyses (Muth, 1971; Polinsky and Elwood, 1977) have used samples of Federal Housing Administration (FHA) appraisal data to derive estimates of "unit prices" for housing which vary by observation, and have used these price estimates in subsequent investigations of the price and income elasticities of housing demand. Analytically, this involves estimating the parameters of the production function (assumed CES, constant elasticity of substitution) relating housing output to land and "non-land" inputs and then substituting the parameters into the cost function to estimate the price per unit of housing, a price which varies for each unit in the sample.[8] Expenditures on housing are then regressed on income and unit prices so derived (in logarithmic form the coefficient on the price term is one plus the price elasticity of demand). The results of both studies, using FHA data from different cities and time periods, suggest a price elasticity of about −.7.

These qualitative results are supported in another study (Hanushek and Quigley, 1977) which uses the results of one part of the housing allowance experiment to estimate the price elasticity of housing demand. In this latter analysis, the un-

observed prices of housing have been reduced experimentally for some households (i.e., some households receive percentage rebates on rental contracts). Price
elasticity estimates, derived within a stock adjustment framework, are replicated
for two independent samples and for two time periods. For the two samples the
price elasticity estimates are about −.5 and −.7, which are quite similar to those
estimated from the parameters of the production function.

There seems to be some professional consensus that over the long run housing
demand is slightly inelastic with respect to income and with respect to price. In
the short run, however, we may expect that there are significant lags in household
adjustment of housing consumption to changes in incomes, prices, or demographic
composition. As noted previously, there are significant search costs and transactions costs associated with changing the amount of housing services consumed.
This implies a high level of inertia in household behaviour and potentially long
lags in adjustment. Evidence from panel data on individual households confirms
the importance of adjustment lags to variations in income for a national sample
of households in the U.S. (cf. Roistacher, 1977) and to variations in income and
price for longitudinal samples of individual households in particular metropolitan
areas (cf. Hanushek and Quigley, 1977 and 1978a). The importance of transaction costs also complicates the analysis of intra-urban mobility, the principal
mechanism by which changes in housing consumption are registered. A recent review of the literature on urban mobility (Quigley and Weinberg, 1977) reveals
many inconsistencies in empirical findings. More recent analyses (Hanushek and
Quigley, 1978b and 1978c) do suggest that local mobility is quite responsive to
changes in housing demand, but we are still a long way from an integrated theory
of housing consumption and local mobility.

THE COMPLEXITY OF "HOUSING SERVICES"

Heterogeneity and Hedonic Measurement

The definition of housing services employed above, the assumption that "housing
services" is a homogeneous good available at a single price, is quite useful in certain instances, since it permits a unique mapping from housing expenditures to
housing quantities. Nevertheless, for many analytic and descriptive purposes,
especially at the microeconomic level, the assumption is clearly unreasonable.
During the past decade, considerable intellectual resources have been devoted to
understanding the relationships between the market prices of rental and owner-
occupied dwelling units and the components of housing services imbedded in them.
This strand of analysis, based on so-called hedonic indices, had seldom been
applied to housing a decade ago; today there is a large descriptive literature on
the dimensionality of housing services. The recent interest in applying these

methods to housing markets owes much to the new theories of consumer behaviour, developed by Lancaster (1966) and by others, which postulates that households have demands for the underlying characteristics inherent in all economic commodities and further that households combine purchased characteristics with time inputs to "produce" satisfactions. Applied to housing markets, the question naturally arises: What subset of the complex and heterogeneous bundle of physical and spatial characteristics enjoyed by the choice of a dwelling unit is reflected in its market price? From observations on the market prices of dwelling units and on these underlying characteristics it is possible to estimate the relationships empirically. The regression of market value or rental price upon the set of characteristics yields their implicit prices. If the market is in equilibrium, in the sense to be discussed below, the ratios of these shadow prices (e.g., the estimated coefficients of the hedonic regression) will indicate the relative supply cost of the underlying characteristics of housing and the marginal rates of substitution in consumption of these characteristics.

Within the discipline of urban economics, this research strategy has been applied to housing markets using the average characteristics of census tracts and later using rich samples of data on the prices paid for individual dwelling units and descriptions of the quantitative and qualitative aspects of these units, their structures, parcels and micro-environments (Grether and Mieszkowski, 1974; Kain and Quigley, 1970a; Lapham, 1971; Ridker and Henning, 1967).

The research strategy requires defining and measuring the set of characteristics and choosing the functional form for analysis. Both issues are largely empirical. With regard to functional form, it has been argued that the semi-log functional form is more plausible (Griliches, 1971) since it is consistent with a rising supply price for individual characteristics.[9] Most authors have chosen the linear, semi-log or logarithmic form for analysis, presumably on grounds of convenience and without rigorous statistical experimentation.[10] (This is hardly surprising, since rigorous analysis of functional form is conditional upon an agreed specification of the independent variables.) So far, this strand of empirical research has been employed: (1) to provide empirical tests of the importance of workplace accessibility, so emphasized in the theoretical literature, in determining housing prices; (2) to investigate the type and importance of local externalities in affecting the market valuation of housing services; (3) to analyze the relationship between local taxes, public services and property values; and (4) to provide a rich description of the components of that heterogeneous commodity called "housing services".[11]

Workplace accessibility With regard to the first question, the empirical evidence is somewhat mixed. Various authors have measured accessibility in different ways; for example, as travel time (or distance or cost) to the central business district or as a generalized workplace accessibility index derived from gravity models. By and large the estimated coefficients of such measures are "significant"; observed market prices vary with accessibility. *Ceteris paribus*, the independent effect of generalized accessibility to workplaces upon housing prices is not large (see Ball, 1973, for a review of some thirteen such studies conducted in the U.K. and the U.S.). Relative to the important structural and qualitative characteristics, it is rather small. In part, these general findings may simply reflect the negative covariance between accessibility and housing quality arising from the historical growth pattern of most cities; the tendency for older, more obsolete and lower quality dwelling units to be located closer to employment centres. In part, however, these results may reflect the limitations of long-run equilibrium analysis applied to durable configurations of residential capital. As noted above, in a temporary equilibrium positive and negative quasi-rents may be associated with particular sites. In many housing markets, these location premiums may be large relative to accessibility premiums.

The importance of externalities With regard to the question of externalities, analyses of hedonic prices have provided direct evidence of the importance of air pollution (Anderson and Crocker, 1971), residential "blight", to use the planners' term (Kain and Quigley, 1970b), and neighbourhood characteristics (Schnare and Struyk, 1976) in affecting property valuation. In addition, and perhaps of much more importance, these analyses have indicated the role of social externalities and racial composition in affecting housing prices.

In the regression relating property values to characteristics of housing services external to the dwelling unit — say measures of ambient air quality (holding the other relevant characteristics of the properties constant) — the regression coefficient provides an estimate of the capitalized value of air quality. It follows then that changes in aggregate property values provide a measure of the market return to policies which improve overall air quality, at least in long-run equilibrium. When such estimates were originally presented (see Freeman, 1971, and Anderson and Crocker, 1971, among others) there was considerable controversy over the principles underlying the assertion that aggregate property values reflected consumers' willingness to pay for improvements in the amenity component of housing services. The set of conditions under which these assertions are formally correct has been shown to be quite restricted. The logic of these sufficient conditions is: without the assumption that the urban area is "small" and that there is perfect equilibration (e.g., residential mobility) between urban areas, the utility levels of residents in one urban area will be affected by any change in the amenity levels provided.

Thus the increase in capitalized values at one location resulting from an increase in the amenity level at that location depends upon changes in the amenity level at all other locations. In an isolated urban area, aggregate increases in amenity levels result in increases in aggregate values, but these changes in values are underestimates of the aggregate willingness to pay (since consumers enjoy higher levels of utility after the general improvement in amenities). With perfect mobility among urban areas, however, the (common) level of utility is exogenous to a change in the amenity level in one city and changes in property values reflect aggregate willingness to pay.

This divergence in implications has led to a distinction in the literature between models of equilibrium in a "closed" (i.e., isolated) urban area and models of equilibrium in an "open" urban area (i.e., a small city whose residents can move without cost to any other city in an equilibrium system of urban areas).

The Demand for the Components of the Housing Commodity

A number of studies have attempted to integrate this complex dimensionality of the housing bundle with the analysis of consumer demand for housing services. There have been three strands to this research which are, in fact, closely related.

1. The demand for bundles of characteristics. Two research efforts have utilized hedonic price indices for a housing market to partition *a priori* the expenditures of a sample of consumers on housing services into implicit payments for a limited number of "composite commodities" or aggregates of underlying characteristics. The earlier of these, by Kain and Quigley (1975), assumes a linear additive form of the metropolitan-wide hedonic price index, implying that the unit price of each underlying component of the housing commodity is constant throughout the housing market. Estimates of the unit prices are used to partition household consumption of "housing services" into several components (in this case four: dwelling unit quality, interior space, neighbourhood quality and exterior space). Finally, household demands for these components are estimated simultaneously as a function of household income and socio-demographic composition. The econometric results suggest a systematic pattern of substitution not only between "housing services" and other goods, but also among components consumed. They reveal, for example, a higher income elasticity of demand for housing quality than for space as well as systematic reallocations in response to variations in family size. The assumptions about the price structure of the market implicit in this analysis are strong, and somewhat unrealistic.

Two recent papers by King (1975, 1976) extend this analysis of the demand for bundles of housing characteristics. King recognizes that the unit prices of particular housing characteristics may vary within the metropolitan housing market, due to excess supplies of particular types of residential housing at specified locations or due to some interaction between accessibility and other housing characteristics. He estimates the implicit prices of the underlying housing characteristics separately for several geographical regions within a single housing market and uses these prices to partition housing expenditures into components (the same four) for a metropolitan sample of households. His subsequent analysis, relating consumption of these commodities to income and *these* prices reveals, not only significant differences in income elasticities across the components of "housing services", but also systematic substitution in consumption in response to intra-market price variation.

The assumptions about household behaviour implicit in this analysis are equally strong. Not only must one assume (as before) that these *a priori* categories exhaust the relevant characteristics valued in housing, but also that there is no substitution among spatial areas by consumers in registering their demands for these components of housing services. Within any housing market, households certainly do make substitutions among spatial locations. However, in this econometric specification, households choose not only levels of consumption of each composite commodity but also the structure of prices. If households choose among price sets by choosing a spatial location, then their consumption opportunities are defined by the envelope of the hedonic price surfaces. In this case, all households would face the same relative prices. Thus, without strong restrictions upon the substitution possibilities among locations, the model is difficult to interpret.

In addition to these attempts to model the household consumption decision simultaneously for an exhaustive set of housing components, a number of studies have concentrated on a single dimension of the housing commodity, the tenure choice decision. As noted previously, for institutional (and historical) reasons home ownership is an attractive vehicle for wealth accumulation, especially by middle-income households. In addition, at least in the United States, a significant fraction of all direct public subsidies to housing consumers has been in the form of tax advantages to home ownership. A number of studies have analyzed the relationship between the demand for owner-occupancy, income, household demographics (and sometimes wealth) (Kain and Quigley, 1972). In the earlier studies analyzing tenure choice within a single housing market, it was implicitly assumed that all households faced the same relative price for renter and owner-occupied dwellings. In similar studies across housing markets, little serious effort was made to evaluate the price sensitivity of choice. More recently, however, Struyk (1976) has attempted to measure variations in the price of owner-occupied relative to rental housing facing individual households by calculating the implicit subsidy to owner occupancy and by measuring differential occupancy costs for the two types of accommodation under alternative assumptions about capitalization. The results suggest that households are highly responsive to relative price variation in their demand for owner occupancy.

2. The influence of workplace-related prices. Two studies have relied upon variations in workplaces to allow the envelope of prices to vary by household, permitting subsequent investigation of the relationship between demand for components of housing services, incomes and intra-market relative prices.

Straszheim (1973, 1975) estimates the price surface for several components of housing services (e.g., structure type, lot size) by the hedonic methods described above. The structure of prices is allowed to vary for a large number of geographic areas within a metropolitan housing market. Assuming that workplaces are predetermined for each household, Straszheim estimates the envelope of prices for each component of housing by summarizing the price level from each workplace at some average distance (commute time).[12] Thus the envelope of housing prices varies in a complex way for different households in the same housing market depending upon the location of the worksites. The subsequent demand analysis relates observed household choices of housing characteristics to incomes and these relative prices. The demand analysis indicates the pattern of direct and cross-price elasticities of demand for several components of "housing services".

Quigley (1976) also relies upon household-specific workplaces to allow the envelope of housing prices to vary for consumers within the same metropolitan housing market. In this case, a workplace-specific travel cost [13] is added to the market price for each of several "types" of housing (i.e., specified combinations of housing components) available at each residential site. [14] The minimum price for each housing type is thus the envelope faced by consumers with different incomes and workplaces.

In this model, the housing demand problem is described as the choice among housing types, a function of the underlying characteristics of the alternative types of housing, the incomes of households and the relative prices they face. The discrete choice model, estimated empirically using maximum likelihood techniques, suggests a strong pattern of substitution among components of "housing services", particularly residential density and housing quality, in response to intra-housing market price variation.

In comparing these two related approaches to the analysis of housing demand, each makes strong but somewhat different assumptions about the nature of housing markets and houshold behaviour. Straszheim assumes that each component of housing services can be purchased separately at any site in the metropolitan area (at varying prices, to be sure), but allows each household to vary in its valuation of travel time. The latter analysis recognizes that households typically do not have the opportunity to purchase any combination of housing components -- they must make a tied purchase of discrete bundles of components. However, Quigley's analysis makes the strong and somewhat artificial assumption that commuting time prices are constant for all households with the same income.[15] In any case, both models suggest that the observed demands of households for the components of "housing services" are highly responsive, not only to income differences but also to intra-metropolitan price variation arising from worksite location.

3. The direct estimation of utility functions for housing components.

Two recent analyses by Wheaton (1977) and Galster (1977) have approached this problem of modelling household demand for the characteristics of dwelling units in a manner complementary to the foregoing classes of models. As noted before, the optimizing choices of housing consumers can be described as points on the lower envelopes of the price surfaces they face. Equivalently, in equilibrium the housing price surface of the urban area itself reflects the upper envelope of the bids different kinds of households are willing to make for alternative locations.

This fact suggests that identical households employed at the same worksite should achieve identical utility levels even though they have chosen different locations and housing components, that is, they should have a common bid-rent function for housing components. The models developed by Wheaton and Galster estimate the common utility function underlying the equilibrium bid-rent function directly. Galster assumes an arbitrary monetary valuation of commute time; Wheaton assumes that commuting time *per se* is valued by consumers. In either case, from information about income, housing payments and out-of-pocket transportation costs, they estimate the parameters of a common utility function defined over housing components and other goods (i.e., income net of housing and transport costs). Conditional upon the form of the utility function (assumed Cobb-Douglas, CES, and in Galster's work also a power transformation) and the assumption about travel time valuation, these analyses provide direct estimates of the marginal rates of substitution between particular components of the housing bundle (e.g., between a measure of the quality and the interior size of dwelling units) for households stratified by income and socio-demographic characteristics.[16] As might be expected, the empirical results of both studies indicate an increasing marginal valuation of most housing components with income (i.e., a decreasing marginal utility of income); however, Wheaton's results also suggest pronounced differences in marginal rates of substitution with income (i.e., *ceteris paribus* an increasing valuation of exterior space relative to interior space with income) and with family size and composition.

In evaluating these models, it should be noted that they assume, as does Straszheim, that households have the opportunity to purchase any combination of housing components and further that the price structure of the urban area is fully adjusted to its temporary equilibrium position. Finally, it should be noted that to apply such models to households in urban areas with decentralized work-

places, some knowledge of the equilibrium wage gradient for identical labour
would be required. [17]

CONCLUSION

As noted at the outset, most of the original work on the analysis of housing
demand proceeds from drastic simplifications about the nature of "housing
services" or about the nature of equilibrium in the housing market. Under the
assumption that housing is a homogeneous good, extensive and sophisticated
analyses of the spatial pattern of urban housing demand in long-run equilibrium
have been undertaken. The more recent extensions appear to have only limited
applicability to   real housing markets, however.

During the past decade, empirical and theoretical research has, in fact,
narrowed considerably the range of uncertainty about the true price and
income elasticities of the aggregate demand function. In the mid-1960s,
on the basis of the evidence produced by Duesenberry (1952) and Reid (1962),
the range of estimates for the income elasticity of demand for the aggregate
commodity was one order of magnitude (that is, from about 0.3 to 3.0). In
the mid-1970s, one may conclude that housing demand is mildly inelastic
with respect to income and relative prices.

Existing evidence on demographic determinants of household demand,
at least the evidence produced by economists, is less convincing, if only because
these important characteristics of households have merely been "held constant"
in ad hoc ways.

Exploitation of the hedonic relationship between rents and housing
characteristics during the decade has provided a rich documentation of the
dimensionality of the housing commodity, has indicated the relative importance
of local externalities in the housing market and promises some practical benefits in reforming tax assessment procedures. Nevertheless, these general research findings have raised more questions than they have answered.

If only because these hedonic representations of the housing commodity
are so convincing, current research on housing demand must consider the substitution possibilities within the housing bundle as well as those between housing and other goods.

Several related approaches have attempted to model this highly complex
choice problem — to investigate the systematic relationship between income and
the choice among particular characteristics or dimensions of housing services —
and to analyze the substitution among these characteristics in response to
intra-metropolitan variation in the relative prices of these characteristics. It
is worth noting that many of these more elaborate economic analyses of con-

sumer demand achieve identification (in a statistical sense) by relying upon somewhat crude versions of current concepts in analytic geography. For example, analyses which relate housing choice to worksite location utilize summary measures of "price geography" (see Apgar and Kain, 1972, for a discussion), a notion closely related to classical gravity concepts. In deriving testable hypotheses of consumer behaviour, these analyses make other strong behavioural assumptions which clearly limit their generality. Nevertheless, within these restrictions, the available empirical evidence suggests that income levels (and demographic characteristics) strongly affect the choice of particular characteristics of "housing services" and that there are strong cross-price effects in demand. There is, apparently, no way to "go back" to the simpler view of demand for a single valued commodity employed in most other specialties in economics.

This review clearly indicates that much remains to be done to understand the economic choice problem facing consumers and still more to quantify the unknown parameters. It is somewhat ironic to note that in the United States and Canada, about 20 per cent of the population moved last year. Thus about one out of five people that economists meet on the streets *actually* solved this complex housing decision problem last year. After a decade of research, professional economists have only crude theories to explain how.

NOTES

1 This last proposition depends also on the plausible assumption that the income elasticity of housing demand exceeds the elasticity of marginal transport costs with respect to income.

2 More precisely, to compute the intercept and the gradient from two pieces of information, leaving no degrees of freedom.

3 See, for example, *Bell Journal of Economics,* March 1972 and *Swedish Journal of Economics,* Autumn 1973.

4 Mills and MacKinnon's review (1973) of this genre questions the cost-benefit ratio of this allocation of research expertise and indicates that the most tempting extensions may not further an understanding of urban economics. A more extreme statement of conflicting judgements may be found in the published views of Richardson, Solow and Mirlees (1973).

5 This follows from a standard errors-in-variables argument.

6 The reasoning here is a bit more subtle. To the extent that average incomes and prices are correlated, an increase in income increases the probability that

a household will locate in a city of higher average income. Since the relative income of the household will be lower after the move, it will locate closer to the city centre, where prices are yet higher. Again, with price inelastic demand, this overstates the change in expenditures with respect to price.

7   Since the bivariate estimates of income elasticity from samples b and c bracket "true" value.

8   This strategy relies upon an exogenous estimate of the value of land for each observation on housing units.

9   This specification is, however, not consistent with equilibrium on the demand side and the diminishing marginal utility of additional units of each characteristic. See Rosen (1974).

10   Indeed, there appears to be only one paper, as yet unpublished (Goodman, 1978), which investigates the functional form of the hedonic relationship. That study concludes on the basis of Box-Cox tests that the appropriate functional form is (roughly) the square root transformation $\sqrt{P} = \beta X$.

11   In addition, it should be emphasised that these research techniques have broad practical application in the assessment of real property and in price indices.

12   The details of this estimation are quite laborious. They are summarized in Straszheim (1973).

13   This assumes that travel time is valued at some constant price (as a proportion of wages) for each household.

14   These household specific price surfaces, termed "gross prices", have subsequently been incorporated in a dynamic framework in the National Bureau's Urban Simulation Model.

15   In addition, the estimation technique used in the latter analysis assumes a specialized property of discrete choice (the so-called independence of irrelevant alternatives). Not too much should be made of this limitation, however, since McFadden has shown in a recent (unpublished) paper on residence choice (1977) that Quigley's empirical model is similar (but not identical) to the true model without this restricted property.

16   The actual estimation technique is slightly more complex and the assumptions are slightly stronger, since income classes (and not identical incomes) are the basis for stratification. See Vaughn (1976) for details.

17   Since the equilibrium bid-rent surface must equalize utility levels for households with different workplaces and hence transport costs to the same residential location.

REFERENCES

Aaron, H. J. 1975. *Who Pays the Property Tax?* Washington, D.C.: Brookings Institution.

Alonso, W. 1961. *Location and Land Use.* Washington, D.C.: Resources for the Future.

Anderson, R.J., and T.D. Crocker. 1971. "Air Pollution and Residential Property Values", *Urban Studies,* 8: 171-180.

Apgar, W.C., and J.F. Kain. 1972. "Neighbourhood Attributes and the Residential Price Geography of Urban Areas". Paper presented at the Winter Meetings of the Econometric Society, Toronto, December 28-30.

Ball, M.J. 1973. "Recent Empirical Work on the Determinants of Relative House Prices", *Urban Studies,* 10: 213-231.

Carliner, G. 1973. "Income Elasticity of Housing Demand", *Review of Economics and Statistics,* 55: 528-532.

De Leeuw, F. 1971. "The Demand for Housing: A Review of the Cross-Sectional Evidence", *Review of Economics and Statistics,* 53, 1: 1-10.

Dixit, A. 1973. "The Optimum Factory Town", *Bell Journal of Economics and Management Science,* 4, 2: 637-651.

Duesenberry, J.S. 1952. *Income, Savings and the Theory of Consumer Behavior.* Cambridge, Mass.: Harvard University Press.

Freeman, A.M. 1971. "Air Pollution and Property Values: A Methodological Comment", *Review of Economics and Statistics,* 53: 415-416.

Galster, G.C. 1977. "A Bid-Rent Analysis of Housing Market Discrimination", *American Economic Review,* 67:144-155.

Goodman, A.C. 1978. "Hedonic Prices, Price Indices, and Housing Markets", *Journal of Urban Economics,* forthcoming.

Gillingham, R. 1975. "Place to Place Rent Comparisons", *Annals of Economic and Social Measurement,* 4: 153-173.

Grether, D.M., and P. Mieszkowski. 1974. "The Determinants of Real Estate Values", *Journal of Urban Economics,* 1, 2: 127-246.

Griliches, Z., ed. 1971. *Price Indices and Quality Change.* Cambridge, Mass.: Harvard University Press.

Hanushek, E.A., and J. M. Quigley. 1977. "What is "the" Price Elasticity of Housing Demand". Institute for Social and Policy Studies, Yale University, New Haven, Conn. (mimeographed).

Hanushek, E.A., and J.M. Quigley. 1978a. "The Dynamics of the Housing Market: A Stock Adjustment Model of Housing Consumption", *Journal of Urban Economics,* forthcoming.

Hanushek, E.A., and J.M. Quigley. 1978b. "An Explicit Model of Residential Mobility", *Land Economics,* forthcoming.

Hanushek, E.A., and J.M. Quigley. 1978c. "Housing Market Disequilibrium and Residential Mobility", in E.A. Moore and W.A.V. Clark, eds., *Population Mobility and Residential Change.* Evanston, Ill.: Northwestern University Press.

Harrison, D., and J.F. Kain. 1974. "Cumulative Urban Growth and Urban Density Functions", *Journal of Urban Economics,* 1: 61-98.

Kain, J.F., and J.M. Quigley. 1970a. "Measuring the Value of Housing Quality", *Journal of the American Statistical Association,* 65: 532-548.

Kain, J.F., and J.M. Quigley. 1970b. "Evaluating the Quality of the Residential Environment", *Environment and Planning,* 2: 23-32.

Kain, J.F., and J.M. Quigley. 1972. "Housing Market Discrimination, Homeownership, and Savings Behavior", *American Economic Review,* 62: 263-277.

Kain, J.F., and J.M. Quigley. 1975. *Housing Markets and Racial Discrimination.* New York: National Bureau of Economic Research.

Kemper, P., and R. Schmenner. 1974. "The Density Gradient for Manufacturing Industry", *Journal of Urban Economics,* 1: 410-427.

King, A.T. 1975. "The Demand For Housing: Integrating the Roles of Journey-to-Work, Neighborhood Quality, and Prices", in *Household Production and Consumption.* New York: National Bureau of Economic Research.

King, A.T. 1976. "The Demand for Housing: A Lancastrian Approach", *Southern Economics Journal,* 43: 1077-1087.

King, A.T., and P. Mieszkowski. 1973. "Racial Discrimination, Segregation, and the Relative Price of Housing", *Journal of Political Economy,* 81, 3: 590-606.

Lancaster, K.J. 1966. "A New Approach to Consumer Theory", *Journal of Political Economy,* 74: 132-157.

Lapham, V. 1971. "Do Blacks Pay More for Housing?" *Journal of Political Economy,* 79: 1244-1257.

Maisel, S.J., J.B. Burnham, and J.S. Austin. 1971. "The Demand for Housing: A Comment", *Review of Economics and Statistics,* 53: 410-412.

McFadden, D. 1977. "Modelling the Choice of Residential Location". University of California, Berkeley (mimeographed).

Mills, E.S. 1967. "An Aggregative Model of Resource Allocation in a Metropolitan Area", *American Economic Review,* 57: 197-210.

Mills, E.S. 1970. "Urban Density Functions", *Urban Studies,* 7: 5-20.

Mills, E.S. 1972. *Studies in the Structure of the Urban Economy.* Baltimore, Md.: Johns Hopkins Press.

Mills, E.S., and J. MacKinnon. 1973. "Notes on the New Urban Economics", *Bell Journal of Economics and Management Science,* 4, 2: 593-601.

Muth, R.F. 1960. "The Demand for Non-Farm Housing", in A.C. Harberger, ed., *The Demand for Durable Goods.* Chicago: University of Chicago Press.

Muth, R.F. 1961. "The Spatial Structure of the Housing Market", *Papers of the Regional Science Association,* 7.

Muth, R.F. 1964. "The Variation of Population Density and its Components in South Chicago", *Papers of the Regional Science Association,* 11.

Muth, R.F. 1969. *Cities and Housing.* Chicago:University of Chicago Press.

Muth, R.F. 1971. "The Derived Demand for Urban Residential Land", *Urban Studies,* 8: 243-254.

Perloff, H.S., and L. Wingo, eds. 1968. *Issues in Urban Economics.* Washington, D.C.: Resources for the Future.

Polinsky, A.M. 1977. "The Demand for Housing: A Study in Specification and Grouping", *Econometrica,* 45: 447-461.

Polinsky, A., and D.T. Elwood. 1977. "An Empirical Reconciliation of Micro and Grouped Estimates of the Demand for Housing". Harvard Institute for Economic Research, Harvard University, Cambridge, Mass. (mimeographed).

Quigley, J.M. 1976. "Housing Demand in the Short Run: An Analysis of Polytomous Choice", *Explorations in Economic Research,* 3, 1: 76-102.

Quigley, J.M., and D.H. Weinberg. 1977. "Intra-Metropolitan Residential Mobility: A Review and Synthesis", *International Regional Science Review,* 2, 2: 41-66.

Reid, M. 1962. *Housing and Income.* Chicago: University of Chicago Press.

Richardson, H.W., R.S. Solow, and J.A. Mirlees. 1973. "Comments on Some Uses of Mathematical Models in Urban Economics", *Urban Studies,* 10: 259-270.

Ridker, R.G., and J.A. Henning. 1967. "The Determinants of Residential Property Values with Special Reference to Air Pollution", *Review of Economics and Statistics,* 49: 246-256.

Roistacher, E.A. 1977. "Short Run Responses to Changes in Income", *American Economic Review,* 67, 1: 381-386.

Rosen, S. 1974. "Hedonic Prices and Implicit Markets: Product Differentiation in Pure Competition", *Journal of Political Economy,* 82: 34-55.

Schnare, A.B., and R.J. Struyk. 1976. "Segmentation in Urban Housing Markets", *Journal of Urban Economics,* 3: 146-166.

Solow, R.S. 1972. "Congestion, Density and the Use of Land in Transportation", *Swedish Journal of Economics,* 74, 1: 161-173.

Straszheim, M.H. 1973. "Estimation of the Demand for Urban Housing Services from Household Interview Data", *Review of Economics and Statistics,* 55: 1-8.

Straszheim, M.H. 1975. *An Econometric Analysis of the Urban Housing Market.* New York: National Bureau of Economic Research.

Struyk, R.J. 1976. *Urban Homeownership.* Lexington, Mass.: D.C. Heath.

Vaughn, G.A. 1976. "Sources of Downward Bias in Estimating the Demand Income Elasticity for Urban Housing", *Journal of Urban Economics,* 3: 45-56.

Wheaton, W.C. 1977. "A Bid Rent Approach to Housing Demand", *Journal of Urban Economics,* 4: 200-217.

White, M.J. 1977. "On Cumulative Urban Growth and Urban Density Functions", *Journal of Urban Economics,* 4: 104-112.

Wingo, L. 1961. *Transportation and Urban Land.* Washington, D.C.: Resources for the Future.

2.2 RESPONSES

1 William G. Grigsby

My comments are triggered by, but not a critique of, John Quigley's paper. The paper has served to clarify in my mind a situation which has been bothering me for some time. It is what might be described as the "Two Separate Worlds of Housing Analysis". These two separate worlds consist of two different groups of researchers, each pursuing similar topics in housing in quite different ways and not really bothering to communicate with each other or, in some cases, even to acknowledge the existence of the other world. Although it is an oversimplification to segment the domain of housing analysis so rigidly, such caricature does lead to some rather interesting insights about the field.

The fact that there really are two worlds was brought home to me when I read John's bibliography. I realized that had I written a paper on the same topic, my bibliography would have overlapped his by no more than 25 per cent. John himself bridges the two worlds of housing analysis. His paper, however, tends to be a history and description of housing demand analysis in what we may term for discussion purposes, World I. This world can be identified from his citations: Alonso, Muth, Mills, Wheaton, and so forth.

The other world, which some persons would characterize as the Netherworld, I will simply refer to as World II. Like World I, it is also most easily identified by reference to several of the individuals in it: Anthony Downs, George Sternlieb, Wallace Smith, Louis Winnick, Chester Rapkin, Frank Kristof, Michael Stegman, Sherman Maisel, Leo Grebler — even Ed Banfield, who most of the occupants of World I would not regard as a housing analyst at all. Obviously there are many persons, such as Jack Lowry and Hugh Nourse, who are hard to classify, but that there are these two separate worlds I will try to demonstrate, using John's paper.

To characterize the World I analysts very loosely, they rely more heavily on secondary data, are much more sophisticated mathematically, and are more "macro and long-term", as John put it, than are their counterparts in World II. They do not have much knowledge, it seems to me, of housing markets except as revealed to them through their regression analyses. They are somewhat removed from policy. John described at least some of their analysis as "uninteresting", a description which I think is both too severe and too charitable. Severe, because without doubt World I analysts have made a substantial contribution to the fund of housing knowledge that the World II group has not; charitable because they have contributed a certain amount of misinformation as well.

The Netherworld is somewhat the opposite of the other world -- more policy oriented, less sophisticated mathematically, and more interested in micro- and submarket relationships, a focus which sometimes leads to conclusions that suffer from fallacy of composition. What is more interesting is the fact that these two different worlds can exist side by side and not communicate with each other very often. This may be due to lack of mutual respect. Judging from remarks made to me by World I and World II scholars, it is my impression that World I looks down on World II, and World II finds World I not only uninteresting but also naive.

With this notion of two worlds of analysis serving as a framework for discussion, let us now turn to the paper itself. John commences his review with the observation that, "Many of the seminal insights about the operation of housing markets were derived in the mid-1960s from the observation that housing and employment accessibility are jointly purchased", and he credits World I analysts with this discovery. In reality, however, this is a World II insight, going back at least to the mid-1950s, when it was the foundation of several large housing market studies. For example, data on journey-to-work were gathered in Philadelphia as part of the supplement to the 1956 National Housing Inventory, precisely for the purpose of implementing the theory of joint accessibility. John also gives Mills credit for a very ingenious study having to do with the changing density gradients of cities from 1880 to the present. These changes, however, were first documented over twenty years ago by Hans Blumenfeld. Mills might have demonstrated the change a little more elegantly, but Blumenfeld's analysis was more timely.

John discusses in considerable technical detail the use of hedonic indices in housing demand analysis, attributing the development of this strand of analysis to Griliches and Lancaster. Actually the notion that consumers of housing purchase varying quantities of different underlying attributes precedes Griliches and Lancaster by some years. What those who have worked on hedonic indices in the housing field have done is to illuminate the value that the market as a whole seems to place on given attributes at any one point in time, and that is a very useful advance in housing knowledge. But it is interesting to note that another group of housing analysts, who would probably regard themselves as in World II, have gone beyond assigning implicit prices to interior space, exterior space and so forth, to suggest that when people demand varying quantities of these characteristics what they really see themselves as buying are status, security, peer group acceptance, etc. These analysts want to understand how and why people relate different housing attributes to their perceived personal physical and psychological needs. I would argue that this area of analysis has considerable policy importance. If the question, for example, is how to stimulate a return of middle-class families to the central city, it is important to recognize that when families buy an acre of land for a home in the suburbs, they are not just buying a good bit of land but rather are attempting to obtain what that land represents to them, possibly beauty, quiet or privacy. In order to persuade families to choose less outdoor space, it is necessary to find out what it is that is represented by such space and how some of the same things could be provided in a more urban environment. This is but one illustration. Demographically similar families differ with respect to the proportion of income they wish to spend for housing, their aversion to racially integrated neighbourhoods and their architectural preferences. We need to devote more attention to these sorts of things and less to hedonic indices themselves.

One of the few subjects that has brought housing analysts from the two worlds together in open dialogue is the income elasticity of demand for housing. The exchange was brief and it was brutal. In 1962, Margaret Reid published *Housing and Income,* in which she attacked Schwab's law, which in effect states that the income elasticity of demand is less than one. She found that the elasticity was not only more than one, but that it might be as much as two. Louis Winnick criticized her analysis and was roundly criticized in return. Since then the quest for the "true" elasticity has been almost exclusively by World I analysts, most of whom now appear to conclude that Winnick was right. Yet the evidence is still not totally convincing, because the various analyses tend to ignore certain important variables, for example, the number of houses that people own, imputed income on equity, and moving and ownership transfer costs. They also have typically ignored possible differences in elasticity across income groups and household attributes, even though aggregate elasticity estimates are close to worthless.

John mentions, almost in passing, the research on locational preferences of various income groups. Since this subject illustrates even better than the others the two separate worlds of housing analysis and since John deals with the matter so briefly, I would like to expand beyond his discussion, using a passage from Wheaton (1977) to highlight the distance between the two worlds.

> ... It is the view of some urban theorists that households of
> greater income select more distant suburban locations as a
> natural consequence of long-run spatial competition. For
> this to be the case, the income elasticity of land consumption
> must exceed the income elasticity of the cost of travel -- in-
> cluding the value of commuting time. Based on cross-section

> data, the results of this study strongly suggest that these two
> elasticities are very similar, in fact so much so that the spatial
> bidding for land of different income groups looks almost identi-
> cal.
>
> The indirect implication of this result is that the long-run
> spatial theory of Alonso, Mills and Muth empirically contributes
> little to the explanation of American location-income patterns.
> This lends strong credence to the view of other urban economists
> that the suburbanization of America's middle and upper classes
> is a response to housing market externalities and the fiscal incen-
> tives of municipal fragmentation.

This passage is especially interesting because in attacking his fellow World I
analysts, Wheaton offers just one alternative theory and does not refer at all to
several other theories which grow out of the world that he either does not hold
in high regard or is not familiar with. But Downs and several other World II
analysts explain urban growth quite differently, emphasizing the cost of newly
constructed housing relative to family income, the cost of vacant versus developed
land, the cost of high-rise housing and the interaction between the markets for
new and existing units.

The final topic discussed by John is the estimation of utility functions. This
is an area where the World I analysis is elegant and interesting — and probably
wrong. The basic question is whether preference functions can be derived from
behavioural data. Several World I researchers say Yes, but there is substantial
evidence to suggest No, a fact which casts doubt on some of the conclusions derived from this analysis. What is alleged is that households with the same socio-
economic characteristics, who work at the same general location, should have
the same housing preference function. Using this assumption, the housing decisions of all these households can be taken together to construct a preference
curve. Without the assumption, one would be faced with the problem of knowing only one point on the preference curve of each household. Since the whole
basis of this analysis derives from the assumption that people with similar socio-
economic characteristics have similar housing preferences, it is fair to ask whether there is any evidence as to whether this is in fact so and, if not, whether any
attempt has been made, in the 12 or so years during which the assumption
has been accepted, to gather such evidence. The answer by those who accept the
assumption is that perhaps similar socio-economic groups do not have exactly the
same preferences but the differences must be very small. Therefore the question
is not worth exploring. So for over a decade World I analysts have massaged
census data on this assumption, when they could have easily assembled a panel
of consumers in order to find out whether the assumption is correct. This casual
attitude is particularly disturbing because limited evidence suggests that the
assumption is not correct. While one can be quite critical of such apparent myo-

pia, perhaps the more important point is that the two groups of housing analysts have differing styles and, associated with these styles, differing sets of skills and differing views as to what is personally rewarding. These divergences contribute to the two separate analytical worlds.

In his conclusion, John points out that much needs to be learned about housing demand, a point with which all persons who make their living by studying housing demand would no doubt agree. But it would seem to me that we are obliged to ask *why* we need to know more about housing demand. Let me, therefore, give several examples of why such knowledge is so essential.

In 1975, the U.S. Congress passed a bill to get rid of an overhang of several hundred thousand new, unsold homes. The bill provided that with respect to any house under construction by March 31, 1975 and purchased by December 31, 1975, the purchaser would be eligible for an income tax rebate of 5 per cent up to $2,000. It is estimated that the aggregate cost of these rebates to the American taxpayer was well above $300 million, but that all but about 12,000 of the new homes would have been sold anyway without the rebate. In other words, the plan cost over $25,000 per household, an expense that could have been avoided if Congress knew a little more about housing demand. Another programme, known as the Targeted Tandem Plan, which has emerged from the Department of Housing and Urban Development within the last year illustrates the same point. The Plan would subsidize mortgage interest rates by about 1 per cent for middle- and upper-income families if they would move into "distressed" city neighbourhoods. This potentially expensive proposal is implicitly premised on assumptions about housing demand elasticities which would appear to be highly questionable and which, in any case, cannot be tested with available data.

Unfortunately, the list of such examples is quite long. Each year new proposals embodying various implicit assumptions about housing demands are brought forward. So we need to know much about housing demand, if for no other reason than to prevent the wasteful expenditure of public funds. Whether the necessary understanding will come primarily from World I or World II analysis, or a third world group, I don't know, but it will come sooner if the several worlds attempt to reduce the distances among them.

REFERENCES

Reid, M. 1962. *Housing and Income.* Chicago: University of Chicago Press.

Wheaton, W.C. 1977. "Income and Urban Residence: An Analysis of Consumer Demand for Locations", *American Economic Review,* 67, 4: 630-631.

RESPONSES

2 Lawrence B. Smith

The thrust of my remarks tonight is to indicate areas for future research in housing markets beyond those identified in John Quigley's excellent paper. Before
doing this I would like to elaborate on a point which I think was implicit in Bill
Grigsby's comments, namely that research today often has a tendency to concentrate excessively on the sophistication of the technique and to overlook institutional considerations. Consequently, economists have come to focus more and more
on narrow esoteric issues which lend themselves to this treatment rather than on
the basic fundamental issues, and non-economists have come to carry out a higher proportion of the work on such issues. This is a trend which I view as quite undesirable in view of the narrowness of policy recommendations that follow from
many of the latter,   and I would hope that as a profession we economists could
return to the approach of such incisive scholars as Leo Grebler, David Blank,
Louis Winnick and Jack Guttentag who combined solid economic analysis and
technique with detailed institutional knowledge to greatly advance our understanding of housing markets and behaviour.
    Turning now to areas for future research, I think there are many topics which
require further investigation. One of the points that ran as an undercurrect in
John's paper, but which was not stressed enough, was the issue of equilibrium in
housing markets. Implicit in much of what John said was that housing markets
are in long-run equilibrium, and I agree with that. But on the other hand, a lot of
work recently by people like Ray Fair and Dwight Jaffe has focused on the possibility of disequilibrium in the market and the implications of such disequilibrium.
This question really goes to the heart of the adjustment mechanism in the housing
market, and is a debate that is far from decided at this point. I think many of the
conclusions that we have drawn by assuming equilibrium are probably appropriate—
i.e., when all the work is in we will probably conclude that there is some long-run
equilibrium and that the adjustment period necessary to this equilibrium is not too
long—but if it turns out that this is not correct a lot of conclusions about the operation of housing markets and policy based on them will have to be revised.
    A second area of uncertainty is that of price adjustment mechanisms, both in
single-family and rental housing. In particular there are two or three areas of the
adjustment process which have surfaced recently and for which we do not as yet
have answers. One aspect is the relationship between price expectations and adjustments in the housing market. Speaking technically for a moment, I think the
application of rational expectations as a procedure for solving some of these
issues is a useful approach, but more work is needed in this direction. Regardless
of the procedure followed, the question of the relationship between price expec-

tations and rapidly rising prices is still a mystery. In fact the whole issue of recent price inflation in the housing sector and the differential rates in the single and multiple sectors of the market is an area very much in need of additional research. Incidentally, this is one area where we in Canada could lead the way, since we experienced our rapid inflation a few years before the U.S. and thus we have a better data base. Another aspect of the price adjustment mechanism that requires additional investigation is the growing acceptance of housing not only as a consumption good but as an investment good, and here I mean not only multiple housing but also single-family housing.

A third area for future research is the whole area of government tax policy, not only property tax policy but income tax, capital gains tax and other tax policies that affect the demand for housing as an investment, since changes in these taxes shift the demand for housing and generate house price movements. This is a particular area of government policy where I think all the answers are not in yet, but where we have at least begun to look at the question.

A fourth and substantially different area that is open to debate is that recently raised by Allan Meltzer, on the role of credit availability in allocating resources to the housing sector. For a long time the view was that interest rates and availability of funds were very important in allocating funds to housing. Meltzer does not really disagree with this in the short run but has recently challenged the proposition by saying that in the long run the availability of funds for housing probably has little or no effect on the transfer of real resources into the housing sector. This proposition has enormous implications for government housing policy, becuase one of the cornerstones of housing policy in North America has been an attempt to increase the long-run availability of funds. But if the primary consequence of that policy is to shift the allocation of housing and real resources from the private sector to the public sector, without any substantial effect on the overall allocation of real resources to the housing sector, then a lot of effort has been devoted to a policy that probably is counterproductive. This proposition is far from proven but it is sufficiently important to warrant considerable investigation.

A fifth area for research very much in the spirit of the Meltzer argument is the implication of government acting as a financial intermediary in the housing field, i.e., the role of federal housing programs in allocating real resources and funds to the housing sector, and the question of whether there are crowding-out effects in capital markets. By crowding-out effects I mean that if funds are being allocated to housing from other sectors as a result of government policy, where are these funds coming from? Are other borrowers being driven out of the capital market because of this intervention? When government intervenes in the capital market it influences the normal allocation of funds by allowing a sector to generate a demand for funds without being constrained by the normal profit and income constraints because of the subsidies it provides. If this intervention reallocates additional real resources and funds into the housing sector, from what other sectors are these funds shifted and what are the implications of this shift?

Some recent work that I have done in the area suggests that there is not much crowding out: it suggests that most of the funds which the government is reallocating are really just coming out of the private housing sector. However, if this is the case it leads to a whole other area of research, namely "why bother?" If all we are doing is taking funds from the private sector, putting them into the government sector and increasing costs while we do it, then why get into the game? Also, I should point out that the game we are talking about is expensive. In work that I have just finished I estimated some of the direct subsidies implicit in federal policies. In 1976, federal housing programs provided direct subsidies (excluding tax concessions) of about $400 million to housing; and provincial programs provided an additional $100 million. On a cash flow basis, the federal gross cash flow to housing in 1976 was over $1.5 billion, and this ignores the provincial and municipal cash flow. Thus, we are talking about very large magnitudes and yet very little is known about the implications and resource consequences of these programs.

Finally, one of the crucial issues in housing market research is the size of price and income elasticities. Considerable work has been undertaken over the years in this area and John Quigley's paper provides a good summary of it. The application of these results to research in the policy areas will be most useful. Moreover, this usefulness for Canada is not diminished by virtue of its concentration on the United States since differences between market responses and behaviour in the two countries are slight, although the role of government in the two markets is quite different. Confirmation of this is the fact that price and income elasticities emerging from work on Canada are very similar to those indicated by John for work on the U.S. If these similarities are representative of the possible extrapolation of research results between the two countries, then considerable benefits can be gained in many of the areas I have discussed by Canadian and American researchers paying more attention to their counterparts and to the results of policy experiements across the border.

RESPONSES

3 Jeffrey Patterson

Let me confirm that what Bill Girgsby has just said with respect to the United States, applies also to Canada. In Metropolitan Toronto, as well as in other housing markets in Canada, we have more unsold housing units on the market than we have had for many years, mostly due to federal and provincial government assisted home ownership programs. I understand that those two levels of government are now financing about 65 per cent of rental starts through one program or another. In Canada as well, then, governments would appear to be in need of considerable additional intelligence with respect to their housing market interventions.

This paper was a very difficult one for me to react to, because it is an overview paper, and all one can comment on in an overview paper is whether the discussion helps one to understand the field and whether the paper is comprehensive or not. And on both these scores it has the limitations that Bill Grigsby described; that is, it is very elaborate in describing what econometricians have contributed to the field but is not adequate in some other areas. By way of putting forth my own views, which will be from the perspective of a social planner and policy analyst, I will just describe briefly what I consider to be some of the attributes of the paper and some of the things that I wish we could go further on and maybe some areas in which I think economists should do further research.

First, I think the paper contains a comprehensive review and analysis of the locational aspects of housing research. I was quite heartened to learn something that I had felt for a long time, but that had been unconfirmed; that accessibility is not all that important a determinant of housing prices and price variations. I think some time ago Straszheim found out that commuters on the whole are indifferent up to about twenty minutes of travelling time.

Probably more than anything else, and I think it has relevance to policy issues that are being debated in Ontario right now, I appreciated the discussion of income elasticity and price concepts. John said in his conclusion that it had profound implications in terms of work on property tax assessments; I think that what he is saying has very immense implications for the current debate on whether or not the province of Ontario is to establish some form of reformed property taxation system in which assessment is related to market value. If the elasticity of demand for housing is less than unity, as concluded by John, then the adoption of market value assessment would result in a regressive property tax in so far as it applies to personal residences.

I think as well that some of the comments that John made on the fact that current market prices may not be a good indicator of ability to pay, or of consumption preferences, may also place some doubt on whether or not any improvements we might make in property value assessments in the province of Ontario would, in fact, result in a better local property tax. I was also heartened by some of the more recent research which John cites on hedonic price functions.

I have several criticisms of the paper: one of them, of course, is that it suffers the consequences of being written mostly for the economists in our audience. That is both good and bad. But, because I happen to be a social planner, I would like to have seen more focus on research that is going on, concerning the demand functions of low-income people. I noted in the paper that John and others have done research on the shelter supplement experiments in the U.S., and I wish that economists had made greater strides in informing us what the elasticity of demand for certain items in the housing package was as a result of this. I wish as well that we knew more about what low-income people prefer when they are less than able to afford adequate housing in the market.

There are a number of questions concerning what we as Canadians can learn from this paper. I would like to know why housing prices in Canada seem to have outpaced those in the U.S., in spite of the fact that we do not give the same subsidy for home ownership as is given in the U.S. I would also like to know, for instance, what determines the decision of a household to live in a single-family house versus an apartment. In the late 1960s we had a glut of apartments on the Canadian market. Many new households who at a previous time would have preferred to go into a single-family house went into apartments in fact in the late 1960s. Of course, the post-war baby boom was partly, but not wholly, responsible for this fact. Now these households seem to be moving into single-family houses. In terms of housing market research I do not think that we know why this pattern was timed as it was. To what extent was it influenced by federal or provincial policies with respect to housing subsidies?

I commented on the fact that I think that land could have been given greater consideration in this report and the fact that we should separate the demand for improvements on land from demand for land itself to learn more about housing markets.

I think we need to know more about the long-term elasticity of housing and housing demand because there are some indications that, in terms of the total economy, long-term elasticity is greater than unity in Canada right now. I think there is evidence that, at least in the short term, greater amounts of our income are going towards paying for the housing package, either to purchase housing or, certainly if you consider what banks get by way of interest rates, to make monthly mortgage payments. We do not know what this means in terms of future markets in Canada.

III

Demand and Income Analysis

3.1 SOME EVIDENCE ON THE RECENT BOOM IN LAND AND HOUSING PRICES[1]

David T. Scheffman

At the risk of belabouring points which may be obvious to Conference participants, in this paper I am going to discuss the recent boom in urban land and housing prices in Canada, and attempt to shed some light on the relative importance
of its various causal factors. Although the majority of academic urban economists
are apparently in agreement that the boom was the result of a large increase in
the demand for housing, brought about principally by inflation, demographic
factors, increasing income, and institutional changes in the mortgage market and
tax policies, this agreement is evidently not shared by the wider circle of professionals interested in urban problems or by the "man in the street".[2] This is unfortunate, since it is politicians, and ultimately the man in the street, who determine
government policies, and policies directed at incorrectly perceived causal factors
may have serious consequences.

Therefore, my first task in this paper will be to present evidence which I hope
will convince the layman as to the basic causes of the boom. The main evidence
considered will be a comparison between different Canadian cities, and a comparison between Canada and other countries. For the reader who already has the
"truth", I believe that some of the data presented will be of interest. My second
task will be to attempt to assess the relative importance of these basic causes.
This assessment will have important implications both for current Canadian policy
and for those wishing to understand the urban land and housing price boom which
has begun in the United States in the last year.

The general outline of the paper is as follows. First, I shall present and discuss
the data on the price and supply of housing and land in Canada during the boom
period, and list and discuss the major factors which contributed to the boom.
Then evidence for three countries (the United States, Great Britain and Australia)

will be presented. This evidence will provide some information on the relative importance of the various factors which caused the boom. Finally, an econometric estimate of the demand for housing in Canada will be presented. This estimate will be used to assess the relative importance of some of the factors contributing to the boom, and to attempt predictions about the future course of house prices.

THE CANADIAN BOOM

Housing and Land Price Data

Perhaps the most important factor leading to incorrect perceptions of the causes of the boom was the feeling in each locality that the boom was a *local* phenomenon. By now it is probably apparent to most people that the boom was in fact a *national* phenomenon, occurring in all major metropolitan areas in Canada. The available data on land and house price trends for several Canadian metropolitan areas is presented in table 1. There are three house "price" and one land "price" data series available.

1. Average Estimated Total Costs (land and structure) of New Single-Detached Dwellings Financed under the National Housing Act (CMHC). This series is an average of total costs as estimated by owner and building applicants at the time of approval for National Housing Act (NHA) financing. There are several problems with this series. First, it is a series of *estimated* costs rather than market prices. Second, NHA-financed new housing has been predominantly low-priced housing in recent years, because of NHA income and loan limits. Finally, there is no control for geographical location in this data series. The typical NHA-financed house in an urban area has moved farther out from the city centre each year, and the NHA data are not confined to urban areas. This results in the land cost component of total estimated costs being increasingly unrepresentative of "average" land costs.

2. Average Dollar Value Per MLS Transaction (Canadian Real Estate Association). These data are an average of all Multiple Listing Service (MLS) transactions, which include houses, apartments, vacant land, and commercial and industrial properties. However, MLS listings are predominantly single-detached houses, so that the average MLS transaction probably only moderately overstates average house prices. Shifts in the composition of low and high priced houses also affect the index. Despite the problems with this series, it is more representative of the trend in *average* house prices in recent years than the NHA series.

3. New House Price Index (Statistics Canada). This is an index of "quality-adjusted" new house prices, available for six cities (Montreal, Toronto, Ottawa-Hull, Winnipeg, Calgary, and Edmonton). Comparing these three house "price" series with my experience with the London and Toronto markets has convinced me that the MLS series is the most representative of the trend of average house

prices during the 1970s: the other two series do not as accurately reflect the timing and magnitude of the boom.

The only available data on land "prices" are:

4. Average Estimated Land Costs of New Single-Detached Dwellings Financed under NHA (CMHC). This is the land cost component of the Average Estimated Total Costs series. It shares the same defects as the total costs series, with the absence of control for location and lot size being even more critical. [3]

In each city the boom period fell between early 1972 and the end of 1976. Table 1 presents the percentage change between the end of 1971 and the end of 1976 of the three house "price" and one land "price" series for ten Canadian cities. [4]

The data on house and land prices demonstrate conclusively that the housing and land price boom occurred throughout the country and resulted in a significant increase in the *real* price of housing and land (the change in the consumer price index (CPI) for 1971-76 was 48.9 per cent).

TABLE 1

Percentage Change in House and Land Prices by Urban Area, 1971-76

	Average estimated total costs[1]	Average MLS transaction[2]	New house price index[3]	Average estimated land cost[4]
Vancouver	76.7	159.5		182.6
Edmonton	138.9	148.8	145.8	187.3
Calgary	151.1	197.1	143.1	233.1
Regina	141.3	153.1		224.6
Winnipeg	137.9	114.9	99.8	264.5
Toronto	75.8	97.3	80.7	134.1
Ottawa-Hull	92.0	85.4	92.5	175.2
Montreal	80.4	67.9	100.9	48.2
Halifax	30.5	73.3		28.0
St. John	72.8	102.3		71.7
Canadian average	80.5	109.0		101.1

SOURCES:

1 CMHC, *Canadian Housing Statistics*
2 Canadian Real Estate Association
3 Statistics Canada
4 CMHC, *Canadian Housing Statistics*

Housing Supply

The most popular media explanations of the real estate boom seem to focus on supply restrictions; for example, monopoly developers and restrictive government approval processes. In table 2 the number of dwelling completions for the periods 1966-71 and 1971-76 for the earlier group of ten cities are represented.

These data understate the increase in the production of non-rental housing because of the slowdown in the production of rental housing in the latter period. This is illustrated by table 3.

These data clearly show that the amount of housing supplied increased during the boom period. It is true that the production of housing was constrained in some cases, such as in the Toronto area where the production of new housing was restricted by a shortage of servicing capacity and the complicated Ontario subdivision approval process. It is also true that the growth of anti-development sentiment among ratepayers (and therefore local governments) seems to be a feature common to many Canadian urban areas. However, despite factors such as these which tend to restrict new supply, housing production was at an all-time high during the period 1971-76, so that it is not clear that the absence of these constraining forces would have resulted in a significant increase in production.

TABLE 2

Dwelling completions, 1966-71, 1971-76
(Total number of units completed)

	1966-71	1971-76
Vancouver	68,956	74,850
Edmonton	36,231	40,476
Calgary	33,114	35,535
Regina	5,894	9,175
Winnipeg	26,804	35,090
Toronto	148,576	170,881
Ottawa-Hull	30,776	56,915
Montreal	117,253	133,086
Halifax	8,512	14,556
St. John	2,312	7,061

SOURCE: CMHC, *Canadian Housing Statistics*

TABLE 3
Total housing completions for centres of population of
10,000 and over, 1966-71, 1971-76 (Units)

	1966-71	1971-76
Single-detached, semi-detached and duplex	274,206	457,197
Row, apartment and other	435,851	487,379
Total	710,057	944,576

SOURCE: CMHC, *Canadian Housing Statistics*

Factors Affecting the Housing Market during the 1970s

Demographic factors The main demographic factor of the 1970s was the increase
in population of the usual home owning age group resulting from the post-World
War II "baby boom". The number of families grew at an annual rate of 2.5 per
cent over the period 1971-76. (The number of families with age of head 25-34
grew at an annual rate of 5.6 per cent, 1971-76; CMHC, *Canadian Housing Statistics*). Therefore there were 672,100 more families and 982,500 more households in 1976 than in 1971.

A comparison of these figures with the earlier data on housing completions
(recall the housing completion data were for centres of population of 10,000 or
more) indicates that the real estate boom was not accompanied by a significant
housing "shortage", at least on a national basis.

Accompanying the increase in families and households during the 1970s was
the continuance of the trend towards increased urbanization. For example, urban
population as a proportion of total population increased from 70 per cent in 1961
to 76 per cent in 1971. Metropolitan population as a proportion of total population increased from 48 per cent in 1971 to 56 per cent in 1976 (CMHC, *Canadian Housing Statistics*). All of these factors indicate that demand forces were
strong in urban areas.

Income Real income grew at an unusually high rate during the 1970s. For
example, real (deflated by the CPI) disposable income per household grew at an
average annual rate of 3.8 per cent over the period 1970-75, while real median

family income grew at an average annual rate of 5.3 per cent over the period 1970-75 (CMHC, *Canadian Housing Statistics*).

Inflation   The 1970s was a period of the highest inflation experienced in Canada since the 1920s. The average annual rate of change of the CPI for the period 1971-76 was 8.3 per cent. Since housing is a prominent *real* asset in consumers' stock of wealth, and financial assets are likely to perform badly in periods of incorrectly anticipated inflation, the *asset* demand for housing would be expected to increase during inflationary periods. The performance of financial assets in Canada in the 1970s is summarized in the next section.

Financial markets   The high rate of inflation was accompanied by very poor performance of most financial assets, as indicated by table 4.

The mortgage market   Several aspects of the mortgage market during the 1970s had an important impact on the housing market. First, the high rates of inflation were accompanied by unusually high nominal, but unusually *low real*, mortgage rates (see table 5). The average conventional mortgage rate was 10.78 per cent over the period 1972-76 and 7.79 per cent over the period 1957-71. However, the average *real* conventional mortgage rate was 2.47 per cent over the period 1972-76, and 5.24 per cent over the period 1957-71 (CMHC, *Canadian Housing Statistics*).

The unusually low real mortgage rates were accompanied by an enormous increase in mortgage financing, as indicated by table 5.

There were three important institutional changes in the mortgage market during the late 1960s and early 1970s which allowed this enormous increase in mortgage financing:

1. The Bank Act was amended in 1967 to allow the chartered banks to engage in conventional mortgage lending for the first time.

2. Several changes were made in 1969 in the regulations governing NHA financing, including allowing the rate on NHA-financed mortgages to be determined by market forces.

3. Through changes in the law, *private* mortgage insurance became possible on a significant scale:

> Until 1970, most institutional lenders were permitted to invest in mortgage loans up to 75 per cent of the appraised value of the property unless the loans were insured by CMHC. In 1970, the federal legislation was extended permitting institutional lenders to invest in mortgage loans in excess of 75 per cent of the appraised value of the property provided that the excess was insured by a private mortgage insurance company or the government of a country, province or

TABLE 4

Real rate of return on various assets, 1970-76
(July annual yield minus percentage change in CPI)

	Federal government bonds %	Corporate bonds %	Common shares[1] %
1970	4.61	5.88	−11.04
1971	4.59	5.78	− 1.79
1972	2.69	3.58	14.00
1973	0.23	1.06	5.38
1974	−1.39	−0.07	−27.68
1975	−1.46	0.12	−17.43
1976	1.87	3.05	

SOURCE: CMHC, *Canadian Housing Statistics*

1   Index of all TSE Industrials, Statistics Canada, *Canadian Statistical Review*

TABLE 5

Mortgage approvals, 1967-76 ($ millions)

	Total value of all mortgage approvals by lending institutions for new residential construction	Total value of all residential mortgage approvals by lending institutions[1]	Real mortgage rate[2] %
1967	1,100.9	1,755.8	4.4
1968	1,794.7	2,366.5	5.1
1969	1,690.1	2,362.4	5.3
1970	1,396.7	2,119.9	7.1
1971	2,470.5	3,829.4	6.6
1972	3,005.5	4,900.5	4.6
1973	3,711.9	6,970.6	2.2
1974	2,880.0	5,954.3	0.7
1975	4,672.9	9,002.1	0.55
1976	5,756.4	10,200.5	4.36

SOURCE: CMHC, *Canadian Housing Statistics*, 1976

1   New and existing housing

2   July conventional mortgage rate minus (calendar) year percentage change in CPI

state in which the mortgage was issued. In the period 1971-73, most of the provinces passed parallel legislation permitting provincially chartered companies to make privately insured high ratio mortgages. These changes in legislation led to an increase in the activity of the only private mortgage insurance company operating in Canada at the time and contributed to the creation in 1972 of two others (Hatch, 1975: 67).

Table 6 illustrates the increasing importance of private mortgage insurance in providing conventional high-ratio mortgages.

Public policies   There were several new national and provincial policies adopted during the early 1970s which affected the housing market, [5] including subsidized rental programs, subsidized home ownership programs, rent control and, in particular, revision of the federal tax statutes. The revisions to the Income Tax Act in 1971 included the introduction of capital gains taxation (with one-half the capital gain treated as earned income) which exempted owner-occupied housing. Although the effect of such a tax on the demand for housing is ambiguous on theoretical grounds, it would be expected to increase the demand for housing (because housing is an asset), as would subsidized home ownership programs.

Some Initial Conclusions

The real estate boom of the 1970s was a *national* phenomenon, indicating that the primary factors causing the boom were common to virtually all parts of the country. Several factors have been discussed which affected the housing market during the 1970s. Each of these factors would be expected to increase the demand for housing (i.e., to increase the demand for housing services, or the demand for housing as an asset). At the same time, it was shown that the quantity of new housing produced during the early 1970s increased over previous periods. Therefore it should be clear that supply-side restrictions did not *cause* the boom, although they may have had an effect on the *magnitude* of the boom.

To test whether differential supply restrictions had an appreciable effect on the magnitude of the boom in various cities, I conducted the following simple test. The group of ten cities which were discussed earlier in this section were ranked by two criteria: (1) in decreasing order of the rate of price (MLS) increase during the period 1971-76; (2) in increasing order of the percentage increase of completions during the period 1971-76 over completions 1966-71. A test of the null hypothesis that differential supply restrictions were *not* important could be conducted by testing of the null hypothesis that the rank correlation of these two rankings is non-positive. The Spearman rank correlation coefficient was .54, which is not significant at the 5 per cent level.

TABLE 6

Sources of mortgage insurance, 1967-75[a]

	Percentage of total value of all mortgage approvals *insured* by NHA and private sources[1]	Percentage of total value of all mortgage approvals insured by private sources[1]	Percentage of total value of all mortgage approvals which are high ratio[2]	Percentage of value of all high-ratio mortgage approvals insured by private sources[2]
1967	20.5		20.5	3.8
1968	32.7		32.7	2.0
1969	26.5		26.5	1.1
1970	36.9		36.9	1.3
1971	45.4	5.4	45.4	5.5
1972	48.6	12.6	48.6	12.8
1973	56.6	34.0	55.4e	59.0e
1974	56.8	37.5	57.5e	69.5e
1975	65.5	30.8	40.7e	69.0e

SOURCES:

1 Dominion Securities Research Notes, *Equity Review*, 1976
2 Canadian Business Service, *Summary Review Service*, April 8, 1975
a Residential and non-residential, new and existing housing
e estimated

Of course this is a very naive test, but it does suggest that the importance of differential supply restrictions on the magnitude of the boom in various cities is arguable. As a naive test of the importance of differential demographic factors, the rank correlation coefficient between the rate of price increase and the population growth rate for the period 1966-74 was computed. It was found to be .783, which is significant at the 1 per cent level.

It is difficult on the basis of such very naive tests to infer much about the relative importance of the various causal factors. However, the behaviour of the stock market during the period raises doubts as to the importance of the effect of the enactment of capital gains taxation in the 1971 revision of the federal taxation statutes. The performance of common shares (as measured by the Toronto Stock Exchange (TSE) Industrials Index) was very good in 1972 and 1973 (see table 4), which is difficult to reconcile with a view that the tax caused significant portfolio reallocations between financial assets and housing.

In the next two sections evidence will be presented which will shed more light on the relative importance of the factors behind the boom.

FOREIGN HOUSING AND LAND PRICE BEHAVIOUR IN THE 1970s

During the Canadian boom period, and perhaps even today, it was not generally recognized that the real estate boom was also an *international* phenomenon. If this fact had been recognized, the causes of the boom would have been more easily understood. In this section we will discuss the experience in the United States, Great Britain and Australia. This discussion will make two contributions: (1) the argument that increases in demand caused the boom will be strengthened, and (2) a comparison of these three countries with Canada will provide some evidence as to the relative importance of the various major factors which caused demand to increase.

United States

Perhaps the major cause of the lack of recognition in Canada of the international nature of the real estate boom was that the boom in the U.S. at the time was much less dramatic. Understanding why this was the case sheds considerable light on the relative importance of the factors which caused the Canadian boom.

Inflation and general demographic trends have been very similar in the U.S. and Canada during the 1970s. However, there are some important differences between the two countries. For example, in Canada in the post-war period there has been rapid growth in almost all major urban areas. In the U.S. general urban growth has been slower, with more variation between urban areas. For example, the West and Southwest have had rapid growth, but this was partially at the ex-

pense of slower growth in the older established major urban areas in the North-
east and North Central regions.

Urban population as a percentage of total population in the U.S. was 69.9 per
cent in 1960, and 73.5 per cent in 1970 (U.S. Bureau of the Census), while in
Canada, urban population as a percentage of total population was 70 per cent in
1961 and 76 per cent in 1971.[6] Total population in the U.S. grew at an average
annual rate of 1.65 per cent between 1961 and 1971. Thus we see that Canada is
growing faster, and evidently urbanizing faster, than the U.S. The median age in
the U.S. fell from 30.2 in 1950 to 28.1 in 1970, exhibiting the effects of the
"baby boom" (U.N., 1975).

There are also important institutional differences affecting the housing markets
in the U.S. and Canada. In the U.S. mortgage interest is tax deductible, but capital gains realized from the sale of owner-occupancy are taxable, at a rate of 25
per cent, although there is no tax liability if the proceeds of the sale are used to
purchase an equally expensive house. Private mortgage insurance has been used
for a longer period and, until recent institutional changes in Canada, more extens-
ively in the U.S.

As with the banking system, there are important differences in the mortgage
markets in the U.S. and Canada. Because of the relative unimportance of national
banks in the U.S., the mortgage market is much more a local or regional entity
than in Canada. Furthermore, the mortgage market in the U.S. is subject to a
great variety of restrictions which do not exist in Canada, such as interest rate
ceilings on deposits in savings and loan institutions, geographical lending restrictions, and usury laws which impose ceilings on mortgage rates in some states.

The effect of these and other restrictions was apparently to make the mortgage
market tighter in the U.S. during the boom period than it was in Canada. However,
as the data in table 7 show, there was a *general* increase in mortgage financing
and easing of terms, combined with low real mortgage rates at about the same
time these things occurred in Canada.

In the U.S. real personal disposable income per capita (PDIC) grew at an average annual rate of 1.9 per cent over the period 1969-74, which is considerably
smaller than the average annual rate of growth of Canadian PDIC over the same
period (4.2 per cent).

Table 8 reports data on new house price trends in the U.S. These data are
probably more representative of all new housing than are the NHA data in Canada. They clearly indicate that there was a significant increase in real house
prices in the U.S. in the early 1970s. Because these data are for *new* house
prices, they probably understate the magnitude of the boom of all house prices
(recall the difference between the new house price and MLS series in Canada).
Furthermore, they may not be definitive for new house prices. For example, in
a study done by the MIT-Harvard Joint Center for Urban Studies (1977), it is

TABLE 7

U.S. mortgage financing, 1963-75

	Annual change in total mortgage debt outstanding on non-farm 1-4 family properties ($U.S. billions)	Loan/price ratio on new homes (conventional first mortgages) %	Loan/price ratio on existing homes (conventional first mortgages) %	Real mortgage rate (new homes) (HUD series minus percentage change in CPI) %
1963	15.7	73.3	70.8	3.8
64	15.4	74.1	71.3	4.8
65	15.3	73.9	72.7	3.8
66	10.7	73.0	72.0	2.9
67	12.5	73.6	72.7	3.4
68	15.1	73.9	73.0	2.4
69	15.6	72.8	71.5	1.9
1970	13.4	71.7	71.1	2.9
71	27.0	74.3	73.9	4.5
72	38.2	76.8	76.0	4.3
73	44.1	77.3	75.2	2.0
74	33.1	74.3	72.4	-1.8
75	41.6	74.7	73.4	0.0

SOURCES: *Federal Reserve Bulletins*; CMHC, *Canadian Housing Statistics*

TABLE 8
Annual percentage change in median new house prices – U.S., by region

	% Change in CPI[1]	All Regions[2]	North-east[2]	North Central[2]	South[2]	West[2]
Average (Geometric) Annual Change 1963-71	3.6	4.3	5.3	5.4	4.3	3.9
1972	3.3	9.5	2.6	7.7	14.7	7.8
1973	6.2	17.8	18.2	12.3	19.8	17.8
1974	11.0	10.5	8.1	9.7	11.7	10.5
1975	9.2	9.5	9.7	9.7	8.1	13.4
Average (Geometric) Annual Change 1971-75	7.4	11.8	9.5	9.8	13.5	12.3

SOURCES:

1   IMF, *International Financial Statistics*
2   U.S. Bureau of the Census, *Characteristics of New Housing,* Construction reports C25-75-13

reported that the average price of a new home increased by nearly 90 per cent in the period 1970-76.[7] (The percentage change from 1970-75 in the U.S. New House Price Series which we have reported was 67.9 per cent.) However, it does appear that the boom was not as rapid or as pronounced as in Canada.

Recent evidence indicates that another house price boom began in 1975 or later in many areas of the U.S. For example, an article in the *Globe and Mail* (1977) indicates that a real estate boom of the type experienced in Toronto in 1972-74 began in California in 1975:

> Los Angeles: Southern California's sizzling real estate market has produced a new kind of commodities speculator who deals in new homes. Investment syndicates are buying homes as fast as they are built in some communities and selling them a year or so later at prices that often double their money.
> Southern California during the past two years has had a real estate market that might be described as bizarre. In many communities, prices for new and used homes have been rising by at least 1 per cent a month, and often at a much higher rate.
> Some builders have resorted to lotteries to choose who among hundreds of would-be customers could buy a limited number of new homes.
> It is not unusual for a home sold for $60,000 one month to bring $80,000 a month later. In Orange County south of here,

where it is all but impossible to buy a new home for less than
$80,000, a recent study by a state legislative committee indicated
that the assessed valuation of single-family homes had shot up
by a third during 1976 to $3.6 billion from $2.6 billion.

In a more recent article (*Wall Street Journal,* 1977) it is suggested that the
boom has spread to other areas:

What started last year in California as a regional flurry of frenzied
home-buying has spread eastward and is developing into the biggest
single-family housing boom on record.
  Instead of a firm sales contract, more and more prospective
buyers in places like Denver, Houston and Washington, D.C. are
being offered only a spot on a waiting list. While the pace is clearly
hottest in the West, 'there are no bad markets anywhere', says
Michael Sumichrast, chief economist of the National Association
of Home Builders. Fueling the boom are favorable mortgage conditions and a growing demand from newly formed households. But
especially important this year is the fear of renewed inflation.
  In 1976 the median sales price of new houses rose 12 per cent
from the previous year.....
  The median existing-home price in March was $41,000, up 10
per cent from a year earlier, according to the National Association
of Realtors.
  But probably the biggest cause of the rising home prices is the
dizzying climb of land costs. In California, 'the top price for a
single-family lot, with improvements, was $12,000 two years ago,
but now the standard price is $20,000, and they go up to $75,000
for a finished lot in the San Francisco Bay area', says John Hensley,
President of Centex Homes in California.

The American evidence raises two questions: (1) Why did house prices rise
much faster in Canada then in the U.S. during the period of the Canadian boom?
and (2) Why has a real estate boom recently begun in the U.S. but not in Canada?
  I believe that the three most important factors explaining the slower growth
of house prices in the U.S. during the early 1970s are:
  1. A significantly smaller growth of real income in the U.S. (real per capita
disposable income grew at an average annual rate of 1.9 per cent over the
period 1969-74 in the U.S., and at an annual average rate of 4.2 per cent in
Canada over the same period).
  2. Institution of wage and price controls in the U.S. for the first time in the
post-war period in August 1971, which probably had a marked dampening effect
on consumers' inflationary expectations, at least in the short run.
  3. A (relatively) tight mortgage market in the U.S.
  I believe the recent real estate boom in the U.S. is primarily the result of four
factors:

1. The weakening of the effect of wage and price controls on inflationary expectations and the eventual removal of controls.

2. A strengthening of demographic pressures resulting from the Vietnam War demobilization.

3. The apparent start of recovery from the severe recession.

4. Institutional changes in the mortgage market which reduced restrictions and made funds more widely available.

Further discussion of the comparison of the U.S. and Canadian booms will be delayed until the end of this section, so that evidence from Great Britain and Australia can be considered.

Great Britain

Great Britain presents an interesting contrast in demographic trends. Although Britain is a more urbanized country than Canada, the *rate* of urbanization has been negative in the post-war period, with urban population as a percentage of total popoulation falling from 80.8 per cent in 1951 to 77.7 per cent in 1973. The average annual growth rate of population was 0.6 per cent from 1960 to 1970 (1.65 per cent for Canada, for 1961-71). The proportion of population between the ages of 20 and 29 has only increased from 13.1 per cent in 1956 to 14.3 per cent in 1970 (U.N., 1975). The demographic forces on demand have thus been weaker in the U.K. than in Canada. By contrast, Great Britain has experienced a higher rate of inflation than Canada in recent times (see tables 9, 10 and 11).

Until the middle 1970s, when upper limits were imposed, mortgage interest was fully deductible. There is no capital gains taxation of owner-occupied residences in Great Britain.

The British financial system in the post-war period has had more restrictions on the level and structure of interest rates than the Canadian financial system. A reform of British monetary institutions was undertaken in 1971 which was largely designed to give market forces a much bigger role in the determination of the level and structure of interest rates, but this reform made an explicit exception of Building Societies. The interest rates Building Societies charge to borrowers and pay to lenders were supposed to be insulated as far as possible from competitive forces in order to keep down housing costs, particularly for first-time buyers. The effect of this insulation of Building Societies' rates is illustrated in table 9.

The Building Societies are by far the largest source of (first) mortgage financing. The only other sources are local authorities (local governments) and insurance companies, which comprise a very small proportion of mortgage financing. Table 10 presents data on mortgage advances by Building Societies. We see from

TABLE 9

Mortgage rates and retail price index changes —
Great Britain, 1965-75

	Building Societies: interest rates on approved mortgages %	Retail price index: annual percentage change %
1965	6.6	4.8
1966	6.9	3.9
1967	7.2	2.5
1968	7.5	4.7
1969	8.0	5.4
1970	8.6	6.4
1971	8.6	9.4
1972	8.3	7.1
1973	9.6	9.2
1974	11.0	16.0
1975	11.1	24.2

SOURCES: Central Statistical Office, *Financial Statistics;* IMF, *International Financial Statistics*

TABLE 10

Mortgage lending — Great Britain, 1965-75

	Net advances by main institutional sources (£ millions)
1965	703
1966	756
1967	966
1968	956
1969	802
1970	1,207
1971	1,748
1972	2,783
1973	2,831
1974	2,282
1975	3,712

SOURCES: Dept. of the Environment, *Housing and Construction Statistics,* no. 17, 1976; Ministry of Housing and Local Government, *Housing Statistics,* no. 18, August 1970

these data that there was an increase in the availability of mortgage funds during the 1970s, although the rate of increase in nominal and, especially, real terms was smaller than it was in Canada. In summary, the British mortgage market during the 1970s was characterized by much lower real mortgage rates but a smaller increase in the (apparent) availability of funds than was true of the Canadian market.

Real personal disposable income per capita grew at an average annual rate of 3.6 per cent over the period 1969-74 in the U.K., while the average rate in Canada was 4.2 per cent.

The U.K. experienced an urban land and housing price boom similar to Canada's, and at approximately the same time. For example, a ministerial statement in the British Parliament estimated that residential land for housing increased from £10,000 per acre in the second half of 1971 to £20,000 per acre in 1972 (Neutze, 1973).

In table 11 the recent trend of house and land prices and retail price index (RPI) in the U.K. is presented. These data indicate an experience very similar to the Canadian one. The magnitude of change in real terms apparently was somewhat lower in the U.K. For example, *real* MLS prices in Canada (average MLS transaction) increased by 34.6 per cent in the period 1970-75 and they were still strongly increasing in 1976. The change in *real* average purchase price of all houses in the U.K. was 27.9 per cent for the period 1970-75. Because of the difference in demographic trends, a comparison of the U.K. and Canadian data provides striking confirmation of the importance of inflation and the growth of real income in generating the real estate boom. This comparison will be discussed in more detail at the end of this section.

Australia[8]

Demographic trends in Australia and Canada in the post-war period have been similar. Australia is the more urbanized country, with the percentage of urban to total population being 81.9 per cent (70 per cent for Canada) in 1961, and 85.6 per cent (76 per cent) in 1971.[9] It also experienced a significant post-war baby boom (U.N., 1975).

Australian rates of inflation have also been higher (see table 12) and there was no attempt to index income taxes until 1976. Australia has no capital gains taxation, and marginal income tax rates are significantly higher than in Canada. Limited mortgage interest deductibility was introduced in 1974 on a sliding scale, with the proportion of mortgage interest which is deductible dependent on family income. (The proportion deductible is zero for families with total incomes greater than A$14,000.)

I have only been able to collect fragmentary evidence about the mortgage

TABLE 11

House and land prices – Great Britain, 1965-75 (Annual percentage change)

	Average purchase price – new houses [1]	Average purchase price – all houses [2]		Private sector housing land – price per plot [3]	Retail price index
		U.K.	Greater London		
1965	9.9				4.8
1966	6.9	5.5		36.0	3.9
1967	6.2	7.3		2.2	2.5
1968	5.0	6.8		15.8	4.7
1969	7.2	7.2	11.3	24.2	5.4
1970	6.4	13.2	14.5	10.0	6.4
1971	12.6	30.9	40.5	13.2	9.4
1972	31.5	34.8	29.7	67.7	7.1
1973	36.2	11.1	3.5	55.0	9.2
1974	6.1	7.3	0.0	0.0	16.0
1975	9.4			−31.0	24.2

SOURCES:

1 Dept. of the Environment, *Housing and Construction Statistics*, no. 17, 1976; Central Statistical Office, *Social Trends*, 1973. Average price, including land, of new dwellings of all types mortgaged with Building Societies by private owners.

2 Central Statistical Office, *Social Trends*, 1976; Ministry of Housing and Local Government, *Housing Statistics*, no. 18, August 1970. Average price of all dwellings mortgaged with Building Societies by private owners.

3 Central Statistical Office, *Social Trends*, 1973; Dept. of the Environment, *Housing and Construction Statistics*, no. 17, 1976 (England and Wales). Private sector housing land (at constant average density). Weighted average price per plot. These data were evidently similar to the NHA estimated land cost data in Canada.

TABLE 12

Rates of inflation — Australia, 1969-74
(Percentage change in CPI)

1969	3.5
1970	4.9
1971	7.0
1972	6.2
1973	9.3
1974	16.0

SOURCE: IMF, *International Financial Statistics*

TABLE 13

Housing financing — Australia, 1970-75
(A$ millions — June to June)

	Dwellings not previously occupied	All dwellings
1970	492.7	1,101.4
1971	569.4	1,251.1
1972	735.6	1,722.6
1973	1,147.1	2,987.6
1974	997.1	2,693.6
1975	909.0	2,910.6

SOURCE: Reserve Bank of Australia, *Statistical Bulletin*. Loans approved to individuals by savings and trading banks, major life offices and permanent building societies

market in Australia. As with Great Britain, Building Societies are a major source of mortgage financing in Australia but their relative importance is less. The evidence presented in tables 13 and 14 indicates that the Australian mortgage market during the early 1970s was similar in the growth and availability of funds, ease of terms and fall in real mortgage rates to the Canadian mortgage market during this period.

The Australian government has recently begun collecting some very good data on residential land prices — a task which the Canadian government should seriously consider undertaking. Table 15 provides data on the recent trend in land prices in major urban areas in Australia. The land price data were compiled from *transactions* on vacant urban residential land of less than one-half acre. It does not control for geographical location, or servicing differences. The starting time

TABLE 14

Mortgage rates – Australia, 1964-75

	%
June 1964 – April 1965	4.75 – 5.50
April 1965 – August 1968	5.00 – 5.75
August 1968 – April 1970	5.50 – 6.25
April 1970 – October 1973	6.25 – 7.00
October 1973 – July 1974	7.25 – 8.00
July 1974 – April 1975	9.25 – 10.00
April 1975 – September 1975	8.75 – 10.00
September 1975 –	9.00 – 10.00

SOURCE: Research Department, Federal Reserve Bank of Australia, Interest Rates on Housing Loans to Individuals (predominantly Savings Banks)

TABLE 15

Inflation and land price changes – Australian metropolitan areas, 1969-74 (Percentages)

	Change in land prices			Change in CPI
	Sydney[a]	Melbourne[a]	Adelaide[b]	
1969	12.2	8.0	5.5	3.5
1970	14.4	1.9	6.1	4.9
1971	20.1	20.2	−3.2	7.0
1972	28.3	22.4	22.3	6.2
1973	34.4	46.2	46.0	9.3
1974	26.8[c]	25.0[c]	29.7[c]	16.0

SOURCES: Australia, Department of Urban and Regional Development, *Urban Land Prices, 1968-74*; IMF, *International Financial Statistics*.

a   Median prices from publicly reported auction sales, all areas.

b   Average prices of all transactions of single vacant residential sites of less than one-half acre in fringe areas, from Land Titles Office Records (in excess of 2,000 transactions per year).

c   Percentage change to May, 1974.

and magnitude of the Australian urban land boom are remarkably similar to the Canadian experience.

I have had less success in acquiring house price data for Australia. Table 16

TABLE 16

Average MLS transaction – Sydney area, 1972–76
(Annual percentage change)

1972	11.2
1973	12.3
1974	18.2
1975	9.0
1976	8.7

SOURCE: Australian Association of Permanent
Building Societies

TABLE 17

Changes in average house prices – Melbourne area, 1972-73

	Suburb	%
Inner:	Brunswick	39.8
	Melbourne	27.4
	Port Melbourne	18.6
	Richmond	40.3
Middle:	Caulfield	37.1
	Heidelberg	30.3
Outer:	Altona	21.3
	Croyden	29.0

SOURCE: Building Science Forum (1975)

reports the annual percentage change in the average MLS transaction in the
Sydney area. These are much less reliable data than the Canadian MLS data,
because the MLS system is much less important in the real estate market in
Australia. This is probably why these data indicate a much smaller magnitude
of the change in house prices than in land prices during the boom.

As a further indication that these house prices are suspect, table 17 shows data
on the percentage change in the average house price between 1972 and 1973 in
several Melbourne suburbs. These data were derived from averages of *all* house
sales in the Melbourne area during this period, compiled by the Valuer General's
Office. [10] These figures are clearly much more in line with the Canadian experience, as represented by the MLS data.

A Comparison of the Foreign and Canadian Booms

Table 18 presents summary data which allow a convenient comparison of Canadian with foreign trends during the early 1970s.

Although I only have fragmentary data on house prices for Australia, based on that and the Australian land price data it would appear that real house prices increased at a faster rate in Australia than in Canada. For example, the average percentage change in real land prices in Sydney over the period 1970-74 was 18.5 per cent. This is a greater increase than the trend of estimated land costs of new NHA-financed housing for any of the ten Canadian cities discussed earlier. (Winnipeg had the fastest average growth rate of real estimated land costs, 14.8 per cent over 1971-75. However, as was pointed out previously, the NHA estimated land costs series underestimates the true trend of land costs. For example, the data on lot transactions in London, Ontario show an average increase of real lot prices of 16.8 per cent over the period 1970-74.)

Comparison of the Melbourne house price data with Canadian MLS data suggests a somewhat larger increase in real house prices in Melbourne; the real MLS average transaction in Toronto increased by 19.1 per cent in 1973 and 16.4 per cent in 1974. Therefore, the land and house price data suggest that Australian real house prices grew at a somewhat higher rate than Canadian real house prices.

In summary, the rate of increase in real house prices was evidently highest in Australia, followed by Canada and Great Britain, with the U.S. having the lowest

TABLE 18

Comparative data — Canada, U.S., U.K., Australia, 1969-74

	Average rate of inflation 1970–74 %	Average rate of growth of real per capita PDI 1979–74 %	Average percentage change in real house prices 1971–75 %
Canada	6.5	4.2	3.8[a] 7.8[b]
U.S.	5.9	1.9	4.4[c]
U.K.	10.4	3.6	6.2[d] 6.5[e]
Australia	8.9	5.1	N.A.

a   Average costs of new NHA-financed houses
b   Average MLS transaction
c   Median new house prices, all regions
d   Average price of new houses mortgaged with Building Societies
e   Average price of all dwellings mortgaged with Building Societies

rate of increase. If it is assumed, as I believe, that supply-side factors had little effect on the boom, the variation in the magnitude of real house price changes between countries is primarily due to the variation in demand-side factors.

Great Britain experienced a smaller growth rate in real income, and weaker demographic trends than did Canada or Australia. It also experienced the highest rate of inflation and lowest real mortgage rates of the four countries. Of the major causal factors behind the boom, Canada and the U.S. differed markedly only with respect to the growth rate of real income. The U.S. was evidently also the only country of the three not to experience a "dramatic" increase in real prices in any one year.

What can be concluded from a comparison of the four countries? That the U.S. experienced a smaller boom is explainable, perhaps, by the slower growth in real income. What must be explained, however, is the evident absence of *dramatic* short-run changes in house prices in the U.S., the absence of the apparent "speculative bubble" phenomenon experienced in the other three countries. At least two hypotheses seem plausible:

1. The higher growth of real income experienced by the other three countries was vital in allowing inflationary expectations to drive the demand for housing. The argument here is that inflationary expectations must be backed by anticipated "affordability"; i.e., consumers must anticipate that the initially high ratio of mortgage payments to disposable income will fall fairly fast.

2. The imposition of wage and price controls in the U.S. in 1971 (for the first time in the post-war period) deflated inflationary expectations.

Presumably both hypotheses have some validity. The current house price boom in the U.S. gives us additional information with which to assess them. If, as it would seem, the U.S. is now experiencing a house price boom similar to those experienced by the other three countries in the early 1970s (characterized by short-run dramatic increases in real house prices), this is occurring in the absence of the high rates of growth of real per capita income experienced by those three countries in the early 1970s – real personal disposable income in the U.S. grew 2.5 per cent during 1976. Therefore, it would appear that the institution of wage and price controls in the U.S. may have had a major dampening effect on the boom.

Irrespective of the importance of institutional factors in the U.S., a comparison of Canada with Australia and Great Britain indicates that institutional factors specific to Canada, such as the enactment of capital gains taxation and changes in mortgage market conditions, probably did not have a major impact on the magnitude of the Canadian boom. This is not to say, however, that these institutional factors will not have an important long-run impact on the housing market.

80 Demand and Income Analysis

SOME ESTIMATES OF THE DEMAND FOR HOUSING IN CANADA

In this section I shall present some estimates of the demand for housing in Canada. The focus of the investigation will be: Was the boom a result of a perturbation in the *demand function* for housing, or was it simply the result of a change in the arguments of a *stable* demand function? The answer to this question will shed some light on two important issues: (1) To what extent were inflationary expectations, speculation and institutional changes such as the enactment of capital gains taxation important in determining the current level of house prices? (2) What is the likely future course of house prices?

Given the available data, I decided to use national aggregates and to estimate the national demand for housing. [11] This is justified, I believe, by two arguments: (1) that the basic causal factors behind the boom were *national* in scope; and (2) I am interested in estimating the *long-run* demand for housing, and in the long run (because of the response of migration to differential levels of economic welfare) the smallest geographical area which can be called a housing *market* may indeed be the whole country.

The Data

Prices There are two series of house "prices" available on a national basis: the average MLS transaction and the Average Estimated Costs of NHA-financed housing. As discussed earlier, the NHA series has become increasingly unrepresentative of average house prices in recent years, so the average real MLS transaction (average MLS transaction divided by the CPI) was used as the house "price" variable. As a further argument supporting the estimation of the *national* demand for housing, it is useful to note that the yearly average MLS transactions for most

TABLE 19

Simple correlation coefficients between yearly average MLS transactions of various cities and national average, 1966–76

Vancouver	.996
Edmonton	.973
Calgary	.974
Regina	.977
Winnipeg	.986
Toronto	.983
Ottawa-Hull	.993
Montreal	.959
Halifax	.985
St John	.997

cities are very highly correlated with the yearly national average MLS transactions. The simple correlation coefficients between city and national average MLS transactions for the period 1966-76 are given in table 19.

Housing stock   Consistent with our price data (which approximates the average price of single-family dwellings), the total stock of "single-family" dwellings (which includes single-detached, semi-detached and duplexes) was used. *Total* stock estimates (as opposed to the occupied stock) were obtained from Statistics Canada for census years. The stock between census years was interpolated using completions and an estimated constant rate of demolitions and conversions.

Families   The consuming unit was taken to be the family, with the number of families derived from Statistics Canada figures.

Income   The income variable used was *real permanent family* income. This variable was estimated from a series of median family income data furnished by Statistics Canada.

Mortgage rates   The mortgage rate variable used was the *real* conventional mortgage rate (end of year conventional mortgage rate minus the percentage change in the CPI, derived from CMHC, *Canadian Housing Statistics*). The NHA rate was subject to ceiling regulations prior to 1970, but the NHA and conventional rates are highly correlated over the whole period and the addition of the real NHA rate (for the whole period, or for the period prior to the lifting of the ceiling) resulted in serious multicollinearity between the rates.

Specification

The specification assumed the usual view of the housing market, i.e., the price of housing in the short run is determined by demand, with the stock of housing given. The use of annual data presumably introduces a greater potential for simultaneity problems than quarterly data, but since our price variable reflects average "used" house prices, these potential problems are probably not serious.

The specification chosen was:

$LRMLS = C + A \cdot LSTF + B \cdot LRPFY + D \cdot LRM$

where

$LRMLS$ = Natural log of the *real* average MLS transaction
$LSTF$ = Natural log of the total stock of "single-family" dwellings per family
$LRPFY$ = Natural log of *real* permanent family income
LRM = Natural log of the *real* conventional mortgage rate

Estimation

The estimation used annual data for the period 1957-76. The estimate of the specified equation was

LRMLS = .945 − 2.7 LSTF + .925 LRPFY − .047 LRM
        (1.15) (−2.46)   (8.61)   (−2.41)

R^2 = .94 (t − statistics in parentheses)

D.W. = .6202

Because of the indicated presence of autocorrelation, the equation was re-estimated using the Cochrane-Orcutt routine. This yielded the estimate:

LRMLS = −1.05 − 2.49 LSTF + 1.15 LRPFY − .03 LRM
        (−.60) (−2.30)   (5.52)   (−2.22)

R^2 = .97 (t − statistics in parentheses)

D.W. = 1.27, Rho-hat = .72

We see the specification yielded an estimate with high explanatory power, and the coefficients of the explanatory variables were statistically significant, and the "right" sign, and implied "reasonable" elasticities. [12]

Inference

Next, a test of the null hypothesis that the demand function had not changed over the period 1971-76 was conducted. This test yielded an F-ratio (with (4, 12) degrees of freedom) of 1.55 which is just significant at the 25 per cent level. Therefore, by usual standards of significance, we cannot reject the hypothesis that the demand function was unchanged over the period.

Is this a believable conclusion? If the conclusion is valid, it means that the ("long"-run) change in house prices was simply the result of a reaction of demand to the growth of real income, low real mortgage rates and demographic factors, and that institutional changes (such as the enactment of capital gains taxation) and the unusual level of speculative activity during the boom had a minor impact. On a national basis, we have not observed a significant fall in real house prices which would signal the bursting of a speculative bubble (although there certainly has been a slowdown in the market), so that it is not unreasonable to conclude that speculation has had a minor impact on the level of prices (although speculation perhaps had a more important impact on the speed of adjustment of prices).

What about institutional changes? Changes in the mortgage market facilitated rather than caused the increase in demand. The major institutional change affecting the demand for housing was the enactment of capital gains taxation. It was argued earlier, on the basis of other evidence, that the case for this change having an important impact on the level of house prices was weak, and this argument is supported by the econometric estimates of this section. The other major institutional changes, such as the treatment of land holding costs for tax purposes, primarily affect the supply side and their impact will not be felt until supply adjusts to a longer-run equilibrium.

If demand has not changed, it is easier to forecast the future path of prices, since it is not then necessary to predict the new long-run demand function. Assuming that real mortgage rates and the growth of real income remain at "normal" levels, I would expect that as supply adjusts to long-run equilibrium, in the short run *real* house prices will fall somewhat before they resume their normal upward trend. This prediction is based on the belief that the current long-run equilibrium supply price of housing is below current house prices.

NOTES

1 Research assistance was provided by Heather Cohen, Glen Copplestone and Bernard Yeung.

2 For a discussion of the popular theories of the causes of the boom, see Bourne (1977).

3 The Average Estimated Land Costs series is deficient in three respects: (1) it represents estimated costs rather than market transactions; (2) it does not control for geographical location; and (3) NHA-financed housing has been almost entirely low priced housing in recent years. Therefore we would expect that these data understate the magnitude of increase in land prices, and this expectation is borne out by data from other sources. For example, the Comay Report (Ontario, Advisory Task Force on Housing Policy, 1973) reported that lot prices in Toronto increased by more than 100 per cent between Spring 1972 and Spring 1973.

I have also obtained a time series on market transactions of subdivision lots in London, Ontario (through the generosity of Professor Gordon Davies of the University of Western Ontario, and Professor Wayne Whitney of Wilfrid Laurier University). This series indicates a change in lot prices of 181.4 per cent over the period 1971-76, while the Average Estimated Land Costs series for London has a change of 105.4 per cent in the same period.

4 For a complete discussion of the problems involved with measuring the change in house prices from the usual house price indices, see Hamilton (1976).

5 For a much more complete discussion of the policy changes which affected the housing market, see Smith (1976).

6 The definition of "urban" is not the same for the two countries.

7 This study has been criticized by several reviewers. For example, the Economics Department of the National Association of Homebuilders (1977) claimed the

90 per cent figure was inaccurate because the "median price of homes in 1970 was badly distorted because of the large production of inexpensive subsidized Section 235 homes".

8 I am indebted to Professor Barry Reece of the University of New England for making the Australian land and house price data available to me.

9 The definition of "urban" is not the same for the two countries.

10 Data reported in Building Science Forum (1975).

11 Smith (1974) developed a quarterly model of the Canadian housing market, in which the demand for housing was estimated for the period 1957-67. For our purposes a longer-run model was necessary.

12 It has been noted in several other studies (e.g., Smith, 1974) that time series estimates generally produce smaller elasticities than cross-section estimates.

REFERENCES

Bourne, L.S. 1977. "The Housing Supply and Price Debate: Divergent Views and Policy Consequences". *Research paper no. 86,* Centre for Urban and Community Studies, University of Toronto.

Building Science Forum. 1975. "Politics of Housing". Summary of the Proceedings of the 23rd Conference of the Building Science Forum of Australia, N.S.W. Division, July.

Globe and Mail. 1977. "Housing is Hot", (April 8).

Hamilton, S.W. 1976. "Measuring House Price Changes", in M. Goldberg, ed., *Recent Perspectives in Urban Land Economics.* Vancouver: University of British Columbia Press.

Hatch, J. 1975. *The Canadian Mortgage Market.* Toronto: Ontario Ministry of Treasury, Economics and Intergovernmental Affairs.

Markusen, J.F. and D.T. Scheffman. 1977. *Speculation and Monopoly in Urban Development: Analytical Foundations with Evidence for Toronto.* Toronto: University of Toronto Press.

MIT-Harvard Joint Center for Urban Studies. 1977. *The Nation's Housing Needs, 1975-1985.* Cambridge, Mass.

National Association of Homebuilders. 1977. *Economic News Notes.* Washington, D.C.: The Association.

Neutze, G. 1973. *The Price of Land and Land Use Planning: Policy Instruments in the Urban Land Market.* Paris: Organization for Economic Cooperation and Development.

Ontario. Advisory Task Force on Housing Policy. 1973. *Report.* (E. Comay, Chairman). Toronto: Queen's Printer.

Smith, L.B. 1974. *The Postwar Canadian Housing and Residential Mortgage Markets and the Role of the Government.* Toronto: University of Toronto Press.

Smith, L.B. 1976. "Recent Shifts in Policies Affecting Housing in Canada", in M. Goldberg, ed., *Recent Perspectives in Urban Land Economics.* Vancouver: University of British Columbia Press.

Smith, L.B., and M. Walker, eds. 1977. *Public Property? The Habitat Debate Continued.* Vancouver: Fraser Institute.

U.N. 1975. *Demographic Yearbook.* New York: United Nations.

U.S. Bureau of the Census. 1975. *Statistical Abstract of the U.S.* Washington, D.C.: U.S. Government Printing Office.

Wall Street Journal. 1977. "Housing Boom Spread from Coast to Coast; Fears of Inflation Help", (May 24).

3.2 HOUSING DEMAND AND HOUSEHOLD WEALTH: EVIDENCE FOR HOME OWNERS[1]

John Bossons

Most work done on household demand for housing implicitly is based on a model in which the demand for housing is assumed to be purely for current consumption purposes, with the household budget constraint being defined as some variant of current income (cf. de Leeuw, 1971). In most applications, "current income" is defined as what a household may reasonably expect to continue to be able to earn (often called "permanent income" to differentiate it from the actual income received by the household in a particular period), reflecting the fact that households will tend to attempt to maintain their consumption at a relatively constant level when transient variations in income receipts occur.

The purpose of this paper is to show that this approach is seriously deficient in two respects: (1) by ignoring the extent to which household consumption choices are affected by household decisions on whether to become homeowners, and (2) by ignoring the importance of wealth as compared to income in defining the household's budget constraint. Wealth has traditionally been assumed to be determined by household savings choices, income and age, varying through a household life cycle in order to allow households to maintain consumption at a relatively uniform level in both working and retirement years (cf. Ando and Modigliani, 1963). It has seldom been assumed to be of importance for household consumption planning (except to the extent that it may in some applications serve as a better proxy for "permanent" income than current measured income), in part because data on household wealth is seldom collected in surveys used for testing consumption models.

The deficiencies in the traditional approach to modelling household demand for housing are discussed in the first major section of this paper. These deficiencies primarily arise because household consumption and investment choices are assumed to be separable, following in the tradition established by Irving Fisher

(1930). This assumption in turn rests on a number of more basic assumptions, which are evaluated in some detail as to their likely realism as well as to the implications of their failing to be realistic.

The discussion in the first major section points out a number of respects in which the traditional assumptions are both unrealistic and significant in their implications. These implications are then elaborated in the following section, which presents a model of household demand for home ownership that reflects a more realistic set of assumptions. This model is then tested in a third section, using data obtained from a U.S. survey that is uniquely appropriate for testing the model.

CONSUMPTION VERSUS PORTFOLIO MOTIVES FOR HOME OWNERSHIP

Under certain restrictive assumptions, the demand for housing services by households and the ownership of housing can be treated as entirely separable. Under these assumptions (described below), the determination of household demand for housing services can be treated as a standard consumer utility maximization problem, subject to a lifetime budget constraint on the household's consumption expenditures. The determination of whether the household owns a home can in such circumstances be treated as an independent problem of maximizing expected portfolio return on the household's assets, subject to constraints on the tolerable levels of uncertainty of the portfolio return.

The assumption of separable household consumption and investment decisions is a very convenient one for analytic purposes and it has consequently often been made by analysts of the demand for housing. It is, however, based on a number of strong assumptions:

1. Complete (and perfect) rental markets for services. All consumption services can be bought and sold at a market-determined rental price; this price is an exogenous parameter in household decisions. The potential empirical importance of violations of this assumption for household consumer durables has been underlined by Watts and Tobin (1960).

2. Perfect capital markets. The return on every asset is independent of household characteristics and household behaviour.

3. No transactions costs in asset portfolio adjustments. Portfolios can be redetermined each period so that no differences between desired and actual portfolios persist.

4. Temporally independent returns on assets. Returns are a martingale; together with assumptions 1-3, this implies that it is necessary only to optimize over a one-year planning horizon in order to obtain a portfolio allocation that is optimal over the remainder of a household lifetime as well (Samuelson, 1969; Merton, 1969).

5. No bankruptcies and no moral hazard in lending. Borrowing against human capital is feasible.

6. Complete asset markets. Marketable investment assets provide a basis over all potential states of nature, so that it is possible to invest in a fully diversified portfolio (Diamond, 1967).

7. No indivisibilities. Intermediation provides access to full diversification without economies of scale.

These assumptions underlie most current work on household savings and asset allocation behaviour.[2] Nevertheless, the assumptions are clearly unrealistic. More important, the results derived from these assumptions are not robust to a relaxation of the assumptions. The likely effects of the more significant failures of these assumptions are described below.

Incomplete Rental Markets

The existence of complete markets for the rental of consumption services is a more critical assumption than is generally realized.[3] Incomplete service markets are particularly important in the case of housing services and attention will be limited to this category of consumption services in this section.

Limitations on the completeness of rental markets for housing services arise from three sources: (1) limitations on the length of rental contracts, (2) the composite nature of housing services and consequent limitations on the availability in rental markets of all possible combinations of attributes contained in the composite good, and (3) the lack of separate markets for services resulting from home improvements whose production is itself a consumption activity. It should be noted that the importance of the third limitation in part arises from the first limitation.

Because of incomplete rental markets for housing services, the consumption opportunity set will differ for two households with given total wealth (including human capital) and differing only in that one household owns rather than rents the dwelling unit in which it resides. Consequently it is no longer possible for a household to obtain an optimal allocation of consumption services independent of its portfolio allocation decision. Likewise, a household's optimal portfolio allocation will depend not only on the investment returns obtainable on assets (along with the household's wealth and risk aversion) but also on the household's demands for consumption services provided by housing.

The major empirical effect of incomplete rental markets for housing services is that the demand for home ownership will depend on variables that are proxies for the demand for the services of housing attributes which cannot easily be rented separately or whose value depend on length of assured tenure.

Capital Market Imperfections

The effect of capital market imperfections is also potentially important. By "imperfect" capital markets is meant those markets for assets in which assumptions 2, 4 and/or 5 are not valid. The invalidity of these assumptions may arise from information costs, from moral hazard problems, from an insufficiency of traders or from a combination of these three considerations. Such invalidity is reflected in illiquid assets and in constraints on borrowing.

It should be noted that illiquidity and borrowing constraints are phenomena which differ from the effects of transaction costs; information costs (unlike transaction costs) do not in general simply reduce the net price received by a seller in a transaction but rather have the effect of also reducing the probability of a seller being able to effect a transaction at any price.

The most illiquid asset is equity in a small business (whether net assets of an unincorporated business or shares in a closely held corporation). Information available to potential investors is both costly and subject to potentially large error. In many cases, potential buyers with sufficient knowledge and experience to evaluate relevant information are limited to competitors, suppliers or large customers. Information problems are moreover enhanced by the extent to which such businesses may depend on the labour input of their owner.

Because of the high cost of information, the market for equity in a small business is not characterizable as a market with many traders. Instead, such assets are normally sold through a sequential bargaining process in which the seller's asking price (and tenacity in holding to this price) partly serve as informative proxy variables for the financial health of the small business or of its owner(s). Consequently the asking price for a small business cannot normally be varied without affecting potential buyers' judgement of the value of the business and of the probability of being able to induce the seller to accept a lower price. The price of an equity position in a small business is consequently not an exogenous parameter at which the asset can be easily sold, as is the case with the price of a marketable security.

It should be noted that the dependence on the owner's labour input of the return on investments in a small business is likely to be a decreasing function of the size of the business, implying a dependence of the rate of return on the length of time the investment is held. [4] A major source of capital gains in such businesses consists of building a self-sustaining management team which reduces the dependence of the business on its owner.

The major empirical effects of the illiquidity of small business equity are: (1) that as the demand for liquidity in an asset portfolio rises (e.g., with age and after retirement), the likelihood of holding small business equity will fall, and (2) that because of the multiplicative interaction of the return to investments of money in a small business, the return to labour input by the owner and the length of the holding period, there may be a tendency for younger investors in a small business to invest a higher fraction of their assets in the business (holding all other factors constant).

Constraints on borrowing have obvious implications. In general, the most realistic assumption is to postulate that borrowings are limited by the value of assets taken as collateral at the time the borrowing is made, and that illiquid assets are not generally taken as collateral. Further, it is possible for the value of assets to decline below the level of loans for which they serve as security. This has the effect of providing that previous as well as current wealth determines the consumption opportunity set for a household, since past borrowings may be maintained even in situations where the household would not be able to obtain credit as a new applicant for a loan.

The dependence of borrowing constraints on past as well as current asset values has several important empirical implications. One of the more important is that households with negative net wealth may have sizeable assets even where credit is given only on the basis of secured loans.

Indivisibilities

Though economies of scale exist with respect to other investments (particularly investments in small businesses), the most obvious indivisibility is with respect to investments in an owner-occupied dwelling unit. This has important implications for the functional form of the relationship between the probability of home ownership and household variables.

The major empirical effect of introducing indivisibilities with no other restrictive assumptions relaxed is to reduce the number of households for whom home ownership is feasible. By thus increasing the relative importance of zero-valued probabilities of home ownership, this increases the potential specification error resulting from use of a linear functional form in predicting the probability of home ownership conditional on household attributes.

In addition, the effects of indivisibilities in home ownership interact with and are accentuated by the effects of incomplete rental markets and imperfect capital markets. In particular, the potential expansion of the household's consumption opportunity set through home ownership, coupled with the requirements for minimum down payments implied by credit rationing imposed by collateral requirements, will result in a tendency for households on the margin of home ownership to allocate an unusually high proportion of their wealth to equity in a home. This will have the empirical effect of causing the fraction of total wealth invested in owned homes to decline as wealth increases.

A further potential empirical effect of indivisibilities combined with incomplete rental markets and collateral-determined borrowing constraints is that the savings rates of young households may be increased where such households have a relatively high demand for the additional consumption services and household productive opportunities provided by home ownership. Such increased savings rates will show up both prior to home ownership (presumably being accumulated in relatively liquid form for use as down payment) and subsequent to home ownership in the form of relatively high"forced" saving in the form of mortgage debt service.

Taking all these factors into consideration, it is clear that consumption and portfolio motives for home ownership cannot be analyzed separately.

THE DEMAND FOR HOME OWNERSHIP

To reflect the considerations described in the previous section, it is necessary to model inter-household differences in the demand for housing in a way that captures both variations in demand for the consumption of housing services and variations in demand for principal residences as an asset. To effect the former, it is necessary to describe how the demand for housing services is related to household characteristics. For the latter, it is necessary to reflect the portfolio balance considerations briefly described in the preceding section.

The problem created by these latter considerations is that consumption demand is not independent of the demand for principal residences as an investment asset. Consequently, the consumption of housing services depends on interdependent consumption and investment decisions. Whether or not a household owns its residence will depend in part on its demand for particular housing characteristics that can only (or more easily) be obtained through home ownership. However, it will also depend on the quantity of housing services demanded and on portfolio balance considerations. Other things being equal, the higher the quantity of services demanded (e.g., because of a larger family), the more portfolio imbalance must be accepted in order to obtain this quantity of housing services in the form of the particular bundles of housing characteristics which are obtainable through home ownership.

Household Characteristics Affecting Demand for Housing Services

A number of identifiable household characteristics can serve as proxies for differences in the demand for the consumption of housing services. Some of these (such as family size) have a direct effect on the demand for housing space and are clearly identifiable through variables such as marital status, numbers and age of children, number of other adults in the household, etc. Others (such as labour force participation of wife, education, etc) have an indirect effect on the demand for particular types of consumption services provided by housing, through affecting the extent to which leisure activities and the use of housing space are viewed as complementary by different households. Still other household characteristics may be related to the likelihood of household preferences reflecting strong and/ or unique tastes. This latter factor will affect the demand for home ownership because of the resultant demand for secure housing tenure in order to reduce the amortized cost per period of renovating housing to accord with the household's tastes; in effect, the more unique a household's preferences, the greater the desired investment in renovation and hence the desirability of secure tenure.

Certain attributes of owner-occupied housing are important complements to home-oriented leisure activities. In particular, the use of leisure time for home production of house improvements (carpentry, gardening, etc.) results in capital improvements whose market value can generally be realized only through home ownership. (This reflects the incompleteness of rental markets noted in the preceding section.) Home ownership is thus of particular value to households for whom home improvement activities are desirable uses of leisure time.

Several household characteristics are likely to be associated with a higher than average demand for home-oriented leisure activities. These include age, retirement status, and whether there are children. Age of household head and spouse together with retirement status are examples of variables which affect the demand for housing attributes which are complementary to the consumption of leisure time. Not only does the older family have more leisure time to consume, but the demand for types of leisure activities that require housing services as inputs to such activities is likely to increase with age.

While the number of children in a family will affect the household's demand for the quantity of housing space, this demand is not in itself likely to affect the demand for particular housing characteristics obtainable through ownership. However, to the extent that the existence of children requires family members to consume leisure time at home, it serves as proxy for (and cause of) higher demand for the consumption of leisure time in ways that are complementary to housing attributes, so that children will be associated with a higher demand for home ownership.

A second group of factors affecting preferences for home ownership is associated with the likely uniqueness of family preferences for particular combinations of housing characteristics. The fact that owner-occupied housing is highly heterogeneous and that "housing services" are a composite of a large number of characteristics of housing is well known. A related factor is that household's relative preferences for these characteristics vary highly and that matching tastes to housing available in the market is costly in time and/or in investments to modify a house. The implicit transactions costs provide a substantial incentive to obtain long-term tenure, and tenure of indefinite length is easily obtainable only through ownership. Accordingly, household attributes that may be correlated with the tendency to uniqueness of a household's preferences will also be associated with a higher demand for home ownership. Such household attributes may include variables such as education. Because very large urban centres attract a particular diversity of households, the fact that a household is located in a large urban centre should also serve as a proxy for uniqueness of household preferences and hence be positively correlated with home ownership. However, this last factor is obscured by the fact that this locational variable is also likely to serve as a proxy for higher housing prices.

The Household Budget Constraint

Because of indivisibilities in home ownership, the household budget constraint is likely to have an important effect on home ownership. However, because these indivisibilities are a constraint on the *minimum* amount of housing that can be purchased by a household, their effect on the demand for home ownership is likely to be in the form of defining a threshold below which it is difficult for a household to own a home.

The effect of the household budget constraint is thus likely to be highly nonlinear. It may be modelled by assuming that the threshold is distributed according to some probability law; the implication of such a model is that the effect of the budget constraint variable will be "S-shaped" in form.

The existence of capital rationing will, as noted in the previous section, have important effects on the nature of the budget constraint faced by households. Without capital rationing (and assuming a household's ability to borrow against human capital), the relevant constraint would be the household's "full wealth" (the sum of its financial wealth and of the capitalized value of future earnings). However, if capital rationing (in the sense of inability to borrow against human capital) is important, the relevant constraint variable is financial wealth. Stronger capital rationing effects (such as the inability to borrow against illiquid business assets or against pension savings) would imply that the constraint variable should be defined as directly controlled financial wealth, or as directly controlled financial wealth less illiquid business assets.

Components of financial wealth are described in table 1. The different definitions of wealth referred to in the previous paragraph as appropriate under different assumptions of capital rationing are (in increasing order of strictness of the constraint):

Full wealth (financial wealth + human capital)

FINW (total financial wealth)

DCWEALTH (financial wealth excluding assets not directly obtainable
        by household, such as accumulated pension rights)

DCWEALTH − A34 (marketable wealth)

The last and strictest definition is what might be termed "bankable" wealth in the sense of conforming to a banker's definition of collateral available as security for new loans.

Portfolio Balance Considerations

Housing units have a number of advantages as investment assets. [5] However, their lumpiness as investments and the relatively high transactions costs associated with their liquidation are important disadvantages. Moreover, the ownership of investment real estate requires a significant managerial input by the owner. The fact that this managerial input is both lessened by and (in some respects) complementary to household leisure activities in the case of investment in owner-occupied housing is a factor that increases the demand for home ownership.

The relative illiquidity of housing as an investment asset and the managerial problems associated with investment real estate that is not occupied by its owner each imply a reduced attractiveness of housing as an investment asset as the head of the household's age rises. However, the latter effect may lead to an increased demand for home ownership by the aged in order to maintain an investment in housing (with its tax and inflation hedge advantages) while reducing the managerial burden associated with investment real estate.

Investments in other illiquid assets (such as illiquid business assets) presumably should reduce the demand for investment in housing in order to maintain liquidity in a household's investment portfolio. However, such portfolio balance effects may be offset by other effects. Owners of unincorporated businesses are likely to expect to be more stable in their location than employees and may consequently have a longer planning horizon in choosing whether to own a home. Since (through amortizing transactions costs over a longer period) this decreases the perceived cost of home ownership, this effect may offset the negative effect on the demand for home ownership of investments in illiquid business assets.

It is likely that any portfolio balance effects arising from the ownership of a business will be captured by variable of the form

$$RA34 = \frac{A34}{A1 + A256 + A34 + A7}$$

in that such balance effects most likely apply to the ratio of business assets to total directly controlled assets. Assuming that households will (other things being equal) attempt to compensate for the holding of illiquid business assets by keeping other assets liquid rather than investing them in home ownership, the ratio RA34 should be negatively related to home ownership. In addition, the existence of illiquid investments (captured by a dummy variable set equal to 1 if $A34 > 0$) should have a negative effect on home ownership.

EMPIRICAL RESULTS

The empirical results presented in this section are based on an analysis of responses to the 1963 U.S. Federal Reserve Board's Survey of Financial Characteristics of Consumers. A total of 2,557 households are included in the sample. The merits of this data base are, first, that the sample was designed in a stratified manner with heavy sampling from high-income households and, second, that unusual care was taken to obtain high-quality data on an extensive number of financial variables

TABLE 1

Components of financial wealth

Symbol	Meaning
A1	Market value of principal residence(s)
Marketable investment assets	
A2	Investment real estate
A5	Traded common stock, and other traded investment contracts (oil royalty contracts, etc.)
A6	Bonds, mortgages, and other long-term debt instruments
A256	Sum of A2, A5, A6
Illiquid business assets	
A3	Shares in closely held corporations
A4	Equity in unincorporated businesses
A34	Sum of A3, A4
Liquid assets	
A7	Cash and short-term investments
Directly controlled assets	
A1-A7	Sum of A1, A2, A3, A4, A5, A6, A7
Assets not directly controlled	
A8	Equity in trusteed pension plans, life insurance, beneficial interest in trusts, estates in probate
Liabilities	
L1	Mortgage(s) on principal residence(s)
L256	Loans secured by marketable investment assets
L3	Loans secured by closely held stocks
L7	Loans secured by liquid assets
L8	Unsecured loans
L1-L8	Total liabilities
Total financial wealth	
DCWEALTH	Directly controlled wealth (A1-A7 less L1-L8)
FINW	Sum of DCWEALTH, A8 (total wealth)

for each household. [6] Median directly controlled wealth as of December 1962 for households in the sample was $15,500; one-quarter of the households sampled had wealth in excess of $78,000.

TABLE 2

The effect of household characteristics on the probability of home ownership

	Regression coefficients	T-statistic	Contribution to R-squared
Rotated principal components:			
1 Large family	.037	4.73[d]	.011
2 Single-person family	−.065	7.38[d]	.094
3 School-age children	.021	2.69[c]	.022
4 Occupation of head professional or managerial	.025	2.54[b]	.023
5 Wife professional or manager	−.006	0.78	−
6 Other adults in household	.033	4.38[d]	.032
7 Location in southern states	.037	3.56[d]	.025
8 Head retired, aged > 74	.021	2.63[c]	.009
9 Little formal education	.021	2.56[b]	−.003
10 Young family	−.053	6.60[d]	.081
11 Head not female	−.008	1.03	−
12 Rural location	.015	1.96[b]	.003
13 Wife working	.011	1.44	−.002
14 Education at one of two extremes (either high or low)	−.010	1.27	−
15 Location in western states	.002	1.31	−
16 Age 55-64		0.01	−
17 Location not a small town	−.017	2.29[b]	.003
18 Young children in family	.001	0.14	−
19 Husband older than wife	−.007	0.96	.001
20 Wife working on farm	−.024	2.97[c]	.011
Other household attributes:			
Inherited wealth significant	.047	1.35	.005
Location in metropolitan area (population > 1 million)	−.115	3.73[c]	.038
Race of head:			
Non-white	.065	1.76[a]	−.006
Not recorded	.021	0.89	.001

NOTES: The regression coefficients measure the additional probability of home ownership conditional on each listed attribute of a household, holding all other attributes constant and also holding constant the financial variables described in table 3.

Principal components are listed in order of importance in summarizing the joint distribution of all 59 household attributes analyzed. A listing of the attributes and of the coefficients of the principal components indicating the relative weight of each attribute is available from the author on request.

a   Significant at 10% level   c   Significant at 1% level
b   Significant at 5% level   d   Significant at 0.1% level

Detailed balance sheet and income statement data were collected from each household surveyed, along with additional data on household characteristics. The balance sheet variables have been summarized in the variables displayed in table 1. Households were characterized by a total of 61 attributes reflecting education, occupational status, labour force participation, family size, marital status, age, number and age of children, and location (region and city size).

TABLE 3

Effects of household income and wealth on the probability of home ownership

	Regression coefficient	T-statistic	Contribution to R-squared
A. *Budget constraint variables*			
Directly controlled wealth:			
Effect at $1,000	–	0.49	.041
Effect at $3,000	–	0.45	.038
Effect at $10,000	.342	13.72^d	.142
Effect at $30,000	.253	12.85^d	−.183
Effect at $100,000	.323	12.77^d	.502
Extended logarithmic transformation of other assets (A8)	.010	2.42^c	.043
Income other than from financial assets:			
Effect at $1,000	−.003	0.13	–
Effect at $3,000	−.001	0.03	–
Effect at $10,000	.038	1.36	−.005
Effect at $30,000	.074	2.16^b	.045
Extended logarithmic transformation of realized capital gains	–	1.15	−.001
B. *Portfolio balance effects*			
Effect of investment in illiquid assets (A34):			
Dummy variable for existence of investment	.423	6.81^d	.199
Logit transformation of ratio of illiquid assets to total assets	−.036	7.91^d	−.167

See Note 8 for description of extended logarithmic transformations and of the cubic spline functions applied to directly controlled wealth and income from non-financial sources. The logit transformation is the logarithm of the odds of the ratio.

Significance levels as in table 2

Results of the analysis of 2,273 households (excluding farmers and households reporting negative business equity) are presented in the form of a regression on these variables of a dummy dependent variable (coded as 1 if the household owns its home, 0 otherwise). The definition of the constraint variable (DCWEALTH) accords with an assumption of no borrowing against human capital. The effect of the more important financial variables (wealth and income) is specified in a form that permits the data to generate a nonlinear functional form consistent with the considerations described in the previous sections.

The interpretation of the effects of household characteristics is clouded by the fact that such characteristics are attributes (i.e., characteristics which are either present or absent) which are both numerous and collinear.

In order to eliminate the problems caused by their collinearity, twenty principal components were extracted from 59 of the 61 attributes and rotated (using a quartimax rotation) to increase identifiability. These components are listed in table 2 in order of their importance in explaining the joint variation of the 59 attributes. The twenty principal components account for approximately two-thirds of the total variance of the attributes.

The regression results are presented in tables 2 and 3. The regression "explains" approximately one-third of the variation in the dependent variable. [7] Because of the dichotomous nature of the dependent variable, a probit function or similar

FIGURE 1: Actual frequency of home ownership versus predicted frequency

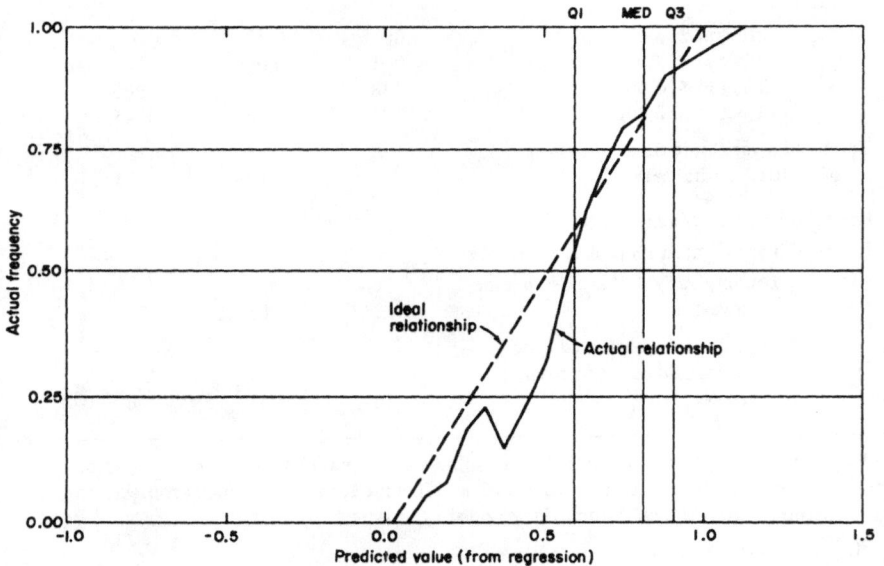

model would provide a more accurate specification of the nature of the relationship. The estimates presented in tables 2 and 3 are of coefficients of a linear probability function which, though nonlinear in its variables, does not restrict predicted values to the range (0, 1). As such, it should be viewed as an approximation; the extent of the approximation is indicated by figure 1, which shows the actual frequency of home ownership at each predicted value of the regression. The dashed line in figure 1 represents what would be seen if the regression predicted values exactly conformed to actual home ownership frequencies.

The relative contribution of variables to explaining the probability of home ownership is as follows:

Budget constraint:		
Directly controlled wealth	54%	
Other assets	4	
Income from non-financial sources	4	62%
Household characteristics:		
20 principal components	31	
Inherited wealth significant	1	
Location in metropolitan area	4	
Race of head	—	36%
Portfolio balance effects:		
Effect of illiquid investments		3%

The extent to which the relationships shown in tables 2 and 3 conform to the implications of the model described in preceding sections will now be discussed.

The Effects of Household Characteristics

The effects of household characteristics which are significantly related to home ownership, presented in table 2, are generally in fairly strong conformity with the predictions made in the preceding section. (As noted earlier, the same variables may serve as proxies for more than one factor, with conflicting effects.) The effects of a few household characteristics conflict with the predictions of the model described in the preceding sections, but in all cases the effect of such variables is not statistically significant. A few of the principal components have an ambiguous interpretation (e.g., components 11, 14 and 17); fortunately, they have little predictive significance.

The principal effect on tenure choice of family size (holding the budget constraint constant) is to increase the quantity of housing services demanded and so to increase the cost of either renting or buying a house, thus reducing the feasible consumption of consumption services other than housing and hence reducing the

use of leisure time in leisure activities outside the home. In this way the budget
constraint (represented by the variables listed in table 3) causes the effect of
quantity demand factors to enhance the relative attractiveness of housing characteristics which are complementary to home-oriented leisure activities. Given
this, the effect of family size on home ownership should be significant. Nevertheless, the degree of significance of components 1 and 2 shown in table 2 is surprising.

The effects of children and of age of the head of the household are as predicted. Components 3 and 18 represent the effect of children; of these, the first is
significant. Components 8, 10 and 16 reflect the effect of age, and show a strongly significant pattern consistent with the predicted effect of age on the orienta-
tion of a household's leisure activities.

Other variables relating to the availability of leisure time include component
6 (reflecting whether adults other than husband and wife are included in the
household) and components 5, 13 and 20 (reflecting the wife's occupational
status). The effect of other adults in a family is similar to that of family size, in
that it increases the stringency of budget constraints on choice of leisure activities and so enhances the attractiveness of home-oriented leisure activities. The
effect of a wife working is partly to reduce the availability of leisure time within
the household; the effect of component 20 (wife working on farm) is probably
to reflect a complementarity of occupational choice and choice of leisure activities.

Factors that may serve as proxies for household preferences for unique bundles
of housing attributes include components 4, 14 and possibly 9. None of them is
highly significant. Component 4 (professional/manager occupation, with high
education) is somewhat significant and may reflect this source of demand.

Differences in household location may serve as proxies either for differences in
household tastes or for differences in housing prices. Components 7 and 15 reflect regional effects that may in both cases be either lower housing prices or a
greater likelihood of household preferences for home-oriented activities; of these,
only the effect of a southern location is significant. Location in a metropolitan
centre with more than a million inhabitants has a negative effect on home ownership, presumably reflecting higher housing prices in most metropolitan housing
markets as well as housing type.

A number of other variables have indeterminate effects or are insignificant.
Among other variables, it is noteworthy that the effect of race is positive (though
not very significant) holding all other variables constant, even though non-white
racial status has a negative zero-order correlation with home ownership in the
sample.

The Effect of Budget Constraints

Financial variables are incorporated within the model by assuming they have a nonlinear effect on the probability of household home ownership. [8] Their effects are shown in table 3.

The primary effect of these variables is to reflect the implications for tenure choice of the budget constraint applicable to all household choices. As such, given the threshold effects discussed in preceding sections, it is not surprising that their effect is highly significant and that a relaxation of the constraint results in a higher probability of home ownership.

The functional form of the effect of directly controlled financial wealth resulting from the model used is shown in figure 2. As this figure indicates, the effect of wealth is highly nonlinear with a substantial threshold effect between wealth of $3,000 and $10,000. In effect, the wealth variable primarily differentiates between households which have sufficient equity to make down payments and those which do not. The importance of this feasibility constraint revealed by figure 2 reflects a likely dominance of consumption motives over investment motives for less wealthy home owners. The effect of the investment motive for households with greater wealth is indicated by the second threshold of wealth at $80,000 shown in figure 2. The dashed line is a hazarded approximation of this second threshold effect; the difference between the fitted function and the dashed line may be regarded as the

FIGURE 2: Functional form of effect of wealth on home ownership

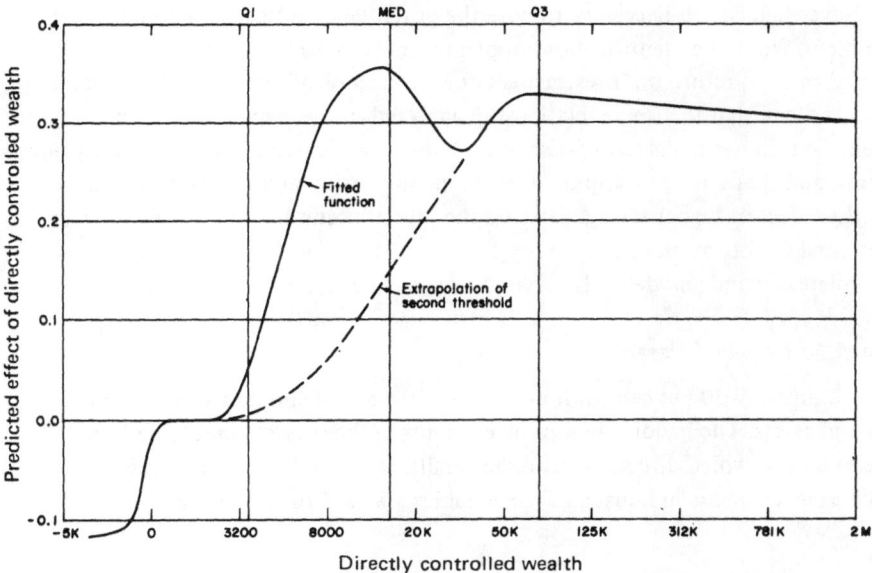

effect of the availability of a down payment for low-wealth households with strongly dominant consumption-motivated demand for home ownership. For households with directly controlled wealth in excess of $80,000 (approximately the upper quartile of the sample), home ownership is a slightly decreasing function of wealth.

The effect of wealth on home ownership is susceptible to misinterpretation, arising from the fact that most households in the sample who owned their homes did so for some period prior to the date of the sample. To the extent that home ownership was *ex post* a better investment choice than other possible investment assets, household wealth in 1962 may have been higher for home owners than for other households. If this were the case, the effect of financial wealth would be subject to a serious identification problem. [9]

For the period prior to 1962, this is unlikely to have been the case for most investors. In the decade prior to 1962, there was little general price inflation and hence little of the inflation-induced distortions in *ex post* rates of return on investment assets that have characterized the 1970s. Evidence presented in Bhatia (1969) indicates that the average rate of increase in housing prices in the United States was approximately 3.5 per cent per year in the early 1960s and earlier, compared to an average rate of increase of stock prices of 11 per cent per year between 1947 and 1964. It would seem doubtful that there can be any presumption that home owners' wealth would have grown at a faster rate than the wealth of other households. From this viewpoint, the date of the sample used (1963, with financial data as of the end of 1962) is fortuitous.

Nevertheless, it is necessary to note the potential qualification raised by this problem. While the identification problem is unlikely to be significant because of higher rates of return on investments in owner-occupied housing, other interacting effects mean that the single relationship analyzed in this paper may not be fully identified. In particular, it is possible that home owners save more than other households, and that a relationship between home ownership and wealth is introduced by the effect of higher savings rates on the rate of accumulation of wealth. This potential qualification can obviously be analyzed only in the context of a more complete dynamic model of household financial behaviour.

Portfolio Balance Effects

Approximately 30 per cent of households in the sample hold investments in illiquid assets. The major effect of investments in these assets should be to reduce the extent to which directly controlled wealth is allocable by households to uses such as investments in housing. Two variables are used to capture the effect of illiquid investments: (1) a dummy variable indicating whether a household has made investments in an unincorporated business or in a closely held corporation, and (2) a variable serving to measure, for households which have made such investments, the relative importance of such investments. The latter variable is measured using a nonlinear logit transformation of the ratio of the value of illiquid assets to total assets. [10]

The dummy variable serves as a proxy for other household attributes relating to demands on household time as well as to occupational and risk-taking choices that may well be related to household preferences. It is thus possible that the high value for the coefficient of this dummy variable may reflect some of these other effects. Further research is required to analyze the extent to which such other influences may be disentangled from the portfolio balance effects of the investment itself. In the absence of such research, it is necessary to conclude that the effect of investments in illiquid assets is more complex than that predicted by the discussion in the preceding sections. In part, this is the result of measurement problems related to the variation between the value of such assets as perceived by owners and their reported book value. This problem is particularly important for such assets precisely because market values are unknown for many of these assets.

CONCLUSIONS

On the whole, the empirical results are consistent with the model of the demand for home ownership described in earlier sections. The one significant exception to this statement is concerned with the effects of the two portfolio balance variables (in particular, the effect of the dummy variable for ownership of illiquid assets). As noted above, this failure of the model may be due to the portfolio balance effect of illiquid assets being confounded with other household characteristics for which the ownership of illiquid assets may serve as a proxy. However, without further work, the model has to be judged deficient in this one respect.

The importance of the wealth constraint is substantial, but its effect is highly nonlinear. This nonlinearity is consistent with the predictions of the model; indeed, if the relationship between wealth and home ownership were not nonlinear with important threshold effects, the model would be severely discredited. The form of the effect of wealth is thus a strong confirmation of the model.

The effects of other variables reflect differences in households' tastes that are embodied in household characteristics. These characteristics differ partly through natural causes (e.g., age) and partly as a result of prior household choices (e.g., occupation, marital status and number of children). Their effects are complex but the model provides a framework for predicting their effects which is generally confirmed by the empirical evidence.

The major conclusions to be drawn from this analysis are twofold: first, the importance of wealth threshold effects and second, the significance of life-cycle related variations in households' demands for particular characteristics of housing that are obtainable only with security of tenure. In effect, home ownership is a variable that must be entered as an argument of the household production function, since it has an important effect on what a household may choose to do in utilizing leisure time and other resources. Because it does, the impact of household consumption preferences on home ownership is substantial, clearly indicating that traditional hypotheses of separable investment decisions are not valid for households.

Because of the implications of home ownership for the feasibility of using leisure time in home improvement activities that cause household wealth to be increased, the significant effect of a wealth threshold on home ownership has an important feedback effect on the accumulation of wealth. The increase in the productivity of leisure time permitted by home ownership is of particular importance for middle-income families with few alternative ways of effectively combining time and monetary resources. The importance of home ownership for lifetime income distribution is thus substantial.

These distributional implications of home ownership have not been generally considered. They imply that encouraging home ownership through tax subsidies or other means can have significant progressive redistributive effects through enhancing the productivity of savings for low-income and middle-income households. However, it is important to note that, because of the importance of wealth threshold effects, the greatest potential redistributive gain arises from programs aimed at accelerating the transition of households from tenancy to home ownership. Policies such as the Canadian AHOP (Assisted Home Ownership Program) which are focused on reducing down payment requirements are most likely to have progressive redistributive effects in the long run.

NOTES

1 I am indebted to Bruce Becker and Les Cseh for programming assistance and to the Connaught Fund's grant to the Centre for Urban and Community Studies for financial support. I am also grateful to John Quigley and Ray Struyk for useful comments.

2 The Ando-Modigliani and Becker-Ghez models of lifetime consumption patterns are examples.

3 An exception to this statement is Watts and Tobin (1960). The Watts-Tobin analysis, though limited to durable goods, carries over easily to the case of housing services.

4 This relationship is in violation of assumption 5 as well as increasing the effective illiquidity of investments in small businesses.

5 These include the availability of significant tax preferences (particularly for owner-occupied housing, in view of the nontaxation of imputable net rent and of the *de facto* exemption in the U.S. of most capital gains realized on the sale of an owner-occupied house) and their relative safety as an inflation hedge. It is noteworthy that these two advantages are mutually reinforcing, in that the taxation of inflation-induced capital gains realized on other assets increases the relative tax preference accorded to owner-occupied housing.

6 The sample is described in detail in Projector and Weiss (1966). The quality of the high-income coverage in the sample is unique and is the result of the use of personal income tax records to design a sampling frame consisting of all U.S. households which filed 1960 tax returns reporting assessable incomes in excess of $50,000. A separate stratified sampling frame based on the 1960 Census was used to derive the remainder of the sample.

7 The R^2 coefficient is .341 with 37 explanatory variables and 2,235 degrees of freedom.

8 This is done using cubic spline functions to allow flexibility in the precise form of the relationship while ensuring that the functional relationship is smooth. Cubic spline functions are piecewise cubic, subject to the restriction that the function and its first two derivatives are continuous where "pieces" of the function are joined; see Poirier (1973). The cubic spline function is further imposed on an extended logarithmic transformation of important financial variables in order to ensure satisfactory properties of the combined function at high wealth levels; this transformation is defined as:

$$F(X) = \ln X, \; x>1$$
$$x-1, \; x\leq 1$$

Regression programs implementing this and similar nonlinear functional forms are available in the MIDAN software package for micro-econometric research; see Bossons (1978).

9 I am grateful to John Quigley for emphasizing the possible importance of this problem in his discussion of my paper at the conference. It must be emphasized,

however, that the relevant question is, "Does having *been* a home owner cause a household to be wealthy?" It is only if the rate of return on investments in housing has historically been *greater* than on common stocks or other potential household investments that an identification problem arises from this cause.

10   The logit transformation is the logarithm of the odds of this ratio, where "odds" denotes the value $R/(1-R)$ where R stands for the ratio. The effect of this transformation is to give greater effect to high and low values of the ratio.

REFERENCES

Ando, A., and F. Modigliani. 1963. "The Life Cycle Hypothesis of Saving: Aggregate Implications and Tests", *American Economic Review,* 53: 55-84.

Bhatia, K.B. 1969. "Individuals' Capital Gains in the United States: An Empirical Study, 1947-64". Unpublished Ph.D. dissertation, University of Chicago.

Bossons, J. 1978. "MIDAN/1.0 User's Manual". Institute for Policy Analysis, University of Toronto.

De Leeuw, F. 1971. "The Demand for Housing: A Review of Cross-Sectional Evidence", *Review of Economics and Statistics,* 53: 1-10.

Diamond, P. 1967. "The Role of a Stock Market in a General Equilibrium Model with Technological Uncertainty", *American Economic Review,* 57, 4: 759-776.

Fisher, I. 1930. *The Theory of Interest.* New York: Augustus M. Kelley.

Merton, R.C. 1969. "Lifetime Portfolio Selection under Uncertainty: The Continuous Time Case", *Review of Economics and Statistics,* 51: 247-257.

Poirier, D.J. 1973. "Piecewise Regression Using Cubic Splines", *Journal of the American Statistical Association,* 68: 515-524.

Projector, D.S., and G. Weiss. 1966. *Survey of Financial Characteristics of Consumers.* Washington, D.C.: Federal Reserve Board.

Samuelson, P.A. 1969. "Lifetime Portfolio Selection by Dynamic Stochastic Programming", *Review of Economics and Statistics,* 51: 239-246.

Watts, H.W., and Tobin. 1960. "Consumer Expenditures and the Capital Account", in Ferber and Jones, eds., *Proceedings of the Conference on Consumption and Savings,* Vol. 2. Pittsburgh: University of Pennsylvania Press.

IV

Supply and Price Considerations

4.1 THE PRICE ELASTICITY OF SUPPLY OF HOUSING SERVICES[1]

Larry Ozanne and Raymond J. Struyk

This paper reports on an empirical investigation of the economic behaviour of the suppliers of housing services over time. Specifically, a long-run (ten-year) price elasticity of housing services from the existing stock is estimated separately for owner-occupied and rental dwellings in the Boston metropolitan area for the 1960-70 decade. Only suppliers utilizing dwellings which were in the stock in 1960 are included; hence, it is a study of changes in the flow of services from the existing stock.

The focus on services sets this work apart from most past econometric analyses of housing supply, which have studied the supply of housing units.[2] Only de Leeuw and Ekanem (1971) have estimated econometrically the price elasticity of housing services, using a cross-SMSA (Standard Metropolitan Statistical Area) analysis employing data on average rents for standard dwelling units, average incomes, prices for non-housing goods, and aggregate measures of the prices for capital and operating inputs employed in producing housing services. The elasticities — found to be in the range of 0.3 to 0.7 — were obtained in a two-step procedure. The price of housing, but not its quantity, was measured across SMSAs using data from the Bureau of Labor Statistics (BLS) on costs of comparable units in different SMSAs in 1967. Consequently, a reduced-form equation could be estimated by regressing price on both supply and demand variables. Then, using demand parameter estimates from prior studies, the supply function parameters were deduced. The elasticities are interpreted as long-run values since differences across SMSAs in rent, incomes, labour costs, etc. tend to persist for years or even decades.[3]

Because of the critical role which the price elasticity of supply of services plays in the evaluation of housing policies which are designed to utilize the existing housing stock — such as housing allowances or unrestricted cash transfers — further analysis of these elasticities seems warranted.[4] The present work uses data on individual dwelling units matched for 1960 and 1970. As such, it differs from the de Leeuw-Ekanem analysis in using microdata for a single market and in being explicitly dynamic.

The first section of this paper presents the conceptual framework. The second briefly describes the main data set — the Components of Inventory Change (CINCH) data from the 1970 Census of Housing. The third section outlines the specification of the variables included in the estimated supply function; special attention is given to the procedure used to estimate the price per unit of housing services and the quantity of services supplied by the individual dwellings. The final section presents and evaluates the estimated supply functions. Special attention is given to the critical procedure involved in doing empirical housing analysis — that used to estimate the price per unit of housing services and the quantity of services supplied by the individual dwellings. It is concluded that the supply elasticity for services from existing stock has a lower-bound value of about 0.3. A more precise estimate was precluded by a series of measurement and econometric problems.

CONCEPTUAL FRAMEWORK

The general premises underlying the entire research effort are that the suppliers of housing services constitute an extremely heterogeneous group, that the housing stock consists of innumerable different bundles of housing components, and that the urban housing market itself is composed of many and varied submarkets. These heterogeneities in some ways greatly hamper efforts to classify and measure the behaviour of housing suppliers empirically, but in other ways they provide the variation needed to estimate the hypothesized relationships.

An urban area is assumed to be a unified housing market such that in the very long run — when housing structures are variable inputs — the price per unit of housing services would reflect area construction costs and preferences. Short of that very long run equilibrium, there will be submarkets within the urban area and the price of housing services will vary among these submarkets. An unanticipated decline in demand for, say, two-bedroom dwellings will result in a lower price for housing services from two-bedroom units. Likewise, an increase in the demand for a specific location or architectural style can result in a higher price for housing services from certain structures. Imperfect information and discrimination can also lead to variations in the price of housing services across submarkets. Landlords respond to such increases or decreases in housing prices by varying the quantity of services they provide. It is these variations in price, and the adjustment of suppliers to them, which permit estimates of supply elasticities.

A second heterogeneity is among producers of housing services. The strategy adopted in this work has been to divide producers into more homogeneous groups for analysis. The most fundamental distinction among suppliers is between the owner-occupant supplier who provides services to his own household and the investor owner, who provides services to tenants.[5]

Initially, it is assumed that all landlords have similar supply (or marginal cost) curves, as do all owner-occupants, and that there is enough competition within every submarket to force all producers to operate along their supply curves. In prior analysis (Ozanne and Struyk, 1976) a ten-year supply function of the following form was derived, which was general enough to apply to both landlords and owner-occupants:

$$Q = \alpha Q_o + \Theta [\frac{P_s(n)}{\mu(w,t)}]^{\gamma}$$

(1)

where Q and Q_o are the end-of-period and initial levels of services provided by the dwelling, exclusive of those services associated with the neighbourhood in which it is located; α is one minus the period depreciation rate applicable if minimum quantities of other factors are employed with the beginning-of-period stock; $P_s(n)$ is the price per unit of housing services which depends on the neighbourhood in which the dwelling is located; $\mu(w,t)$ is the weighted average of factor prices; Θ is a parameter incorporating the effects of expectations and the returns to scale on output; and γ is a term having to do with the rate of substitution among factors and returns to scale. The slope of the supply curve is determined by Θ, μ, and γ. This model was derived from a constant elasticity of substitution production function formulated to imply less than constant returns to scale with the initial stock, labour and capital as inputs, and a profit function that considers both current net returns and future (discounted) net returns.

Because of data limitations, it has not been possible to estimate this exact model. A supply model which can be estimated, though, is of the same general form and can be written as:

$$\ln(Q) = B_o + B_1 \ln(Q_o) + B_2 \ln(P) + B_3 \ln(P_o) + B_4 \ln(E)$$

(2)

where P is the price per unit of housing services, P_o is a proxy for factor input prices, and E reflects producer expectations. Since all observations are from the same market in which input prices are generally identical, P_o represents deviations from the market-wide average input price, $\overline{P}_o$, and is implicitly expressed as the ratio, $P_o/\overline{P}_o$.

Some additional aspects of this supply function can be appreciated by studying the curves in figure 1 which are ten-year supply curves for services from existing dwellings, corresponding to the supply function stated in equation (2). There is a different curve for each initial level of services (Q_o) as variation in Q_o produces a shift in the entire function; curve S_3 is the supply curve for the dwelling having the greatest Q_o. The three curves all have the same slope, as indicated by the linear price term in equation (2). It is because of the intra-market variation in the price per unit of services, and suppliers' adjustments to this variation, that it is possible to observe a supply curve rather than simply a point at any Q_o level.

The dash line in figure 1 represents the price per unit of housing service in 1960. For simplicity, the price is assumed to be the same for the three dwellings shown, although this is clearly not required. The point to the right of each supply curve is the beginning-of-period quantity (Q_o) for the dwelling referred to by the similarly numbered supply curve. The distance between the point and the curve is the amount of depreciation over the decade, $(1-\alpha)Q_o$, assuming minumum amounts of other inputs are used.

The specification in equation (2) does not take full advantage of the data available on the prices of housing services. It should be possible with the CINCH data to obtain observations on housing prices in both 1960 and 1970. The additional data can be used by specifying the supply equation entirely in change form:

$$\Delta Q/Q = K_1 \frac{\Delta Q_o}{Q_o} + K_2 \frac{\Delta P}{P} + K_3 \frac{\Delta P_o}{P_o} + K_4 \frac{\Delta E}{E}$$

$$(3)$$

Supply curves can be inferred by observing changes in price and output. While the change specification takes fuller advantage of the available housing price data, it also requires further data which cannot be obtained. The output of sample dwellings in 1950 is not known; hence ΔQ_o is unknown. Also, input factor prices applicable to individual dwellings are not accurately known in either 1960 or 1970; hence, changes in P_o over the decade are not known. The problem caused by these omissions is demonstrated in figure 2 which shows the actual supply curve of dwellings in 1960 and 1970. Assume the shift between the two periods is caused by an increase in factor prices. S^1 is the supply curve which would be estimated with the time series data, given the lack of proper data on the change in P_o. It clearly underestimates the true elasticity. On the other hand, the omission of ΔQ_o could produce a bias in either direction, so that the expected relationship between

FIGURE 1: Alternative supply curves

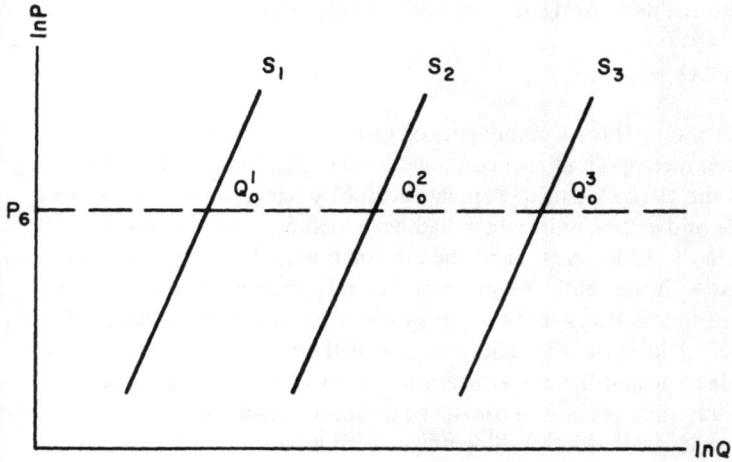

FIGURE 2: Time series supply function with changing factor prices

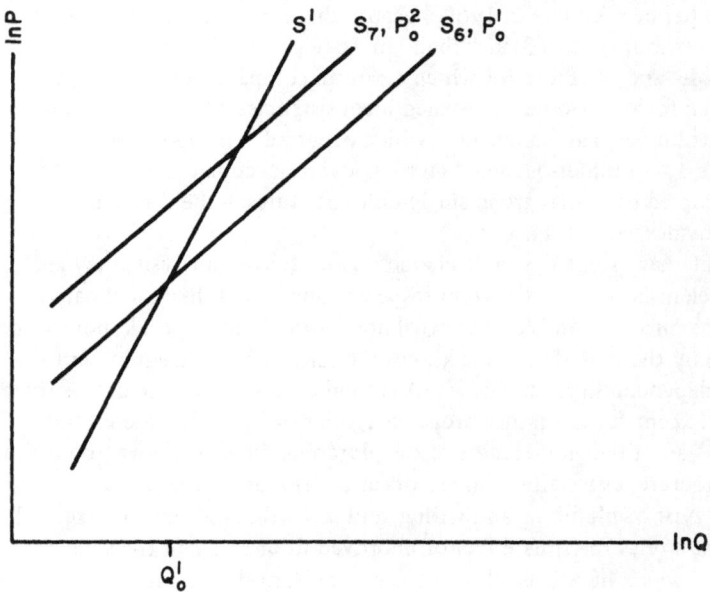

the true and estimated elasticities is ambiguous. These problems may seem to make estimation of the change formulation of the model questionable; fortunately, we have in practice been able to mitigate their severity substantially.

THE CINCH DATA

The principle data source is the Components of Inventory Change (CINCH) survey data for the Boston metropolitan area compiled by the U.S. Bureau of the Census (1973) as part of the 1970 Census of Population and Housing. In 1970 the Bureau surveyed a sample of dwelling units which had been included in either the 5 or 20 per cent samples in the 1960 census, and the information gathered was coded so as to be consistent with that obtained in 1960. The information covers three distinct areas relevant to this study: (1) the physical attributes of the dwelling; (2) gross rents or house values; and (3) characteristics of the occupants including number, total family income and the age, education and sex of the household head.

The present study involves only those 4,810 dwellings classified by the Census Bureau as the *same* units; that is, dwelling units which in both years existed as one, and only one, housing unit. It thus excludes units changed by merger or conversion over the decade, as well as units built or demolished since 1960. The sample actually used in the analysis was reduced to 2,465 dwellings by excluding those dwellings that: (1) were vacant in either 1960 or 1970, because occupant characteristics are missing and data on physical attributes are less reliable; (2) were included in the 5 per cent sample in 1960, because this sample omitted some important physical attribute data; (3) switched tenure (e.g., rental to owner-occupancy) over the decade; and (4) those for which a careful comparison of the physical attributes reported for the two years revealed inconsistencies which were greater than might be attributed to actual changes which occurred. The 2,465 observations remaining include 1,474 renter-occupied and 991 owner-occupied dwellings. All of the owner-occupied dwellings are in single-unit structures — the dwellings for which Census provides value data.

While these data have some desirable characteristics for our analysis, they are nevertheless deficient in several important respects. One is that, like most data on dwelling units, the information is on the attributes of the housing stock, not on the services provided by the unit. Thus, one knows the kind of heating equipment the unit has, but its dependability is unknown. A second deficiency of the data is their incompleteness. Except for the rather broad categories of "sound," "deteriorating" and "dilapidated" and the completeness of the plumbing, little is known about the quality of the structure, especially such factors as interior and exterior painting, modern kitchen, type of plumbing and wiring, and so forth. Also omitted are such measures of house size as the square feet of improved floor area and the square footage of the lot, which have been shown to be important determinants of rents and house values in prior studies. It would seem that the most damaging of the above omissions for our purposes are those measures of condition susceptible to change at moderate expense by the landlord, such as quality of the appliances and the decor.

A further limitation is the lack of precise data on the neighbourhood in which the dwelling is located. Census disclosure rules prohibit the identification of any area containing less than 250,000 persons. The Bureau agreed to identify the location of each dwelling in a "neighbourhood" meeting the disclosure rules, and the basis for designing the neighbourhoods was left for us to specify. Since a number of prior studies had shown the educational level, occupational status and incomes of households in a neighbourhood to be significantly related to rents and house values, an index containing these three factors was constructed using census tract data for suburban tracts from the 1970 census.[6] The tracts were then ranked and each group of successive tracts with a combined population of 250,000 was defined as a "neighbourhood." Eight suburban neighbourhoods were thus defined. Note that these areas are relatively homogeneous with respect to the index variables but are composed of spatially noncontiguous tracts. The location of the sample dwellings by census tract in the central city had not been coded by the census, so two areas within Boston city were defined on the basis of the race of the head of the household. While far from ideal, this division is still useful in light of the pervasive residential segregation by race in the city.[7] Thus, the entire metropolitan area has been divided into ten "neighbourhoods", and a number of variables specifying the characteristics of these have been computed using data travel times, land use, public expenditures and census tract level socio-economic data. While these data certainly are an improvement over effectively no information, they are nevertheless only broad indications of the actual neighbourhood situations associated with individual dwelling units.

SPECIFICATION OF THE VARIABLES

Measuring Changes in Price and Quantity

Definitions Because of the lack of direct observations on the price per unit and quantity of services provided by a dwelling, it has been necessary to devise a procedure for using the information available — data on rents or values, and structural, neighbourhood and household characteristics. The basic vehicle for separating changes in "rents" over the decade into changes in price and quantity is a hedonic index, a model which relates the cross-sectional variation in rents to the attributes of the dwelling, the neighbourhood in which it is located and its occupants.[8] The typical hedonic regression model is of the form

$$R_t^j = \sum_i P_t^i X_t^{ij} + u_t^j$$

(4)

where R_t^j is the rent of the jth dwelling at the time t; p_t^i is the regression coefficient and is interpreted as the price of an incremental unit of attribute i at time t; X_t^{ij} is the quantity of the ith attribute possessed by the jth dwelling at time t; and, u_t^j is the error term. The price coefficients represent the market-wide average price of the attributes. Hedonic models are estimated for 1960 and 1970 for rental and owner-occupied structures separately, although this discussion is in terms of "rents".

Given the estimated hedonic models, the quantity of services produced from a dwelling in each period can be defined as:

$$Q_{60}^j = \sum_i P_{60}^i X_{60}^{ij} \qquad Q_{70}^j = \sum_i P_{60}^i X_{70}^{ij}$$

(5)

which yields in change form:

$$\Delta Q^j / Q^j = [\sum_i P_{60}^i (X_{70}^{ij} - X_{60}^{ij})] / \sum_i P_{60}^i X_{60}^{ij}$$

(6)

Equation (6) is a Laspeyres index of the change in quantity. Measures of the price per unit of service for the full housing bundle corresponding to equations (5) and (6) are:

$$P_{60}^j = \frac{R_{60}^j}{Q_{60}^j} \; ; \qquad P_{70}^j = \frac{R_{70}^j}{Q_{70}^j}$$

(7)

$$\frac{\Delta P^j}{P_{60}{}^j} = \frac{\Delta R^j}{R_{60}{}^j} - \frac{\Delta Q^j}{Q_{60}{}^j}$$

(8)

where $Q_{60}{}^j$ and $Q_{70}{}^j$ are defined in equations (5) and (6) and equation (8) yields an approximation to the exact value of the relative price change.[9] Thus, the variation in price among dwellings in each period is measured by that portion of the residual in the hedonic regression which cannot be accounted for by the measured quantity. This is in keeping with the assumption that the price of housing differs among submarkets. The hedonic equation estimated across the whole market reflects the market-wide average price of housing services. Deviations in price among submarkets are reflected in the residual terms for each dwelling.

Measurement problems   There are several measurement problems in estimating a supply function from the preceding specifications of quantity and price, especially when the measures are based on Census Bureau housing data. Because of some of these problems, the price variables ultimately used in the supply regressions are several steps removed from those specified in equations (7) and (8).

The hedonic measurement of quantity is subject to at least three types of error. One results from errors in the Census data. Rents are the Census Bureau's estimates of gross rents (i.e., rent plus utility) based on contract rents; house values are the owners' estimates.[10] Dwelling unit characteristics can be misreported as well. A second problem is the use of attributes of the stock to measure the flow of services, as when type of furnace is used to reflect the flow of heating services.[11] A third problem in the hedonic measurement of quantity is the Census Bureau's relatively brief list of dwelling unit and neighbourhood characteristics. Thus, differences among dwellings, or in the same dwelling over time, in characteristics which are omitted (and not highly correlated with included variables) are not reflected in differences in Q, the calculated measure of housing services.

The errors in measuring the quantity of housing services are mirrored by errors in the measurement of the price of housing services, since price measures are obtained from the identity that price times quantity equals rent. The result is the building in of a spurious negative relation between quantity and price, and also between changes in quantity and price. Since a supply function, which presumably has a positive slope, is to be estimated, the effect of this measurement problem is to bias downward the estimated elasticity.

It is possible to avoid the above problem in part by reformulating the supply function in terms of rent rather than price. If the supply function is specified logarithmically as

$$\ln(Q) = \gamma_0 + \gamma_1 \ln(Q_0) + \gamma_2 \ln(P) + \gamma_3 P_0 + \gamma_4 E + U \tag{9}$$

then adding $\gamma_2 \ln Q$ to both sides and rearranging gives

$$\ln(Q) = \alpha_0 + \alpha_1 \ln(Q_0) + \alpha_2 \ln(R) + \alpha_3 P_0 + \alpha_4 E + V \tag{10}$$

where the price elasticity of supply, γ_2, is given by $\alpha_2/(1-\alpha_2)$. In this formulation, when rents are measured without error and independently of quantity, the errors in Q need not bias the regression estimate of α. Of course, actual rents (and house values) are not known precisely, but use of their Census-reported values avoids the built-in, but spurious, negative relation between the quantity and price variables.

Use of rents in place of the derived prices does not entirely avoid the measurement problems. The reason is that Q and R are not measured independently; the reformulated supply curve in (10) embodies the hedonic relationship in equation (4), since Q is defined as in (5). Errors that entered the original hedonic regression of characteristics on rents are likely to re-enter when the same rents are regressed on an aggregate of the characteristics. Another way of stating the problem is that equations (4) and (10) form a simultaneous set of equations — albeit an unusual one — and that the coefficients estimated in (10) are therefore biased.

To avoid this problem a two-stage estimation procedure has been used. An independent set of variables is used to create a measure of R purged of those elements which are correlated with the measured Q because of the hedonic relation. Specifically, a household expenditure function is estimated for the occupants of the dwellings in the CINCH sample, and the predicted rents ($\tilde{R}$) from this demand-side relation are substituted for the reported rents. The functions were actually estimated under the assumption of a unitary price elasticity of demand, an assumption consistent with the available evidence (de Leeuw, 1971) which permits omission of a housing price variable. It should also be noted that use of the variable $\tilde{R}$ in the supply functions means that an instrumental variable estimation technique is being used which therefore insures the identification of the supply function.[12]

While the above definitions of the quantity and price of housing services introduce the basic concepts and their measurement problems, one further conceptual refinement to the quantity measure is still required. Quantity as defined in (5) includes characteristics of the dwelling and the neighbourhood yet individual housing producers generally cannot alter their neighbourhoods through their own actions. Since the objective is to measure producers' responses, quantity is redefined to include dwelling-specific measures only. Neighbourhood values cannot be excluded entirely from the definition of quantity, so the average value of neighbourhood characteristics across all dwellings in 1960 is assigned to each dwelling.[13] The resultant definition of the quantity of structural services is

$$Q_t^{js} = \sum_{i \varepsilon s} P_t^i X_t^{ij} + \sum_{i \varepsilon n} P_{60}^i \overline{X}_{60}^i$$

(11)

where s is the set of dwelling characteristics, n is the set of neighbourhood characteristics, and $\overline{X}_{60}^i$ gives the average value of the ith neighbourhood characteristic in 1960.

The corresponding variable for the price of housing services is defined as

$$P_t^{js} = R_t^j / Q_t^{js}$$

(12)

Since the quantity of neighbourhood characteristics is held constant in the definition of quantity in equation (11), all changes in the characteristics of a neighbourhood that affect the values appear as a price change in (12). Thus, for example, if a neighbourhood improves, causing the rents to rise for dwellings located within it, producers are assumed to treat this as an increase in price and, because of competition within the submarket, to increase their supply of structural services.

To some extent, producers may act as though rents are divided into structural and neighbourhood components. In that case changes in the price or quantity of neighbourhood services might not lead to a response in the quantity of structural services. The rise in neighbourhood value would simply be capitalized in the total value of the dwelling. To the extent that the rise in value of a neighbourhood is not treated as a rise in the price of structural services, the price measure in (12) will be overstated. Hence, the supply elasticity estimated, using the quantity of structural services as defined in (11) and total rents, will be biased downward.

Of great importance to the entire procedure is the ability of the hedonic index to explain most of the variation in rents and house values. The estimated hedonic models are presented in Appendix A for 1960 and 1970 owner-occupied and rental units. The coefficients agree generally in sign and order of magnitude with estimates made by Schnare (1974) for Boston using the Census public use samples. The single most important point for current considerations is that the models explain only between 38 and 61 per cent of the variance in the dependent variables, which in turn means that the unexplained residuals of the individual observations are large. Hence a major element of variation is passed on to the measurement of P_t^j. The quality of fit in these models is about the same as we have found in our earlier work with Census data, and attempts to improve the fit by refining the data base made only marginal improvements.[14]

Not shown in the table, but of interest for the price and quantity calculations, is that the residuals from 1960 and 1970 hedonic regressions are fairly highly correlated, r of about 0.6, for both owner-occupied and rental properties. This implies that units which rented for more (or less) than predicted in the 1960 regression were likely to have rented for more (or less) than predicted in the 1970 regression. To some degree, then, the residuals will cancel each other in the change formulation when "loaded" into the price terms and subtracted one from the other.

Other Variables

Factor input prices   The general form of the supply function naturally includes input prices as well as output prices. Thus, for estimation of the function, one would like to have data on the factor input prices paid by each supplier, and in fact some information on these prices is required to assure econometric identification of the supply function. There is, however, no such information available in the CINCH data. Further, since all the sample housing units are drawn from the same market, the variation in factor prices to be measured is supplier-specific, not market-specific.

The strategy adopted in the econometric analysis is based on the assumption that there are average market-wide prices for factor inputs which apply in most segments of the market, and the purpose of the factor input variables included in the regression model is to capture deviations from the average market price. These deviations are likely to be associated with the unit's locational features, the characteristics of the housing supplier, or the characteristics of the factors.[15]

Non-tenant wage rates   In general it can be argued that the Boston labour market is unified; for skilled occupations in particular there is convincing evidence that this is the case.[16] At the same time, there is some suggestive evidence that among unskilled workers, such as janitors, there is spatial variation in wage rates which arises from increased compensation being required for commuting greater distance.[17] There are also more tentative indications of Boston central city painting, repair and maintenance contractors charging higher rates for suburban jobs, again apparently as compensation for greater travel times.[18] Both of these patterns, if founded in fact, argue for suburban housing suppliers paying a premium for unskilled labourers like janitors, lawn men and the like, and for some semiskilled workers. To capture this, a dummy variable for the two "neighbourhoods" identified as distant surburbs was specified.

Non-labour inputs   Among managers of rental property, whether owner-managers or management firms, there are measurable differences in the average cost of non-labour inputs with the number of units managed. Such differences stem from the trade and quantity discounts available to managers when purchasing expendables, such as cleaning aids and paint; durable goods, such as replacement household appliances; and capital equipment, such as floor polishers and lawnmowers. The presence of real savings to the larger manager was the clear consensus of the limited number of operators we interviewed.

The data on the rental dwellings in our sample do not include information on the number of units owned by the owner(s) of the property or on the number of units the manager, if different from the owner, manages. The data do include, however, the number of units in the structure in which the dwelling is located. For units-in-structure to be an effective indicator of the size of operation there must be a reasonably high correlation between units-in-structure and number of units owned and managed by one landlord; that is, structures with few units connote small operators.

Several people knowledgeable about the Boston rental housing market were questioned on this point to determine if this correspondence exists. Specialization of large operators in large properties seems to be the case, although numerous exceptions to this rule exist. The small operators, on the other hand, were consistently characterized as owning small properties. Further, a strong aversion by management firms to handling small holdings was reported, so that the general association between a structure with few units and a small operation seems to be supported. In designing a dummy variable to capture the higher price per unit paid by the small operators, it is necessary to limit the units-in-structure size to from one to four units in the specification because many large garden apartment complexes consist of six-to-eight unit structures.[19]

Roxbury   There was a clear consensus among those interviewed that the factor input prices for mortgage funds, skilled labour services and contracted services are significantly higher in poor black neighbourhoods than elsewhere in the city of Boston. For the latter two types of service, the higher prices were caused by the unwillingness of a large portion of those providing the service to go into these areas, with the remaining firms or individuals apparently recognizing their market

power.[20] Unfortunately, the same variable may be associated with other phenomena affecting housing supply in the area. For example, the rate of decay of revenues less costs may be anticipated to be greater in such neighbourhoods, which
would also lead to lower levels of output at a given price than would be found in
other areas.

Expectations The supplier's determination of the profit-maximizing quantity of
services to provide at a given price is affected by his expectations regarding the
future. Because of the lack of precise information on expectations, they have been
approximated by variables which can be observed and which are expected to be
correlated with the factors themselves. More specifically, expectations were measured by variables characterizing neighbourhood conditions at the start of the decade (1960) and changes in these conditions over time. The neighbourhood measures include the racial composition of the population, the vacancy rate, the
amount of new construction in the area during the decade and the proportion of
units that are owner-occupied. Change in the average income of household in the
neighbourhood is not used because this variable could cause confusion with a demand function.

ESTIMATED SUPPLY FUNCTIONS

The general form of the supply function derived on theoretical grounds was set
out earlier, and the data limitations which confront estimation of this form have
been described. The basic model estimated is of the following form:

$$\ln(Q_{70}) = \alpha_0 + \alpha_1 \ln(Q_{60}) + \alpha_2 \ln(\tilde{R}_{70}) + \alpha_3 P_o + \alpha_4 E + \mu$$

$$(13)$$

where Q_{70} is the quantity of structural services provided by the dwelling in 1970,
$\tilde{R}_{70}$ is the rent or house value predicted by the tenure-specific expenditure functions, P_o is a proxy for factor input prices and E is a proxy for producer expectations. Q_{60} is included in the model as the initial flow of services from the dwelling.
The price elasticity of supply, obtained by substitution for prices in the underlying
model, is $\alpha_2/(1-\alpha_2)$.[21]
    The second formulation of the supply function uses percentage changes in ser-
vice quantities and rents over the decade. As noted, data on the change in Q_o, P_o
and E are unavailable. Consequently the formulation estimated is

$$Q^* = \beta_0 + \beta_1 R^* + \beta_2 P_o + \beta_3 E + \mu$$

$$(14)$$

where an asterisk indicates relative change over the period. Parallel to the "cross-sectional" model just discussed, the price elasticity of supply in the "dynamic", or percentage change, model is $\beta_1/(1-\beta_1)$. P_o again refers to end-of-period intra-market variations in factor prices. As noted earlier, the lack of information on changes in input prices over the decade clearly creates problems of bias in the esti- . mation of the supply elasticity.

Basic Results

The basic supply models for both owner-occupied and rental properties are presented in table 1. These models omit those independent variables which were consistently insignificant; a number of these were highly co-linear with the variables which are included in the reported models. The most important data in the table, the price elasticities, are given in the next-to-last row; they are uniformly extremely low, varying from 0.07 to 0.22. The elasticity estimates from the percentage change models are consistently lower than those from the cross-sectional models. This could be caused by either the bias from omission of changes in factor prices over the decade and ΔQ_o both being biased downwards, or by the downward bias from omitting ΔP_o being greater than the upward bias from excluding ΔQ_o.

Although we do not have information on changes in the factor prices faced by the individual producers, it is possible to make an adjustment in the percentage change model for the average change in factor prices over the decade and then to compare the two sets of estimates. The adjustment to the estimated elasticities entails two steps: (1) obtaining an estimate of the change in mean factor input prices over the decade; and (2) applying the actual adjustment.

In determining the change in factor prices, it is the change in the price of the marginal unit of each factor which is relevant, since it is on this basis that the producer makes the decision on providing additional services. For most factors the distinction between average and marginal prices is not important, but for capital services it is, because of the substantial periods of time which can elapse between factor purchases. The home owner cost index component of the consumer price index, compiled and published by the Bureau of Labor Statistics, has the virtue of being an index of home ownership costs of homes purchased in the current year. As a consequence, it embodies the marginal cost of capital as well as other goods and services. On the other hand, it may be subject to some upward biases as an index of input prices for rental housing.[22] In spite of these shortcomings, the home owner index still seemed to be the best available.[23]

Using the change in home owner costs in the Boston area with the procedure outlined in Appendix B, the adjusted elasticities shown in the final line of the table, where appropriate, were computed. The elasticities are now quite close to those from the cross-sectional models for rental properties. For owner-occupants, the changed elasticities are now twice those from the cross-sectional models. These

TABLE 1

Estimated supply functions for owner-occupied and rental dwellings

Variable	Owner-occupied Dwellings				Rental Dwellings			
	Type of Model				Type of Model			
	Cross-Sectional		Percentage Changed		Cross-Sectional		Percentage Changed	
	(1)	(2)	(1)	(2)	(1)	(2)	(1)	(2)
Constant	.686 (2.39)[c]	.677 (2.38)	474 (4.00)	680 (5.33)	-.244 (1.63)	-.132 (.91)	-.419 (4.57)	-21.6 (1.63)
$\ln Q_{60}$	.788 (41.51)	.786 (44.2)			.847 (50.89)	.826 (49.5)		
$\ln \tilde{R}_{70}$	.157 (6.47)	.160 (6.71)			.173 (8.82)	.184 (9.51)		
(Change in proportion units built in past 10 years)*1000[a]		.0002 (3.46)		.253 (3.17)				
Elderly head of house		-.033 (4.03)		-35.7 (3.14)				
$[(\tilde{R}_{70} - \tilde{R}_{60})/\tilde{R}_{60}]*1000$			.083 (4.12)	.082 (4.07)			.065 (5.13)	.066 (5.24)
Unit in structure with under 5 dwelling units						-.013 (1.91)		-10.9 (1.27)

TABLE 1 (Cotinued)

(Change in proportion households black, 1970-1960)*1000[a]						-.0002 (6.63)		-.212 (5.83)
1970 occupant household headed by black						.034 (1.80)		53.0 (2.23)
Average persons per room 1960 and 1970						-.0007 (4.92)		-.118 (.72)
R^2	.713	.721	.168	.199	.673	.692	.047	.072
F	986	506	14.3	10.1	1176	416	24.7	12.4
Implied price elasticity of supply	.19	.19	.09	.09	.21	.22	.07	.07
Elasticity adjusted for factor price changes	b	b	.40	.40	b	b	.20	.20

a Neighbourhood variable.

b Adjustment not applicable.

c The numbers in parentheses are the t-statistics from the ordinary least squares regressions, adjusted for the bias in the standard errors of the estimate caused by (1) the implicit use of a two-stage least squares procedure by including the instrumental variable $\tilde{R}$ and (2) the scalar heterogeneity caused by use of rents instead of prices (see Note 21).

d Dependent variable is $[(Q_{70} - Q_{60})/Q_{60}]$ *1000.

comparisons suggest that the bias from omitting ΔQ_o may be quite modest, as would be the case if the change in Q from 1950 to 1960 were small.

Since it is probable that the estimates are biased downward, the elasticities obtained indicate the lower bound to the true elasticity to be in the range of 0.2 to 0.3.[24] Also, there do not appear to be any dramatic differences between the elasticities for owner-occupied and rental units, but some of the same factors biasing the estimates downward may be distorting the true pattern here as well.

The coefficients of the variables representing the initial level of services can be used to obtain estimates of the rate of depreciation. Note, though, that the depreciation applies to services, not to the stock of housing. The estimates indicate that if all prices and expectations were unchanged over the decade, services from owner-occupied dwellings would depreciate at an average annual rate of about 1 per cent, and rental dwellings would depreciate negligibly. Unfortunately, it is not possible to base any statement about comparative maintenance of owner-occupied and rental dwellings on these estimates because the owner-occupied stock is on average much more recently built than the rental stock. New owner-occupied units may depreciate more quickly in their first couple of decades of existence, and then approach the depreciation rates of rental units. Also, it is especially important for this older rental stock to recall that the dwellings included in our sample for this older rental stock are those that survived the decade, so that the most rapidly depreciating rental dwellings may have been removed from the sample.

The remaining variables in the model are those which reflect variations in factor input costs (number of units in structure, age of head) and variations in producer expectations (neighbourhood conditions). There are two general points to be made regarding these variables. One is that the price elasticities are very robust when such variables are included in the model. The other is that no variable exerts a quantitatively large impact on Q_{70}. Nevertheless, the high levels of statistical significance of some of these coefficients serve to indicate systematic variations within the Boston SMSA in expectations and input prices.

Further Results

One of the complexities of estimating housing supply functions derives from the heterogeneity of producers of housing services. It is this complexity which led to the strategy of estimating separate functions for owner-occupied and rental dwellings. The increased homogeneity effected by this stratification of producers may not have been sufficient. The estimated average supply elasticities reported may suppress important variation among producers, and in fact may contribute to a downward bias in the supply elasticity estimates. Further disaggregation of housing suppliers could yield improved estimates of supply elasticities.

There are, in summary, four ways in which producers may vary systematically from each other: (1) expectations; (2) production technology; (3) input factor prices; and (4) the initial quantity of services (and composition — capital versus other services).[25] Of these, stratification of expectations would seem to have the least advantage in the present analysis, given the very broad definitions of neighbourhoods. Among rental properties, however, there is a convenient potential correlation between factor prices and production technology on the one hand, and the size of the property or number of units in the structure on the other. Inclusion of the variable for under five units in the structure in the supply regression model for renters is an attempt to control for such differences.

Variations in these aspects of the circumstances of producers of rental housing seem more important than those associated with the initial quantity of services; therefore stratification of the rental sample by the number of units per structure was undertaken. Owner-occupants, by contrast, should utilize fairly uniform production technologies and should face largely the same factor prices, with the notable exception being their own wage rate for producing housing net of the utility derived from such activity. Wage rates and differing factor-mixes may be reflected by the size of the home; hence, stratification for owner-occupants was tried by the level of initial quantity of services (which is approximated by the number of rooms in the dwelling) in the initial year.

The estimated supply elasticities for the two stratification schemes just outlined did not increase overall, but substantial variation around the average elasticity is evident from both stratification schemes (table 2). Among the cross-sectional estimates, rental duplexes and small owner-occupied dwellings exhibit elasticities significantly higher than the average, while the largest rental structures and largest owner-occupied dwellings have highly inelastic supply functions. For the percentage change models, though, the medium-sized rental structures have larger elasticities.

It would be a mistake to place much credence in the comparative results since increasing the homogeneity in one dimension may increase the importance of differences in some other dimension (e.g., expectations). These results seem to imply that, while too much aggregation probably is not the cause of the low elasticity estimates, there are nonetheless important differences among suppliers in both the owner-occupant and rental markets.

SUMMARY OF FINDINGS

We have established the lower bound of the long-run price elasticity of the supply of housing services to be on the order of 0.3; according to the Census CINCH data, this estimate applies nationally to about 70 per cent of the housing stock over a ten-year period. To establish the value of the elasticity more precisely will require substantially better data than is presently available on the physical and neighbour-

TABLE 2

Estimated supply elasticities from stratified samples[a]

Model type	Size of structure				
		Renter-occupied dwellings			
	Duplex	3-4 unit structure	5-9 unit structure	10-19 unit structure	20+ unit structure
Cross-sectional model	.32	.18	.15[b]	.25	.09
Percentage change model unadjusted	.07	.06	.09	.12	c
adjusted for factor price changes	.18	.18	.28	.36	c

	Owner-occupied dwellings		
	Small units	Medium units	Large units
Cross-sectional model	.42	.16	.08
Percentage change model unadjusted	.22	.07	c
adjusted for factor price changes	1.60	.30	c

a Full results are given in appendix tables B-3 to B-6 in Ozanne and Struyk (1976). All coefficients are significant at .05 level or higher unless otherwise indicated. Note that there are both upward and downward biases in these t-statistics as discussed in footnote c to table 1.

b Significant at .10 to .05 level

c Coefficient insignificant at .10 level

hood attributes of housing and on the characteristics of producers, although the general methodology developed here should remain applicable. The lower bound estimate is, however, quite consistent with the results of the deLeeuw-Ekanem analysis.

Combined, the elasticity estimates emphasize that existing structures constitute major impediments to changes in the quantity of services provided by the dwelling. Further, they indicate that government actions which greatly increase the demand for housing by the poor — a demand which will mainly be satisfied by housing already available to the poor, due to building code restrictions and the length of time required for units to filter downward — will also be accompanied by significant rise in housing prices. For example, assuming income and price elasticities of demand of 1.0 and -1.0 respectively and a price elasticity of supply of housing services of 0.3, a 10 per cent increase in income to low-income households will produce a 7 per cent increase in prices and only a 3 per cent increase in the quantity of housing service consumed. A supply elasticity of 1.5 — a value we believe may be a realistic upper bound — shifts these values markedly to a 4 per cent price increase and a 6 per cent quantity increase; but the implied inflation is still substantial.

Little difference was found in the elasticity estimates for owner-occupied and rental properties. It seems likely, however, that further stratification of producers into more homogeneous groups in terms of their expectations, production technologies and the factor prices they face may show significant differences in supplier responsiveness to price changes.

NOTES

1 This research was conducted under contract with the Office of Policy Development and Research, U.S. Department of Housing and Urban Development; opinions expressed, though, are those of the authors and not necessarily those of the sponsoring agency.

2 Muth (1960) analyzed the long-run demand for, and supply of, new units nationally; Swan (1973), among others, has studied shorter-run effects of the same problem; and Bradbury, et al. (1974) have studied the number of units converted from one structure type to another within an urban area.

3 For further discussion of these estimates see Grieson (1973), and de Leeuw and Ekanem (1973).

4 Other analyses are currently being carried out as part of the experimental housing allowance program; see Lowry, et al. (1973).

5 Even this distinction is not clear cut, however. A supplier with some characteristics of both groups is one who owns and resides in a multi-unit structure, renting the units other than his own.

6 The index for tract i is

$$I^i = (Y^i/\overline{Y}) * (WHC^i/\overline{WHC}) * (E^i/\overline{E})$$

where bars refer to SMSA averages and Y is mean family income, E is the mean number of school years completed by the population, and WHC is the fraction of males working in white-collar occupations.

7 See Schnare and Struyk (1975) for a description of racial segregation in Boston over the 1950-70 period.

8 For a complete description of the properties of a hedonic index see Rosen (1974). Examples of prior use of these indices are reviewed in Ball (1973), and

Schnare and Struyk (1976).

The definition of price change we develop in equation (8) is equivalent to one of the measures of "pure price" change used by Dhrymes (1971: 110-112).

9   Note that in the following exposition, p^j will refer to the price per unit of the bundle of services and p^i will refer to the price of the ith item or attribute in the bundle.

10   Owners' estimates of value have been found to be unbiased but with a considerable variance by Kish and Lansing (1954), and Kain and Quigley (1972).

11   In the estimation of hedonic indices the stock characteristics and the flow of services have been assumed to be highly correlated, but to the extent to which this is not the case, errors are introduced.

12   A few additional points about these estimates are worth noting. First, use of predicted house values for home owners may reduce some of the measurement error in owners' estimates of current house values. Owners whose homes have not been sold recently may not be able to report the value of their homes as precisely as they can their ages, incomes, education and number of children. Thus, an accurate expenditure function may provide better estimates of house values.

Estimation of our instrument, $\tilde{R}$, from demand determinants alone leaves open the possibility that the residual, $R-\tilde{R}$, is correlated with the exogenous variables in our supply equation. Because $R-\tilde{R}$ is implicitly included in the residual term of our supply equation with $\tilde{R}$, this correlation could bias our estimates. From our experience with the estimated $\tilde{R}$ we are confident that no significant correlations exist between $R-\tilde{R}$ and the other supply determinants.

Finally, we estimate an instrument for R_t but use $\ln R_t$ and $(R_{70}-R_{60})/R_{60}$ in our supply equations. More appropriate formulations would be to estimate instruments for the transformed R_t variables as used in the supply equations or to include nonlinear terms of the transformed variables constructed from $\tilde{R}_t$.

13   Neighbourhood characteristics cannot be entirely removed from the hedonic measure of quantity since the constant term in the hedonic regression includes the value of a basic set of both structural and neighbourhood characteristics. Intuitively, the problem is that dwellings are never observed outside of their neighbourhoods; hence it is difficult to separate dwelling-specific and neighbourhood-specific contributions to rent and value.

14   The earlier Census estimates are reported in Struyk and Marshall (1973), and Schnare and Struyk (1975).

Two further analyses were undertaken in attempts to improve the quality of fit. One attempted to refine the sample through identification of outlying observations using a type of discriminant function to determine such observations. About 1 per cent of the observations were identified. Also, from prior analysis with Boston data, problems with using one value for the open-ended house value interval were evident, so observations in this class were also dropped. Re-estimation of the hedonic indices with the refined samples produced very small changes in the ratios of the standard error of the estimates to the mean value of the dependent variable. The second type of analysis involved fitting separate hedonic models to the individual neighbourhoods. Again, little improvement in the quality of fit was obtained.

15 In addition to the three measures discussed in the text, it had been planned to include the wage rate of the "tenant" in the analysis. Specifically, the wage rate of the head of the household was to be included to capture the major difference between dwellings in factor prices faced by suppliers. Although the Census did collect earnings data for each household member, it was not coded; the only income data included is total household income. Use of total income, a principal determinant of demand, as a measure of factor prices in a supply function would raise serious identifications problems, so the tenant wage variable had to be omitted.

16 This is the conclusion of both Wachter (1972), and Hamer (1973).

17 This is based on Hamer's (1973) interview data for janitors and material handlers among a broad sample of Boston manufacturers. Wachter found no difference; however, his sample of thirty firms was restricted to firms with over 500 employees. There is substantial literature on "dual labour markets" which argues that one would expect no differences among the largest firms which offer preferred jobs, while finding substantial variations among smaller firms which provide inferior fringe benefits, working conditions, and job stability. See, for example, Gordon (1972).

18 The basis for this contention is at best fragmentary, and is contained in Schafer, et al. (1974).

19 For a further discussion of this point see Ozanne and Struyk (1976).

20 Schafer, et al. (1974) found evidence of higher prices in Roxbury. One, which was well-documented, not mentioned in this text, was insurance rates; but since this is an element of fixed costs which does not affect marginal supply decisions, it does not bear directly on the present problem.

21 That is, if the underlying model is

$$\ln(Q_{70}) = \gamma_o + \gamma_1 \ln(Q_{60}) + \gamma_2 \ln(P_{70}) + \ldots$$

then substituting $\ln R_{70}$ for $\ln P_{70}$ yields $\gamma_2/(1 + \gamma_2)$ instead of γ_2. Using this result and the estimated value of α_2 from $(13)^2$, γ_2 is solved from the relation $\alpha_2 = \gamma_2/(1 + \gamma_2)$ which yields the result given in the text. Similarly, the initial quantity of services elasticity of final output is $\alpha_1 + \alpha_1(\alpha_2/(1 - \alpha_2))$.

It might be noted that in deriving this expression, it is necessary to divide all terms in the model by $(1 + \gamma_2)$, including the disturbance term, μ. This causes a scaling problem in the disturbance term. This problem is easily overcome, however, since one need only adjust the variance of the errors by the constant $\gamma_2 + 1$.

22 One bias stems from the higher land-to structure ratio of owner-occupied dwellings compared to rental dwellings. If the price of urban land is increasing at a greater rate than other factors, the index will be biased upwards for renters. Another problem with the index is that while strong attempts are made to keep sample dwellings of a fixed quantity of services, this cannot be done perfectly under the BLS procedures; this produces some unknown period-to-period bias. A final problem is that the weights used to combine the five components of the home owner index appear to differ significantly from the expenditure share figures for rental properties as reported for properties in New York and Baltimore by Sternlieb (1971) and Stegman (1972). For a discussion of the CPI procedures, see Weicher and Simonson (1975).

23 The rent index is a measure of output prices, not inputs. It has other problems as well. It is the average over all rental dwellings, regardless of time of purchase. One could argue, however, that in a competitive market rents should not pose a problem. While this may be the case, there are reasons for believing the rent index to be downward biased. Weicher and Simonson (1975) outline these reasons which have to do with improper accounting for reduction in structural services due to dwelling depreciation, and in neighbourhood services.

24 A comparison of a purely cross-sectional model, one regressing $\ln \widetilde{R}_{70}$ on $\ln Q_{70}$, with the cross-sectional models in table 1, indicates that not using the time series data $(\ln Q_{60})$ produces a sizeable upward bias in the estimated elasticities. For renters, the difference in the elasticities between the purely cross-sectional model and the model reported in table 1 (column 5) is 0.9 versus 0.2; for owner-occupants it is 1.2 versus 0.2. The potential upward bias in the purely cross-sectional estimates, then, appears to be quite large. Estimates based on such data should be viewed in this context.

25 It is instructive in this regard to look at the data used in the only prior econometric estimation of service supply elasticities, that made by de Leeuw and Ekanem. The data were SMSA average values of rents and input factor prices for the very homogeneous group of rental dwellings sampled in thirty SMSAs by the Bureau of Labor Statistics. These dwellings are homogeneous, not only with regard to their physical characteristics, but also in terms of the kind of neighbourhoods in which they are located, at least to the extent that some minimal level of neighbourhood quality must be exceeded. The problem of deter-

mining differences in quantity of services and producer expectations was obviated by the homogeneity of the sample. Further, since between-market variation in factor prices probably greatly exceeds the within-market variation, the majority of this variation could be directly captured.

APPENDIX A

Estimated hedonic indices for dwellings included in Boston cinch data, 1960 and 1970

| | Dependent variable: value of owner-occupied dwellings | | | | Dependent variable: gross monthly rent | | | |
| | 1960 | | 1970 | | 1960 | | 1970 | |
	coeff	t-stat	coeff	t-stat	coeff	t-stat	coeff	t-stat
Constant	-5556	3.55	-3102	1.10	-229	2.31	-43.3	.36
A. Structure Variables								
Number of rooms	1518	11.5	1480	7.57	4.93	8.75	4.84	5.09
Year built								
1955-1960	5340	10.9	4114	5.83	14.2	2.06	-4.17	.36
1950-1954	3332	7.00	3111	4.48	-19.9	7.06	-37.4	7.84
1940-1949	2306	4.15	2531	3.08	-11.9	4.22	-28.8	6.03
1930-1939	2568	4.80	1827	2.29	c		c	
Number of bathrooms								
3 or more	b		23336	16.1	b		430.	14.3
2½	b		11629	9.77	b		285.	9.63
2	7426	12.1	4922	5.54	89.4	14.2	77.4	6.93
1½	2030	4.98	4441	7.95	17.8	2.15	28.9	3.11
Heating equipment								
central, air or electric	2537	2.41	3993	1.64	16.4	6.59	24.8	5.56
steam	3862	3.74	5102	2.11	17.2	8.59	21.6	5.84
Sound condition	1612	2.02	3984	3.97	4.69	2.32	12.0	4.63
Hot and cold piped water	c		c		9.87	2.37	12.3	1.04
Private toilet	c		c		25.6	6.80	30.6	3.10
Unit in duplex	a		a		-4.51	2.25	-5.58	1.64
Unit in 3 or 4 unit structure	a		a		-6.43	3.78	-8.93	3.14

APPENDIX A (Cotinued)

B. Occupant Variables

Elderly head of house	-327	.81	570	.99	-2.82	1.92	-15.9	6.38
Black household head	-2589	.73	-3918	.97	-6.27	1.73	9.93	.72
Male household head	538	1.15	2365	3.84	c		c	
Non-relative present	-297	2.46	853	.67	.18	.26	30.3	10.9
Children per room (*100)	-12.7	2.15	-21.8	2.05	c		c	

C. Neighborhood Variables

Per cent of households headed by a black	-80.0	1.04	30.7	.43	.11	1.14	-.08	.33
Per cent of Population having attended college	207	13.9	217	10.5	.63	5.95	1.24	7.73
Per cent of dwellings occupied	c		c		2.37	2.31	.70	.55
Per cent of dwellings in 5+ unit structures	-23.5	1.98	-59.4	3.41	c		c	
R^2	.60		.58		.38		.44	
F	84.8		69.2		48.8		57.1	
N	991		991		1473		1473	

a All owner-occupied units are in single unit structures.

b Data not available for 1960.

c Variable not included in model.

APPENDIX B

Adjustment of estimated coefficients for average price factor changes

---

If it is assumed in making the adjustment that the fully specified model to be estimated is

$$Q^* = b_o + b_1 \tilde{R}^* + b_2 P_o^* \qquad \text{(B-1)}$$

where the notation is the same as that in the text.
Estimation of the model omitting P_o^* results in a biased estimate of $\hat{b}_1$. Assuming that the only source of bias in $\hat{b}_1$ is from this specification error, the true value of b_1 is

$$b_1 = \hat{b}_1 - \tau b_2 \qquad \text{(B-2)}$$

where τ is the coefficient of the regression.[a]

$$P_o^* = \tau R^* \qquad \text{(B-3)}$$

The coefficient τ can be estimated using the percentage change in factor prices just described for P_o^*, the mean values of $\tilde{R}^*$ for owner-occupied and rental property, and the requirement that the regression line pass through the mean values of the dependent and independent variables.[b] Further, if it is assumed that $b_1 = -b_2$, that is, that changes in output and input prices have equivalent but opposite effects on output, then

$$b_1 = \hat{b}_1/(1-\tau). \qquad \text{(B-4)}$$

Finally, the price elasticity of supply is computed as $b_1/(1 - b_1)$.

---

a See Goldberger (1965: 194-197) for a discussion of specification errors.

b The coefficient is simply the ratio of the mean values of the dependent and independent variables. The estimates of τ are: .615 for owner-occupied dwellings and .524 for rental dwellings.

REFERENCES

Ball, M.J. 1973. "Recent Empirical Work on the Deteminants of Relative House Prices", *Urban Studies*, 10: 213-233.

Bradbury, K., R. Engle, O. Irvine, and J. Rothenberg. 1974. "Simultaneous Estimation of the Supply and Demand for Household Location in a Multizoned Metropolitan Area". Paper presented at the Econometric Society Meeting.

De Leeuw, F. 1971. "The Demand for Housing: A Review of Cross-Sectional Evidence", *Review of Economics and Statistics*, 53, 1: 1-10.

De Leeuw, F., and N. Ekanem. 1971. "The Supply of Rental Housing", *American Economic Review*, 61: 814-826.

De Leeuw, F. and N. Ekanem. 1973. "The Supply of Rental Housing: Reply", *American Economic Review*, 63: 437-438.

Dhrymes, P. 1971. "Price and Quality Changes in Consumer Goods: An Empirical Study", in Z. Griliches, ed., *Price Indexes and Quality Change*. Cambridge, Mass.: Harvard University Press.

Goldberger, A. 1965. *Econometric Theory*. New York: John Wiley.

Gordon, D. 1972. *Theories of Poverty and Unemployment*. Lexington, Mass.: D.C. Heath.

Grieson, R.E. 1973. "The Supply of Rental Housing: Comment", *American Economic Review*, 63: 433-436.

Hamer, A. 1973. *Industrial Exodus from the Central City*. Cambridge, Mass.: Lexington Books.

Kain, J.F., and J.M. Quigley. 1972. "Notes on Owner's Estimate of House Value", *Journal of the American Statistical Association*: 803-806.

Kish, L. and J.B. Lansing. 1954. "Response Errors in Estimating the Value of Homes", *Journal of the American Statistical Association*: 520-538.

Lowry, I.S. 1973. "The General Design Report". WN-8198-HUD. Santa Monica: Rand Corporation.

Muth, R.F. 1960. "Demand for Non-Farm Housing", in A. Harberger, ed., *The Demand for Durable Goods*. Chicago: University of Chicago Press.

Ozanne, L., and R.J. Struyk. 1976. "Housing from the Existing Stock: Comparative Economic Analyses of Owner Occupants and Landlords". Washington, D.C.: Urban Institute.

Rosen, S. 1974. "Hedonic Prices and Implicit Markets: Product Differentiation in Price Competition", *Journal of Political Economy*, 82: 34-55.

Schafer, R., W. Holshauser, K. Moore, and R. Santer. 1974. "Spatial Variation in the Operating Costs of Rental Housing". Cambridge, Mass.: Harvard University (processed, unpublished).

Schnare, A.B. 1974. *Externalities, Segregation and Housing Prices.* Washington, D.C.: Urban Institute.

Schnare, A.B., and R.J. Struyk. 1975. "Changes in Ghetto Housing Prices over Time". Paper presented at the National Bureau of Economic Research Conference on Income and Wealth.

Schnare, A.B., and R.J. Struyk. 1976. "Segmentation in Urban Housing Markets", *Journal of Urban Economics:* 146-166.

Sternlieb, G. 1971. *The Urban Housing Dilemma.* New York: City of New York Department of Rent and Housing Maintenance.

Stegman, M. 1972. *Housing Investment in the Inner City.* Cambridge, Mass.: MIT Press.

Struyk, R.J., and S. Marshall. 1973. "Estimating the Value of Housing Services with the Census User's Sample: Results for Five Areas". *Working paper 208-10.* Washington, D.C.: Urban Institute.

Swan, C. 1973. "Housing Subsidies and Housing Starts", *American Real Estate and Urban Economics Journal,* 1, 2: 119-140.

U.S. Bureau of the Census. 1973. Census of Housing, 1970. *Components of Inventory Change.* Final report H C(4)-3, Boston, Mass. SMSA. Washington, D.C.: U.S. Government Printing Office.

Wachter, M.L. 1972. "Wage Determination in a Local Market", *Journal of Human Resources:* 89-103.

Weicher, J.C., and J.C. Simonson. 1975. "Recent Trends in Housing Costs", *Journal of Economics and Business:* 177-185.

4.2 THEORETICAL APPROACHES TO FILTERING IN THE URBAN HOUSING MARKET[1]

Gordon W. Davies

There are a variety of definitions of filtering in the urban housing market, some chosen for different empirical purposes.[2] Here we propose a more general definition, as follows:

> Filtering in the housing market is the process in which the real housing consumption of families or households changes over time, whether by the depreciation or renovation of the same dwelling unit or the choice of a different dwelling unit (which may be newly constructed or have experienced depreciation, renovation, or conversion from a different type). The process may involve changes in real incomes and in the relative price of housing services.

The term "filtering" comes from the observable process in which a dwelling unit previously occupied by a higher-income household depreciates and is passed down to a household with a lower income, although the term is not necessarily restricted to movements in this particular direction.

The process is important in analyzing housing policy, because one alternative to public housing as a source of accommodation for low-income families is existing housing which is vacated by families who move into newer units. It is usually assumed that the private market will not directly supply new housing for low-income families, either because this construction is unprofitable or because it is less profitable than the construction of higher quality units. But if policies which encourage construction of units for higher-income households also result in improved housing conditions for lower-income households, then public housing may not be the most effective way of providing low-income households with "adequate" housing. This view is also supported by the argument that public housing almost necessarily entails a welfare loss to society because it distorts the relative prices facing the consumer and offers him an all-

or-nothing choice between a fixed quantity of housing services, in the public housing project, and the quantities he could consume at unsubsidized rates, given his income.

The importance of filtering has been acknowledged in the debate on housing policy in the United States but not to any great extent in Canada, although the issues are the same in either country. The purpose of this paper is to review existing theoretical models of filtering to determine the state of the art and to glean suggestions for application of a model of filtering to the analysis of selected housing policies operating in Ontario. We plan in subsequent empirical work to use the 1974 Central Mortgage and Housing Corporation (CMHC) Survey of Housing Units (SHU) linked, by individual dwelling unit, to the 1971 Census of Canada. The SHU survey contains information on the dwelling units and on the demographic and economic characteristics of the occupants.

History of the Concept

One of the first references to the filtering process is found in a British special committee report on slum housing. The 1929 report stated that:

> When post-war building began it was hoped that there would be a gradual movement of the working-class population out of the slums into better houses. This might occur in two ways, either the slum dweller might go direct into a new house or a process of "filtering up" might occur under which the slum dweller would move from the slum into a better pre-war house, the tenant of which would, in his turn, move into a new house. Both of these processes have of course occurred, but on a disappointingly small scale (National Housing and Town Planning Council, 1929: 15).

Hoyt (1939) has been credited with providing the first systematic approach to neighbourhood change with his introduction of the "sector" theory. By charting the distribution and growth patterns of 142 American cities (using average rents by block as his standard of measurement) he discovered that areas of increasing rental levels did not form concentric circles as was believed, but that different rent levels occupied different sectors of the city.

As the city expanded, he determined that

> the different types of residential areas tend to grow outward along rather distinct radii, and new growth on the arc of a given sector tends to take on the character of the initial growth in that sector (Hoyt, 1939: 114).

Hoyt emphasized the importance of high-rent neighbourhoods whose movement he believed "pulled" city growth in the same direction. He found that occupants of high-rent units moved to the periphery of the city to new homes constructed on the outward edge of the sectors which they originally occupied.

Members of lesser income groups, in their desire to remain as close as possible to the high-rent areas, successively occupied the vacated homes, now less desirable and less expensive because of age, quality decline, etc. This process he refers to as filtering, whereby all groups "move up a step, leaving the oldest and cheapest houses to be occupied by the poorest families or to be vacated" (Hoyt, 1939: 122). Thus, in the sectors in which the high-rent groups form the periphery, there appears a downward succession of rents because of the filtering process.

Obsolescence of the higher-priced dwellings and population growth were cited by Hoyt as the major contributors to neighbourhood movement. In a "reconstruction" of neighbourhood forecasting, Smith estimated Hoyt's model to include another factor — changing composition of demand. Three aspects of neighbourhood characteristics (proportion of non-white occupants, proportion of owner-occupied dwellings and monthly dwelling value) were identified for seventy-six residential neighbourhoods in Oakland, California, and their movement was traced over three time periods between 1936 and 1960. Using a technique similar to that employed earlier by Fisher and Winnick (1951), Smith calculated the change of these neighbourhood factors in relation to the city as a whole, and determined that not only was transition a gradual process, but that "neighbourhood changes required to accommodate a shift in aggregate housing demand composition were more likely to occur in neighbourhoods already in the process of transition" (Smith, 1963: 292-293). That neighbourhoods were more likely to move from a "high" to a "medium" rather than "low" value classification is a particularly important result in the discussion of the filtering process.

The foregoing constitutes a brief description of the applied studies which preceded subsequent approaches to filtering which may be characterized as being theoretical. These approaches are (1) the matrix method, (2) the assignment problem, (3) the commodity hierarchy model, (4) simulation models, and (5) Markov processes. These approaches are discussed *seriatim* in the next five sections.

Matrix Method

The first reasonably formal model of the filtering process was Grigsby (1963). Previously, studies had tended to look at either the supply or demand sectors of the housing market (or submarkets). Grigsby (1963: 31) attempted to bring these two sectors together in order to observe their interaction as part of a "composite whole". By the use of matrices Grigsby intended that the supply and demand interrelationships could be viewed systematically.

Grigsby divides the housing market into various distinct submarkets, all of which are interdependent to some degree. Although the exact concept of a submarket is somewhat vague, Grigsby borrows his definition from Rapkin, Winnick and Blank (1953: 10) and defines two houses as being in the same submarket if they compete as alternatives for those demanding housing space (i.e., there is a high degree of substitutability between the two houses).

The various submarkets which comprise the housing market in a given area are tied together by "linkages". Some linkages may be thought of as representing characteristics that would distinguish one submarket (or, what is the same thing, one more or less homogeneous group of dwelling units) from another, and it is these linkages that act as the agents in establishing the submarket interdependencies. They need not be direct, i.e.:

> Bargain house prices in Area A might be completely ignored by potential home buyers in Area C if the latter area were too far distant. These prices might, however, attract a segment of the market from Area B to Area A. This shift might in turn create values in B which would serve to capture a segment of the potential in C (Grigsby, 1963: 34-35)

nor need they be of the same "length", i.e., strength. Other linkages are established by the movements of households through the supply of dwellings. These movements also "cause values to shift, areas to improve or decay, and housing to become available or unavailable to lower-income groups" (Grigsby, 1963: 56).

In order to understand fully the concepts underlying the matrix analysis, it is useful briefly to review the steps that were followed in constructing the model. Commonly, certain household characteristics are associated with certain submarkets. By employing unpublished National Housing Inventory (NHI) data, Grigsby constructs a matrix that relates the characteristics of recent home purchasers in the Philadelphia metropolitan area to the characteristics of the homes which were purchased. Purchasers are grouped according to family income and employment location of household head, and the accommodations purchased are grouped by value and location.

This matrix (which is no more than a simple cross-tabulation) allows us to see actual movements, but it does not provide any information about the alternative choices considered by buyers when they make the decision to acquire a new dwelling. Such data on alternative choices are useful in order to determine the interdependence between submarkets. Unfortunately, this information is not available and Grigsby is forced to employ some simplifying assumptions concerning the household's second choice of dwelling units. From these assumptions and the NHI data, he constructs a hypothetical table cross-tabulating the number of households making second choices for dwelling units in different submarkets by the characteristics of the units in the submarkets. This gives an indication of potential demand in different submarkets and of the degree of interdependence between submarkets, but it does not provide any information as to the reasons *why* families change accommodation, i.e., to what change in market conditions they are reacting.

Because potential moves from one submarket to another release dwelling units in the original submarket, the above approach leads to an input-output matrix which shows the potential net flows of existing, net out-migrant, newly formed, and newly dissolved households between submarkets. The gross flows are first shown in a purely hypothetical input-output matrix in which each element a_{ij} represents the gross flows from area i to area j. The net flows between submarkets, a'_{ij} are then calculated as

$$a'_{ij} = a_{ij} - a_{ji}$$

Inspection of this matrix reveals which submarkets are gaining (or losing) households at the expense (to the benefit) of other submarkets, and summation along a row gives the overall change in demand for units within the submarket. Again, there is no behavioural content to the model in the sense that the reasons for household moves have not been determined, nor does the model show the responses of price, maintenance and new construction in the submarkets although these aspects are certainly thoroughly discussed by Grigsby in other parts of the study. The model is therefore not operational in a realistic sense, in part also because suitable data are not available. The assignment problem approach to filtering considered below, may be viewed as an attempt to breathe more formal behavioural and normative content into the type of framework developed by Grigsby.

Assignment Problem

The assignment problem, which is the simplest form of the linear programming problem, is a relatively powerful approach which determines an optimal configuration of house values and incomes, shows the response of the allocation to various sorts of changes, and permits an assessment of the normative implications of the results.

In his study, Smith (1964) uses the assignment approach to match hypothetical families and housing units. Initially he assumes five families, identical except for income, and five housing units differing only in quality. The families are numbered 1 through 5, with 1 designated as the family with the lowest income, 2 with the second lowest income, etc. In a similar manner, the housing units are assigned the letters A to E, with A representing the unit with the lowest quality and E the dwelling of highest quality. It is assumed that all families rank the quality of the dwelling units the same.

Smith then constructs a "market demand matrix" which is illustrated in table 1. The elements of the matrix represent the differential bids which households with different incomes are willing to make for the various house types. L is the

TABLE 1

Smith's market demand matrix

Income of Families	Low	Houses (Quality)			High
	A	B	C	D	E
1 Low	L	+5	+10	+15	+20
2	+10	+16	+22	+28	+34
3	+20	+27	+34	+41	+48
4	+30	+38	+46	+54	+62
5 High	+40	+49	+58	+67	+76

SOURCE: W.F. Smith, 1965

minimum amount that would be offered by any household for any house type, and the other elements in the matrix represent the premiums households are willing to pay over the reference bid L. These elements in the matrix may be described by noting: (a) for a family with a given income, the increment in the offer is constant as we move to higher quality houses; (b) the constant increment in (a) is larger for families with higher incomes. These two features of the matrix necessarily imply that for a given house type, the increments in the bids as income increases are fixed, but that these increments are larger for houses of higher quality.

The value to be maximized by the model is the aggregate of rental offers and, given the conditions of the demand matrix, any assignment of families to dwellings that does not lie on the diagonal can be shown to be non-optimal, i.e., aggregate rental offers are not maximized in the off-diagonal assignment. This pattern of occupancy gives us the result that we might expect − the lowest quality dwelling is inhabited by the family with the lowest income and the second lowest quality is occupied by the family having the second lowest income, etc.

The concept of "filtering" can be simply demonstrated in the basic assignment problem. By altering the income distribution of the hypothetical community, it is possible to show how the families will redistribute themselves among the dwelling units to once again maximize aggregate rental offers. In the case of removing the highest income family and replacing it by a family with an income equivalent to that of family 1, all families (except family 1 or its equal) will now occupy the dwelling of the next highest quality level (i.e., family 2 will move to dwelling C, family 3 to dwelling D and 4 to E). Housing units have filtered down to lower income groups.

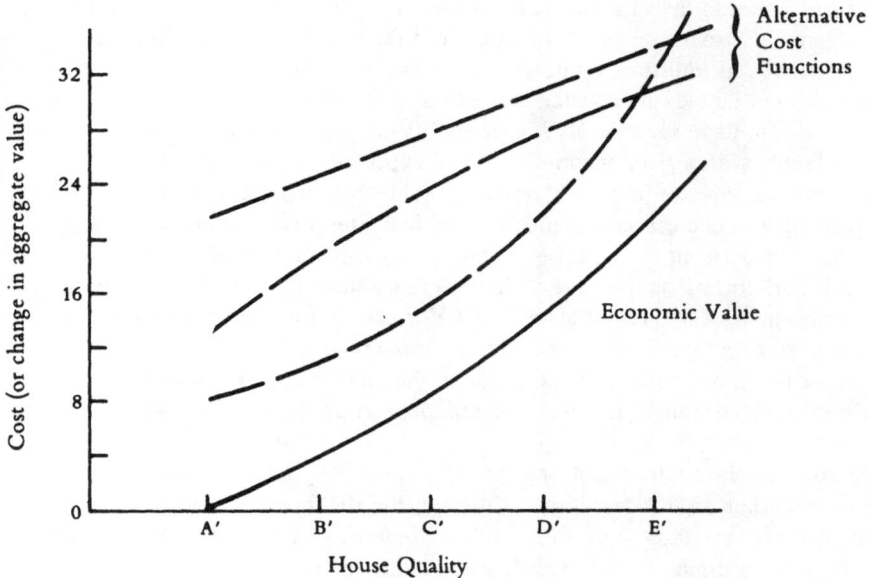

FIGURE 1: Selecting quality level for new construction – replacement case
Source: W.F. Smith, 1964

In a similar manner, it is possible to simulate the reaction of the community to new construction. By introducing a new home of each quality level in turn, a table of change in aggregate value is constructed, this change designated as the economic value (EV) of each quality level. As the quality of the dwelling type constructed increases, so too does the economic value, at an increasing rate. The EV function, shown in figure 1, is convex (i.e., increases at an increasing rate). Also shown in figure 1 are alternative cost curves, which relate the cost of new construction to the differing quality levels. These curves, as shown, may be convex, concave or linear.

Assuming that the community in Smith's model has a constant population with an unchanged distribution of income, new construction will be of the replacement type due to general deterioration or obsolescence of the existing stock. Those desiring new housing, Smith argues, will be willing to pay premiums for it, because of depreciation of existing units, and these premiums may be viewed as moving the cost curve (whatever its shape) downward. New construction will only be warranted at the intersection of the cost curve and the EV curve. Unless the former were more convex than the latter, there is small chance of middle-quality construction.

The shape of the economic value function shown in figure 1 obviously depends entirely on the differential bids which households with different incomes make for houses in the various quality classes. The set of bids shown in table 1 indeed gives rise to a convex EV function, but the structure of these bids does not appeal to our intuition. As noted, Smith has assumed that the increments in the differential bids are constant for a household with a given income bidding for dwelling units in successively higher quality classes. This is unreasonable since a family with a given income would be expected to bid smaller absolute increments for units of increasing quality.[3] Table 2 shows incremental bids which are positive, but decrease as the quality level increases. For the bids shown in table 2, if we perform the exercise of adding a dwelling unit of each type, determining an optimal assignment of families to dwelling units, and calculating the change in aggregate rental offers, the EV function, for these particular bids, is linear. Because these incremental bids are more realistic, Smith's conclusion about the likelihood of new construction in the middle quality ranges is therefore weakened, although the result will still depend on the particular shape of the cost function.

Smith then shows the effect of population growth by removing one house from the market. In this case houses filter *up,* and the family offering the lowest bid is left without a dwelling unit. By removing each house from A to E in turn, a curve similar to the preceding economic value curve is produced. However, as the community finds itself short of housing space, all families find that they must now bid more for the houses which they occupy. The economic value curve will rise as the rental offers increase and will flatten as the rich find that their real incomes are falling (hence the premiums paid for extra quality also fall or disappear). Construction is therefore most likely to occur in the lowest quality range.

In a commentary on Smith's assignment model, Edel (1972) has pointed out that Smith's maximand implies that all housing is owned and produced by one firm, or housing trust. Housing ownership is in reality highly decentralized and this affects Smith's conclusions about new construction. Edel also discusses the implications of filtering combined with decentralized ownership on economic and social welfare. Edel's first point is that private decentralized builders, when they decide whether to construct new units, do not take into consideration the loss in the property values of existing owners occasioned by a general decline in price as a result of a larger stock of housing. In Smith's model this general decline in value is implicitly recognized in the sense that he compares the value of the maximand (aggregate rental offers), with and without construction of dwelling units in the different quality classes. We may therefore expect a higher level of construction with decentralized ownership.

Edel also maintains that the distribution of new construction will be dif-

TABLE 2

Alternative market demand matrix

| Income of Families | Low | Houses (Quality) | | | High |
	A	B	C	D	E
1 Low	L	+5	+9	+12	+14
2	+10	+16	+21	+25	+28
3	+20	+27	+33	+38	+42
4	+30	+38	+45	+51	+56
5 High	+40	+49	+57	+64	+70

ferent with decentralized ownership because (as in the general case) builders of any house type are not concerned with the decline in property values which should ensue. Of course, this decline in property values will in itself ultimately restrict construction (because new houses compete in the market with existing ones), but the construction which occurs in this process should still be greater than the amount which would occur if the property decline were taken into account before construction occurs, as in Smith's model.

Concerning the welfare aspects of decentralized ownership combined with filtering, Edel suggests that aggregate welfare will be higher because of private, individual ownership. This would be true because decentralized ownership would result in more construction, a higher stock of housing, lower prices for dwelling unit services, and therefore a greater excess of consumer's and producer's surpluses over costs than would occur with a monopolist housing authority which restricted output in order, implicitly, to increase aggregate property values (rental offers). These issues are certainly interesting and relevant, but they are not at all formally developed by Edel, or pursued to any great extent. The remaining approaches to filtering discussed here appear to sidestep the issue by assuming that all dwelling units are rented and by excluding consideration of the position of the landlord or existing owner.

Commodity Hierarchy Model

The analytical literature on filtering took a quantum leap forward with the recent publication of two papers on commodity hierarchies by Sweeney (1974a; 1974b). The definition of a commodity hierarchy is

> a class of commodities characterized by mutual exclusivity . . . (where) each consumer's partial preference ranking defined over the elements of the class is identical to the partial ranking of every other consumer and is independent of the other components of the consumption bundle (Sweeney, 1974a: 148).

Sweeney's model is extremely general as it determines endogenously depreciation and demolition, new construction, filtering and prices. The hierarchy approach is equally applicable, with few modifications, to the analysis of any durable good (such as automobiles) for which depreciation is associated with a decline in quality.

When applying the hierarchy concept to the rental housing market, the dwellings comprising the market in any given area are grouped into discrete quality levels, the ranking of which is agreed upon by all consumers. Any differences characterizing the units that cannot be classified under the heading of quality are abstracted from, so that dwelling aspects such as location are not dealt with.

The notion of quality is made rigorous in Sweeney's model, as units of different qualities are defined to be distinct gross substitutes. N different levels of quality exist (where N can be any integer greater than zero) and they are assigned numbers from 1 to N. The least preferred dwelling group (i.e., that with the lowest quality) is designated as 1, and the most preferred level of quality is assigned N. Each level is described by a market rental price, this price varying directly with the dwelling quality described by that level. Hence dwellings in the highest level, N, have the highest market value.

Over time, houses deteriorate and pass through progressively lower levels of quality. The rate at which homes deteriorate from any given level is directly proportional to the number of units in that level and varies inversely with the average time which a consumer occupies a unit in that quality bracket. The supply of housing at any quality level is determined by construction of new dwellings in i, and the rate at which units enter and leave i because of depreciation. The demand for a unit in quality bracket i is implicitly a function of consumers' tastes and incomes, and of the prices prevailing in all quality levels.

By specifying a variety of functions, Sweeney develops "a closed, dynamic system that will determine endogenously, as a function of time, all prices, stocks, deterioration rates, and construction rates once initial conditions are given" (1974b: 301). He then determines the conditions for three equilibria states — the short-run, stationary and long-run — and proves their existence and uniqueness.

It is useful to examine one type of long-run equilibrium, that of a "normal equilibrium", which is defined as a long-run equilibrium in which construction occurs at, and only at, contiguous levels in the hierarchy. This type of equilibrium presumably closely resembles real world equilibrium. A housing market in normal equilibrium is illustrated in figure 2 in which P_i is price in the ith quality level, and E_i is new construction in the ith level. At the highest quality levels no new construction occurs so no housing will exist in the long run at these levels. Those who demand housing in the lower quality regions must, in the absence of public housing, rely on dwellings filtering down from higher levels because of deterioration. Rents or prices will fall as these dwellings move into lower quality brackets, and will con-

FIGURE 2: Normal equilibrium in Sweeney's model
　　　　Source: J.L. Sweeney, 1974b

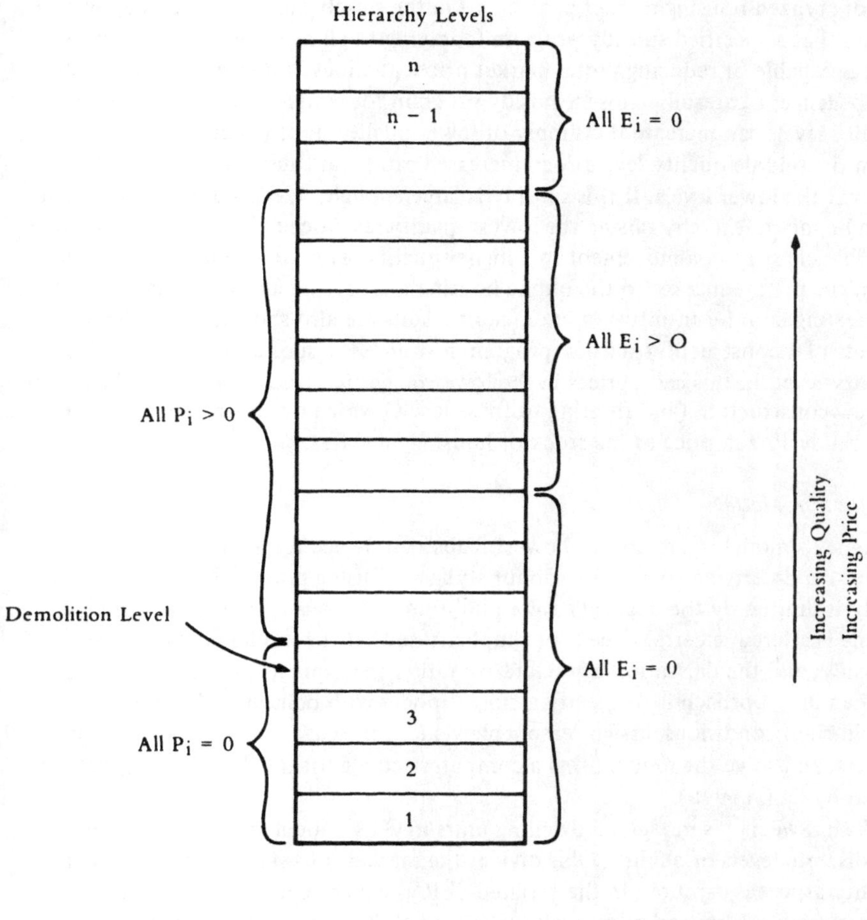

Hierarchy Levels

tinue to fall until market price or rent becomes zero. When this price reaches zero the unit is effectively removed from the stock by abandonment, which is equivalent in the model to demolition. (This formulation is for simplicity only; Sweeney, 1974b: 301.)

The usefulness of Sweeney's commodity hierarchy approach to housing lies in its ability to explain how the abstract market will respond in the long run to a number of stylized housing market programs. On the supply side, for example, Sweeney shows that a specified subsidy program (applying to all new construction) exists that is capable of reducing rental market prices at all levels above the demolition level. Hence, a carefully chosen subsidy program for construction at moderate quality levels can increase the supply of lower quality units (as units deteriorate from the middle quality levels at an increased rate) and thus lower the price of units at the lower levels. If this subsidy is large enough, the demolition level might even be raised, thereby raising the lowest quality level occupied. Demand subsidies, which can result in a movement to a higher quality level, or a complete movement from the private market to the public housing market, are also examined. Some interesting counter-intuitive or anomalous results are also shown, for example, the effects of a construction subsidy program in which the subsidy increases with the quality level. In this case, prices in the lower ranges *increase,* as a result of a decline in new construction (and filtering to these levels) which occurs in response to a general decline in price as the stock of housing increases.

Simulation Models

Sweeney's model is a relatively powerful abstract device for analyzing the filtering process and deriving conclusions about stylized housing programs, but its applicability is limited by the necessity for equilibrium solutions in which one variable at a time is altered, a certain need for simplicity so that the model may be solved analytically, and the derivation of qualitative rather than quantitative results. A complementary approach is to specify a closed model with behavioural functions and equilibrium conditions, assign reasonable values for exogenous variables and parameters, and solve the model using a computerized algorithm. This is the approach taken by Ohls (1975).

As in Sweeney's model, all dwelling units in Ohls' model are rented and there are discrete levels of quality. Ohls divides the market into sixty such levels. This quality aspect is captured in the variable SERV, which represents the output of housing services offered by a dwelling unit. SERV(J), therefore, denotes the bundle of services associated with quality level J. It is assumed that more services represent a proportionally higher quality dwelling. It is only this bundle of services which is relevant to the consumer when he decides upon the desirability of a certain dwelling unit.

The consumers in the model are 8,100 computer-generated families, each of which is assigned an income such that the total distribution of these incomes is lognormal. Each consumer is assumed to maximize utility, as defined by the function (with parameter values assigned in the reference solution),

$$U(Y,J) = (Y - P)^{0.8} SERV(J)^{0.2}$$

where Y represents family income and P is the total rental price of the consumed dwelling. Note that, because of the form of the utility function, it is assumed that a family spends 20 per cent of its income on accommodation, which is not unreasonable. Thus, families with higher incomes spend more for housing in absolute terms, but the same proportion on housing services, as do those with lower incomes.

The stock of housing at any of the sixty quality levels may be altered by new construction, or by entrances to and exits from the quality level because of depreciation. The cost of construction varies in fixed proportion to the quantity of housing services supplied by the dwelling unit. Functionally, the construction cost curve, C(J), is given by

$$C(J) = 2400 \cdot SERV(J).$$

Ohls has therefore assumed that the cost curve is linear, but he points out (as did Smith) that there is no reason to believe that it necessarily takes this shape, as opposed to being convex or concave. Builders and owners are assumed to maximize profits.

As noted, the stock of rental housing at each quality level is also altered by depreciation of the existing units; this depreciation is characterized as production of a lower quantity of housing services from the unit. In order to formalize this process, Ohls assumes that the rate of depreciation experienced by a dwelling unit is determined by the amount of maintenance expenditure on that unit which would be required to keep the unit at the Jth quality level. Specifically, he uses the function

$$M(J,T) = 70 + 0.5e^{0.058T} [SERV(J)]$$

where M(J,T) represents the monthly expenditure necessary in order that a unit in quality class J will remain in that quality bracket for a time period of length T. Note that one portion of the expenditure ($70) is independent of the level of SERV. This might represent necessary fixed minimal expenditures on items such as heating. The other component is an increasing proportion of the level of housing services, the proportion itself varying directly with the length of time T during which the unit is maintained in the Jth quality class. This specification assumes that it costs more, at the margin of time in the quality class, to maintain higher quality units.

A number of equilibrium conditions and market clearing mechanisms are also specified in the model. A solution is determined for variables such as the distribution of families to dwelling units in the different quality levels (such that all families are housed), maintenance expenditure requirements, M(Y,J), and construction rates. With level 1 designated as the lowest quality level (in that it provides the smallest quantity of housing services), and 60 assigned to the highest level, Ohls calculates that no family will choose to live in units below level 5, and that no construction will occur below level 34. This latter result obtains because it is cheaper, for the same low quantity of housing services to be produced, to let existing units in higher quality ranges depreciate and filter down than it is to build new units for those demanding lower quality accommodation.

The model is also used to compare the effects of a rent voucher program and a public housing program on the housing consumption patterns of low-income families. The former offers to the families occupying the bottom 20 per cent of the income distribution a rent subsidy which covers one-half of their rental payments, P. The only constraint attached to this program is a subsidy ceiling of $91 per month per family. Subsidized families under this program increase their housing consumption level by an average of three classes, even though no low-quality housing is constructed; units below level 8 are no longer occupied in this solution. Construction levels at middle quality ranges increase and the rate at which dwellings filter to lower levels also increases. Maintenance expenditures are also higher in the lower levels, with the result that units remain in these classes for longer periods of time before filtering to an even lower quality class.

An alternative program investigated, public housing, is handled by removing the poor from the private market altogether. Low-income families therefore no longer occupy houses which have filtered down to them. This policy simulation assumes that the bottom 20 per cent of the income distribution is removed. In this solution, if it is assumed that enough public housing is constructed in order to upgrade the housing consumption of low-income families by the same amount on average as in the rent subsidy program, it is shown that the former entails a higher cost to the government, which is assumed to fund either program.

An interesting application of an applied filtering model is as a component of a larger simulation model of urban growth and locations of residence and unemployment, the NBER (National Bureau of Economic Research) urban simulation model. Using data for Detroit and San Francisco, Ingram, Kain and Ginn (1972) develop a prototype model consisting of nineteen workplace and forty-four residence zones. The housing market has three basic sectors — the demand sector, the supply sector, and the price formation and market clearing sector. The activities within each sector are carried out in one or more of seven "submodels". Figure 3 represents the

FIGURE 3: Components of NBER urban simulation model
        Source: Adapted from Ingram, *et al.*, 1972

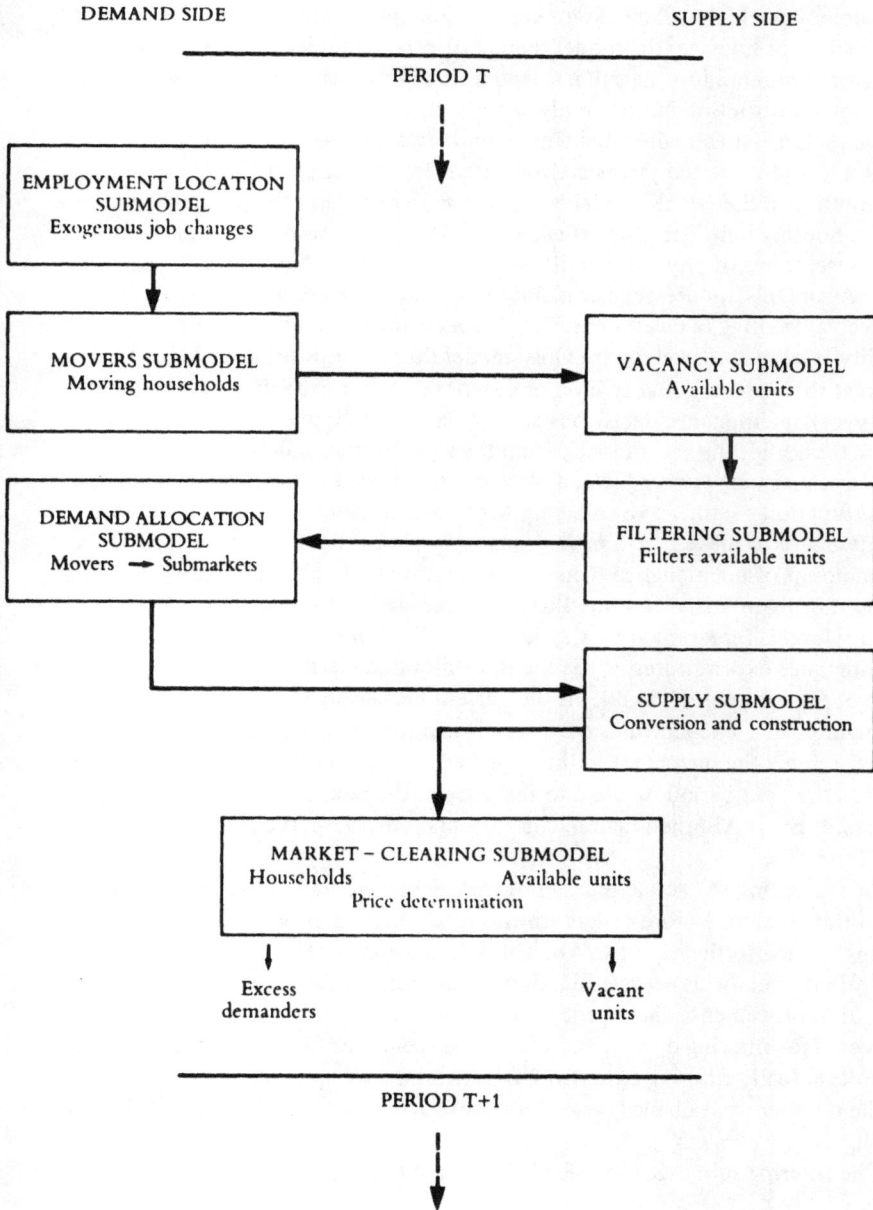

model schematically. Exogenous changes in the location of employment first generate household moves on the supply side. Movers generate vacancies in the various submarkets. These vacant units are then allowed to filter up or down in the filtering submodel which will be explored more fully in a moment. With the newly filtered stock of housing, the model then performs a complex forecast demand allocation of household to the submarkets, which in turn is used to generate conversion and construction in the supply submodel. In the market-clearing submodel, households are then reallocated among units to satisfy certain equilibrium conditions and end-of-period prices are generated (Ingram, *et al.*, 1972: 26-27).

Filtering in the NBER model is defined as "a change in the physical condition of the housing unit" (Ingram, *et al.*, 1972: 44). It is assumed that quality, which is representative of physical condition, is an objective and measurable characteristic. As in Ohls' model, regular maintenance expenditures are necessary in order to keep a dwelling in a certain quality bracket. Increased expenditure can raise the quality level of the dwelling (in Ohls' model this is not possible, as units either remain at their present quality level or deteriorate). For each time period (which is one year), maintenance decisions are simulated for 20 per cent of the housing stock (basically, the vacant stock from the vacancy submodel).

The underlying *conceptual* maintenance relationship is a relatively simple, discrete function -- either a dwelling unit receives enough, or more than enough, maintenance to move it to a *higher* quality level or it does not. If it does not receive this amount of maintenance then it may filter down to a lower quality level. The amount of maintenance required to raise a representative dwelling unit to a higher quality level is represented by the distance AB in figure 4 in which M is annual maintenance expenditures, P_m is the price prevailing in the next period if maintenance occurs this period, and P_n is the current period price which would prevail if no maintenance expenditures occurred. If maintenance equal to AB occurs, then BC represents the increment in the expected price of the unit at the higher quality level in the next period, relative to the price in the next period if no maintenance occurs. If BC > AB, then maintenance occurs; otherwise, it does not (Ingram, *et al.*, 1972: 45-50).

In calculating the actual number of units which actually filter up or down in a given time period, a more or less arbitrary, continuous, probabilistic filtering function is applied to the ratio BC/AB. This relationship generates the probability of a unit filtering up or down as a function of the ratio of the quality premium to the cost of improvement. These probabilities are constrained to be between minus 10 per cent (for filtering down), and plus 10 per cent (for filtering up). The number of units actually filtering either way is determined by applying these probabilities to the number of available (vacant) units of each type (Ingram, *et al.*, 1972: 109-113).

The filtering submodel described above simulates only a portion of the housing

FIGURE 4: Conceptual filtering function in NBER urban simulation model
Source: Ingram, *et al.*, 1972

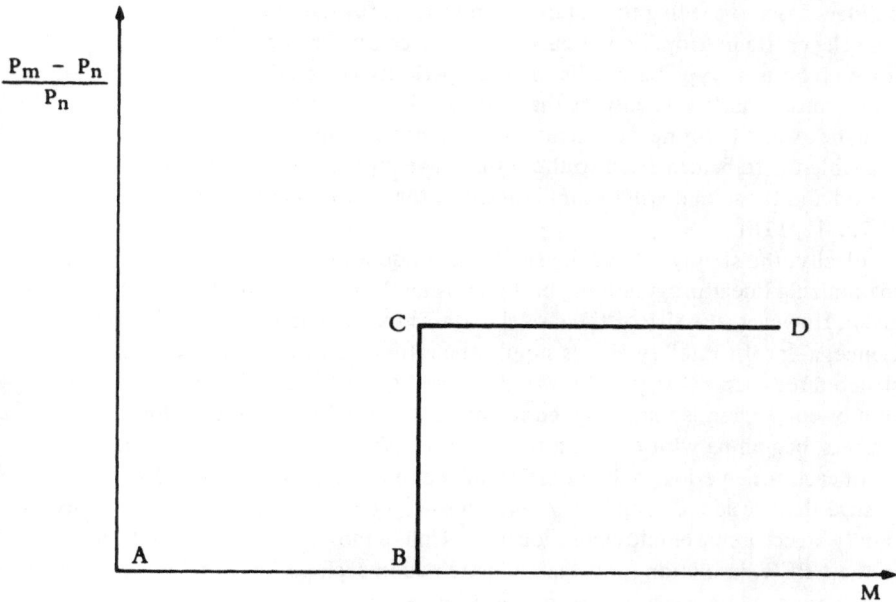

market alterations which are possible in the entire NBER model in any given time period. The other supply activities — new construction and the conversion of existing dwellings — are defined in the model as a supply activity which uses vacant land as an input, and conversions involve the use of an existing dwelling as an input to production. Structural changes such as home enlargement or conversions from single to multiple dwelling unit type constitute supply activities of the latter type.

The construction industry exhibits characteristics of perfect competition in that it consists of numerous small builders, all of whom are profit maximizers and who act as price takers in both the input and output markets. There are twenty-eight available inputs (twenty-seven different housing types and vacant land) and twenty-seven possible outputs (the different housing types). The outputs can be created by new construction or they can result from the transformation of existing units. An input-output matrix tabulates a set of efficient technologies and costs for transforming vacant land, or existing structures, into new or other structures (Ingram, *et al.*, 1972: 114). Expected selling prices for each type of structure are exogenous in each time period, and builders' profits for each type of supply activity are simply calculated as the difference between revenues and costs.

Builders in the NBER model operate under three constraints. The first of these is a zoning constraint in which exogenous zoning policies prohibit or limit certain types of construction or transformation in some areas. The second type constrains builders from exceeding the total demand that is forecast for each housing type over the entire metropolitan area. (It is not necessary, however, that the demand for each housing type be satisfied in each period.) The second constraint operates on the input market. It ensures that only 10 per cent of the vacant land in each zone be available for new construction each period, and it limits the dwelling units available for transformation to those that have sat vacant for more than one time period and those that will become vacant in the current period (Ingram, *et al.,* 1972: 41, 118).

Ideally, the supply side of the simulation model would be structured as a profit maximizing linear programming problem using the expected profits and contraints given. However, the size of the model dictates that a simpler method be used. Hence, a "profit rate" (which is simply the ratio of profit to total cost) is constructed for each activity and these rates are listed in descending order. Construction or conversion is then assigned to each activity subject to the building constraints, beginning with the most profitable (Ingram, *et al.,* 1972: 42-43).

In each time period, only a portion of the modelled households are allowed to change their residences, and they may do so as a result of a change in taste, income, family structure or employment location. Unlike movers in other models, movers in the NBER simulation model are constrained in each period to relocate to houses which are newly constructed or currently vacant.

Markov Processes

In addition to the assignment problem approach previously discussed, the methods of operations research provide another technique for modelling the housing market and the filtering process. The dynamic aspects of the process may be described analytically by a Markov chain using transition matrices of probabilities. Sharpe (1976, footnote 264) describes a Markov chain as a simplification of a Markov process, the latter being

> . . . any stochastic process such that the outcome at time 't' depends
> on the outcome at time t-1, and not on anything that occurred at any
> earlier time.

In a Markov chain, it is furthermore assumed that the probabilities of these outcomes do not change over time, i.e., "$P(t) = P$ for all t" (Sharpe, 1976: footnote 264).

We assume a hypothetical city of 400 housing units and classify each of the units as being in excellent, good, fair, or poor condition. Let these quality conditions be represented by "states" S_1, S_2, S_3 and S_4 respectively and assume

TABLE 3

Movement of units from time t to t+1

States	S_1	S_2	S_3	S_4
S_1	70	25	5	0
S_2	10	50	20	20
S_3	5	15	50	30
S_4	0	0	20	80

that there are exactly 100 housing units in each state in the initial time period t. Now, say that in time period t+1 (which is twenty years later) we want to see how these 400 units have changed with respect to their quality classifications because of depreciation and/or improvements carried out in the twenty-year period.[4] By constructing a matrix (table 3) in which the rows and columns represent the quality states in periods t and t+1 respectively, we may tabulate the hypothetical movements from S_i to S_j over time, where i represents a row and j a column. For simplicity only it is assumed that no housing units have entered or left the system.

Of the 100 units initially in state S_2 (good condition), 10 move up one classification to excellent condition, perhaps because of extensive improvements such as new plumbing or heating, 50 remain in S_2, 20 depreciate to state S_3, and 20 units are now in poor condition in time t+1. A similar analysis may be carried out for the movements of the 100 units initially in each of states S_1, S_3, and S_4.

A transition matrix, as noted above, is a matrix of probabilities. If we know that, of the 100 units initially in S_2, 10 have moved to S_1 in the next period, we may calculate the probability of this move (P_{21}) to be 10/100 = .1. Generally, the probability of any move P_{ij} may be calculated as

$$P_{ij} = S_{ij} / \sum_i S_i$$

where S_{ij} is the number of units moving from S_i to S_j, and $\sum_i S_i$ is the total number of units in state i at time t. The transition matrix for our example is shown in table 4. Note that the probabilities in each row sum to 1, and that each cell has an entry greater than or equal to zero (but less than or equal to unity).

This transition matrix shows us a first-order Markov chain, i.e., movement taking place over one time period. Finding the probability that a unit presently in state S_i will be in state S_j two time periods from now (a second-order Markov chain)

TABLE 4

Matrix of Transitional Probabilities

States	S_1	S_2	S_3	S_4
S_1	.70	.25	.05	0
S_2	.10	.50	.20	.20
S_3	.05	.15	.50	.30
S_4	0	0	.20	.80

involves multiplication of the matrix by itself. Note that this self-multiplication implies that the probabilities have not changed.[5]

The simplicity and adaptability of the approach have made Markov chain techniques useful in many studies, particularly in view of their ability to project future movements of urban characteristics. It is not necessary that houses be grouped according to quality states or that Markov chains be used to analyze only the movement of houses. Bourne (1976) uses transition matrices to describe the pattern of land use conversion in the City of Toronto over two time periods, and Clark (1965) traces the value changes of rental units in the census tracts of four large American cities. Each state in Clark's study represents a rent interval of $10. These rents were deflated to a 1940 base by the consumer price index for rents and their movement was traced over the two ten-year periods from 1940 to 1960. A general pattern of upward shifting of tract value was found, although some tracts had a high probability of remaining in their initial value states. As well, rental units initially in the highest value stratum showed a somewhat higher probability of shifting downwards (Clark, 1965: 355), an important result when discussing a process of filtering. Another housing market study of this type is Maher (1976) in which the probabilities of houses in Toronto moving from one selling price stratum to another over several time periods are calculated.

An interesting application of the Markov chain approach may be found in White (1971). He argues that it is not price changes alone that are the dynamic force in the housing market, but that chains of vacancies allow families to move through the market. A family (or individual) cannot move into a house unless that house is vacant or newly constructed, and when the family does move, it too leaves behind a vacancy that can be filled by yet another group of people. This chain of moves, instigated by a corresponding chain of vacancies, continues until the final vacancy formed occurs in a house that leaves the system (perhaps because of conversion or demolition). The total number of moves caused by the initial arrival of a vacancy, or what is termed the average chain length, is denoted as the "multiplier" (White, 1971: 89).

White illustrates the Markov approach by dividing housing units in a hypothetical market into three price categories (high, medium and low) and by treating vacancies as the active entities — the "individuals" that jump from house to house. Probabilistic estimates of a vacancy's movement are then calculated. By introducing a vacancy into each of the price categories, the respective chain lengths may be determined, based on these probabilistic estimates, with the result that the longest chain occurs when a vacancy is introduced into the high price category. This finding leads White to conclude that subsidized new housing, in that it has a smaller multiplier effect, is not as useful as new housing units built for middle and higher income groups in allowing families generally to improve their housing situation. The longer chains of vacancies created by upper-priced construction allow more low-income families to take part voluntarily in the filtering process (White, 1971: 90-93).

Kristof (1965) and Lansing, Clifton, and Morgan (1969) provide pioneering works in the study of vacancy chains. Kristof (1965: 241) found a chain of housing turnover generated by the construction of sixty-four new dwelling units in New York to have a multiplier in the order of 2.4. As he points out, however, the rent controls in effect in New York City constrain this estimate from being used as a measure of the amount of filtering occurring in the city.

Lansing, *et al.* contribute the most extensive discussion of vacancy chains in their study tracing nationwide chains initiated by the construction of 1,133 new housing units in seventeen standard metropolitan statistical areas. Although this study, like that of Kristof, is not explicitly presented in a Markov chain framework, the results are valuable when discussing the success of the filtering process in satisfactorily housing those with low incomes. Following Kristof's lead, extensive interviews were conducted with the new occupants at each link of every chain until the termination of the chain occurred due to the unit's removal from the system or because the new occupant had left behind no vacancy. On average, for every 1,000 new units constructed, approximately 3,500 families were able to adjust their housing situation, thus implying a multiplier of 3.5 (Lansing, *et al.*, 1969: 13). The length of a chain was found to be positively related to the value of the constructed unit that initiated it, and chains begun with rented units tended to be a full link shorter than those begun with owner-occupied dwellings.

It was also found that as a chain became longer, at each successive link poor people (where poor was defined as a yearly income less than $1,000 plus $500 per family member) comprised a higher proportion of the new occupants, and it was estimated that 333 poor families were able to move because of the construction of 1,000 new units. Overall, 55 per cent of the dwellings were occupied by people with lower incomes after the move and 25 per cent by people with higher incomes (Lansing, *et al.*, 1969: 45). Values and rents also tended to fall through the links of the chains — from the first to the sixth or later link the median home value fell from $25,900 to $17,300 and median rents declined from $135 to $100.

Sharpe (1976) who used the vacancy chain approach to examine the Toronto CMA, finds an average chain length of 1.54, based on vacancy data initiated by over 24,000 newly constructed units. While Lansing, *et al.* find that chains begun with owner-occupied housing tend to be longer, Sharpe finds the opposite to hold for Toronto. Rental units have chains of 1.7 links whereas new owner-occupied dwellings are followed by chains of length 1.3. Several demographic characteristics that are peculiar to the Toronto housing market are cited for this difference and Sharpe emphasizes the fact that comparisons of the results of different studies cannot be made because of the varying samples, techniques, and areas used. Finally, a Markov chain formulation is calculated to substantiate his results, and to investigate patterns of inter-submarket movement.

Summary

In this section we summarize briefly the approaches reviewed above and offer a general evaluation of the different models. The early studies by Hoyt and Smith on neighbourhood change constitute the foundation of a descriptive model on filtering. We may view Grigsby as having contributed a more general formulation of the filtering process, without the mathematical rigour which characterizes more recent approaches. Smith's assignment problem approach introduces a more formal, normative model. His use of a formal maximand and Edel's commentary on his work preceded models of filtering with more detailed, precise and normatively-based specifications of the interdependencies in housing submarkets. The most rigorous of the recent formulations is the commodity hierarchy approach which achieves mathematical tractability only through a high degree of abstraction and logical simplicity. Sweeney's approach, along with those taken by Ohls and the NBER group, are more realistic in that they entail general equilibrium specifications of the housing market. Ohls' approach strikes us as achieving a practical compromise between theoretical and empirical considerations, although the model is probably not well enough developed to be applied to a real housing market to develop reasonably firm policy prescriptions. The NBER model is more applied but the absence of a firm conceptual basis for the model and of suitable data introduces a very ad hoc procedure for calibrating the model. The Markov formulation has proven useful for descriptive survey work and the results of studies using this approach are interesting to pursue. The approach is, however, somewhat mechanical and we think that there is a considerable risk of reading too much normative content into results from these sorts of studies, particularly if they use the vacancy chain as a basis for policy prescriptions.

The entire literature on filtering is interesting and instructive in its own right. Future research work might usefully be directed towards extending the type of approach taken by Ohls. A more applied model, with a satisfactory theoretical foundation, would contribute greatly to the discussion of housing policy, although it should be recognized that such an exercise is currently constrained for Canada by the lack of the very detailed data which would be necessary to calibrate such a model more realistically.

NOTES

1 Printed by permission of the author and the Ontario Economic Council. This paper, which forms part of a study being prepared for the Council, 'Housing Economics and Public Policy', reflects the views of the author and not necessarily those of the Council. The author wishes to thank Mary E. Broderick for diligent research work, which included drafting the first version of the paper. Responsibility for the content rests, however, with the author.

2 A considered review of these definitions is given by Grigsby (1963: 84-99). He points out that, on one definition, a house may be described as having filtered up and, on a different definition, as having filtered down.

3 We are assuming, of course, that the real quality differences between the five quality classes are equal and that the differences between income levels are constant.

4 The choice of twenty years as a time period is strictly arbitrary, as any number of years could have been used. However, the change in quality of housing units is not an overnight phenomenon since it usually takes several years for a dwelling to depreciate from, for example, good to poor condition. A time period of, for example, one year would therefore not have been useful in our example, although use of such a period would be meaningful if the number of states were increased.

5 Gilbert (1972) discusses the loss of reality occasioned by the use of transition matrices that remain constant over time, and offers a "non-homogeneous" Markov model in which the probability of a housing unit moving from state i to state j from period t to t+1 depends upon t. This type of model accounts for the fact that a unit that has been in state S_3 for, say, two time periods is more likely to deteriorate than a dwelling occupying this state for only one period. A non-homogeneous Markov process, however, carries with it the disadvantage that a dwelling may be in only one of two possible occupancy states at any time. Gilbert also discusses at length a "Markov renewal model" which is conceptually similar to a Markov chain in which the transition times for any one dwelling unit are random occurrences which follow an arbitrary probability distribution.

REFERENCES

Bourne, L.S. 1976. "Monitoring Change and Evaluating the Impact of Planning Policy on Urban Structure: A Markov Chain Experiment", *Plan Canada*, 16, 1: 5-14.

Clark, W.A.V. 1965. "Markov Chain Analysis in Geography: An Application to the Movement of Rental Housing Areas", *Annals of the Association of American Geographers*, 55,2: 351-359.

Edel, M. 1972. "Filtering in a Private Housing Market", in M. Edel and J. Rothenberg, eds., *Readings in Urban Economics*. New York: Macmillan.

Fisher, E. and L. Winnick. 1951. "A Reformulation of the Filtering Concept", *Journal of Social Issues*, 17, 1-2: 47-58.

Gilbert, G. 1972. "Two Markov Models of Neighbourhood Housing Turnover", *Environment and Planning*, 4,2: 133-146.

Grigsby, W.G. 1963. *Housing Markets and Public Policy*. Philadelphia: University of Pennsylvania Press.

Hoyt, H. 1939. *The Structure and Growth of Residential Neighbourhoods in American Cities*. Washington, D.C.: U.S. Government Printing Office.

Ingram, G., J.F. Kain, and J.R. Ginn. 1972. *The Detroit Prototype of the NBER Urban Simulation Model*. New York: National Bureau of Economic Research.

Kristof, F.S. 1965. "Housing Policy Goals and the Turnover of Housing", *Journal of the American Institute of Planners*, 31,3: 232-245.

Lansing, J.B., C.W. Clifton, and J.N. Morgan. 1969. *New Homes and Poor People: A Study of Chains of Moves*. Ann Arbor: Survey Research Center.

Maher, C.A. 1976. "Residential Change and the Filtering Process: Central Toronto, 1953-1971". Unpublished doctoral thesis, Department of Geography, University of Toronto.

National Housing and Town Planning Council. 1929. *A Policy for the Slums*. Report of a Special Committee. London: D.Ş. King.

Ohls, J.C. 1975. "Public Policy Toward Low Income Housing and Filtering in Housing Markets", *Journal of Urban Economics*, 2,2: 144-171.

Rapkin, C., L. Winnick, and D. Blank. 1953. *Housing Market Analysis: A Study of Theory and Methods*. Washington, D.C.: Housing and Home Finance Agency.

Sharpe, C.A. 1976. "Vacancy Chains and Residential Relocation. The Response to New Construction in the Toronto Housing Market Area". Unpublished doctoral thesis, Department of Geography, University of Toronto.

Smith, W.F. 1963. "Forecasting Neighbourhood Change", *Land Economics,* 39, 3: 292-297.

Smith, W.F. 1964. *Filtering and Neighbourhood Change.* Research report no. 24, Center for Real Estate and Urban Economics, University of California Institute of Urban and Regional Development, Berkeley.

Sweeney, J.L. 1974a. "Quality, Commodity Hierarchies, and Housing Markets", *Econometrica,* 42, 1: 147-167.

Sweeney, J.L. 1974b. "A Commodity Hierarchy Model of the Rental Housing Market", *Journal of Urban Economics,* 1, 3: 288-323.

White, H.C. 1971. "Multipliers, Vacancy Chains and Filtering in Housing", *Journal of the American Institute of Planners,* 32, 2: 88-94.

4.3 INFLATION AND URBAN HOME OWNERSHIP

Stuart M. McFadyen and Robert J. Hobart

During the rapid inflation of the early 1970s, housing prices in Canada rose much more rapidly than the general price level. Statistics Canada data on housing prices in six Canadian cities showed increases ranging from 68 per cent in the case of Calgary to 83 per cent in the case of Montreal for the period 1971-74 (Statistics Canada, 1974: 7). Over the same period the consumer price index only rose 25 per cent.

These rapid increases in the price of houses resulted from significant increases in housing demand during a period of constrained supply. Supply constraints are not examined in this paper. The reasons for the significant shift in demand away from other goods and services and towards houses in this period include the large increase in the twenty-five to thirty-five year age group in the population, the increased availability of high ratio mortgages, the extension of mortgage insurance to conventional mortgages, the exemption of owner-occupied housing from the 1972 income taxation of capital gains, and the flight of investors during steep general inflation into real assets such as housing and land.

This paper examines the last of these factors — the effect of inflation and inflationary expectations in increasing the demand for home ownership. This examination involves an analysis of the economic aspects of the decision to invest in a house. Non-economic factors such as security of tenure and pride of ownership may be important factors in individual decisions but, since they cannot be readily measured, they have been excluded from this analysis. Also, since both the demand and supply factors differ in the case of multiple housing, this examination is restricted to the detached housing traditionally favoured by owner-occupants.

The economic and financial aspects of the basic rental/ownership decision are analyzed through an examination of annual housing costs. Whereas market rents may maintain a fixed relationship with market value over time, certain elements of ownership cost such as closing costs on purchase or capital gain on sale occur only once during the ownership period, while other elements such as mortgage interest vary in size over the ownership period. To permit comparisons these costs have been annualized using a capital budget type of housing cost model.

The analysis of the basic rental/ownership decision proceeds in three stages. First, the real resource costs of the housing services which flow from a dwelling of any given value are established on the basis of housing cost data derived from various secondary sources. Second, the relationship between the market rent and the market value for a dwelling of any given value is estimated using data on homes rented and sold in the west end of Ottawa during the years 1968-71.

Once the conditions required to establish equivalence between the rental and ownership markets have been established, a sensitivity analysis is carried out to quantify the impact of variations in the rate of increase in housing prices on the housing investment decision.

The Real Resource Costs of Housing Services

Many of the real resource costs of housing services will not be affected by the form of tenure. But if an individual chooses to rent rather than own, he must expect to bear slightly greater maintenance expenses, and to cover management costs and vacancy allowances. On the other hand, upon moving he avoids the sales transaction costs which would have been incurred had he chosen ownership.

Precision in the estimation of the real resource costs of housing services is impossible since each house differs, each household differs, and adequate accounting information does not exist. The cost estimates in this study are based on aggregate data supplied by Statistics Canada and on previous work by Shelton (1969), and Clayton (1974).

Imputed opportunity income   For an investment in housing to be economically justified, it must be possible for the investor, whether he purchases as a landlord for subsequent rental or as an owner-occupant, to earn a rate of return on his investment equal to that obtainable in his next best alternative. In the analysis of the basic rental/ownership decision this rate of return has been assumed equal to the mortgage interest rate of 10 per cent (see following paragraph).[1] This assumption is premised in part on the view that for most investors in housing the investment alternative with the highest yield will be repayment of their mortgage indebtedness. In addition, the use of a single rate obviates the need for an annual recalculation of the owner's equity and outstanding mortgage balance components of total value, since the one rate can be applied against total value.

Mortgage interest   Mortgage interest costs can be calculated by multiplying the outstanding mortgage indebtedness by the relevant borrowing rate. The average interest rate on conventional mortgages for the years 1968-71 varied from a low of 9.1 per cent in 1968 to a high of 10.4 per cent in 1970.[2] A rate of 10 per cent is assumed as representative of lending costs during this period.

Property taxes   The 1970 survey of household income, assets and indebtedness estimated the market value of the average owner-occupied house at $18,636 (Statistics Canada, 1970a). Property taxes of the average home owner were $301, according to the 1970 family expenditure survey (Statistics Canada, 1970b). Accordingly, property taxes have been estimated at 1.6 per cent of value.[3]

Depreciation   A wide variety of approaches to measuring depreciation have been used in previous studies. Laidler (1969) used an annual depreciation rate of 2.25 per cent based on the forty-five year life allowed rental buildings under U.S. tax law. Sunley (1970) and Clayton (1974) allowed zero economic depreciation on the argument that buildings appear to decline little, if any, in value, at least during the first twenty-five years.

Since in our analysis physical depreciation and general appreciation in property values are disaggregated, the approach of Clayton and Sunley appears inappropriate. The Laidler approach appears to involve the depreciation of land. Shelton has argued that if land is assumed to represent 25 per cent of total property value and if building life is assumed equal to fifty years, then a straight-line depreciation of 1.5 per cent of initial property value is the appropriate charge. This 1.5 estimate has been used in this study.

Maintenance   Shelton (1969: 63) estimates that maintenance in the long run averages 1.0 to 1.5 per cent of dwelling value per year. He uses the lower-point estimate of 1.0 per cent. Using the average owner-occupied house value of $18,636, and average home owner maintenance expenditure of $202 (Statistics Canada, 1970a and 1970b), maintenance expenditures have been estimated in this study at 1.1 per cent.[4]

Shelton (1969: 65) has argued that maintenance costs must be expected to be slightly higher in the case of rental properties on the basis that renters will take less care of property than owner-occupants. An allowance of 0.4 per cent has been made for this factor in the case of renters in this study.

Vacancy allowance and management costs   Shelton (1969: 64) estimates the vacancy allowance for single-family housing in "normal" markets to be 3 per cent of total units. Vacancy data for single-family housing are not published in Canada. Data for 1968-71, covering privately initiated rental structures of six or more units, shows average vacancy rates ranging from 2.7 per cent in 1968 to 5.0 per cent in 1971.[5] Since these data are compatible with the Shelton estimate, a vacancy allowance of 3 per cent of gross rents has been adopted in this study.

The market price of property management services is estimated by Shelton (1969: 64) at 5 per cent of gross rentals. This figure accords with recent practice in National Housing Act-financed privately owned rental projects. Accordingly, an estimate of 5 per cent of gross rentals has been adopted in this study.

To facilitate cost calculation, both of these estimates must be converted from a gross rent basis to a property value basis. If gross annual rents are known to equal .072 as a fraction of property value, this conversion yields estimates of approximately 0.2 per cent in the case of vacancy allowance, and 0.4 per cent in the case of management costs.[6]

Transfer costs   The most significant difference between the real resource costs of renters and owners occurs in the area of transfer costs. While it is true that a landlord incurs transfer costs upon liquidating his investment, these costs are avoided when an individual renter gives up his occupancy. On the other hand, each time an owner-occupant moves, unless he chooses to convert the dwelling to a rental property, property transfer costs will be incurred. These transfer costs consist of real estate commissions, legal fees and various title transfer charges. Real estate commissions vary according to the nature of the listing (exclusive or multiple) and by city, but 6 per cent is a representative rate. A 1 per cent estimate for the remaining elements would bring the total estimate of transfer costs to 7 per cent of sales value.[7] These costs occur only once during the ownership period, at time of sale; therefore their importance on an annual basis decreases as the period of ownership increases.

Summary of annual real resource costs of housing services   The annual cost estimates developed in the foregoing sections are summarized in table 1. Historical cost depreciation must be calculated on the basis of original cost but, if property appreciation is ignored, it becomes possible to aggregate costs to a total of 15.2 per cent of annual value for renters and 14.2 per cent of annual value for owner-occupants. The owner-occupant total must, of course, be supplemented by the applicable portion of transfer costs but, without information on the holding period, these transfer costs cannot be converted to fractions of annual value.

The Market Rent for Housing Services

The relationship between market rents and market values has been established for the Ottawa market using data obtained from the National Capital Commission on all dwellings in Ward Nine in Ottawa[8] which were either sold or rented during the period January 1, 1968 to December 31, 1971.[9]

The relationship between market values and assessed values was estimated by regressing, for each of the years 1968-71, the market prices[10] of dwelling units that were sold against their assessed values. Applying these results to the assessed value of each rented dwelling permits an estimation of its market value. The ratio of rent[11] to estimated market value for each property was calculated and the mean ratio computed for each year. The mean ratio of market rent to estimated market property value was extremely stable over the four-year period ranging from a high of 7.36 per cent in 1969 to a low of 7.14 per cent in the years 1968 and 1970. These results are consistent with those obtained by Fulton (1977) using 1972 data and an alternative estimation procedure.[12]

Comparison of the Annualized Costs of Renting versus Owning

The opportunity income component of the real costs of housing services has been developed on the basis of the argument that, unless market rents provide a return on investment capital equal to the return on the next best available alternative, capital will not be attracted to the industry. The opportunity rate of return has been estimated previously at 10 per cent of value. When the remaining elements

TABLE 1

Annual Real Resource Cost of Housing

	Owner-occupant	Renter
Imputed opportunity income		
Mortgage interest [1]	.10 value	.10 value
Property taxes	.016 value	.016 value
Depreciation[2]	.015 cost	.015 cost
Maintenance	.011 value	.015 value
Vacancy allowance	ϕ	.002 value
Management costs	ϕ	.004 value
Transfer costs	.07 sales price	ϕ
Total [3]	.142 value plus applicable transfer costs	.152 value

1   Value may be subdivided into two components: (i) the outstanding mortgage balance and (ii) owner's equity. If the mortgage interest rate is equal to the opportunity rate of return on owner's equity, a single rate may be applied to total value as shown. In cases where the rates are not equal, the appropriate rate must be applied to each component of total value.

2   Depreciation is calculated on the basis of historical cost which provides for return of the owner's original dollar investment over the life of the asset rather than a replacement cost basis which in time of rising price would provide for replacement of the asset.

3   This addition in terms of percentages of value assumes that depreciation as a percentage of cost accurately reflects depreciation as a percentage of value (see note 2). Property values must remain unchanged for a given percentage of cost to remain equal to a given percentage of value over the entire holding period.

of real resource cost are considered, the housing investor requires an annual return sufficient to cover 15.2 per cent of value on a rental basis or 14.2 per cent plus applicable transfer costs on an owner-occupant basis. The market rent analysis, however, has revealed annual market rents, at least in the case of Ottawa, to be of the order of only 7.2 per cent of property value.

In a high interest rate, non-inflationary situation, there would clearly be little incentive to shift to owner-occupancy status. However, when allowance is made for inflation, capital gains on owner-occupied housing may, or may be expected to, more than offset higher annual real resource costs. This section examines the nature and magnitude of the role of inflation in shifting demand towards owner-occupancy type housing.

There are a variety of methods of placing cost and revenue items which occur irregularly over time on a common basis. This study follows Gaumnitz (1974) in using an average annual cost method which transforms all flows occurring at different times into an equivalent annual cost, assuming a given cost of capital or required rate of return. Sums occurring at different times and in varying amounts can be expressed in terms of a present value figure as shown in equation (1).

$$PV = \frac{C_1}{(1+r)} + \frac{C_2}{(1+r)^2} + \frac{C_3}{(1+r)^3} + \dots \frac{C_N}{(1+r)^N} \tag{1}$$

where PV — is the present value of the stream of costs occurring over n periods
   C_1 — is costs in year 1
   C_2 — is costs in year 2
   C_N — is costs in year N
   r — is the cost of capital
Similarly, the present value figure (PV) can be expressed in terms of equal annual costs as shown in equation (2).

$$PV = \frac{AC_A}{(1+r)} + \frac{AC_A}{(1+r)^2} + \frac{AC_A}{(1+r)^3} + \dots \frac{AC_A}{(1+r)^N} \tag{2}$$

where PV — is the present value of a stream of identical costs occurring over n periods
   AC_A — is the constant cost associated with a given asset in each period
   r — is the cost of capital
A rearrangement of equation (2) to solve for AC_A can be established by finding the present value of all sums and applying a capital recovery factor at a given discount rate for the specified number of periods. Using equation (2) above, and representing the annualizing formula as:

$$\Phi = \frac{r\ (1+n)^t}{(1+r)^t - 1}$$

it is possible, where rents are assumed to equal .072 of property value, to denote annualized housing cost on a rental basis AC_R as:

$$AC_R = \Phi \sum_{t=1}^{n} \frac{.072\ Co\ (1+g)^{t-1}}{(1+r)^t}$$

Similarly, using the cost parameters developed in the previous section, the annualized housing cost of an equivalent dwelling on an ownership basis (AC_H) can be shown as:

$$AC_H = \Phi \sum_{t=1}^{n} \frac{1}{(1+r)^t} \cdot \frac{z}{1 - \frac{1}{(1+z)^k}} \cdot (Co-DP) +$$

$$\Phi \sum_{t=1}^{n} \frac{.016\ Co\ (1+g)^{t-1}}{(1+r)^t} +$$

$$\Phi \sum_{t=1}^{n} \frac{.015\ Co}{(1+r)^t} + \Phi \sum_{t=1}^{n} \frac{.011\ Co\ (1+g)^{t-1}}{(1+r)^t} +$$

$$\Phi\ DP - \Phi \frac{Co\ (1+g)^n - .07\ Co\ (1+g)^n - Co}{(1+r)^n} -$$

$$\frac{\Phi \sum_{t=0}^{n} PR_t}{(1+r)^n}$$

where: r — is the rate of return on alternative investments
n — is the holding period or length of tenure
Co — is the market value of the dwelling at time of purchase
g — is the expected growth rate in dwelling values
z — is the rate of interest on mortgage debt
k — is the amortization period of the mortgage debt
DP — is the downpayment made for dwelling purchase
PR_t — is the principal recovery portion of a mortgage payment in time period t.

The annualized cost saving available from home ownership as compared to rental tenure (AC_{net}) is determined by:

$$AC_{Net} = AC_R - AC_H$$

A negative result of such a calculation would, for instance, denote an annualized cost for home ownership in excess of the cost of renting equivalent accommodation. This general annualized housing cost model has the advantage of comprehensiveness. Its principal disadvantage is the concomitant complexity which makes it impossible to derive explicit solutions. In order to examine the model, it is necessary to proceed by way of sensitivity analysis. First, as a baseline for all comparisons, the annualized cost of renting and owning a standard dwelling unit under a particular set of assumptions must be calculated. Then the impacts of alternative rates of inflation on the net annualized cost of owning as compared to renting are calculated. For example, the impact which rates of growth of property values of 5 per cent and 0 per cent would have on net costs is compared to the situation prevailing in the standard case.

1. Annualized costs of renting versus owning: the standard case. The standard case deals with a dwelling valued at $40,000 and purchased with a 10 per cent downpayment of $4,000. These basic data provide only a scale factor to all results. Therefore, if the annualized cost saving of home ownership in any particular set of circumstances is required for a $100,000 house, one need only multiply the value shown in the appropriate table by a factor of 2.5.

A mortgage amortization period of thirty years has been assumed throughout. The market interest rate on mortgages, and the discount rate, have been assumed to equal 12 per cent. The latter is equivalent to the assumption of a zero marginal income tax rate where opportunity investments offer a 12 per cent taxable, before-tax rate of return. The rate of growth of property values has been assumed to equal 10 per cent. The mortgage interest rate and discount rate have been selected as reasonably typical for 1975; the rate of growth of property values has been assumed at a level which approximates the implicit rate of capital gain identified using the Ottawa housing market data.

Table 2 presents the results of the cost calculations and comparisons for this standard case. The stub of the table shows the holding time over which the costs are annualized. Column 1 shows the annualized rental costs. In the first year these are found to be $2,880. This is 7.2 per cent of the $40,000 property value. Annualizing has no effect over a one-year period. In the second year, property value rises by 10 per cent to $44,000. Rent at 7.2 per cent equals, in the second year, $3,168. Rent at $2,880 for one year, and $3,168 for a second year, when considered over a two-year holding period, is equivalent to a constant annualized rent of $3,019 as shown in the table. Each year the amount of rent paid increases by 10 per cent as a result of the assumed 10 per cent per year increase in property values. Accordingly, annualized rental costs rise as the time horizon of the holding period is extended. In the standard case, the increase is from $2,880 in the case of a one-year holding period, to $6,659 in the case of a twenty-five year holding period.

The calculation of annualized home ownership costs, although involving a multiplicity of cost elements, proceeds along similar lines with the results shown in column 2. The net difference between the annualized rental costs and the annualized home ownership costs for any given holding period are shown in column 3. The negative net differences shown in the standard case for holding periods of five years and less indicates that, under the assumed circumstances, if the prospective

TABLE 2
Annualized costs of renting versus owning: The standard case[1]

Holding time (n years)	Annualized rental costs (AC$_R$ dollars)	Annualized home ownership costs[1] (AC$_H$ dollars)	Annualized cost saving for home ownership[2]	
			(AC$_{net}$ dollars)	Percentage of annualized rental costs
1	2,880	5,560	−2,680	−93
2	3,019	4,171	−1,152	−38
3	3,154	3,762	−608	−19
4	3,294	3,607	−313	−10
5	3,441	3,556	−115	−3
6	3,587	3,552	35	1
7	3,737	3,580	157	4
8	3,891	3,628	263	7
9	4,044	3,686	358	9
10	4,191	3,747	444	11
15	5,006	4,181	825	17
20	5,830	4,667	1,163	20
25	6,659	5,174	1,485	22

1 Assumptions: Purchase price = $40,000
Downpayment = $4,000
Amortization period = 30 years
Discount rate = 12%
Market interest rate on mortgage = 12%
Growth of property values = 10%
Marginal tax rate = 0%

2 A negative figure denotes an annualized cost for home ownership in excess of the cost of renting equivalent accommodation.

home owner anticipated a holding period of five years or less, it would be advisable to rent rather than purchase.

Column 4, where annualized cost savings for home ownership are calculated as a percentage of the corresponding annualized rental cost, shows ownership costs to exceed rental costs by 93 per cent for a one-year holding period. Costs are roughly equal for a six-year holding period and 22 per cent lower for home ownership in the case of a twenty-five year holding period.

The large negative numbers for shorter holding periods result principally from the favourable rent levels which are available and the short period over which home ownership transfer costs may be amortized. For longer holding periods these factors are swamped by the influence of the large tax-exempt capital gains reaped by home owners.

2. The effect of the rate of growth in property values on annualized housing costs. Expected growth rates in property values are important in the ownership/tenancy decision process. At growth rates less than 9 per cent, under conditions of 12 per cent mortgage interest and discount rates, the costs of ownership exceed those of tenancy regardless of the length of the holding period.

Table 3 presents the results of an analysis of the impact on the annualized cost saving from home ownership of a rate of growth in property values of 5 per cent per year rather than the 10 per cent assumed in the standard case. Table 4 presents corresponding data for the case of zero increase in property values. The case of a fall in property values is not analyzed but the reader should keep in mind that the cost impacts identified in these cases will apply *a fortiori* in such circumstances.

Both the costs of tenancy and home ownership are affected by the growth rate. Column 3 of table 3 reveals that if property values increase at only 5 per cent per annum, while the remaining assumptions of the standard case hold, the annualized cost of tenancy will increase from $2,880 for a one-year tenancy period to $4,201 in the case of a twenty-five year holding period. Column 4 of the same table illustrates the annualized cost differential between renting and owning. In all cases, tenancy is clearly the superior alternative. The excess costs of home ownership range from 158 per cent for a one-year hold, to 53 per cent for a holding period of twenty-five years.

These cost consequences are, of course, even more pronounced in the case of a zero increase in property values. With no growth in property values, annualized rental costs remain constant at $2,880 regardless of the tenancy period as is shown in column 3 of table 4. The annualized cost advantage of tenancy relative to ownership (column 2) is $6,400 for a one-year hold, decreases to $3,674 for a fifteen-year holding period and then increases to $4,000 for a holding period of twenty-five years. Column 4 indicates that excess home ownership costs are 222 per cent, 128 per cent and 139 per cent of rental costs for the three holding periods respectively. The extreme values in the shorter periods reflect the absence of any important negative costs to offset the influence of heavy ownership transfer costs which must be amortized quickly. In the no-growth case, the relative costs of home ownership increase in the later periods because of the rapid decrease in the present value of the proceeds realized from the sale of the dwelling.

Conclusion

The divergence between real resource costs and market rents for a given housing unit demonstrates the extent to which expectations of inflation in housing prices

TABLE 3
Annualized costs of renting versus owning: [1]
Sensitivity to reduction on rate of growth in property values from 10% to 5%

Holding time (n years)	Annualized cost saving for home ownership[2]		Annualized rental costs $g = 5\%$	Cost saving for home ownership as a percentage of annualized rental costs
	Growth of property values $g = 10\%$	Growth of property values $g = 5\%$		
1	−2,680	−4,539	2,880	−158
2	−1,152	−3,083	2,951	−104
3	−608	−2,607	3,014	−86
4	−313	−2,381	3,080	−77
5	−115	−2,255	3,148	−72
6	35	−2,177	3,211	−68
7	157	−2,127	3,275	−65
8	263	−2,096	3,340	−63
9	358	−2,074	3,401	−61
10	444	−2,057	3,453	−60
15	825	−2,057	3,746	−55
20	1,163	−2,088	3,991	−53
25	1,485	−2,235	4,201	−53

1 Assumptions: Purchase price   = $40,000
                  Downpayment   = $4,000
                  Amortization period   = 30 years
                  Discount rate   = 12%
                  Market interest rate
                     on mortgage   = 12%
                  Growth of property
                     values   = variable
                  Marginal tax rate   = 0%

2 A negative figure denotes an annualized cost for home ownership in excess of the cost of renting equivalent accommodation.

have been built into the existing price structure. It is only expected capital gains which can justify the *purchase* of owner-occupancy type housing when it is available at market rents much below the real resource costs of ownership.

The sensitivity of ownership costs to changes in the expected rate of housing price inflation, demonstrates the crucial role which inflationary expectations may be presumed to play in shifting demand away from other goods and services and towards owner-occupied housing.

TABLE 4

Annualized costs of renting versus owning:[1]

Sensitivity to reduction øn rate of growth in property values from 10% to 0%

Holding time (n years)	Annualized cost saving for home ownership[2]		Annualized rental costs g = 0%	Cost saving for home ownership as a percentage of annualized rental costs
	Growth of property values g = 10%	Growth of property values g = 0%		
1	−2,680	−6,400	2,880	−222
2	−1,152	−4,926	2,880	−171
3	−608	−4,428	2,880	−154
4	−313	−4,183	2,880	−145
5	−115	−4,041	2,880	−140
6	35	−3,943	2,880	−137
7	157	−3,875	2,880	−135
8	263	−3,828	2,880	−133
9	358	−3,789	2,880	−131
10	444	−3,749	2,880	−130
15	825	−3,674	2,880	−128
20	1,163	−3,990	2,880	−139
25	1,485	−4,000	2,880	−139

1   Assumptions: Purchase price   = $40,000
                   Downpayment   = $4,000
                   Amortization period =   30 years
                   Discount rate   =   12%
                   Market interest rate
                      on mortgage   =   12%
                   Growth of property
                      values   =   variable
                   Marginal tax rate   =   0%

2   A negative figure denotes an annualized cost for home ownership in excess of the cost of renting equivalent accommodation.

NOTES

1 The implications of differences between the opportunity rate of return and the mortgage interest rate are not analyzed here; the present discussion abstracts from income tax considerations which provide for the deduction of mortgage interest only in the case of rental housing.

2 The average of monthly rates for each year were: 1968, 9.1%; 1969, 9.85%; 1970, 10.4%; 1971, 9.4% (CMHC, 1973: 68). Data on the mortgage interest expenditures of sitting owners is not relevant since this analysis focuses on the rental/ownership decision, which is a decision point where only current mortgage rates are of concern.

3 This procedure follows Clayton (1974: 301). American data are not comparable for this item.

4 As in the case of property taxes this procedure follows Clayton (1974: 301).

5 The average rate for each year was: 1968, 2.7%; 1969, 4.0%; 1970, 5.0%; 1971, 5.0% (CMHC, 1973: 20).

6 The basis of this .072 value for gross annual rents as a fraction of property value is disclosed in the following chapter. Shelton, who estimates gross annual rents at 11.4 per cent of property value, uses percentage of value estimates of 0.3 per cent and 0.6 per cent for vacancy allowances and management costs respectively (1969: 64-65).

7 Shelton (1969: 65-66) also uses a 7 per cent estimate. The fact that private sales do not involve real estate commissions does not necessarily demonstrate a saving in real resource costs. The owner himself must expend personal services and other resources on the sales function.

8 Ward Nine is a middle- to upper-middle class district approximately six square miles in area on the west side of Ottawa. It stretches from Merrivale Road west to the city limits and north from Baseline Road to the Ottawa River.

9 Years subsequent to 1971 cannot be examined using this data base since collection of rental data was discontinued in 1972.

10 Observations where the sales price was less than $10,000 were excluded from the study on the assumption that they represented non-arm's length transactions. Only the higher price transaction was recorded for houses sold more than once in a given year or for houses sold at a price escalation of over 100 per cent within four years.

11 The rents for various properties were put on a common base by including the

amount of property taxes when these were paid separately by the tenant and by excluding utility payments in all cases. The property tax adjustment was calculated by applying the mill rate to the assessed value. Utility adjustments were based on the average Ottawa utility expenditures per household contained in Statistics Canada (1967: 50-65; 1971: 56-71).

12 Using the 1972 Statistics Canada Household Incomes and Facilities Data File, rents paid on dwellings in urban areas were regressed against the physical and locational characteristics of the dwellings. The resultant regression equation was then used to estimate market rents on owner-occupied dwellings. Using this procedure, Fulton found that the ratio of gross rents to market value was 8.5 per cent. The difference between this result and our result of between 7.14 and 7.36 per cent would appear to be largely attributable to Fulton's inclusion of utilities costs in the rent data. The rent data used in this study exclude utility costs.

REFERENCES

CMHC. 1973. *Canadian Housing Statistics.* Ottawa: Central Mortgage and Housing Corporation.

Clayton, F.A. 1974. "Income Taxes and Subsidies to Homeowners and Renters: A Comparison of U.S. and Canadian Experience", *Canadian Tax Journal,* 22, 2: 295-305.

Fulton, P. 1977. "The Income Distribution Effects of Tax Related Housing Policies". Doctoral thesis in progress, Department of Economics, University of Western Ontario, London.

Gaumnitz, J.E. 1974. "Mobile Home and Conventional Homeownership: An Economic Perspective", *Nebraska Journal of Economics and Business,* 13, 4: 130-143.

Laidler, D. 1969. "Income Tax Incentives for Owner-Occupied Housing", in A. Harberger and M. Bailey, eds., *The Taxation of Income from Capital.* Washington, D.C.: Brookings Institution.

Shelton, J.P. 1969. "The Cost of Renting versus Owning a Home", *Land Economics,* 44, 1: 59-71.

Statistics Canada. 1967. *Urban Family Expenditure on Shelter and Household Durables.* Catalogue no. 62-530. Ottawa: Information Canada.

Statistics Canada. 1970a. *Incomes, Assets and Indebtedness of Families in Canada, 1969.* Catalogue no. 13-547. Ottawa: Information Canada.

Statistics Canada. 1970b. *Family Expenditure in Canada, 1969.* Vol. 1. Catalogue no. 62-535. Ottawa: Information Canada.

Statistics Canada. 1971. *Urban Family Expenditure on Shelter and Household Durables.* Catalogue no. 62-540. Ottawa: Information Canada.

Statistics Canada. 1974. *Construction Price Statistics: New House Prices.* Catalogue no. 62-007. Ottawa: Information Canada.

Sunley, E.M., Jr. 1970. "Tax Advantages of Homeownership versus Renting: A Cause of Suburban Migration?" in *Proceedings of the Sixty-Third Annual Conference on Taxation.* National Tax Association.

V

Studies of Local Markets and Information Systems

5.1 DEVELOPER BEHAVIOUR AND URBAN GROWTH: ANALYSIS AND SYNTHESIS

Michael A. Goldberg

As more rigorous and sophisticated tools of analysis have become available to professionals in the social sciences we have greatly expanded our knowledge about our social systems on a macroscale as well as our knowledge of the microcomponents of these systems.[1] Unfortunately, until recently little attention has been paid to the compatibility of these micro- and macroanalyses. The problem is neither new nor trivial. In economics the aggregation problem is one of long duration and of some stature.[2] It explicitly acknowledges the difficulties faced in attempting to generalize from specifics.

With the advent of the most recent generation of computing machinery, it has become possible to contruct large-scale models of complex systems to begin to unravel the aggregation problem in its various disguises.[3] More specifically, urban simulation models provide a most useful framework for exploring the macro-impact on metropolitan regions of micro-behaviour of commuters, households, real estate developers and industrial and commercial firms. Through studying the location behaviour of these micro-units it becomes possible, in theory at least, to aggregate these behaviours to study patterns, and changes in patterns, of metropolitan development.

This paper explores one such micro-behaviour in detail, that of residential developers in choosing locations for their developments. Analyses of the location behaviour of residential developers are then incorporated into a working urban simulation model to explore the consequences of such behaviour for simulated metropolitan growth and structure. Analogies with actual metropolitan growth and structure flow directly from these findings.

Some Antecedents

Nearly a decade ago, a group of researchers at the University of British Columbia in Vancouver set out to develop a large-scale simulation model for the Vancouver region. That effort ultimately gave rise to the work being reported on here.[4]

During the 1960s great strides were taken in modelling urban development. Most models were developed in conjunction with either metropolitan transportation plans or community renewal programs.[5] By the end of the decade more than a dozen operational models were being used, several in two or more different cities (see Pack, 1975; Goldner, 1971). These efforts suffered in general from similar shortcomings. They tended to be difficult to use, to operate quite outside the traditional bureaucratic/political framework and to be of highly variable quality.[6]

In response to these shortcomings, model builders at the University of British Columbia teamed up with representatives of several levels of government to develop jointly an urban and environmental simulation model capable of providing needed policy insights prior to taking large-scale decisions. The study was called IIPS (Inter-Institutional Policy Simulator). By bringing together academics and civil servants it was hoped that more useful and realistic policy models might be designed and used (see Goldberg, 1977a). Accordingly, the objectives of the IIPS project were two-fold: to develop a *modelling framework* for model building that included representatives from various levels of government and various departments of the university, and to develop models capable of dealing with key environmental sub-systems subject to policy intervention in the Greater Vancouver region but potentially transferable elsewhere.

Figure 1 provides an overview of the various interacting model elements that were to be included in the original IIPS effort. It can be seen from the overlapping of the elements that models of intra-urban transportation and land use were central to the model system. These sub-models distributed activities spatially and therefore were the prime vehicle for analyzing the spatial impacts of various land use, transportation and environmental policies. Of greatest importance was housing, since residences represent the largest single user of developed urban land. Accordingly, development of a useful housing model took priority. The modelling problem was partitioned four ways, into macrospatial and microspatial elements, demand and supply.

Macrospatial elements   The housing model proceeds in a series of distinct steps. First, regional demand and supply are forecast. Lacking a suitable set of sub-models to forecast regional supply and demand separately, demand and supply (i.e., the flow of new units and new demand) are assumed to be equal. Demand/supply (i.e., $D \equiv S$) is estimated for each year in the simulation by reasonably straightfor-

FIGURE 1: Diagram of relationship between the IIPS subgroups

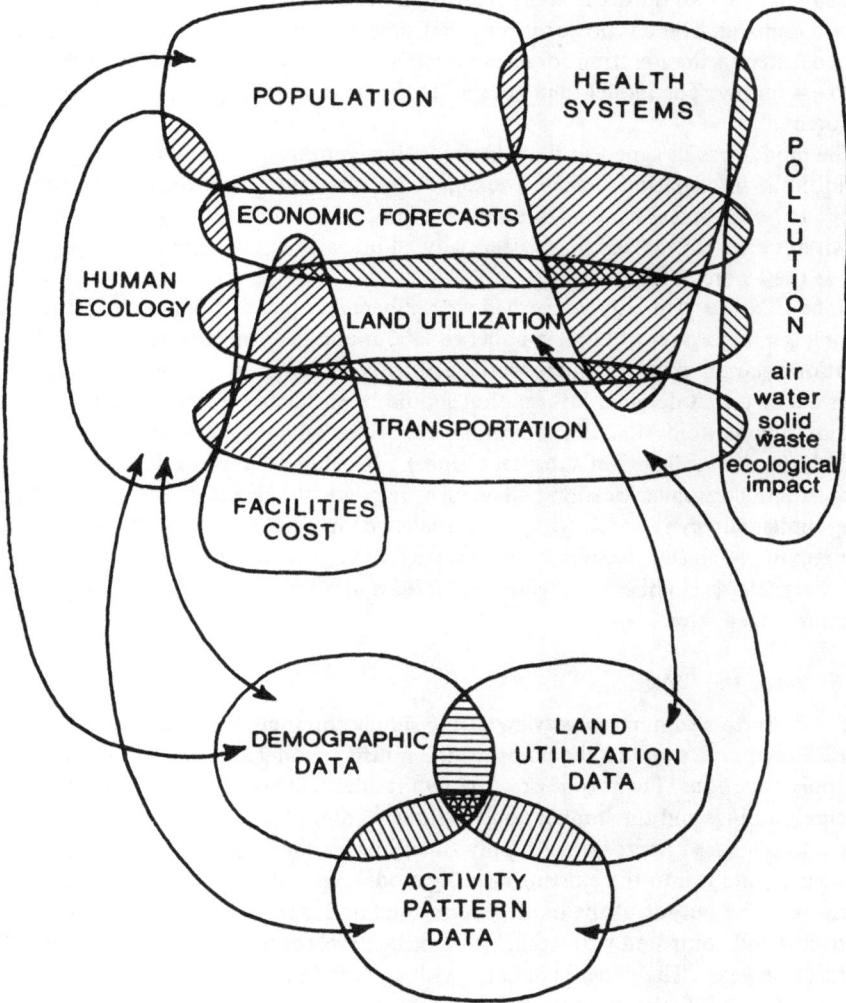

ward trend procedures. Demand/supply is then disaggregated into single-family/ row housing, and multi-family housing based on characteristics of the forecast population and past demand.

Microspatial elements   Given regional totals, the microspatial components of the model allocate these totals to the subareas of the region (presently there are 167 such subareas.) Two quite different algorithms are used to determine subareal supply and demand. There is no constraint that subareal supply and demand be equal. The final step in the iteration for each period allocates excess demand to subareas of excess supply. The model then goes on to the next year's regional demand/supply forecast.

The model was designed so that the foregoing components could be improved as additional information became available. The initial models of regional demand/supply and of subareal demand/supply were largely intuitive conceptualizations. The strategy was to replace these essentially ad hoc algorithms with more rigorous ones as they were developed.

Since IIPS was primarily concerned with subareal impacts of policy, and since housing is a major user of land, supplier of labour and determinant of urban form, attention focused upon the microspatial elements of the housing model. Initially it was decided that detailed information should be gathered on the location behaviour of households (i.e., the determinants of subareal demand) and of developers (i.e., the determinants of subareal supply).[7] Because the cost of doing a statistically sound consumer location behaviour survey greatly exceeded the cost of doing similar survey research with residential developers, it was decided to begin by surveying the latter. Resources were sufficient to conduct two separate surveys (Goldberg, 1974; Goldberg and Ulinder, 1976a and 1976b). The results of both are summarized later.

The Scope of the Paper

First we turn to a summary overview of the simulation models developed under the IIPS aegis and, more to the point, to the housing model and the evolution of its supply functions. Then we review the two residential developer surveys, their principal findings and the implications of these findings for the construction of a behaviourally based microspatial supply function. We then derive this function and incorporate it into the existing housing model replacing the previous intuitive algorithms. The output of the model is discussed under these two quite different algorithms and compared with actual residential development in the region during the past five years. The paper concludes with an agenda of work that remains to be done and a brief summary of what has been accomplished to date.

THE SIMULATION FRAMEWORK

Overview of the Model

Just as the residential development process occurs in the context of urban development, so does the modelling of residential development occur in the context of,

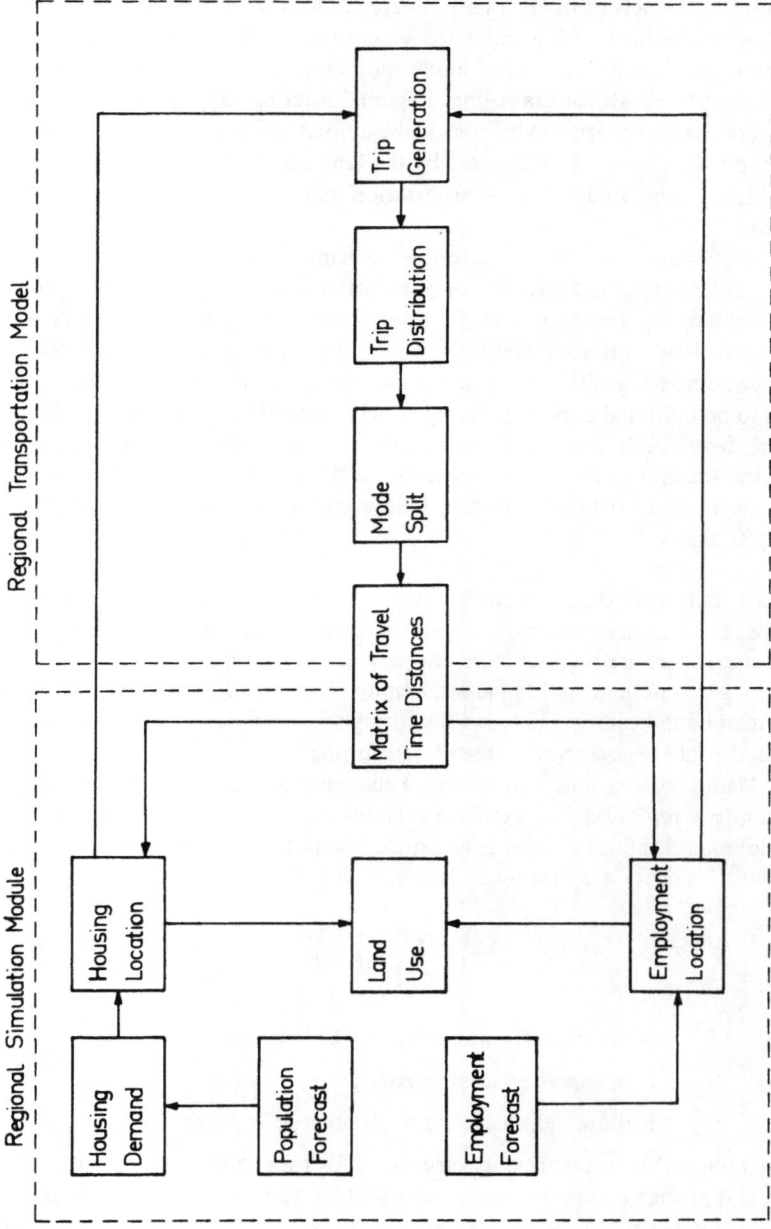

FIGURE 2: The interaction between the module and the regional transportation model

modelling urban development. Figure 2 sets out diagrammatically the context of the housing models of interest here. There are four interacting models represented: land use, including housing and employment location; transportation, including trip generation, distribution and mode split; employment forecasts for the region; population forecasts for the region. Regional forecasts of population and employment are used to provide estimates of the amount of new economic activity and housing to be allocated to subareas by the land use models. These models also use travel times generated by the transportation model as inputs to the allocation algorithms.

Activities are allocated in the following manner: given the matrix of time distances and the regional forecasts of population and employment, the model first allocates employment (up to 18 different types) to subareas and calculates the amount of land thus used. Next, the population estimate is combined with previous period housing activity to provide an estimate of the total number of housing units to be built and allocated during the iteration. The details of this allocation will be described in more detail below. Finally, given the location of people and jobs, the transportation model recalculates trips and travel times, and the model then moves on to the next iteration. These land use models are set out schematically in figure 3.

Employment location sub-models   Employment in each of eighteen industry groups is allocated on the basis of the locational criteria of that industry. However, since there are regularities in the way certain groups of employment choose locations within metropolitan areas, employment location was dealt with under four major sub-headings: (1) manufacturing and wholesaling; (2) retail trade; (3) services; (4) agriculture, forestry and fishing.

1. Manufacturing and wholesaling. These employment activities are disaggregated into seven industrial sectors (see Goldberg and Davis, 1973; Davis, 1974). Employment is allocated to a zone on the basis of its attractiveness for a given industry.[8] The attractiveness index is given by:

$$A_j^k = \sum_{k=1}^{k} S_{ij} \ w_i^k \qquad (1)$$

where A_j^k is the attractiveness of zone j to industry k

   S_{ij} is the *i*th site factor in zone j

   w_i^k is the weight attached to site factor i by industry k.

These indices, however, are only calculated for those zones with industrially zoned land, and possess certain essential factors which vary by industry such as deep water access for petroleum refining and railroad access for wholesaling, warehousing and

FIGURE 3: Land use models

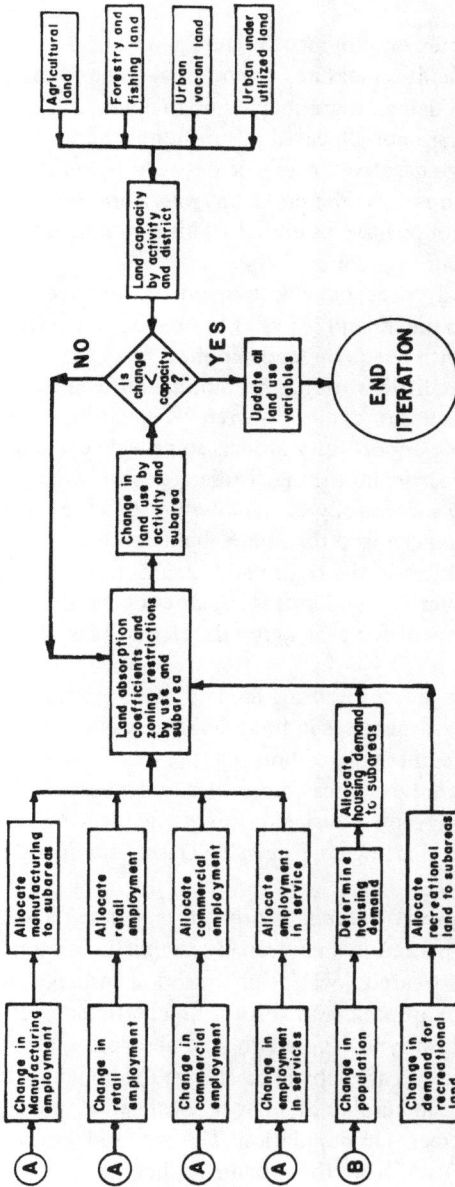

LAND USE MODELS

(A) Employment changes from Economic Model
(B) Change in Population from Population Model

storage. These attractiveness indices are then normalized and used to allocate employment subareas. The allocated employment is converted to land use via a land absorption coefficient (LAC) for each industry. If sufficient land is lacking, excesses are reallocated.

2. Retail trade. Retail employment is allocated using a gravity model formulation.[9] The model generates measures of potential demand for retail trade in each zone. These potential demands are then compared with actual trade in each zone. Excesses and deficits are not allocated instantly but rather phased in over time. Thus, if there is a large negative difference between potential demand and actual demand, only a portion of the deficit is removed from the zone in each time period allocated to zones with positive potentials. This is intended to account for the lags and inertia which occur in practice.

As before, the newly allocated employment is converted to land use via the appropriate LAC. If too much land is found to be required, excess employment is reallocated to areas with adequate land supplies.

3. Services. To date little work has been done in the area of service employment location.[10] In the absence of extant research we are attempting to calibrate the gravity and intervening-opportunity models to provide estimates of service location.

4. Agriculture, forestry and fishing. These are primary activities which have not been able to compete successfully for land with urban uses. The recent Land Commission Act in B.C. has changed this somewhat (Baxter, 1974). All three industries are experiencing a decline in the region and the assumption that these declines allow for conversion to urban land uses is consistent with the idea that they are a significant supply element for urban growth (Harris, 1966; Clawson, 1977).

Housing models   The present housing models, to be discussed at greater length below, allocate forecast increases in households to each of the 167 traffic zones for each of eight different types of housing (i.e., two structure types and four value classes). The structure types correspond to densities and are roughly equivalent to (a) single-family, row housing or low-rise garden type apartments, and (b) medium and high-rise apartments. The value classes are quartile values.

Recreation and open-space models   At the present time recreation and open-space determination is carried out in an extremely simplistic fashion. Two different kinds of parkland are treated, local/neighbourhood and regional parks. For each there is a 4 X 2 matrix of park land absorption coefficients, one for each housing value class and structure type. These two land absorption matrices represent current planning practice and are subject to change for policy testing purposes. They are used to calculate the number of acres of local and regional parks required to serve the forecast increases in population. The required land is taken from each subarea (traffic zone) and from the urban periphery.

FIGURE 4: Housing model

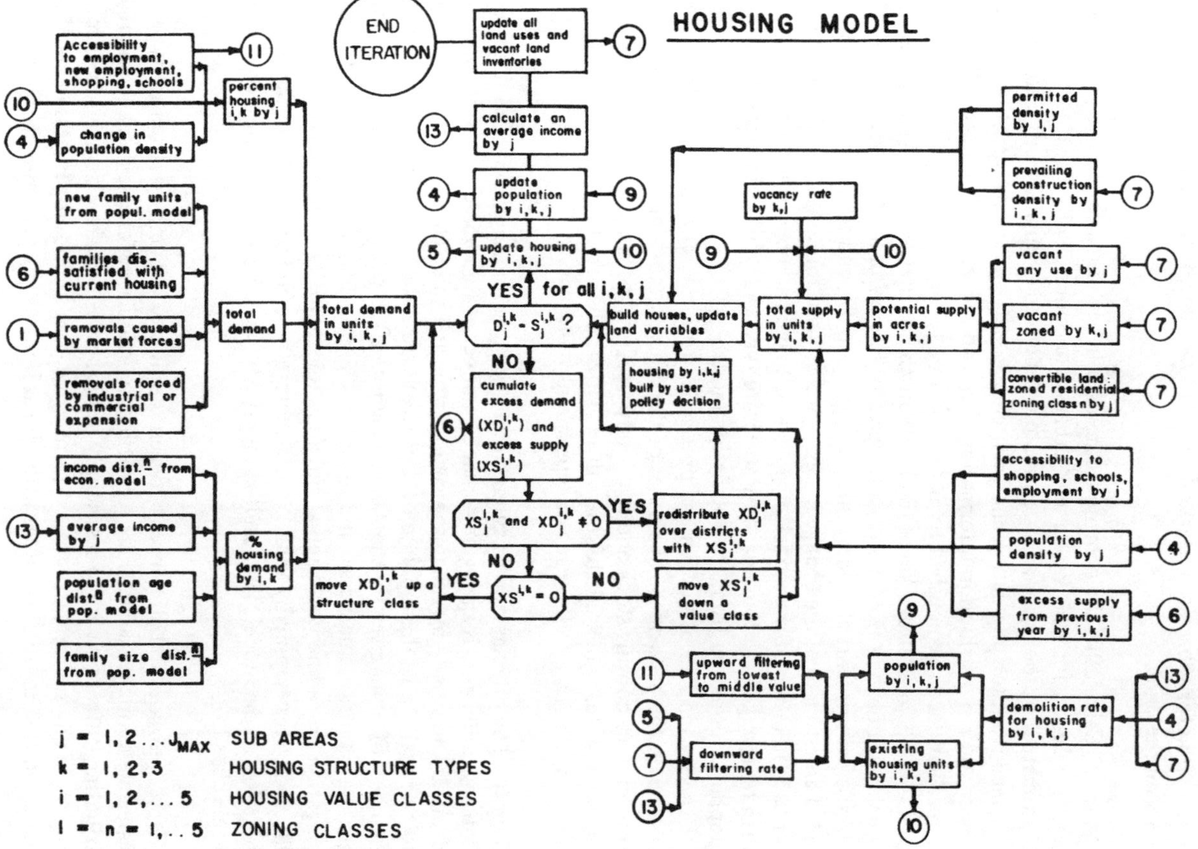

The Original Housing Model

In the microspatial model of figure 4, we see two distinct elements: demand determination for subareas appears on the left hand side of the diagram, supply appears on the right.

Demand   Calculating the demand for housing in each subarea is a two-step process (see Center for Real Estate and Urban Economics, 1968). First, total demand is estimated for the region. This estimate was derived originally from information obtained from the population and economic models on income distribution, family size and age distribution information. Demand also comes from people whose homes have been demolished to make way for additional housing or for another land use. The model also keeps track of households that were put in housing which was not their first choice in the previous iteration of the model. These dissatisfied residents also enter into the aggregate demand for housing. This provided an estimate of the change in aggregate demand for housing in the region for each iteration of the model. Aggregate demand (number of households) was then disaggregated into demand by structure type and value class using demographic information from the population model.

The second step of the demand process is to allocate demand to subareas. This is done on the basis of the attributes of the subarea, most important being its access, current housing stock and the family size, income and age characteristics of the households which inhabit the subarea stock. The resulting demand, $D_j^{i,k}$ is demand in subarea j, for housing of type k, and value class i.

Supply   The original model assumed that aggregate housing supply (number of housing units) equals aggregate demand (number of household units). However, demand and supply by subarea, structure type and value class are not constrained to be equal. Thus, the supply model proceeds from the total regional supply in numbers of units(given by the demand algorithm) to disaggregate this supply into structure types, value classes and subareas. The principal data inputs to this disaggregation procedure were: actual and allowable densities, available land, accessibility and excess supply by value class, structure type and subarea from the previous iteration of the model. The result is supply $S_j^{i,k}$, by subarea j, structure type k, and value class i.

Market resolution   Differences between supply and demand by structure type and value class for each subarea are reconciled by cumulating excess demand and redistributing it to areas with excess supply until there is no excess demand or excess supply in any subarea, structure type or value class of housing. Excess demand is allocated first to other subareas with similar housing (by type and class). If no similar housing is available, demand is allocated to those areas that have housing of the same value class but any structure type. If there is no such housing available, the excess is allocated to subareas with the originally desired structure type but the next lower value class. This process continues until all excess demands are allocated. If, on the other hand, there are excess supplies in certain subareas, the excess housing is assigned to the next lower value class. In this way excess supply moves down through value classes, which is what happens in practice where high vacancy rates lead to price cutting. Excess demand, however, moves across structure types within the same value class, unless no housing exists in any subarea in the desired value class, in which case demand moves down one value class and then across the structure types again if necessary, thus raising the value class of that housing.

Recent and Ongoing Revisions to the Original Model

Despite the reasonableness of the assumptions, input data and results, there were a number of problems surrounding the model. The initial strategy entailed building the models in a modular fashion so that they could be readily replaced and refined. This section reports on two areas of refinement, one macrospatial, the other microspatial.

It was decided early in the modelling exercise to concentrate first on the supply side. This was done because it was less expensive to do such work and also because the location of new supply by builders determines the future growth of the metropolitan region. To the extent that developers are merely following their own estimate of consumer demands, then the supply response also includes the consumer's demand for housing in the long run.

Macrospatial supply evolution   In keeping with the strategy of modular evolution of the major components of the housing model, the macrospatial regional forecasting algorithms have undergone significant change during the past several years. Initially, since demand and supply were assumed equal for each year (iteration), it was possible to estimate crudely the demand/supply increment directly from the regional population models. Equating households with housing units provided a quick, if dirty, means for deriving rough forecasts of the demand/supply increment each simulated year. Since this approach does not allow for the existence of vacancies, the next phase of our work included vacancies as a determinant of new supply (demand).

New supply was now assumed equal to the change in the number of households plus a demand for vacancies to allow for equilibration of short-term disturbances (i.e., some inventories for short-run adjustments).

Equation (2) sets out the supply relationship:

$$NS_t = THH_t - THH_{t-1} + VACRAT_t(THH_t) - VACRAT_{t-1}(THH_{t-1}) \qquad (2)$$

where;

NS_t = new supply in period t

$THH_{t,t-1}$ = total household in period t and t-1 respectively

$VACRAT_{t,t-1}$ = weighted average vacancy rate over the preceding three periods.

If NS_t is negative then a small number of units is still built. This reflects the fact that the construction of residential units does not stop even given the existence of high unsold or unoccupied inventories of housing stock.[11]

This largely ad hoc procedure was improved by estimating two equations to replace equation (2), one for single starts, one for multiple. These generate regional totals which are further disaggregated into the value classes and are then allocated to subareas. Refinement of the allocation algorithm depends on the development of the behavioural data summarized below under microspatial evolution.

Equations (2a) and (2b) replace the single aggregate equation (2):[12]

$$HS_t^m = \underset{(0.132)}{0.139\ HS_{t-1}^m} + \underset{(0.087)}{0.397\ HS_{t-2}^m} + \underset{(0.039)}{0.095\ Pop_{t-1}} - \underset{(0.038)}{0.047\ Pop_{t-2}} \qquad (2a)$$

$$R^2 = 0.358 \quad \text{F-Statistic } (5,107) = 100.443$$

$$HS_t^s = -31.0 + \underset{(0.112)}{0.25\ HS_{t-1}^s} - \underset{(0.117)}{0.129\ HS_{t-2}^s} + \underset{(0.023)}{0.051\ Pop_t} + \underset{(0.025)}{0.070\ Pop_{t-1}}$$

$$+ \underset{(0.023)}{0.045\ Pop_{t-2}} \qquad (2b)$$

$$R^2 = 0.894 \quad \text{F-Statistic } (6,106) = 283.939$$

where:

$HS_{t,t-1,t-2}^m$ = Multi-family housing starts for periods t,t-1 and t-2 for the region

$HS_{t,t-1,t-2}^s$ = Single-family housing starts for periods t,t-1 and t-2 for the region

$Pop_{t,t-1,t-2}$ = Population for periods t, t-1 and t-2 for the region.

Microspatial supply evolution Forecasting sub-regional growth in housing is significantly more complex than developing estimates of regional totals. This complexity stems from the greater diversity of variables that impact on residential location, including such disparate forces as community attitudes, zoning and administrative procedures, availability of vacant land, availability of sewers, water supply and other needed infrastructure, and a host of other site-specific and community-specific variables. The microspatial supply algorithms have accordingly gone through several stages to reach their present state.

Stage 1 was a largely ad hoc formulation based on intuition and rules of thumb in common use in the region. The functional forms of the variables were essentially unproven hypotheses about the likely relationship between the zonal variables and the development of single-family and multi-family housing. Independent variables included access to employment, access to shopping, vacant land, occupied housing units and allowable and actual densities, all of the above by subareas (i.e. by each of the 167 traffic zones in the region).

An immediate problem encountered with these crude specifications related to the demolition of existing units as developed areas became ripe for redevelopment. The health of the core areas of the region, resulting from both small-scale and large-scale private development and reinvestment, could not be adequately mimicked by the model.[13] It was difficult in the first stages of development to derive an intuitively sensible yet operational algorithm to handle demolitions of existing structures other than through direct policy intervention. Thus, as areas were rezoned to allow for higher densities, the bulk of the existing structures was unaffected. This was a serious weakness. However, after studying a number of areas in this region that have been rezoned, we established that a demolition rate of 2-3 per cent per year of the stock existing at the time of rezoning prevailed over the last decade in such rezoned areas (Vancouver, City Planning Department, 1969). The demolition algorithm is then applied to the existing stock in subareas where the actual density is less than the allowable density. Demolitions begin with the lowest value class housing, which in practice is the most easily assembled, and move up through the value classes and structure types until the stock has been rebuilt at the new densities and there is no additional vacant land or underutilized land remaining. Another option we are experimenting with is applying a saturation variable to affect the demolition rate, reasoning that the higher the level of saturation (i.e., the smaller the percentage of developable of redevelopable land), the higher the rate at which underutilized structures are demolished. This option is still being developed and is not discussed below.

Stage 2 followed directly from the original model with a number of apparently minor changes which, as will be shown later, had some significant impacts on the quality of the output. To begin with, coding errors were corrected and data bases revised to take account of the most recent available data. One very important new data source was the 1971 land use data from the Greater Vancouver Regional District (GVRD), which represented a major improvement over the 1970 land use data initially used in the model. Finally, following in part on the improved land use data bank, the land supply variable for each subarea in the microspatial allocation routines was changed from vacant land to vacant, zoned and sewered land. This was to make a major improvement in the output of the model.

The ad hoc formulations in Stage 1 were replaced in Stage 3 by two single equation estimators of the percentage of the regional total increment of single and multi-family development that each subarea of the region obtained. The microspatial allocation function was thus reduced to the following two equations:

$$PCDEV_{jt}^s = 0.189 + 0.00182(POTSUP_{jt}^s) \quad R^2 = 0.246 \quad F(2,165) = 51,208$$
$$(0.00025) \hspace{8cm} (3a)$$

$$PCDEV_{jt}^m = 0.304 + 0.007(POTSUP_{jt}^m) \quad R^2 = 0.703 \quad F(2,165) = 371,964$$
$$(0.00004) \hspace{8cm} (3b)$$

where

$PCDEV_{jt}^s$ = percentage of 1966-1971 single-family housing development in GVRD that was accounted for by subarea j

$PCDEV_{jt}^m$ = percentage of 1966-1971 multiple-family housing development that was accounted for by subarea j

$POTSUP_{jt}^s$ = potential supply of land for single-family development in subarea j as given by the number of acres of properly zoned, sewered and vacant land in j

$POTSUP_{jt}^m$ = potential supply of land for multiple-family development given by number of acres of properly zoned, sewered and vacant land in subarea j and by the allowable density of development.

The most recent stage of evolution builds directly on Stage 3 with an important change; $PCDEV_{jt}^s$ is now deemed to be a function of the municipality within which the development takes place, as well as the POTSUP variable (i.e., the possibility that municipal politics affects development is considered explicitly). The rationale for this specification derives from the behavioural work alluded to at the outset, wherein developers attested to difficulties with certain municipal governments and good working relationships with others. A review of the developer surveys is therefore in order to allow for a better understanding of the behavioural basis for Stages 3 and 4.

DEVELOPER EMPIRICS

From the very beginning of the survey work our interest went beyond the surveys *per se* to their application in the simulation framework. Two surveys were conducted, one in the summer of 1972, the other in the summer of 1975 (see Goldberg, 1974; Goldberg and Ulinder, 1976a and 1976b). To provide a structure for comparing the findings, the results are discussed in terms of industry characteristics and their location criteria.

Developer Behaviour 1972

The 1972 study differed from the 1975 study in that it was much smaller in scope and confined to developers in the Greater Vancouver region. Only 63 developers were interviewed in 1972 compared with 140 in 1975.

TABLE 1

Dwelling units initiated by developers in sample, 1972 survey

| | Starts of multiple dwelling units | | | Starts of single family units | | | Total starts | | | Lots subdivided | |
	Sample	Regional total	%	Sample	Regional total	%	Sample	Regional total	%	Sample	Regional total
1972	4,329	6,957	62.2	2,132	7,451	28.6	6,461	14,408	44.8	2,204	—
1971	3,332	9,760	34.1	1,373	5,216	26.3	4,705	14,976	31.4	1,216	—
1970	2,834	8,760	32.4	1,035	4,365	23.7	3,869	13,125	29.5	965	—

TABLE 2

Dwelling units initiated by developers in sample, 1975 survey

| | Multiple unit starts | | | Single unit starts | | | Total starts | | | Lots subdivided | |
	sample	prov. total	%	sample	prov. total	%	sample	prov. total	%	sample	prov. total
1974	5,238	12,116	43.2	1,797	19,304	9.3	7,035	31,420	22.4	6,874	—
1973	3,776	15,413	24.5	1,743	22,214	7.8	5,519	37,627	14.7	6,294	—
1972	2,912	15,609	18.7	1,449	19,708	7.4	4,361	35,317	12.3	3,858	—

TABLE 3

Geographic distribution of 1975 sample

	Metropolitan area developers	Mixed area developers	Non-metropolitan area developers	Total
Multiple unit developers	27	4	9	40
Single unit developers	43	6	16	65
Residential subdividers	32	11	20	63
Total	102	21	45	168 [a]

a   168 responses received from 140 developers; some were involved in more than one
activity

Industry characteristics   Of the 63 participants in the survey, 46 were involved in the development of single-family units, 38 in multiple-unit development and 27 were active in residential subdivision. Table 1 summarizes the magnitude of the building activity of the sample and the GVRD total as descriptors of the industry characteristics.

Location criteria   Developers were asked to indicate the relative importance, on a scale from unimportant to essential, of a dozen location factors. In each case, independent of developer type, four factors were considered to be significantly more important than the others: proper zoning, access to trunk sewer, price of land and availability of developable land. Of these, proper zoning was the most important factor, followed closely by access to trunk sewer lines.

Summary of the Principal Findings of the 1972 Survey

1. Developers require adequate supplies of zoned and sewered land *before* development can be considered.

2. Developers are not engaged in land hoarding, generally holding land sufficient for the normal course of their development activities.

3. A substantial number of public and private organizations exist through which the developer must proceed in order to carry out any given project.

4. Debt financing is extremely important in financing residential property development.

5. Developers are tending towards new structural forms of residential housing that make more efficient use of urban land through higher average densities.

Developer Behaviour 1975

Industry characteristics   A total of 140 developers were interviewed in 1975 from many different areas of the province; the earlier study focused on developers in the Greater Vancouver region. Table 3 sets out the geographical distribution of the sample.

That the responses included in the study are representative of the industry as a whole is borne out by the sizeable portion of units constructed and lots subdivided by the sample as shown in table 2. This table seriously understates single-family developer behaviour since many of the development decisions in the single-family home building industry are in fact made by the subdivider from whom the builder buys land.[14] Subdividers estimated that 60-80 per cent of the lots they subdivided were sold to builders for housing construction. Taking the lower figure of 60 per cent implies that in 1974 the location criteria could be applied to over 4,000 single-family homes built in the province. Thus, behavioural information is provided by the sample for nearly 6,000 single-family units in 1974, over 30 per cent of the starts in that year — a credible representation for our purposes.

Location criteria   (see table 4) From the survey it was found that the same four factors were of overriding importance in the developer's location decision: proper zoning, price of land, access to trunk sewer and availability of developable land.

Summary of Principal Findings of the 1975 Survey

1. Developers require adequately serviced and appropriately zoned land.

2. Developers are primarily involved in the development of residential property. The high cost of land in conjunction with limited capital reserves and high financing costs make land banking an uncertain and high-risk undertaking.

3. Developers are most concerned with factors affecting their development costs and place less emphasis on variables that affect the ultimate value of their product.

4. There has been a marked change in the tenure composition in the flow of new units. This trend became apparent in 1973 and accelerated in 1974, with condominium units gaining favour.

Implicit in these findings is the role of government, since government provides infrastructure and zoning. In the 1975 survey, questions were asked about difficulties in obtaining approvals. It was found that nearly half of those surveyed had encountered such difficulties and that over 80 per cent of these difficulties lay with local government. It became clear as a result that some proxy for government attitudes would also weigh heavily in the location decision as many developers confined their activities to one or two municipalities. Accordingly, for purposes of simulating developer behaviour below, we felt that a fifth location criterion should be added, namely, local government attitudes.[15]

TABLE 4

Evaluation of location factors by all developers, 1975 survey
(140 respondents: per cent of respondents in parentheses)

Location factors	Unimportant (0)	Fairly important (1)	Average importance (2)	Very important (3)	Essential (4)	No response	Mean	Standard deviation
Proper zoning	6(4.3)	2(1.4)	11(7.0)	43(30.7)	67(47.9)	11(7.9)	3.26	1.01
Price of land	4(2.9)	2(1.4)	9(6.4)	63(45.0)	51(36.4)	11(7.9)	3.20	0.88
Availability of developable land	7(5.0)	9(6.4)	9(6.4)	66(47.1)	38(27.1)	11(7.9)	2.92	1.07
Access to trunk sewer	14(10.0)	5(3.6)	8(5.7)	53(37.9)	49(35.0)	11(7.9)	2.91	1.26
Size of site	19(13.6)	13(9.3)	36(25.7)	51(36.4)	9(6.4)	12(8.6)	2.14	1.17
Nearness to schools	14(10.0)	20(14.3)	42(30.0)	44(31.4)	7(5.0)	13(9.3)	2.08	1.08
Nearness to major road	14(10.0)	21(15.0)	43(30.7)	41(29.3)	9(6.4)	12(8.6)	2.08	1.10
Character of surrounding area	16(11.4)	20(14.3)	30(27.1)	45(32.1)	8(5.7)	13(9.3)	2.07	1.13

PUTTING THE FINDINGS TO WORK: APPROACHING A SYNTHESIS

Residential location as perceived by residential developers is considerably different from residential location as described in the literature on the subject and as simulated in the early versions of the housing model. Accessibility in its various forms dominates the literature,[16] yet received scant attention in both developer surveys (see Appendix A). The original subareal allocation functions in the housing model were based on a number of accessibility measures. However, the survey results argue against placing such heavy weight on these measures.

Applying the Survey Results

Available zoned and sewered vacant land was the key locational variable stressed by developers. Accordingly, it was necessary to get reliable land use information for the base year of the simulations in order to identify vacant land. Current zoning had to be overlaid on these vacant land estimates for each of the 167 subareas. Lastly, a map of trunk and lateral sewers had to be superimposed on the composite of appropriately zoned vacant land.

Gathering the necessary data   By changing our base year from 1970 to 1971 we were able to make use of the 1971 land use data prepared by the GVRD. These data were more accurate than our original 1970 base and provided as well compatibility with the 1966 land data also gathered by the GVRD. These data are of high quality and are updated virtually on an annual basis at the present time for some 10,000 grid cells which span the region.

Current zoning information as of 1971 presented a more substantial problem. Difficulties arose because there does not exist a standard zoning by-law or map for the entire region. Zoning definitions vary from one municipality to the next. However, since we were primarily concerned with single-family versus multi-family land uses, there was no difficulty in converting the widely varying definitions into one of our two types of residential land use. Placing the zoning information on a map of uniform scale represented a time consuming activity but one which involved no other problems.

Deriving the information on sewered land presented the greatest difficulty. Each municipality in the region provided us with detailed maps of trunk and lateral sewers. From consultation with several engineering firms who were actively involved in subdivision and development work we ascertained that land within 500 feet of a trunk or lateral sewer was usable. More distant land was too expensive to service with sewers. For each municipality we overlaid sewer maps onto the zoned and vacant land maps previously discussed. Vacant and zoned land lying within 500 feet of existing sewers (or those presently under construction in 1971) was then measured for each of the 167 subareas in the region.

Estimating the microspatial allocation functions   Three sets of independent variables were used to estimate these functions:

1. A measure of potential supply (either vacant, zoned and sewered land or multi-family densities depending on whether single-family or multi-family units were being allocated).

2. A variety of accessibility measures were also employed ranging from accessibility to employment and shopping, to straight line distances to the Vancouver central business district (CBD) or the nearest other CBD.

3. Dummy variables were the last group of variables used, one for each of the seventeen municipalities in the region. These dummy variables were suggested by the developer surveys and the consistent complaints about municipal attitudes towards residential development.

Two dependent variables were employed:

1. The percentage of total regional, single-family development which each of the 167 subareas actually received from 1966 to 1971 (denoted $PCDEV_j^{sf}$).

2. The percentage of total regional multiple-family development that each of the 167 subareas actually received from 1966 to 1971 (denoted $PCDEV_j^{mf}$).

Two surprising results were obtained from regressing the independent variables as measured by subarea against the two dependent variables. First, no measure of accessibility materially improved the explanatory power of the regression equations, which contrasts markedly with other studies.[17] Second, zoned, sewered and vacant land explained over 70 per cent of the variance in multiple-family development but slightly less than 25 per cent of the variance in single-family development during the 1966-71 period. However, when the dummy variables were added, nearly 50 per cent of the variance of single-family development could be explained, as will be seen below.

In summary, based on the regresssion results, the variables cited by developers as being important appear to be important. Traditional accessibility measures, on the other hand, were of little help in explaining where and how much residential development occurred during the 1966-71 period.[18]

Given these interim findings, it was possible to estimate the spatial allocation functions using the two sets of variables identified by the developers: vacant, zoned and sewered land, and dummy variables for municipal attitudes towards development. No accessibility measures appear in these allocation functions as measured since they added only slightly to explaining the variance in development within the region.

The allocation functions   As noted above, using zoned, vacant and sewered land as a measure of potential supply of development in each subarea accounted for more than 70 per cent of the variance in multiple-family development but less than 25 per cent of the variance of single-family development. Using dummy variables improved this significantly for single-family development only. Equation (4a) includes dummy variables for municipalities and replaces equation (3a) which did not.

$$PCDEV_{jt}^{sf} = 0.229 + 0.0017\, POTSUP_{jt}^{sf} - 0.359\, DUMMY1 - 0.508\, DUMMY2$$
$$(0.00024) \qquad\qquad (0.283) \qquad\qquad (0.303)$$

$$+ 1.608\, DUMMY3 - 0.789\, DUMMY4 - 0.371\, DUMMY5$$
$$(0.313) \qquad\qquad (0.419) \qquad\qquad (0.512)$$

$$- 0.191\, DUMMY6 + 0.730\, DUMMY7 - 0.173\, DUMMY8$$
$$(0.315) \qquad\qquad (0.524) \qquad\qquad (2.33)$$

$$- 0.094\, DUMMY9 - 0.0495\, DUMMY10 + 0.834\, DUMMY11$$
$$(0.233) \qquad\qquad (0.350) \qquad\qquad (0.869)$$

$$- 0.453\, DUMMY12$$
$$(0.523)$$

$R^2 = 0.451 \qquad F(14,153) = 9.167$ \hfill (4a)

where:

$PCDEV_{jt}^{sf}$ = per cent of 1966-71 single-family development occurring in subarea j

$POTSUP_{jt}^{sf}$ = potential supply of land measured by vacant, zoned and sewered acres in subarea j

DUMMY 1 = Burnaby
DUMMY 2 = Coquitlam
DUMMY 3 = Delta
DUMMY 4 = New Westminster
DUMMY 5 = North Vancouver City
DUMMY 6 = North Vancouver District
DUMMY 7 = Port Coquitlam
DUMMY 8 = Surrey
DUMMY 9 = Vancouver
DUMMY 10 = West Vancouver
DUMMY 11 = White Rock
DUMMY 12 = University Endowment Lands

Dummy variables proved to be insignificant for the other municipalities in the region and as a result were not included.

Using dummy variables did not materially improve the explanatory power of the equation for multiple-family development, and it remains unchanged as presented above (equation 3b). These equations form the basis for the simulations presented below where output from Model 1 and Model 4 are compared with actual development and each other for the period 1971-75.

Simulation Output: Comparing the Models

Four variants of the housing model were developed as set out previously. Since Model 3 and Model 4 were based on 1966-71 data, more recent data was needed to test the output of the various models. This was accomplished using 1975 housing and land use data gathered by the GVRD. The test was a straightforward one and entailed running the models for four simulated years beginning in 1971 and ending in 1975, and then comparing the resulting outputs with the observed housing and land use totals for 1975.

The four models represented below all relied on forecasts of one sort or another of housing starts to drive the models. However, as can be seen from table 5, these macro-forecasts of regional starts compare unfavourably with the actual experience over the period 1972-76. Most important, they are low in every instance. Since we could benefit from hindsight, we re-ran the model using the actual housing starts in the years 1971 through 1975 as obtained from Central Mortgage and Housing Corporation. We call this Model 5, which is identical to Model 4 in terms of the microspatial allocation functions and differs only in that it uses actual as opposed to forecast estimates of housing starts.

Testing the models   To test the relationship between the predicted and actual forecasts in each of the 157 subareas in our study (10 of the 167 traffic zones were exit zones, containing no land use) we ran the following regressions:

$$PH^{sf}_{j,1975} = a_1 + b_1 AH^{sf}_{j,1975} + \mu_1 \tag{5a}$$

$$PH^{mf}_{j,1975} = a_2 + b_2 AH^{mf}_{j,1975} + \mu_2 \tag{5b}$$

where:

$PH^{sf}_{j,1975}$ = predicted stock of single-family housing in subarea j in 1975

$AH^{sf}_{j,1975}$ = actual stock of single-family housing in subarea j in 1975

$PH^{mf}_{j,1975}$ = predicted stock of multi-family housing in subarea j in 1975

$AH^{mf}_{j,1975}$ = actual stock of multi-family housing in subarea j in 1975

a_i, b_i = parameters to be estimated

u_i = error terms

The results in table 6a show that all the models perform reasonably well. The R^2 are high and the relevant F-statistics are all significant at the 0.001 level. Table 6b presents other measures of the goodness of fit between predicted and actual values, such as Theil's inequality coefficient, Spearman's rank correlation coeffi-

TABLE 5

Macro-model comparisons

	Actual completions		Model completions		% deviation	
	SF	MF	SF	MF	SF	MF
1972	6,073	8,103	4,615	6,752	−0.23	−0.17
1973	7,088	7,865	3,998	6,715	−0.44	−0.15
1974	5,451	6,586	4,074	5,584	−0.25	−0.15
1975	5,762	6,070	4,256	5,524	−0.26	−0.09
1976	6,751	7,955	4,374	5,176	−0.35	−0.35

SOURCE: CMHC, *Canadian Housing Statistics*

SF   single-family
MF   multi-family

cient and several measures of error terms between predicted and actual values.

Using stock data as in equations (5a) and (5b) is not, however, a true test of performance, since the stock of housing is unlikely to change greatly in a four-year period, and much of the 1975 single-family and multi-family stock will be made up of stock extant in 1971. A more rigorous test, therefore, is to look at how well the models dealt with changes in the stocks of housing in each subarea as opposed to merely looking at the levels of the stocks. Models to predict changes in single-family and multi-family stocks by subarea are set out in equations (6a) and (6b).

$$\Delta PH^{sf}_{j,1975} = a_3 + b_3 \Delta AH^{sf}_{j,1975} + \mu_3 \tag{6a}$$

$$\Delta PH^{mf}_{j,1975} = a_4 + b_4 \Delta AH^{mf}_{j,1975} + \mu_4 \tag{6b}$$

where

$\Delta PH^{sf}_{j,1975}$ = predicted change in stock of single-family houses in subarea j between 1971 and 1975

$\Delta AH^{sf}_{j,1975}$ = actual change in stock of single-family houses in subarea j between 1971 and 1975

$\Delta PH^{mf}_{j,1975}$ = predicted change in stock of multi-family housing in subarea j between 1971 and 1975

$\Delta AH^{mf}_{j,1975}$ = actual change in stock of multi-family housing in subarea j between 1971 and 1975

a_i, b_i = parameters to be estimated

μ_i = error terms

The results of these regressions, in table 7a, are much less impressive than previously. For predicting change in single-family housing the initial ad hoc model

TABLE 6a

Model test regression results for stock of units

Dependent
variable – model prediction

Independent
variable – actual data

TEST	R	R^2	Standard error of estimate	F	Significance level of F	Intercept	Coefficient	Standard error of coefficient
Stock of single family units								
Model 1	0.973	0.948	317.54	2804.91	0.001	−7.086	0.898	0.017
2	0.970	0.941	375.98	2493.61	0.001	104.716	1.003	0.020
3	0.974	0.947	358.02	2864.15	0.001	91.591	1.023	0.019
4	0.976	0.954	341.48	3207.19	0.001	72.872	1.033	0.018
5	0.976	0.952	347.06	3099.42	0.001	78.500	1.032	0.019
Stock of multi family units								
Model 1	0.978	0.956	451.200	3337.81	0.001	46.402	0.891	0.015
2	0.991	0.981	296.691	8145.20	0.001	−42.108	0.916	0.010
3	0.990	0.980	286.569	7632.18	0.001	−6.296	0.856	0.010
4	0.989	0.978	301.254	6920.60	0.001	−1.985	0.857	0.010
5	0.986	0.973	337.045	5615.54	0.001	60.601	0.864	0.012

(N = 157)

TABLE 6b

Model test results actual against model forecasts for the stock of units

TEST	Spearman correlation	Mean error	Mean square error	Root mean square error	Theil U statistic	Fraction of error due to:		
						Bias	Different variation	Different co-variation
Stock of single family units								
Model 1	0.9469	153.2	257.3	382.3	0.097	0.061	0.091	0.748
2	0.9668	-108.8	229.5	389.1	0.091	0.078	0.017	0.905
3	0.9713	-125.3	224.3	378.8	0.088	0.110	0.040	0.850
4	0.9720	-120.3	204.1	363.3	0.085	0.110	0.056	0.834
5	0.9721	-124.6	209.1	369.8	0.086	0.114	0.054	0.832
Stock of multi-family units								
Model 1	0.8772	49.1	277.0	517.4	0.108	0.009	0.158	0.833
2	0.9101	116.3	205.7	373.1	0.078	0.097	0.224	0.679
3	0.9040	132.8	239.8	459.9	0.099	0.083	0.471	0.446
4	0.8975	127.7	247.7	466.2	0.100	0.075	0.447	0.478
5	0.8761	59.2	266.1	465.8	0.099	0.016	0.389	0.595

TABLE 7a

Model test regression results for change in the stock of units

Dependent variable – model prediction

Independent variable – actual data

TEST	R	R^2	Standard error of estimate	F	Significance level of F	Intercept	Coefficient	Standard error of coefficient
Change in single family units								
Model 1	0.457	0.209	253.802	40.954	0.001	−140.090	0.348	0.054
2	0.116	0.013	94.284	2.112	0.148	128.376	0.029	0.020
3	0.286	0.082	119.268	13.795	0.001	143.541	0.095	0.026
4	0.392	0.154	141.319	28.129	0.001	137.157	0.161	0.030
5	0.359	0.123	139.819	22.866	0.001	141.844	0.143	0.030
Change in multi family units								
Model 1	0.447	0.120	446.568	38.721	0.001	87.160	0.459	0.074
2	0.713	0.508	169.495	160.495	0.001	46.252	0.352	0.028
3	0.422	0.178	146.376	33.588	0.001	83.735	0.140	0.024
4	0.373	0.139	127.711	25.088	0.001	88.100	0.143	0.029
5	0.354	0.126	251.614	22.293	0.001	143.144	0.196	0.042

(N = 157)

TABLE 7b

Model test results actual against model forecasts for change in the stock of units

TEST	Spearman correlation	Mean error	Mean square error	Root mean square error	Theil U statistic	Bias	Different variation	Different co-variation
Change in single family units								
Model 1	0.1256	153.2	257.3	382.2	0.557	0.161	0.054	0.785
2	0.1256	−108.8	229.5	389.1	0.730	0.078	0.511	0.411
3	0.4148	−125.3	224.3	378.8	0.672	0.110	0.432	0.458
4	0.4738	−120.3	204.1	363.3	0.626	0.110	0.367	0.523
5	0.4632	−124.6	209.1	369.8	0.637	0.114	0.366	0.520
Change in multi-family units								
Model 1	0.2504	49.08	277.0	517.4	0.479	0.009	0.001	0.990
2	0.4790	116.3	205.7	373.1	0.455	0.097	0.424	0.479
3	0.4772	132.8	239.8	459.9	0.618	0.083	0.493	0.424
4	0.4526	127.7	247.7	466.2	0.607	0.075	0.410	0.515
5	0.4629	59.23	266.1	465.8	0.533	0.016	0.215	0.769

(N = 157)

performs best. For multi-family changes Model 2 does significantly better than the others. Overall, however, Model 4 is most consistent, followed by Model 5.[19] Essentially the same pattern emerges when looking at other measures of fit found in table 7b.

Two sets of questions come to mind after reviewing these results. First, has there been a significant improvement in the performance of the models resulting from the use of the behavioural data for estimating the microspatial allocation functions? Second, independent of the degree of difference among these models, how does the model set perform compared with other predictive land use models?

In answering the first question one must rely heavily on personal taste and judgment. Improvements did occur in model performance as can be seen from tables 6 and 7. Whether or not these improvements were worth the resources devoted to them remains a more open question. I think they were. A great deal of experience was gained from working with the models and in refining the codes. The developer behaviour studies were valid research undertakings in their own right quite independent of the modelling effort. Finally, as will be noted below, the present work identifies further areas of conceptual and empirical weakness and therefore allows us to focus on these areas in the ongoing model development process.

Finding an answer to the second question is ironically more difficult because of the paucity of literature comparing actual and predicted output from urban models. Although there is no shortage of models, as we have noted earlier, there is a severe shortage of model output. A careful screening of the modelling literature turns up a great deal of work on calibration and fitting of models to historical or cross-sectional data. The fits in general are impressive. Calibration methods are even more ingenious and the goodness of fit measures reported in the literature are invariably statistically significant within very high levels of confidence (Putman, 1976).

Finding information with which to compare the present performance of predicted versus actual values was most trying. The following few examples alone were available for present purposes. In a report on testing of land use models, Stephen Putman (1976) compared the output from his model against the output from the widely used EMPIRIC model, both calibrated for the Minneapolis-St. Paul region. Over the 1960-70 period the two models produced the following R^2 of actual versus predicted zonal estimates by income class of housing. The results appear as table 8. While the R^2 are reasonably high, it should be remembered that they refer to 1960 versus 1970 stocks. A more stringent test, which Putman does not perform, would be on the changes between 1960 and 1970 as we have presented in tables 7.

Another quite sketchy piece of evidence comes from the work done at the Oak Ridge National Laboratory by A.H. Voelker (1976). In his paper on "A Cell-Based Land-Use Model", he alludes to several tests of the model's performance. No time

TABLE 8

1960 and 1970 comparisons of EMPIRIC and DRAM: Actual versus predicted

Household type	Empiric R^2	Dram R^2
LIQ – lower income	0.918	0.750
LMIQ – lower middle	0.941	0.828
UMIQ – upper middle	0.889	0.844
HIQ – upper income	0.829	0.699

SOURCE: Putman, 1976: 32

period is given, nor is the nature of the "test" described in any detail. It appears that the forecast period is well under a decade. For selected test areas the model over the forecast period consumed 20 per cent more land than was actually consumed. No detail is given as to whether or not this 20 per cent over consumption was with respect to the stock of land or the change in land. Voelker concludes (1976: 17-19) by noting that serious testing of the model against actual outcomes awaits development of suitable data bases and is an important future priority task.

These two studies are the only ones that look at predicted versus actual outcomes of land use models. A variety of national econometric models have been subjected to rigorous testing of predicted against actual magnitudes and the results have not been overwhelmingly good. This is the case even given that these models are highly aggregated and therefore likely to yield more stable forecasts, and that they look at variables such as GNP, which shows a large amount of inertia from one period to the next.[20] Errors on changes in GNP and other macro-aggregates have averaged as much as 40 per cent over as short a period as eight quarters.[21]

Viewed against these other studies, the present output is not so bleak. Rather it tends to raise more general questions about our ability to forecast anything very well. Accordingly, considerably more attention should be paid to forecasting models and to their limitations. Perhaps the models are really quite reasonable, but our expectations of their roles and reliability are not. The process of forecasting deserves closer scrutiny, not just the forecasts. Appropriate forecasting processes and processors are very much needed. Development of more reasonable and realistic expectations is likely to be as important as the development of more reasonable and realistic models.

Summary of Model Results and an Overview of Future Micro-Supply Efforts

The analyses presented above point to some significant improvements in the workings of the model. Progress has been made in refining the computer codes and the land use, housing and employment data that underlie the models. In addition, using the behavioural data from the developer studies we have constructed an interesting and reasonable allocation function to allocate new single-family and multi-family housing in the 157 subareas of the region.

Several problems remain. First, the microspatial supply functions were estimated using changes in single- and multiple-family housing *stocks* in each subarea between 1966 and 1971. Thus, they include not only new additions to the stock (starts) but also demolitions and conversions of existing units. However, since the allocations run on single-family and multi-family starts, there is an inconsistency. It would have been desirable to estimate the allocation functions by subarea using 1966-71 starts. Such data are not available. Alternatively, we could have stayed with the present formulation if in addition we had information on demolitions and conversions by subarea. These data are also not available.

Without demolition and conversion algorithms (and data) we are continually building new stock without removing or converting existing stock. Positive and negative errors result. We are likely to overestimate the 1975 stock in those areas where there is sufficient land to locate new stock but in which significant demolitions also occurred between 1971 and 1975. We are likely to underestimate the 1975 stock in those areas where existing structures precluded building on the occupied land and where there was little, if any, vacant available land. Our model would show minimal new stock where in practice demolitions could have cleared the way for significant quantities of new housing. This we know is happening because an examination of the residuals shows that the errors are worst in the high density older areas of the region where demolitions are an important factor.[22] Similar difficulties arise as a result of conversions where we might have no room to build between 1971 and 1975, and little or no new building in fact, but where sizeable numbers of existing single detached houses were converted to apartments. In such a case our model would show no activity but there would be a change (an increase) in actual numbers of units between 1971 and 1975 as a result of conversion activity.

The net result of the foregoing considerations is that there is a pressing need, not only in the present models but also in other simulation efforts, to begin to understand the dynamics of the standing stock of housing with respect to demolitions and conversion. Somewhat further down the road is the need to study renovation and rehabilitation of the new standing stock, as such activities, while not necessarily changing the numbers of units or densities, can have considerable impact on the character and viability of the urban area.

A second area of concern relates to the land absorption coefficients which convert housing units to acres and which are at the heart of the market mechanism which measures the availability of vacant land for building. Inaccurate LACs combine with the dynamics of the standing stock noted above to use land too rapidly or not rapidly enough; they therefore lead to inaccurate estimates of land using, and thus housebuilding activity, in each subarea. Land absorption, while distinct from demolitions and conversions, interacts with both to constrain or to encourage units to be built in subareas at rates different from the actual rates. Better estimates of land absorption are essential if the present, and similar, models are to fulfill their promise as land use and not merely housing allocation models. The allocation functions estimated here yield estimates of number of units which are then multiplied by the LACs to produce land needs and are then tested against capacity constraints. Inaccurate LACs can lead to violation of the capacity constraints and therefore force the apparent excess units to be reallocated to areas different from those determined by the allocation function. The LACs and the allocation functions must be consistent or the estimation of the allocation functions is an exercise in futility. Over the four-year time span of the present test, these capacity constraints were not a consistent problem, though they did override the allocation function frequently enough to cause divergence between the allocations as realized in the models and the allocations as specified by the microspatial supply equations.[23]

One last point should be made. If one were to pick a hazardous period for forecasting housing, that period would have been 1971 to 1975 when the Vancouver housing market took off on a major inflationary spiral.[24] Housing types and housing densities changed dramatically with the shift to condominiums, townhouses and smaller suburban lots. Thus, even assuming away problems of LACs, demolitions and conversions, it is unlikely that a model estimated over the period 1966 to 1971 would do very well in the 1971 to 1975 Vancouver housing market.

Taking the preceding into account, several points come to the surface. First, the models are not unreasonable and, given better mechanisms for dealing with demolitions and conversions, would probably perform markedly better. Second, demolition and conversion algorithms are worth pursuing, not only in the context of the present discussion, but more generally given the emergent steady-state of most large North American metropolitan areas. The spatial dynamics of the standing stock of housing deserve the kind of attention reserved in the past for new housing construction. Finally, the models should be retested using more recent data than 1975 to enable further refinements to be made and to allow the use of the full range of 1966 to 1975 data in the microspatial estimation procedures.

ADDITIONAL WORK LYING AHEAD

During the past seven years the models have evolved significantly from their earliest largely intuitive beginnings. A great deal more remains to be done, as noted above, and the modular design of the model set described here is well designed for refining and replacing weak elements.

Supply Functions

While the microspatial supply functions have been improved over the recent past there is still room for additional refinement as discussed. Independent of improvements in the microspatial supply functions, if they allocate inaccurate regional totals then their utility is severely restricted. Improving the regional macro-supply' functions becomes a high priority accordingly. Such work is already progressing independently.[25] As that work becomes usable it can be plugged into the appropriate place in the housing model without difficulty.

Demand Functions

On the assumption of an improved macrospatial housing supply function, and given the satisfactory performance and refinement of the currently operating Model 4 microspatial allocation functions, attention must of necessity turn to demand. Breaking the problem into micro- and macro-components seems appropriate in light of the progress to date on the supply side outlined above. We hope to be able to implement our earlier study design and conduct a large-scale behavioural study of consumer residential location behaviour to parallel the developer studies. These behavioural data would then be used to estimate behaviourally based microspatial demand allocation algorithms analogous to those detailed in this paper. Carrying out regional macro-demand research would also provide a nice parallel to the recently begun work on regional housing supply functions.

Demand and Supply Interactions: The Market

Mechanisms for reconciling demand and supply in the market are imperfectly understood and require considerably more study. Because of the complexity of the task we are not optimistic about achieving sound analyses of the price/quantity relationship which result from demand and supply interactions. Indeed, the present model set has avoided the use of prices explicitly because of the difficulty in obtaining accurate base data, let alone simulating price behaviour over time. Equally important, prices in the context of simulation models are likely to be misleading indicators to potential users. They imply a degree of precision and sophistication that models do not deserve. Including prices in models such as those described here is not a high priority, as we are fearful of the difficulties such prices will create in the minds of users and in estimating the models given the paucity of reliable price data.[26]

Nonetheless, work is proceeding on price/quantity relationships in our area. We are focusing in particular on the impacts of existing housing stocks on prices and trying to reconcile two competing schools of thought.[27] While not of direct relevance for the models of interest here, any knowledge we gain about the market mechanism, both regionally and more locally, will be of significant value.

Related Components Requiring Further Work

Housing and land development processes do not operate in isolation in either the real or simulated world. In the present case, the housing model is intimately tied to other land use models which allocate employment to subareas and consume land for employment and for such public purposes as recreation and parks. Accordingly, it is important to improve the quality of the employment location models, most notably those dealing with industrial location, as they are non-trivial consumers of urban land. Greater emphasis must also be placed on the development of operational location algorithms for service employment which is of overwhelming importance in urban areas in terms of the percentage of the work force that it employs. Given journey-to-work relationships, service employment location is thus of potential importance to housing location as well, although the present work casts doubt on those relationships in the GVRD.

The macro-employment and population forecasting models also need revision and updating. The transportation model could do with similar scrutiny. In sum, the same sort of evolutionary strategy and review of components that applies to the development of the housing model is required for these other interacting components.

Prospects for Success

As the work on the microspatial supply functions has demonstrated, continued efforts do pay off. The same doubtless holds true for these other areas which are in need of further work. Ultimately, the degree of effort expended on these areas, and on these types of models, depends upon the expected utility of the models themselves. This utility in turn depends vitally upon careful development and ongoing refinement.[28] And so it goes.

By opening efforts such as ours to careful scrutiny perhaps the utility can be improved through demystifying the models and the model building process and through benefiting from the input of interested and knowledgable colleagues and potential users. In this way it is hoped that the above model building process can be directed to the benefit of models, users and perhaps even the affected public and our cities.

ACKNOWLEDGEMENTS

I want to express my appreciation to a number of individuals and organizations for their assistance. First, the British Columbia Real Estate Association has generously supported the modelling work reported on here over the past half dozen years. Their support has enabled the work to proceed. In addition, they funded the two developer surveys which form the behavioural base for the present paper. The Faculty of Commerce and Business Administration has provided all necessary secretarial assistance, equipment and space to carry out this work. To Mr. Blake Allan I owe a special debt of gratitude for his untiring efforts in getting the models to work, in deriving the developer based allocation functions, in testing the output and identifying meaningful ways to present the results. Without his dogged determination the effort could never have progressed as far as it has. I also want to thank Mr. Douglas A. Ash who has worked with me over the past eight years on these models and provided valuable linkages with earlier model developments. Finally, my colleague Professor Robert H. Zerbst read the previous versions of this paper and provided much-needed criticism and guidelines for improvement. As with all acknowledgements, I also have to acknowledge my own errors and accept the blame for the remaining weaknesses.

NOTES

1 A similar point is made by Bourne (1976). Much of the underlying rationale for the work by Forrester and his associates is predicated on this "micro-macro" interaction. See Forrester (1969).

2 The aggregation problem is neatly summed up and discussed in Ackley (1961).

3 See Forrester (1969) for one of the more forceful presentations of the "systems" approach to modelling. Forrester (1971) extends this theme. A pioneering effort in the social sciences at using micro-level analyses to forecast macro-level phenomena is Orcutt, et al. (1961).

4 The IIPS project and its major components and objectives have been documented at some length elsewhere. See Goldberg (1973), Goldberg and Stander (1976), and Goldberg and Ash (1977).

5 There are now many excellent reveiews of the literature of urban simulation modelling. See, for example, Putman (1975), Batty (1972), and Wilson (1974).

6 A number of reflective and sometimes critical papers have recently appeared in the literature to argue for a reorientation and for greater perspective in urban modelling. See Lee (1973), and Voelker (1975). Guarded optimism and expressions of changing the emphasis of modelling can be found in Schneider, et al. (1974), Lee (1977), and, most recently, Goldberg (1977a).

7 An early working paper established the strategy we would be following in the modelling of housing development. See Baxter, et al. (1972).

8 The approach being followed here draws heavily on earlier work by Putman (1972), and Goldberg (1968).

9 The models closely parallel those done previously by Huff (1963), Lakshmanan and Hansen (1965), and Forbes and Fowler (1969).

10 Some research has been focused on descriptions of changing patterns of office location (Armstrong, 1972; Goddard, 1968) and some on office location criteria (Bannon, 1973).

11 This is a characteristic of the residential development industry, where a certain level of building continues almost independently of vacancies and unsold inventory to keep work crews and overhead staff employed. See Herzog (1963).

12 Biernacki (1977) has amply observed some of the difficulties in modelling a metropolitan housing market. Given the difficulties, the present study opted for relatively simple descriptors such as equations (2a) and (2b). It should be noted that since these equations formed part of a simulation modelling system, the independent variables had to be capable of being forecast endogenously. This precluded the use of monetary and financial variables such as interest rates, money supply and other measures of credit conditions since they could not be generated within the model. Equations (2a) and (2b) are based on pooled cross-section time-series data on housing starts compiled by Central Mortgage and Housing Corporation for the Greater Vancouver Region and the seven subareas which comprise the region. Annual data were used by aggregating monthly data over a calendar year.

13 This problem occurs when modelling most Canadian cities due to the abundance of private reinvestment and redevelopment of central cities. See Collier (1974), for example.

14 A number of authors have commented upon the predominance of small builders in the residential development industry. See Herzog (1963) and, for the British Columbia experience, Price (1970), and Ratcliff and Hamilton (1972).

15 The work by Bourne (1976) supports this as does the earlier work by Kaiser and Weiss (1970).

16 Previously cited modelling work by Goldner (1971), and Putman (1975) stresses the importance of accessibility, as does the pioneering work of Lowry (1964), and the more recent work by Kain and Quigley (1975). A complementary body of literature which has also traditionally placed significant weight on accessibility is that dealing with house price determination. Kain and Quigley (1975) build on hedonic notions of pricing durables. Other recent examples of this stream are provided by Wilkinson and Archer (1973), Richardson, et al. (1974), and Mark (1977). The recent work in the real estate appraisal/assessment area includes Stenehjem (1974), Walsh and Stenehjem (1975), Zerbst (1976) and, most recently, Zerbst and Eldred (1977).

17 Looking at the results from all developers (multiple-family, single-family and residential lot developers) the only accessibility criterion mentioned of any im-

portance to developers was nearness to schools which had a mean importance of 2.08 (out of 4.0) compared with proper zoning (3.26), price of land (3.20), availability of land (2.92) and, finally, access to trunk sewer (2.91). Here again we are faced with the distinction between stock pricing, where accessibility can be seen as conceptually important, and flow location models where other factors, such as zoning, can be seen to dominate.

18   The importance previously ascribed to accessibility derives from *ex post* observations of density and rent gradients. The geometry of circumferential expansion about a city centre produces this pattern since rings get geometrically larger with distance and it is not unreasonable to expect densities to get geometrically smaller. However, as a predictor of residential development its utility appears to be much more severely limited.

19   At first glance it is strange that Model 5 has a poorer fit in all instances than Model 4, since the number of starts in Model 5 is known to be correct and the number in Model 4 is incorrect. The problem is not difficult to resolve when we see that Model 4, using estimates of starts that are consistently low, leads to subarea totals that are nearer to the actuals, since the actuals include demolitions whereas the present model does not. Model 5, being in essence reliable on starts, seriously overstates the total stock of units in the region since it does not demolish any units.

20   The evidence on econometric model performance is reasonably large at the level of national forecasts. Work by Theil pioneered the field of analyzing the accuracy of forecasts (see Theil, 1965, which is a basic reference). A recent survey of the reliability of national forecasts using expectations data is provided by Maital (1977). At the regional and urban level of aggregation the number of studies providing assessments of forecast reliability is more limited. Walter (1969) provides an accuracy analysis of a regional econometric model for the San Francisco Bay Area economy. Most recently Robertson (1977) has modelled a regional housing market in Florida. Looking at these sources leads one to conclude that forecasting has not proven to be a uniformly successful undertaking, and that more disaggregated and local forecasts are less reliable. Against this background the present work stands as acceptable.

21   Work done by Zarnowitz at the National Bureau of Economic Research showed that moving from forecast totals to forecast changes pointed up serious deficiencies in a variety of short-term economic forecasting models. Zarnowitz (1967) found that even over as short a period as eight quarters (two years) the models showed tremendous variability in their performance. Moreover, when their ability to forecast changes was analyzed, their performance slipped significantly. As the forecast period increased from one and two quarters to four or more

quarters, performance fell. Similarly, as attention moved from forecasting aggregates such as GNP to components of GNP, reliability declined. Given this experience, it is understandable that forecasts for 167 subareas and two housing types over four years will be a risky venture.

22 A recent study by Vancouver City Planning Department (1977) showed that during the period January 1, 1973 to February 1, 1977 there were 4,492 demolitions in the city of Vancouver, while during the same period there were just over 12,000 housing starts. Demolitions are therefore non-trivial in the city of Vancouver. In outlying areas of the GVRD demolitions are not important. However, in the city they are, and it is in the central areas of the city that the model has experienced its greatest difficulties in accurately forecasting the housing stock.

23 The problems associated with land absorption coefficients can be seen from examining Appendix B tables I and II on the predictive accuracy of the models with respect to acres of single-family and multi-family land use. They are analogous to tables 6 and 7. Significantly, the results are much poorer, illustrating the major error introduced by using unreliable LACs.

24 Dramatic changes in house prices during the 1971-75 period caused alarm throughout Canada. At the federal level the "Federal/Provincial Task Force on the Supply and Price of Serviced Residential Land" was created late in 1976 with a $500,000 plus budget to look into the national housing "crises". The federal government responded with major housing programs such as AHOP (Assisted Home Ownership Program) and ARP (Assisted Rental Program). For analysis of the "crises" see Goldberg (1977b). For a review and analysis of the policy response to the "crises" see Smith (1977).

25 This work is being done in stages, beginning with multiple-family units because of their susceptibility to government policy. See Zerbst and Johnston (1977).

26 This aversion to using prices in the present models has been stressed in Goldberg (1977c).

27 Of interest here is the so-called stock-flow model wherein prices are determined solely by demand since supply is assumed totally inelastic and dominated by the existing stock. See Hamilton and Baxter (1975), for example. The more traditional margin cost pricing mechanism of microeconomics is the other leading contender in this debate.

28 This point has been stressed repeatedly in writing on this and other models. See Goldberg (1973 and 1977c).

APPENDIX A

When a variety of access measures were used to explain residential development in the 1971-75 period none, either singly or in combination, could explain more than 15 per cent of the variance in residential development. This appears to support the findings of the developer survey mentioned in Note 17, even though evidence concerning relationship between location (accessibility) and real property values speaks strongly for the inclusion of accessibility measures. However, there is little *a priori* reason to assume that such measures weigh heavily in developer decisions concerning the location of new residential developments. Developers will attempt to satisfy consumer preferences in housing, and access is certainly a variable in the preference map of consumers. Given the obvious fact that most new residential development takes place on vacant land, and that vacant land is usually less accessible than developed land, developers are at an immediate disadvantage relative to the existing stock when it comes to location, and therefore are essentially forced to choose sites from among virtually equally inaccessible sites relative to the standing stock. What the price determination models cited above appear to be picking up is the pricing of the stock wherein access does hope to explain price differentials in the stock. What developers are dealing with is the *flow* of new units, which will generally be small relative to the stock (perhaps 3-5 per cent of the stock in any given year). Price determination models will therefore be predominantly stock-oriented. Our current work looks at the flow. All things being equal, it is probably true that developers will value and choose more accessible over less accessible locations. However, in the development of new housing in existing urban areas all things cannot be considered constant. Developers are forced to develop on available usable land. The developer surveys conclude that available usable land is taken by developers to mean vacant, zoned and sewered land. Such land generally will lie on the urban periphery and differences in accessibility among such parcels are likely to be small. New development can be seen as occurring in peripheral rings within which accessibility differences are not likely to be very great.

There is another, and perhaps more convincing reason, for doubting the importance of accessibility in the location behaviour of developers of housing. The argument follows directly from the basic tenets of urban land economics where in a competitive market situation developers will bid up the prices of more accessible land to such a price that profits are equalized throughout a metropolitan land (housing) market. In such a case developers will be indifferent whether they develop at accessible high priced locations or at less accessible and therefore lower price locations. In a competitive equilibrium developers will be indifferent to accessibility since the trade-off between access and price will be such that economic rents will be reduced to zero (or near zero) and profits will be identical at all locations, differences in land values soaking up excess profits.

Given this competitive situation, and the evidence in the GVRD is that land is widely held and that markets are competitive, developers will focus attention on the type of housing they want to develop and then the competitive market will predetermine whether this development is to be on expensive accessible land or less accessible, less expensive surburban land. We should expect to find that development in this situation should be quite different at different accessibilities since changing land prices imply different combinations of land, labour and capital to satisfy housing consumers' tastes and budget constraints. Moreover, in a residential development industry characterized by small builders, especially for single-family homes, we could reasonably expect that these developers will be specialized with respect to the type of residential developments they undertake and thus quite localized in this competitive market setting. This is in fact the picture that emerges from developer responses (see Goldberg and Ulinder, 1976b: 259). Since developers tend to work in specific municipalities, it is reasonable to see them as taking accessibility as given.

Extending this argument further we can properly interpret the findings of the developer surveys as providing conditional conclusions since developers either explicitly or implicitly hold accessibility as constant and given. There is good reason for their taking access as given, especially in the GVRD. First, as previously stressed, development is likely to occur in peripheral locations with roughly equal accessibility. Secondly, in the GVRD there have been no significant transportation improvements during the past two decades roughly (the Trans-Canada Highway opened in 1961), so that travel patterns and accessibility measures can reasonably be taken as constant over that period. This should be contrasted with the process of urban development in the United States where investments have been made since 1956 on freeways in urban areas which have quite dramatically changed travel and accessibility patterns. It should be noted that most of the work cited previously showing the importance of accessibility was done in the United States and its relevance for Canadian cities is, I suspect, limited given the relative paucity of freeway development. Furthermore, it would be a most interesting test of the points being made here to look at the determinants of residential development in the United States to see if accessibility is among them. I would venture that it would not be for reasons given in Note 17 relating to differences between real property price determination models (stock dominated) and the present real property development model (flow dominated).

Summing up, while accessibility is generally treated as an important variable in location decisions of households and therefore impacts on models of house price determination, accessibility need not represent an important location variable to developers. They are primarily interested in land availability, which is generally to be found at the urban periphery where accessibility is neither very great nor very different among potentially developable sites and land prices are correspondingly low. These developers preferring greater access and higher land prices will locate more centrally. In any case the competition in the market place for land assures us of developer indifference to accessibility in equilibrium.

APPENDIX B

TABLE I

Model test regression results for the stock of acres

Dependent Variable — Model Prediction
Independent Variable — Actual Data

TEST	R	R^2	Standard error of Estimate	F	Significance level of F	Intercept	Coefficient	Standard error of. coefficient
Stock of single-family								
Model 1	0.892	0.795	118.694	602.220	0.001	17.015	0.963	0.039
2	0.967	0.934	64.473	2211.064	0.001	15.773	1.002	0.021
3	0.970	0.940	63.518	2446.537	0.001	5.447	1.039	0.021
4	0.974	0.948	59.948	2812.053	0.001	1.585	1.051	0.020
5	0.973	0.947	61.870	2776.307	0.001	2.122	1.078	0.020
Stock of multi-family								
Model 1	0.788	0.620	20.625	253.133	0.001	3.290	0.821	0.052
2	0.897	0.804	11.848	636.598	0.001	1.090	0.748	0.030
3	0.912	0.832	9.605	770.264	0.001	0.811	0.667	0.024
4	0.912	0.832	9.667	766.708	0.001	0.878	0.670	0.024
5	0.910	0.828	10.031	747.085	0.001	1.084	0.686	0.025

($N = 157$)

TABLE II

Model test results: actual against model forecasts for the change in stock of acres

TEST	Spearman correlation	Mean error	Mean absolute error	Root mean square error	Theil U statistic	Fraction of error due to:		
						Bias	Different variation	Different co-variation
Change in single-family								
Model 1	0.1923	−6.98	60.73	118.50	0.703	0.003	0.123	0.874
2	0.2008	−16.41	49.80	66.13	0.657	0.062	0.352	0.586
3	0.1012	−15.96	46.86	65.77	0.631	0.059	0.255	0.686
4	0.1397	−15.44	44.64	62.76	0.571	0.061	0.162	0.777
5	0.1393	−23.24	48.85	68.35	0.558	0.116	0.049	0.835
Change in multi-family								
Model 1	0.1895	0.62	11.98	21.28	0.565	0.001	0.027	0.972
2	0.4561	4.42	7.99	14.92	0.565	0.088	0.230	0.682
3	0.4665	6.48	8.20	15.67	0.735	0.171	0.573	0.256
4	0.4669	6.35	8.17	15.59	0.723	0.166	0.558	0.276
5	0.4548	5.79	8.06	15.26	0.673	0.144	0.489	0.368

(N = 157)

REFERENCES

Ackley, G. 1961 *Macroeconomic Theory.* New York: Macmillan.

Armstrong, R.B. 1972. *The Office Industry.* Cambridge, Mass.: MIT Press.

Bannon, M., ed. 1973. *Office Location and Regional Development.* Dublin: A Foras Forbatha.

Batty, M. 1972. "Recent Developments in Land Use Modelling: A Review of British Research", *Urban Studies,* 9: 151-177.

Baxter, D.E. 1974. "The British Columbia Land Commission Act — A Review". *Report series no. 8,* Urban Land Economics Division, Faculty of Commerce and Business Administration, University of British Columbia, Vancouver.

Baxter, D.E., M.A. Goldberg, D. Lach, and G. Mason. 1972. "Toward a Regional Housing Model". Vancouver: Urban Land Economics Division, Faculty of Commerce and Business Administration, University of British Columbia (mimeographed).

Biernacki, C.M. 1977. "Tests of Temporal Sensitivity of the Toronto Housing Market". *Major report no. 12,* Centre for Urban and Community Studies, University of Toronto (mimeographed).

Bourne, L.S. 1976. "Urban Structure and Land Use Decisions", *Annals of the Association of American Geographers,* 66, 4: 531-547.

Center for Real Estate and Urban Economics. 1968. *Jobs, People and Land: Bay Area Simulation Study.* Berkeley: Center for Real Estate and Urban Economics, University of California.

Clawson, M. 1977. *Suburban Land Conversion in the United States.* Baltimore: Johns Hopkins University Press.

Collier, R.W. 1974. *Contemporary Cathedrals.* Montreal: Harvest House.

Davis, H.C. 1974. "An Inter-Industry Study of the Metropolitan Vancouver Economy". *Report series no. 6,* Urban Land Economics Division, Faculty of Commerce and Business Administration, University of British Columbia, Vancouver.

Forbes, J.D., and A.G. Fowler. 1969. "Simulation of a Gravity Model", *The Annals of Regional Science,* 3, 1: 86-95.

Forrester, J.W. 1969. *Urban Dynamics.* Cambridge, Mass.: MIT Press.

Forrester, J.W. 1971. "Counterintuitive Behaviour of Social Systems", *Technology Review,* 73: 53-68.

Goddard, J.B. 1968. "A Multivariate Analysis of Office Location Patterns in the City Centre", *Regional Studies,* 2: 69-85.

Goldberg, M.A. 1968. "Bay Area Simulation Study: Employment Location Models", *The Annals of Regional Science,* 2, 2: 161-176.

Goldberg, M.A. 1973. "Simulation, Synthesis and Urban Public Decision-Making", *Management Science,* 20, 4(part II): 629-643.

Goldberg, M.A. 1974. "Residential Developer Behaviour: Some Empirical Findings", *Land Economics,* 50, 4: 85-89.

Goldberg, M.A. 1977a. "Simulating Cities: Process, Product and Prognosis", *Journal of the American Institute of Planners,* 43, 2: 148-157.

Goldberg, M.A. 1977b. "Housing and Land Prices in Canada and the U.S.", in L.B. Smith and M. Walker, eds., *Public Property? The Habitat Debate Continued.* Vancouver: Fraser Institute.

Goldberg, M.A. 1977c. "Urban Simulation – the Vancouver Experience", in D.B. Massey and P.W.J. Batey, eds., *Alternative Frameworks for Analysis.* London Papers in Regional Science, 7. London: Pion.

Goldberg, M.A., and D.A. Ash. 1977. "Continued Development of the Vancouver Model", *Transportation Research Record,* 617: 55-61.

Goldberg, M.A., and H.C. Davis. 1973. "An Approach to Modeling Urban Growth and Spatial Structure", *Highway Research Record,* 435: 42-55.

Goldberg, M.A., and J.M. Stander. 1976. "Analysis of Output and Policy Applications of an Urban Simulation Model", *Transportation Research Record,* 582: 61-71.

Goldberg, M.A., and D.D. Ulinder. 1976a. "Residential Developer Behaviour 1975: Additional Empirical Findings", *Land Economics,* 52, 3: 363-370.

Goldberg, M.A., and D.D. Ulinder. 1976b. "Residential Developer Behaviour: 1975", in *Housing: It's Your Move.* Vancouver: Urban Land Economics Division, Faculty of Commerce and Business Administration, University of British Columbia.

Goldner, W. 1971. "The Lowry Model Heritage", *Journal of the American Institute of Planners,* 37, 2: 100-111.

Hamilton, S.W., and D. Baxter. 1975. *Capital Taxes Pertaining to Real Property.* Vancouver: Real Estate Institute of B.C.

Harris, C.C. 1966. *A Stochastic Process of Suburban Development.* Technical report no. 1. Berkeley: Center for Real Estate and Urban Economics, University of California.

Herzog, J.P. 1963. *The Dynamics of Large-Scale Housebuilding.* Research report no. 22. Berkeley: Center for Real Estate and Urban Economics, University of California.

Huff, D.L. 1963. "A Probability Analysis of Shopping Center Trading Areas", *Land Economics,* 53, 1: 81-90.

Kain, J.F., and J.M. Quigley. 1975. *Housing Markets and Racial Discrimination.* New York: National Bureau of Economic Research.

Kaiser, E., and S.F. Weiss. 1970. "Public Policy and the Residential Development Process", *Journal of the American Institute of Planners,* 36, 1: 30-37.

Lakshmanan, T.R., and W.G. Hansen. 1965. "A Retail Market Potential Model", *Journal of the American Institute of Planners,* 31, 2: 134-143.

Lee, D.B., Jr. 1973. "Requiem for Large-Scale Models", *Journal of the American Institute of Planners,* 39, 3: 163-178.

Lee, D.B., Jr. 1977. *Improving Communication among Researchers, Professionals and Policy Makers in Land Use and Transportation Planning.* Washington, D.C.: U.S. Department of Transportation.

Lowry, I.S. 1964. *A Model of Metropolis.* Santa Monica: Rand Corporation.

Maital, S. 1977. "What do Economists Know: Predictive Accuracy, Causality and Structure of Experts' Expectations". Jerusalem: Foerder Institute of Economic Research (mimeographed).

Mark, J. 1977. "Determinants of Urban House Prices: A Methodological Comment", *Urban Studies,* 14: 359-363.

Orcutt, G.H., M. Greenberger, J. Korbel, and A.M. Rivlin. 1961. *Microanalysis of Socioeconomic Systems: A Simulation Study.* New York: Harper.

Pack, J.R. 1975. "The Use of Urban Models: Report on a Survey of Planning Organizations", *Journal of the American Institute of Planners,* 41, 3: 191-199.

Price, E.V. 1970. "The Housebuilding Industry in Metropolitan Vancouver". Unpublished M.B.A. thesis, Faculty of Commerce and Business Administration, University of British Columbia, Vancouver.

Putman, S.H. 1972. "Intra-Urban Employment Forecasting Models: A Review and a Suggested New Model Construct", *Journal of the American Institute of Planners,* 38, 4: 216-230.

Putman, S.H. 1975. "Urban Land Use and Transportation Models: A State of the Art Summary", *Transportation Research,* 9: 187-202.

Putman, S.H. 1976. *Laboratory Testing of Predictive Land-Use Models: Some Comparisons.* Washington, D.C.: U.S. Department of Transportation.

Ratcliff, R.U., and S.W. Hamilton. 1972. *Suburban Land Development.* Vancouver: Faculty of Commerce and Business Administration, University of British Columbia.

Richardson, H., J. Vipond, and R. Furbey. 1974. "Determinants of Urban Housing Prices", *Urban Studies,* 11: 189-199.

Robertson, T. 1977. "A Local Housing Market: An Econometric Model". Paper presented at the Meetings of the American Real Estate and Urban Economics Association, New York (mimeographed).

Schneider, J.B., D.B. Lee, Jr., and B. Harris. 1974. "National Bureau of Economic Research Models: A Review Forum", *Journal of the American Institute of Planners,* 40, 3: 212-215.

Smith, L.B. 1977. *Anatomy of a Crisis: Canadian Housing Policy in the Seventies.* Vancouver: Fraser Institute.

Stenehjem, E. 1974. "A Scientific Approach to the Mass Appraisal of Residential Properties". *Automated Mass Appraisal of Real Property.* Chicago: International Association of Assessing Officers.

Theil, H. 1965. *Economic Forecasts and Policy.* 2nd rev. ed. Amsterdam: North Holland Publishing Company.

Vancouver. City Planning Department. 1969. *Vancouver Urban Renewal Study.* Vancouver: City Planning Department.

Vancouver. City Planning Department. 1977. "Demolition Report". Vancouver: City Planning Department.

Voelker, A.H. 1975. *Some Pitfalls of Land-Use Model Building.* ORNL-RUS-1. Oak Ridge, Tenn.: Oak Ridge National Laboratory.

Voelker, A.H. 1976. "A Cell-Based Land-Use Model". ORNL-RUS-16. Oak Ridge, Tenn.: Oak Ridge National Laboratory.

Walsh, T.J., and E. Stenehjem. 1975. "Neighbourhood Influences on Residential Property Values", *Assessors Journal,* 10: 23-31.

Walter, G.R. 1969. "Judging regional Forecasting Accuracy — Sectoral Employment in the San Francisco Bay Area", *The Annals of Regional Science,* 3, 1: 156-166.

Wilkinson, R., and C. Archer. 1973. "Measuring the Determinants of Relative House Prices", *Environment and Planning,* 5: 357-367.

Wilson, A.G. 1974. *Urban and Regional Models in Geography and Planning.* London: John Wiley.

Zarnowitz, V. 1967. *An Appraisal of Short-Term Economic Forecasts.* Occasional paper no. 104. New York: National Bureau of Economic Research.

Zerbst, R.H. 1976. "Locational Attributes of Property Values", *Real Estate Appraiser,* 42, 3: 19-22.

Zerbst, R.H., and G.W. Eldred. 1977. "Improving Multiple Regression Valuation Models Using Location and Housing Quality Variables", *Assessors Journal,* 10: 23-31.

Zerbst, R.H., and K. Johnston. 1977. "The Effects of Changes in Income Tax Laws on Multi-Family Housing Starts in British Columbia". Paper presented at the Annual Meetings of the American Real Estate and Urban Economics Association, New York.

5.2 THE ROLE OF URBAN DATA SYSTEMS IN THE ANALYSIS OF HOUSING ISSUES

Eric G. Moore and Stewart J. Clatworthy

We begin with the contention that many housing programs in urban areas have weak analytic foundations. This is meant in the sense that the interactions between a given program and the broad spectrum of social, economic and demographic processes in the city are poorly understood. For example, we still do not have a sufficient grasp of the complexities of real market structures to be able to say with any degree of confidence what the impacts of such programs as rent control, income subsidy or public ownership of land will be in a particular city. Under these circumstances it is difficult for either the policy maker or the social scientist to assess whether a particular program will be effective. One consequence is that programs then tend to be evaluated in terms of whether specific political goals are being met (such as satisfying certain groups that the problem is being tackled) rather than whether substantive social benefits are being attained. This argument, of course, is not new and has been pursued at length in the debate on the relative utility of input and output indicators in program evaluation (Land, 1975).

It is reasonable to ask why we find ourselves in this situation. It is partly because the dominant emphasis has been on the elaboration of micro-level models of household and producer behaviour set within a framework of limiting assumptions necessary to make ensuing analysis tractable. Most outcomes are expressed in terms of average or expected behaviour of individuals with well-defined characteristics acting under institutional constraints which are either ill-defined or assumed to be of a very restrictive form, namely conditions of perfect competition. Certainly it can be argued that this work has contributed a great deal to our general understanding of urban housing markets and that it is relevant to local issues in the sense of providing both a language and a logic for addressing complex social and economic problems. However, it is a contribution to a general structural argument, divested of the specifics of local institutional arrangements, details of local zoning ordinances, patterns of land ownership, the available mix of federal and provincial programs, and of the broad range of political, cultural and business interests which permeate the local community.

There are a variety of perspectives that could be taken with respect to these comments. It might be argued, for example, that this is merely a restatement of the problem of translating general theories into specific cases (Scriven, 1959; Heilbroner and Ford, 1971) and as such is certainly not limited to housing issues. Yet we believe there is more to it than this, in that the general style of research has imposed constraints on our ability to learn about the systems for which we make decisions. First, many researchers have emphasized equilibrium-oriented arguments, arguments which have been particularly suited to empirical test using cross-sectional data from census or survey material. In other words, the analytic style has been reinforced by the nature of available data and has slowed the development of alternative conceptual approaches to the modelling of urban structure and change. Second, we have failed to consider explicitly that the institutional constraints of programs and policies are integral to the processes we analyze. Two major consequences of these biases have been: (1) that the results of local housing analyses have been phrased at a level of generality inappropriate to the detailed context in which most planners and policy makers operate, even when the original data are for a single city; and (2) since most of our analyses do not include those instrumental variables embedded in program structures (such as the institutional details of controls on rents or the provision of income supplements), we are hard pressed to offer advice on the possible impacts of a given policy.[1]

A fundamental point which arises in this context is that the way in which we answer questions depends on the presuppositions which underlie the questions, the structural representations (models) chosen, the data available, and the specific decision-making or theory-building context in which the question is posed. From this perspective the questions addressed in planning contexts are different from those posed in a theory-building situation. Which groups in the city are experiencing the greatest problems in finding suitable housing? To what extent have different groups been affected by recent programs and policies? What programs are most likely to achieve specific goals with respect to occupancy characteristics? In an academic context we may claim that these questions cannot be readily answered because the underlying theory is poorly developed. In a planning environment, answers will be provided to these questions whether the knowledge base is sound or not, and the less we understand of the relevant processes the more likely it will be that political considerations dominate.

The questions which are addressed within a planning context are clearly also questions about process. Emphasis is on the nature of change, the response of individuals and organizations to a changing institutional environment, a recognition that problems emerge and dissipate, often in a short period of time, and that local decision-making is, to a large degree, incremental and reactive (Niner, 1976). However, concern with process over the typical time horizons of local planning activities demands both new data and new methodologies. As Dunn (1974) has argued so persuasively, concern with process takes us beyond the state descriptors of most census or survey data, and demands that activity and programmatic descriptors be added to our data base. In other words, in order to understand process we need to consider both transactional data and the set of institutional rules, regulations and constraints which influence the nature and outcome of the transactions.

New data alone are not sufficient to guide us to an expanded knowledge of process. We do not gather observations at random nor discard what we already know; clearly the latter provides us with guidelines as to what observations we might seek and how they might be organized. However, existing ideas do not provide the sole basis for future structures. There must be a substantial learning process involved in finding out not only *what* is happening in a local housing system but also *why*. Thus there will be a continual feedback between the development of new data, ways of interpreting such data, understanding the nature of urban dynamics and the design of improved data bases.

The paths to improved understanding of process are undoubtedly varied. One such approach is explicitly to include transactions within the existing framework of microeconomic analysis, as in the study by Hanushek and Quigley (1976). A second approach is to develop a theoretical framework which stresses the central role of social and political institutions in influencing the outcomes of housing market transactions (Harvey, 1974; Duncan, 1976). A third strategy, more in the spirit of the local planning questions raised above, is the development of a monitoring framework which incorporates a broad range of transactional and institutional information as well as characteristics of the occupancy of the stock (Forrest, 1976).

Each of these procedures holds considerable promise but is likely to take time to achieve substantial results, particularly at the local level. Furthermore, the expense of developing data bases with detailed records of transactions is likely to be extremely high and we might ask whether the costs of special purpose systems for housing analysis at the local level can be justified. At the least, we should consider whether contributions to the questions raised above can be obtained from other sources of public data, primarily those collected for other administrative and planning purposes at the local government level.

The remainder of this paper is concerned with an examination of the types of insight regarding local housing systems which can be obtained from one type of public data, the annual enumeration. The following section discusses one example of an annual enumeration, that of Wichita, Kansas. Two examples of analysis based on these data are provided in the third section and the final section discusses more general issues of development and use of urban information for planning purposes.

THE WICHITA DATA BASE

Given the planning questions raised in the previous section, what types of public data are likely to provide a useful contribution? The most fundamental requirement is the ability to link dwelling and household characteristics at the level of the individual unit on a regular basis (preferably at least once a year). This can be accomplished either at the original collection stage or via the more cumbersome procedure of linking different files on the basis of individual identifiers such as address. Although it would appear that the latter procedure is the more likely solution in the North American context (Symons, 1974; Moore and Tinline, 1977), one system which uses the first approach has been developed in Wichita, Kansas. Since this system has a richer set of data relative to housing issues than currently accessible linked file systems, it is fruitful to examine its properties to identify some of the potential uses of microdata systems in general.

In 1971 Wichita began a series of annual enumerations of households and dwellings, built around the basic requirement of Kansas law that each individual be enumerated once a year for assessment purposes (the similarity with the situation in Ontario is striking). A number of questions were added to those needed for assessment purposes as a response to a common set of needs expressed by a variety of social agencies in Wichita, which individually felt that they were spending too much on data collection. The outcome has been a sequence of seven annual enumerations with a core of questions on the characteristics of each dwelling (size, condition, structure type, value or rent) and household (age, sex, education, family income, employment and migration experience) asked   each year, together with additional variable questions focusing on current planning issues (garbage pick-up, basement drainage, travel time to work). As such, these data provide a unique statement of the recent residential history of the city from which the structure of transactions can be inferred by comparison of successive enumerations.[2]

EXAMPLES OF USES OF MICRODATA IN HOUSING STUDIES

The great bulk of the work that we have so far on the Wichita Enumeration has focused on the development of longitudinal data files spanning the years 1971-76. These files have only just been prepared and are currently being edited, a process which is far more complicated than cross-sectional editing, as logical inconsistencies between successive household records must be reconciled.

Although we have not yet analyzed these particular files for the entire period, we have undertaken a number of preliminary studies based on single enumerations or comparisons of pairs of enumerations which provide illustrations of the utility of this data base.

The advantages of the Wichita data lie primarily in two areas. First, the coverage, for most practical purposes, is complete with regard to both dwelling units and households, although the response rates vary from question to question on the enumeration form (table 1). Given this coverage (approximately 100,000

TABLE 1

Response rates for variables in the Wichita-Sedgwick county
Annual enumeration, 1971-75 (percentages)

Variable	1971	1972	1973	1974	1975
Race	95	97	92	98	98
Structure	NA	NA	77	97	94
Own/rent	88	89	90	95	92
Value	88	82	94	94	89
Rent	88	82	98	98	96
Bedrooms	92	86	97	99	96
Utilities	88	74	96	NC	NC
Building condition	93	84	86	89	88
Sewage disposal	NC	NC	NC	93	NC
Refuse	NC	83	NC	NC	NC
Refuse collection	NC	85	88	NC	NC
Animals	NA	83	91	100	100
Vehicles	NC	81	86	NC	NC
Insurance	NC	80	NC	NC	NC
Income	73	67	59	71	70
Fixed income	NC	79	75	92	NC
Person interviewed	NC	NC	NC	75	67
Migration	72	NC	69	68	53
Occupation of HOH	NC	NC	63	NC	NC
Age	94	97	96	96	95
Sex	99	99	98	99	99
Employment	88	90	88	92	92
Relationship to HOH	NC	NC	96	98	99
Education	NC	NC	88	90	89
Military service	NC	NC	94	NC	NC

NA   Not available
NC   Not collected
HOH Head of household

household records per year), it is possible to identify, by appropriate aggregation of individual records, the housing attributes of a large number of well-defined subgroups in the population as they vary over both time and local neighbourhood. Second, the linkage of individuals over time permits strong inferences to be made about the structure of transactions, and thereby provides a better understanding of the mechanics of change in consumption for both population subgroups and subareas from one year to the next. The two examples provided below illustrate the type of insight which can be obtained in taking advantage of these properties.

Housing Consumption of Low-Income Households

An issue of current concern to the planning department in Wichita concerns the definition of future strategies for providing housing for low-income households. With inflation still proceeding apace it is important for them to identify the relative success of different socio-economic and demographic groups in obtaining adequate housing within the urban area. We have explored this issue from a comparative static perspective, using data from the 1973 and 1975 enumerations.

In the first instance, the problem was clearly one of how to characterize the low-income population and its consumption. Here we were limited, of course, by the data collected in the enumeration, but it still provided a far richer source than either the census or the majority of surveys. The first step was to consider alternative classifications of households. The possibilities are legion and therefore it seemed reasonable to make a first cut by using existing notions of the life-cycle stage which are already embedded in other discussions of household budgets and consumption patterns (e.g., Glick and Parke, 1965; Duncan and Newman, 1975). We began with 130 household groups, and gradually refined them on the basis of both relative frequency and patterns of consumption to the twenty-one groups in table 2, which are based on data on age, sex of household head, supplemented by data on race, household size and age of children. Using this classification, we examined income and consumption changes over the two-year period.

The various household groups exhibited different patterns of income change between 1973 and 1975. Although the income of blacks had increased proportionately more than that of whites, the average increase was less (table 3). Furthermore, both the structure of low incomes (less than $7,000) and the internal distribution of that income increase was markedly different within each racial group (figs. 1-6). In particular older singles and older couples in the black population, and single-parent families in general, have become relatively worse off during this inflationary period. When this is translated into consumption indices, we find similar results emerging with respect to changes in ownership rates, shelter cost-to-income ratios and the relative quality of services acquired. For example, although the average increases in house prices and rents were consistently greater for units occupied by whites (figs. 7 and 8), when these increases were combined

TABLE 2

Classification of household types

Household type number	Description
1	Single male. < 40 yrs.
2	Single male. > 40 yrs.
3	Single female. < 40 yrs.
4	Single female. > 40 yrs.
5	All other non-family households
6	Married couples. Household head < 35 yrs.
7	Married couples. Household head 36–50 yrs.
8	Married couples. Household head 51–64 yrs.
9	Married couples. Household head > 65 yrs.
10	Married couples. Oldest child < 5 yrs., 3 persons, household head < 25 yrs.
11	Married couples. Oldest child < 5 yrs., 3 persons, household head > 25 yrs.
12	Married couples. Oldest child < 5 yrs., > 3 persons, household head < 25 yrs.
13	Married couples. Oldest child < 5 yrs., > 3 persons, household head > 25 yrs.
14	Married couples. Oldest child < 17 yrs., 3 persons, household head < 35 yrs.
15	Married couples. Oldest child < 17 yrs., 3 persons, household head > 35 yrs.
16	Married couples. Oldest child < 17 yrs., > 3 persons, household head < 35 yrs.
17	Married couples. Oldest child < 17 yrs., > 3 persons, household head > 35 yrs.
18	Married couples. Oldest child > 17 yrs.
19	Single-parent family. Oldest child < 5 yrs.
20	Single-parent family. Oldest child < 17 yrs.
21	Single-parent family. Oldest child > 17 yrs.

TABLE 3

Approximate average household income by race,
Wichita, Kansas, 1973 and 1975

Race	Income ($ per annum)		
	1973	1975	% change
Black	6,210	8,950	44.1
White	10,230	13,200	29.0
Total	10,010	12,930	29.2

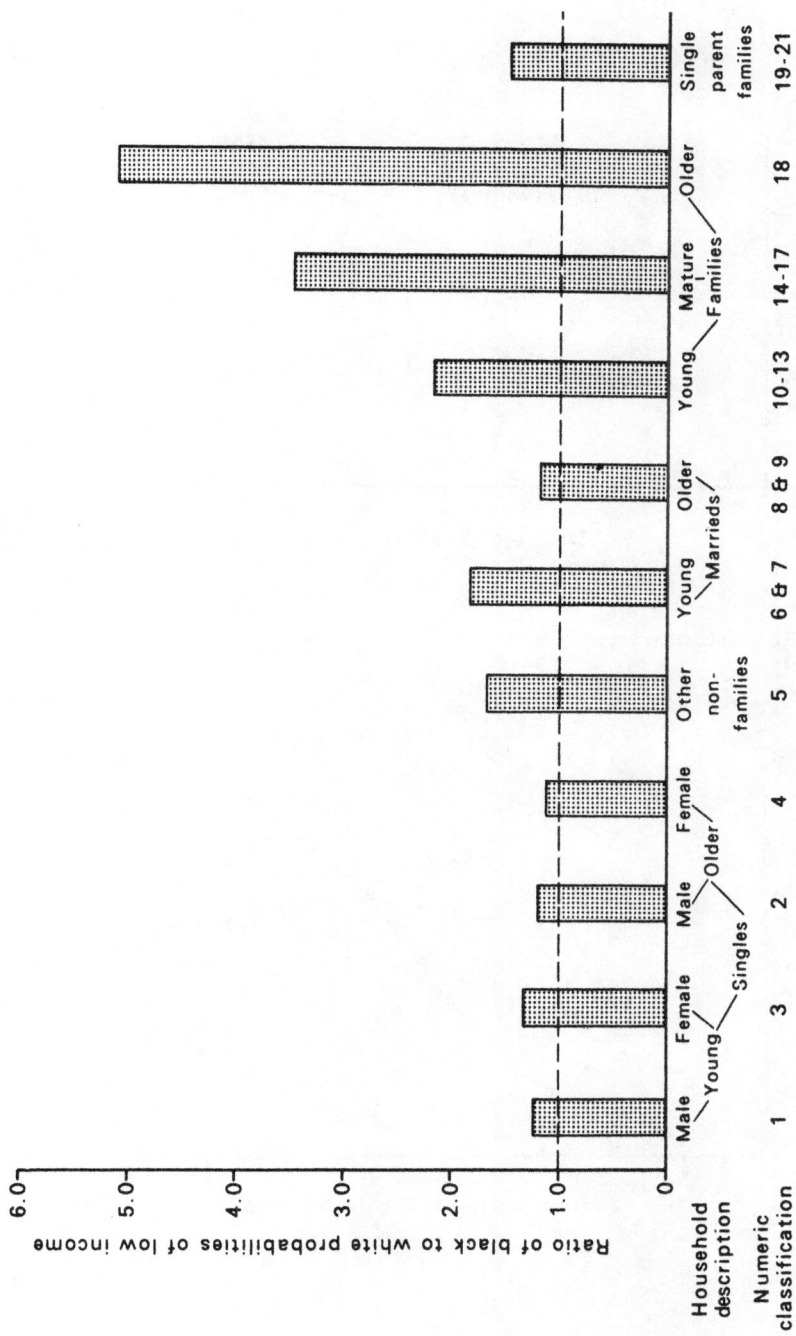

FIGURE 1: Racial and demographic differences in the incidence of low income: Wichita, Kansas, 1973

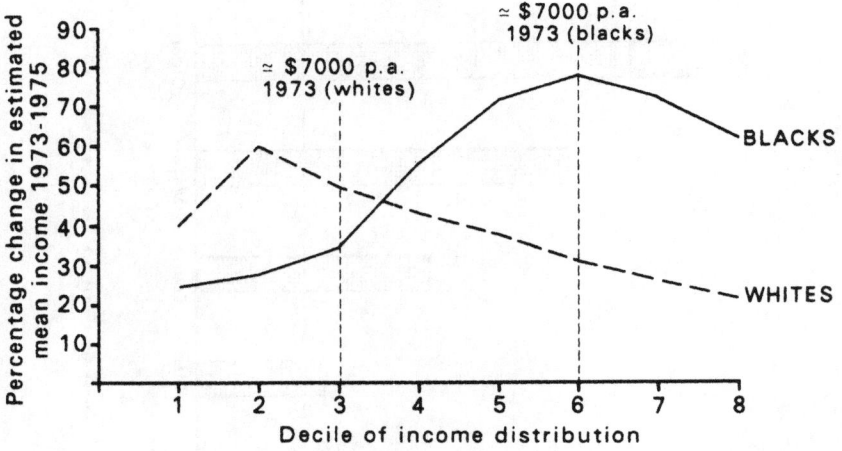

FIGURE 2: Income changes by race, 1973-75

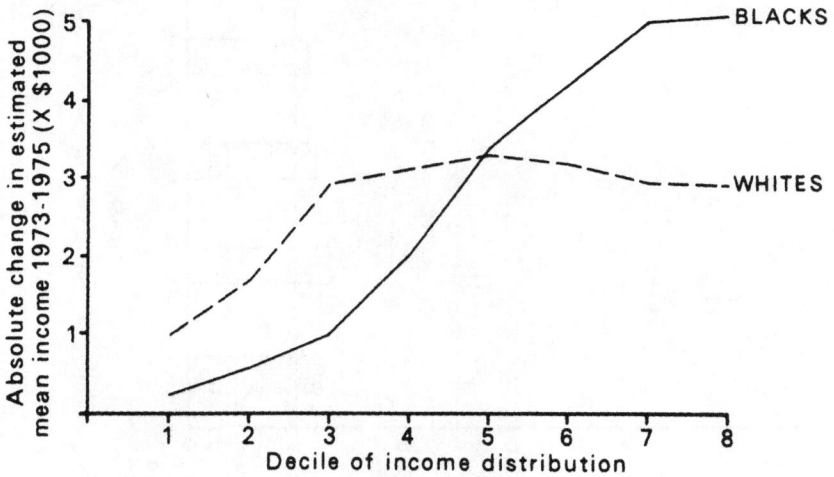

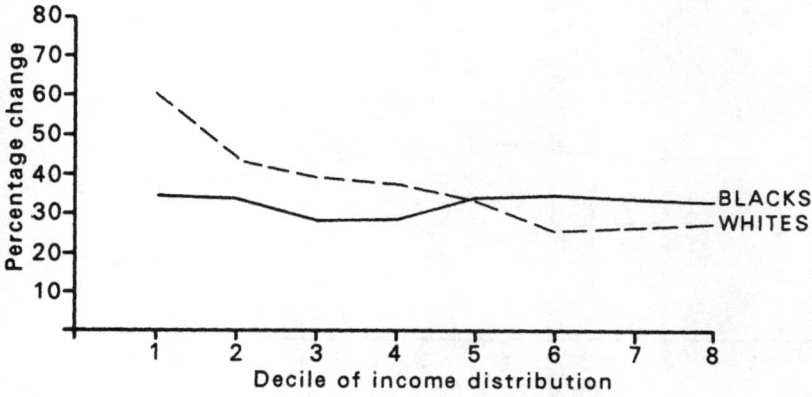

FIGURE 3: Income changes among young, single males, 1973-75

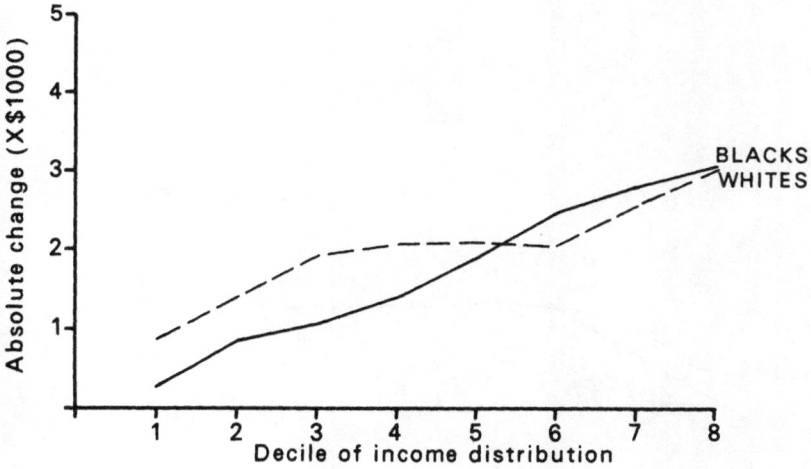

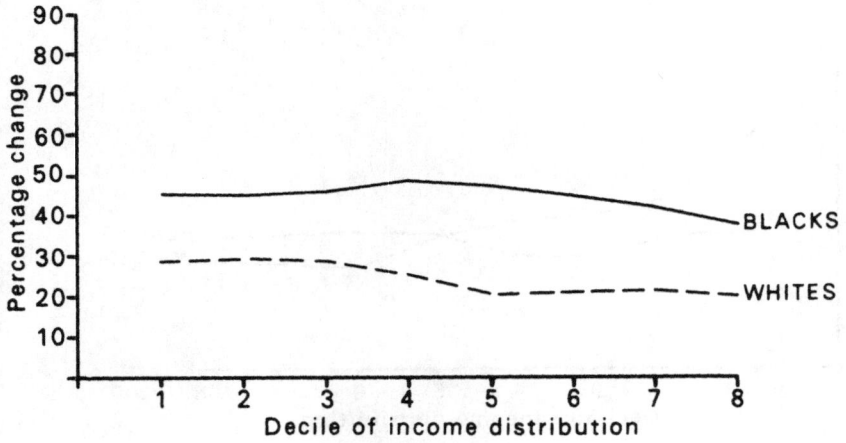

FIGURE 4: Income changes among mature families, 1973-75

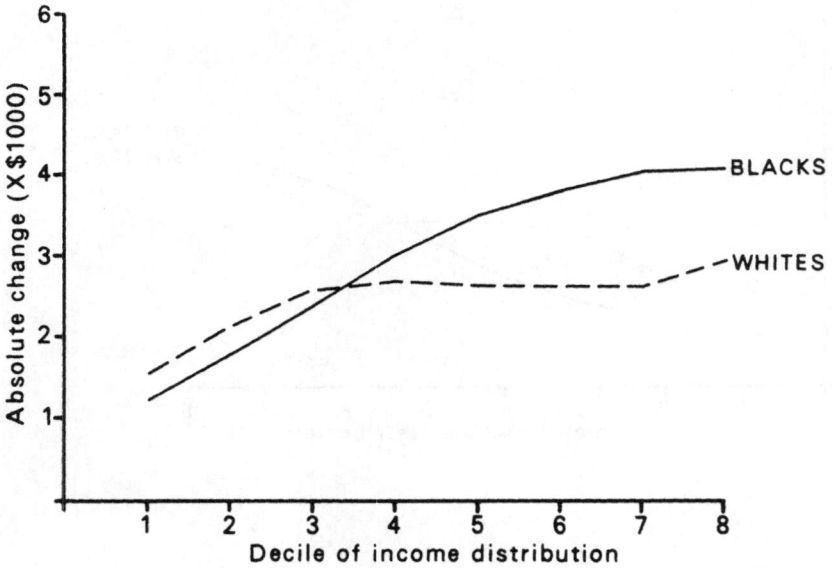

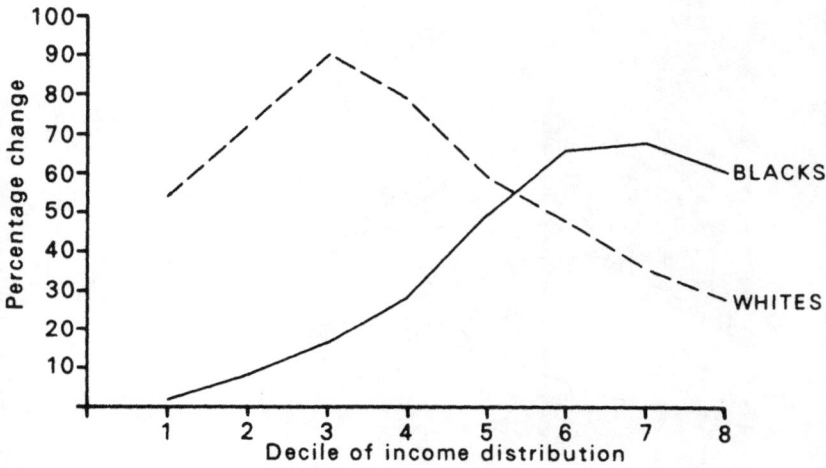

FIGURE 5: Income changes among older marrieds, 1973-75

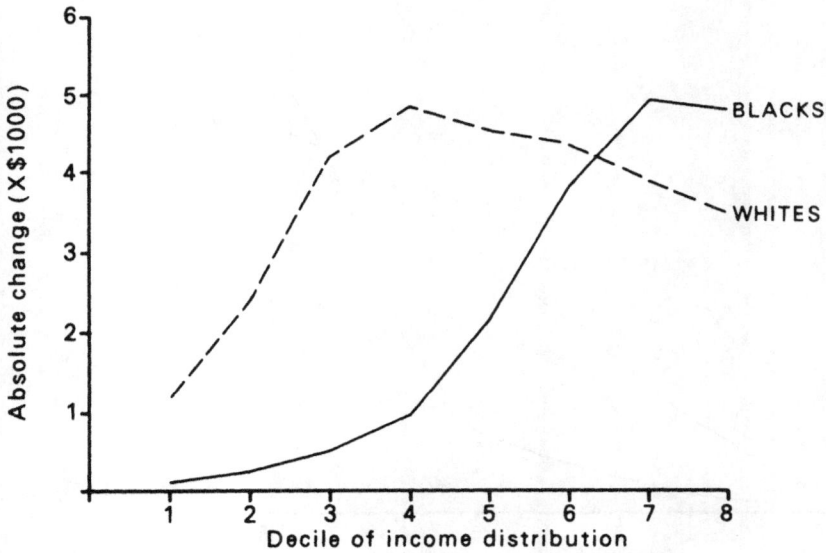

FIGURE 6: Income changes among single-parent families, 1973-75

FIGURE 7: Change in value of recently purchased homes by race, 1973-75

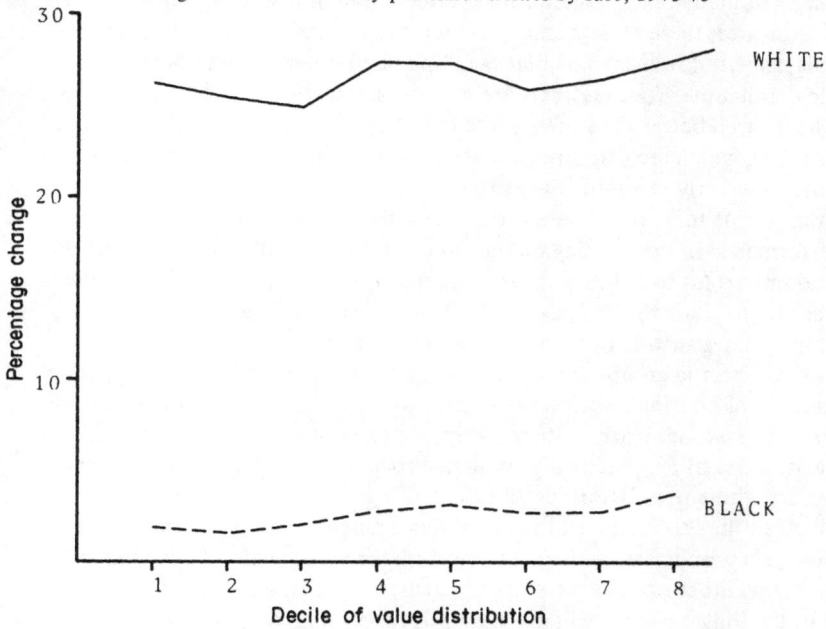

FIGURE 8: Change in monthly rent by race, 1973-75

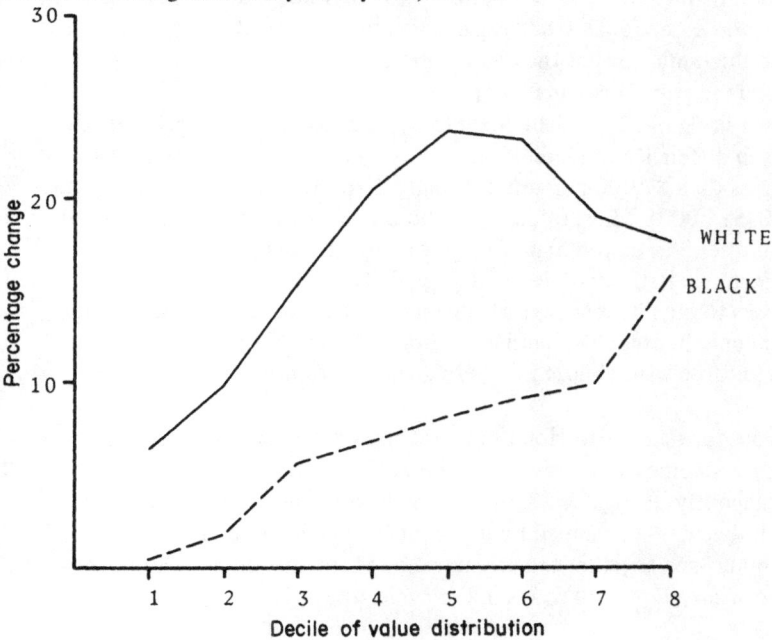

with changes in income, the distributional effects were not so straightforward. As figure 9a indicates, these effects among renters are primarily confined to higher-income blacks with lower-income blacks falling further behind over the two years. Among lower-income groups, effects are not uniformly distributed: young black families have fared better than their white counterparts (fig. 9b), while for single-parent families, which are disproportionately represented in the black population, the situation is clearly reversed (fig. 9c).

The main point to be made here is that these data permit problems of differential performance in the housing market to be identified with greater specificity. It is just as important to identify those marginal groups which do not seem able to cope as it is to chart the progress of the average household which, in this case, seems to have more than kept up with inflationary trends.

Even when specific groups are identified as possessing some need for attention in designing local housing policies, the impacts of different types of programs are still poorly understood. Until quite recently, for example, the bulk of research on income elasticities of demand for housing had focused on estimation of one parameter for the whole population (de Leeuw, 1971; Paldam, 1970). Straszheim (1975) showed that elasticity estimates for San Francisco vary substantially between life-cycle groups, yet perhaps the most important question from a policy standpoint is whether responses to income changes are themselves a function of income. In the longer run we will examine this issue using the longitudinal household file, but in the meantime we have attempted to estimate differences between responses using cross-sectional data disaggregated by household category and income. Despite the limitations of the enumeration data[3] some interesting conclusions were obtained from these analyses:

1. As shown in figures 10 and 11 the impact on housing consumption resulting from a given difference in income was markedly less for those receiving a very low income (less than $7,000 per annum) than for those in the moderate income range ($7,000–$15,000). Thus, estimates of housing response to income subsidy programs would tend to be too high if they were based on standard population estimates of income elasticity of demand (e.g., de Leeuw, 1971).

2. Responses to income increases are different for different life-cycle groups. Among low-income households, families without children have higher income elasticities than those with children, a finding which also has implications for public policy.

Using a procedure similar to Holm's (1967) analysis of variation of housing consumption by income, we consider the two attributes of dwelling size and condition simultaneously. In figures 12 and 13 we show the average condition and average size of dwellings consumed by different life-cycle groups at different income levels; by linking together the consumption points for the income classes we trace the *consumption path* for each life-cycle group. The diagrams indicate

FIGURE 9 a, b, c: Reduction of rent-to-income ratios by race, 1973-75

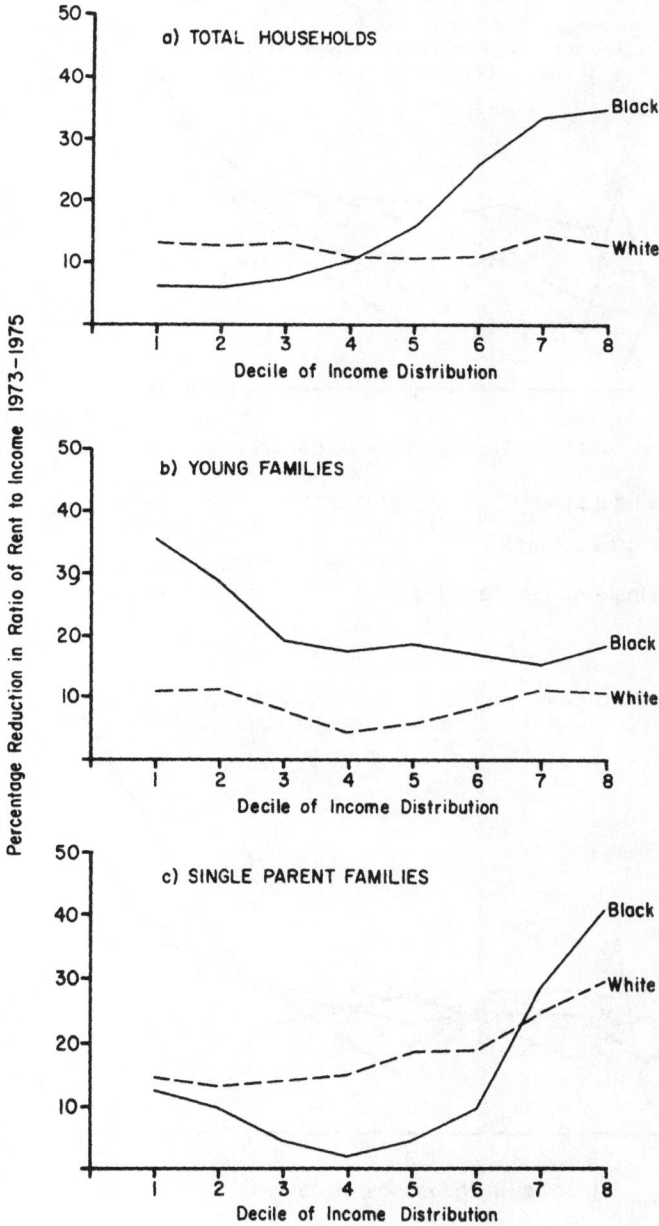

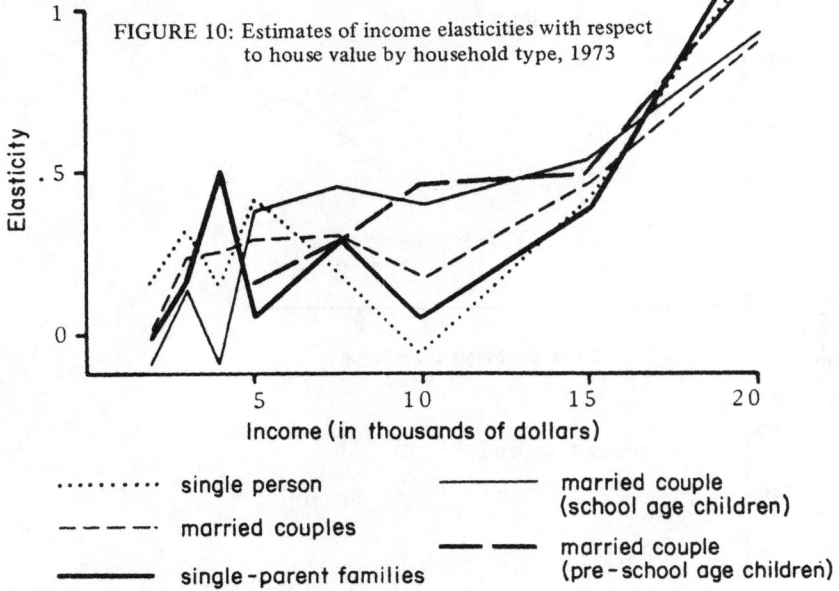

FIGURE 10: Estimates of income elasticities with respect to house value by household type, 1973

.... single person

– – – – · married couples

——— single-parent families

——— married couple (school age children)

— — married couple (pre-school age children)

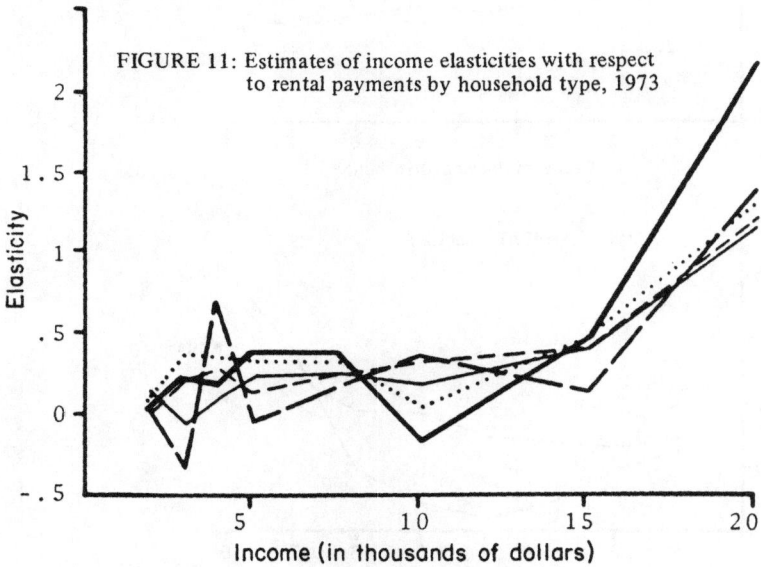

FIGURE 11: Estimates of income elasticities with respect to rental payments by household type, 1973

FIGURE 12: Changing levels of housing consumtion with increasing income in single-family owned units: Wichita, 1973

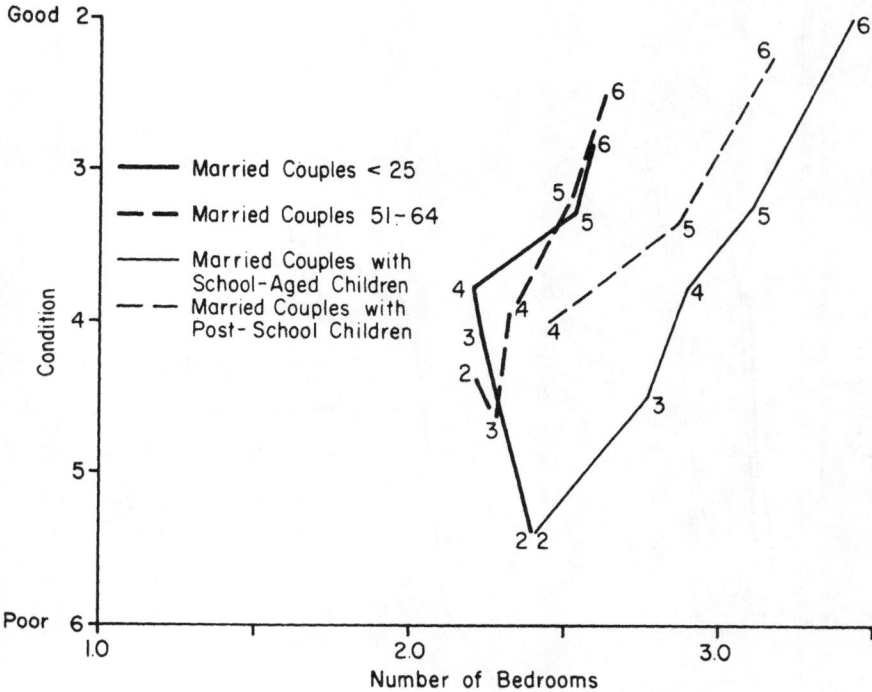

Income classes:

1 = $0 – 1,999		4 =	7,000 – 9,999
2 = 2,000 – 3,999		5 =	10,000 – 14,999
3 = 4,000 – 6,999		6 =	15,000 and over

that, not only do marked differences exist in the types of housing consumed by different household groups, but also that the nature of the trade-off between these two housing attributes varies by household type as income increases. For example, the steep slope of the curves obtained for renters (fig. 13) indicates that, for most households, income increases are spent to acquire better quality units. However, among large lower-income families additional income appears more likely to be directed towards obtaining larger dwellings, suggesting that these households are

FIGURE 13: Changing levels of housing consumption with increasing income in
multiple-family rental units: Wichita, 1973

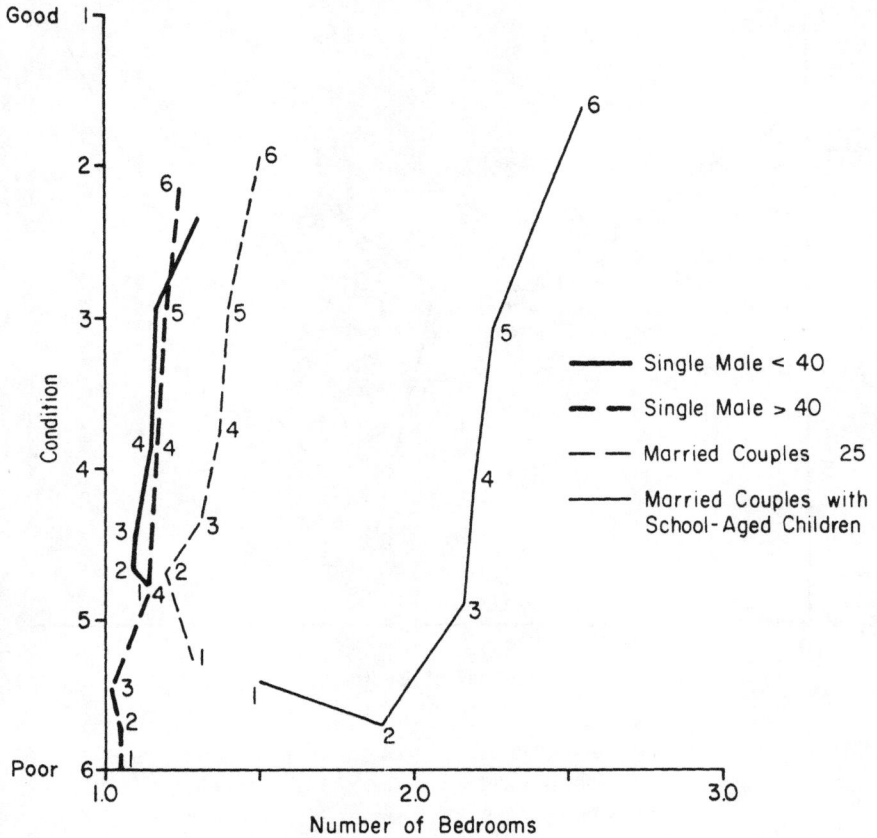

Income classes:
1 = $0 – 1,999   4 = 7,000 – 9,999
2 = 2,000 – 3,999   5 = 10,000 – 14,999
3 = 4,000 – 6,999   6 = 15,000 and over

experiencing some difficulty in acquiring rental units suitable for their space
needs. As compared with renters, the results for home owners suggest that a more
balanced trade-off between the housing attributes occurs as income increases.

It is important to remember that these measures are presented as a class of indicators of existing differentials. At present their properties are not known in the sense that the effects of response bias, and of using this type of categorical data, particularly for income, are unclear. Nevertheless, the general structure of these responses suggests the need for more critical analysis of income elasticity measures if they are to be used as guidelines for anticipating the effects of public programs.

Changes in Levels of Overcrowding

A second class of problem arises in the case of overcrowding of dwellings. Although it is often cited as a major concern for housing policy (e.g., Dennis and Fish, 1972), its definition is almost always in terms of cross-sectional observations such as those provided by the decennial Census. However, as Grigsby and Rosenberg point out (1975: 4),

> Since there is a continual flow of families into and out of an over-crowded status as their household composition changes and as moves are made, cross-sectional data on crowding overstate the problem.

Unfortunately, once we attempt to look beyond this caveat, there is little to enlighten us. Many unanswered questions arise. At what rate do households of different types flow into and out of such a state in different types of neighbourhoods? What would constitute a dynamic measure of the problem and what types of policy inference would ensue? Even more important, how would we conceptualize the process of change in overcrowding in such a way as to facilitate the collection, organization and analysis of appropriate data?

From a planning perspective, a major question concerns the changes in occupancy of the stock in a given neighbourhood. If a policy were to be oriented towards reducing overcrowding, it would be desirable to identify the way in which current processes are affecting existing levels of overcrowding in different neighbourhoods. In order to provide some insights into the nature of these processes, one neighbourhood in Wichita was selected for more detailed analysis using the 1971 and 1972 enumerations which were linked at the individual dwelling level. The area is located in an older segment of the city and its general characteristics are described in table 4. Each dwelling was classified by tenure and by the specific association between dwelling size (measured in number of bedrooms) and household size (in number of persons). Those units having a ratio of greater than two persons per bedroom were classed as overcrowded for the purposes of this study (fig. 14).

At the beginning of 1971, approximately 6 per cent of the one- and two-bedroom owned units were overcrowded, while 10 per cent of rented units were in the same condition. Table 5 indicates what happened to them during the ensu-

TABLE 4

Characteristics of study area, 1970

A	Demographic characteristics	
	Total population	17,512
	Total black population	12
	Average household size	2.57
	Per cent population > 65	12.5
	Per cent population < 18	27.4
	Per cent population > 14 single	18.3
	Per cent same residence 1965	51.9
B	Socio-economic characteristics	
	Median school years	11.6
	Per cent unemployed	9.2
	Median income ($)	7,881
	Per cent below poverty level	10.0
C	Housing characteristics	
	Per cent dwellings owner-occupied	55.2
	Median number of rooms	4.5
	Median persons/dwelling unit	2.2
	Median value ($)	10,440
	Median rent per month ($)	78

SOURCE: U.S. Bureau of the Census, 1970 Census of Population and Housing: Census Tracts -- Wichita, Kansas.

FIGURE 14:

Classification of dwelling units in the study of overcrowding

Dwelling type	Household type	Number of persons in household					Vacant
		1	2	3	4	> 5	
Owned	1 bedroom	1	5	9[a]	13[a]	17[a]	
	2 bedroom	2	6	10	14	18[a]	
	3 bedrooms	3	7	11	15	19	
	4 bedrooms or more	4	8	12	16	20	
							41
Rented	1 bedroom	21	25	29[a]	33[a]	37[a]	
	2 bedroom	22	26	30	34	38[a]	
	3 bedrooms	23	27	31	35	39	
	4 bedrooms or more	24	28	32	36	40	

a   Overcrowded states

TABLE 5

Transition behaviour of overcrowded units, 1971-72

Type		N	Proportions to various states					Per cent overcrowded in dwelling size class
			Demolished	Household moved	Unit not overcrowded	Remained overcrowded		
Owned	1 bedroom (> 2 persons)	25	.04	.20	.20	.56		8.96
	2 bedroom (> 4 persons)	119	.02	.17	.14	.67		4.91
Rented	1 bedroom (> 2 persons)	111	.03	.73	.04	.21		10.53
	2 bedroom (> 4 persons)	113	.04	.55	.07	.34		9.96

TABLE 6

Origins of overcrowded units, 1972

| Type | | N | New construction | Proportions from various states | | | | Per cent overcrowded in dwelling size class |
| | | | | Stayers | | Movers | | |
				No change	Change in household	Previously overcrowded	Not previously overcrowded	
Owned	1 bedroom	18	.06	.78	.06	0	.10	7.14
	2 bedroom	99	.01	.78	.11	.02	.08	4.15
Rented	1 bedroom	91	.04	.25	.09	.12	.50	8.88
	2 bedroom	99	.03	.39	.10	.10	.37	9.10

ing twelve months. The most dramatic finding is that only 65 per cent of the owned units and 27 per cent of the rented units remained in the same state (occupied by the *same* family in overcrowded conditions). Beyond that, further important differences exist with regard to tenure. For renters, the overwhelming number of changes are associated with household relocations, whereas for owner-occupied units changes are about equally divided between relocations and reductions in household size among stayers. In other words, the natural thinning out of an older owner population is just as important as mobility in effecting a reduction in overcrowding in this area.

However, from the point of view of changes in a given neighbourhood, one must also consider the origins of those units which are overcrowded at the end of the period (table 6). Again, there are strong differences between owners and renters: among the former, the dominant source of overcrowded units is provided by those who remain in the same state during the entire twelve months, whereas for renters, households moving into dwellings which were not previously overcrowded constitute a major flow, particularly for one-bedroom units. This observation strongly suggests that some difficulty is being experienced by a significant segment of the population in finding adequately sized units at a reasonable price in the rental market.

The general pattern of contribution to changes in overcrowding is summarized in table 7, in which the role of mobility in rental units is readily apparent, contributing more than 60 per cent of the overall reduction in overcrowding during 1971-72. Further light is cast on these changes in table 8, in which some of the shifts in patterns of overcrowding can be seen as reflecting more basic changes in household size within the area. Among the owned units, the sizes of households which stayed in the area became slightly smaller while the families moving into units in the area were slightly larger (and presumably younger) than those leaving. Among rented units, on the other hand, while stayers remained the same size, the average size of those moving into units was smaller than those moving out.

It would clearly not make a great deal of sense to attempt to provide specific policy recommendations regarding overcrowding based on a study such as this. The definition of overcrowding is far too simplistic for the results to be convincing in a decision-making context, as well as being prone to measurement error. Nevertheless, a number of general conclusions may be drawn which do have important implications for policy:

1. Whatever definition of overcrowding is used, the structure of transactions in a neighbourhood will have a substantial effect on the degree to which overcrowding is regarded as a problem. In this study area, almost 60 per cent of the overcrowded units changed their occupancy state within twelve months. Forty-six per cent of overcrowded units experienced household relocations but only 10 per cent of these remained in an overcrowded state. Thus, it can be argued that

TABLE 7

Contribution of different classes of events to change in overcrowded units, 1971-72

| | Component | Number of overcrowded units | | | Proportionate change in total overcrowding by component |
		A 1971	B 1972	B-A	$\frac{B-A}{TOT. A}$
Owned units	No household relocation	115	103	-12	-.083
	Household relocation	25	12	-13	-.090
	Demolitions/new construction	4	2	- 2	-.013
	Total	144	117	-27	-.188
Rented units	No household relocation	73	80	+ 7	+.031
	Household relocation	143	103	-40	-.179
	Demolitions/new construction	8	7	- 1	-.004
	Total	224	190	-34	-.152

the cross-sectional measure of overcrowding does over-estimate the extent of the problem, although the degree of over-estimation is difficult to determine. To place the overcrowding measure in clearer perspective, it should be pointed out that the overwhelming majority of those units classified as overcrowded fall into two categories: three persons in a one-bedroom unit, and five persons in a two-bedroom unit. In 1972, 286 out of the 307 overcrowded units fell in one of these two categories, and it would be desirable to ascertain from a study in greater depth the extent to which these two conditions are perceived as overcrowded by the occupants.

2. The impact of crowding on movement response without any public sector involvement is clearly demonstrated in figure 15. However, more than 50 per cent of overcrowded units remained in that state, most of them in the owner-occupied sector, and further analysis is required to assess the degree to which various subgroups of these households are unable to gain access to the market.

3. In addition to those overcrowded households which do not move, the number of households which moved into units in an overcrowded state during the year may constitute a further problem. In particular, this observation suggests that a certain segment of the population is unable to find accommodation more suited to its needs.

TABLE 8

Transitions in household sizes, 1971-72

(1) Owned units – stayers

		1972 State					Av. size 1972
		1	2	3	4	5	
1971 State (no. persons)	1	619	28	5	0	1	1.06
	2	63	1325	58	6	3	2.01
	3	4	83	390	41	4	2.92
	4	4	9	38	277	16	3.85
	5	2	3	13	30	267	4.77

Av. household size 1971 = 2.46 1972 = 2.42

(2) Owned units – movers

		1972 State					Av. size 1972
		1	2	3	4	5	
1971 State (no. persons)	1	20	24	6	5	1	1.98
	2	12	34	18	11	5	2.54
	3	1	11	11	8	4	3.09
	4	4	8	7	11	4	3.09
	5	2	10	5	2	14	3.45

Av. household size 1971 = 2.61 1972 = 2.70

(3) Rented units – stayers

		1972 State					Av. size 1972
		1	2	3	4	5	
1		393	19	3	2	1	1.08
2		22	360	29	1	0	2.02
3		2	23	141	19	1	2.97
4		2	2	17	90	13	3.87
5		1	0	2	9	90	4.83

Av. household size 1971 = 2.26 1972 = 2.26

(4) Rented units – movers

		1972 State					Av. size 1972
		1	2	3	4	5	
1		89	77	20	6	2	1.74
2		95	158	58	29	14	2.18
3		31	73	45	27	12	2.55
4		9	33	25	24	11	2.95
5		11	16	18	18	31	3.45

Av. household size 1971 = 2.54 1972 = 2.37

FIGURE 15: Changes in overcrowding, 1971-72

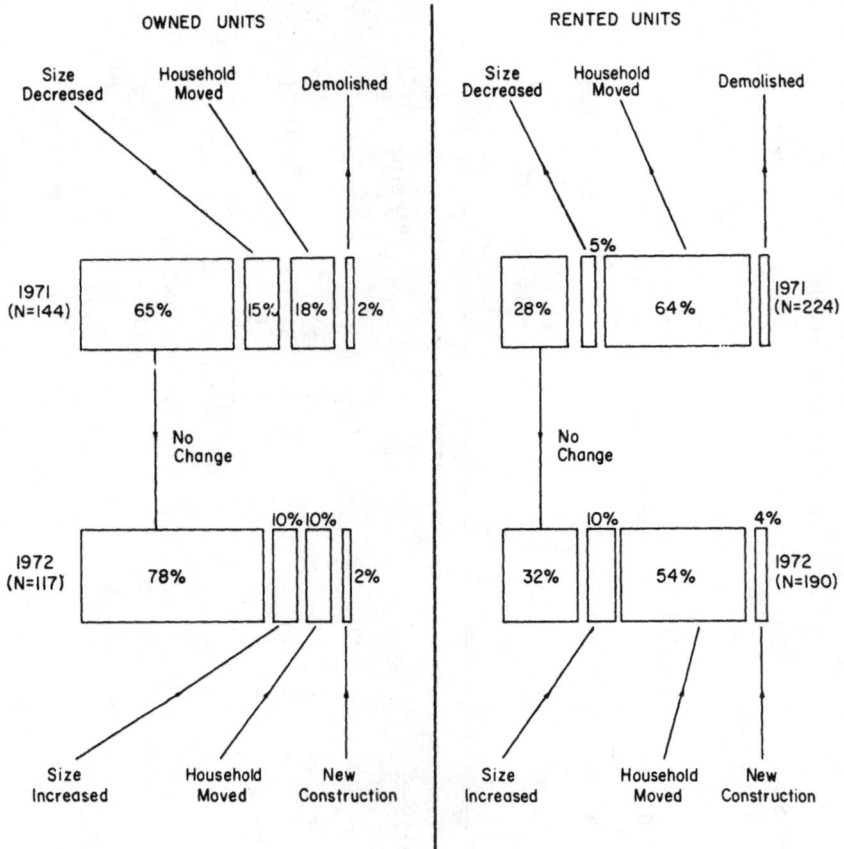

4. The results reported here clearly illustrate the difficulties of evaluating a program aimed at reducing overcrowding. Such a program, initiated in this area in 1971, might have claimed to be successful on the basis that the number of over-crowded units fell by 20 per cent in a single year. Yet, for proper evaluation, it would be necessary to separate the program effects from those changes induced by ongoing demographic and other events, which in this case are entirely re-sponsible for the reduction.

5. From a substantive viewpoint, a main deficiency of the analysis concerns the lack of a more detailed treatment of the composition of the household and, even more important, of information on incomes and prices. A major problem in Wichita seems to be a lack of larger units at a price accessible to low-income households, a situation which will be exacerbated by continued construction of small units in the rental market. However, price and income data are needed to document this argument.

Perhaps the most important outcome is an appreciation of the complexity of the transitions in a single subarea of the city. In an area containing 6,184 households, there were 2,996 transitions involving changes in household, dwelling size and tenure, relocation, and the activities of the construction industry. The bulk of these transitions produced a complex set of balances and counter-balances with relatively small net effects. Yet it is these transitions which will be influenced by any public policy and in order to assess possible effects of different types of programs at the local level, understanding of their structure is desirable together with indicators of how they change over time in different local contexts.

CONCLUSIONS

What have we learnt so far from these and other micro-level analyses of the housing market in Wichita? As might be expected at this stage, our results have mainly served to demonstrate that the extent of many existing housing problems is difficult to measure, that programs would be more effective if directed at specific subgroups rather than very general classes of the population and that it is virtually impossible to say what impact a particular program is having unless one has some conception of the direction in which other processes are carrying the system.

If stronger statements are to be made about such impacts, we also need to associate the type of transitional analysis pursued here with additional data on the nature of public programs and the specifics of their implementation at the neighbourhood level. Certainly, improvements in the data themselves would also be desirable from a theoretical standpoint, particularly with regard to information on household income; however, there are substantial practical problems regarding the types of data which can be collected in an enumeration such as Wichita's, in which responses to the bulk of questions are voluntary.

At a more general level, the development of data bases to support the type of indicators outlined in the above examples is likely to be a slow process. Although there has been a dramatic growth of urban information systems over the last decade (Kraemer, *et al.*, 1976), the great majority have been constructed for administrative rather than planning purposes. Their design is such as to promote efficiency in individual record retrieval and this efficiency is achieved at the expense of the types of uses which planners might envisage (Moore, *et al.*, 1974). The task of building systems which are responsive to the needs of local planners, not only in the area of housing but also in regard to a wide range of public services, is a complex one, including not only problems of gaining access to data which are collected for other purposes, but also of training planners in methods of accessing and using microdata (Moore and Tinline, 1977). However, unless there is the commitment to develop such systems we are likely to continue to experience a considerable gap between theories of housing markets and the needs of planners and policy makers in rapidly changing, institutionally bound local environments.

NOTES

1 The recent work by Hanushek and Quigley (1976) and by the Rand Corporation (Lowry, 1976) are obvious exceptions.

2 For details of the enumeration structure and associated procedures, see Gschwind (1973).

3 The original questions relating to income record responses by income classes. Estimates for income responses to each consumption variable (rent, number of bedrooms, conditions, etc.) were obtained over the nth income range using the relation

$$n_n = \frac{\log(^{y}h_{(n+1)}/^{y}h_n)}{\log(i_{n+1}/i_n)}$$

where $y_{h_{(j)}}$ is the average value of the hth consumption variable for the jth income class. This procedure produces lower values then the true ones. A second set of estimates were derived for selected groups by computing the average income for specific housing consumption categories (of value, rent, size, etc.). These estimates are generally higher than the true values but, for the purposes of this discussion, they retain the same general order properties over different income groups and household types.

REFERENCES

De Leeuw, F. 1971. "The Demand for Housing: A Review of Cross-Sectional Evidence". *Review of Economics and Statistics*, 53, 1: 1-10.

Dennis, M., and S. Fish. 1972. *Programs in Search of a Policy*. Toronto: Hakkert.

Duncan, G., and S. Newman. 1975. "People as Planners: The Fulfillment of Residential Mobility Expectations". Chapter 8 in G. Duncan and J.

N. Morgan, eds., *Five Thousand American Families: Patterns of Economic Progress,* Vol. 3, Ann Arbor: Institute of Social Research.

Duncan, S.S. 1976. "Research Directions in Social Geography: Housing Opportunities and Constraints", *Transactions of the Institute of British Geographers* (New Series), 1, 1: 10-19.

Dunn, E.S., Jr. 1974. *Social Information Processing and Statistical Systems – Change and Reform.* New York: John Wiley.

Forrest, R. 1976. "Monitoring: Some Conceptual Issues in Relation to Housing Research". *Working paper no. 42,* Centre for Urban and Regional Studies, University of Birmingham.

Glick, P.C., and R. Parke. 1965. "New Approaches in Studying the Life-Cycle of the Family", *Demography,* 2: 187-202.

Grigsby, W.G., and L. Rosenberg. 1975. *Urban Housing Policy.* Center for Urban Policy Research, Rutgers University, New Brunswick, N.J.

Gschwind, R.A. 1973. "The Intergovernmental Enumeration, Wichita-Sedgewick County, 1971-1973". *Working paper no. 2,* Research on Metropolitan Change and Conflict Resolution, Peace Science Department, University of Pennsylvania.

Hanushek, E.A., and J.M. Quigley. 1976. "A Stock Adjustment Model of Residential Mobility". Paper presented at the Mathematical Social Sciences Board Seminar on Models of Residential Mobility, University of California, Los Angeles.

Harvey, D. 1974. "Class-Monopoly, Rent, Finance Capital and the Urban Revolution", *Regional Studies,* 8: 239-255.

Heilbroner, R.L., and A. Ford. 1971. *Is Economics Relevant?* Pacific Palisades, Calif.: Goodyear.

Holm, P. 1967. "A Disaggregated Housing Market Model", in A.A. Nevitt, ed., *The Economic Problems of Housing.* London: Macmillan.

Kraemer, K.L., J.N. Danziger, and J.L. King. 1976. "Information Technology and Urban Management in the United States". *Working paper no. 76-14,* Public Policy Research Organization, University of California, Irvine.

Land, K.C. 1975. "Social Indicator Models: An Overview", in K.C. Land and S. Silerman, eds., *Social Indicator Models.* New York: Russell Sage.

Lowry, I.R. 1976. "The Housing Assistance Supply Experiment: An Overview". *Papers of the Regional Science Association,* 37: 21-30.

Moore, E.G. 1977. "The Impact of Residential Mobility on Population Characteristics at the Neighbourhood Level". Department of Geography, Queen's University, Kingston, Ontario (mimeographed).

Moore, E.G., *et al.* 1974. "The Role of Micro-Level Data Systems in the Urban Planning Process: A Comment and a Case Study". *Proceedings of the Fourth European Symposium on Urban Data Management,* Madrid.

Moore, E.G. and R. Tinline. 1977. *The PRISSA Project: An Overview.* Population Research on Information Systems for Small Areas, Department of Geography, Queen's University, Kingston, Ontario.

Niner, P. 1976. "A Review of Approaches to Estimating Housing Needs", *Working paper no. 41,* Centre for Urban and Regional Studies, University of Birmingham.

Paldam, M. 1970. "What is Known about the Housing Demand", *Swedish Journal of Economics,* 2: 130-148.

Scriven, M. 1959. "The Covering Law Position: A Critique and an Alternative Analysis", in P. Gardiner, ed., *Theories of History.* New York: Free Press.

Straszheim, M.H. 1975. *An Econometric Analysis of the Urban Housing Market.* New York: National Bureau of Economic Research.

Symons, D.C. 1974. "An Urban Information System". *Proceedings of the Fourth European Symposium on Urban Data Management,* Madrid.

VI

Social Policy Considerations

Albert Rose

All housing policy is social policy in the sense that it is designed to help people meet a basic human need. Moreover, housing policy is societal in nature since the decisions of major private entrepreneurs, as well as significant agencies of the several levels of government in a federal state, affect the entire society.

In Canada such enunciation of policy and consequent legislation for nearly fifty years have had both economic and social objectives. At one time, the economic objective may have been predominant; at other times, more attention was directed towards social objectives. In most years the capital investment in what has come to be known as "social housing" was quite insignificant by comparison with investment in private housing markets.

Nevertheless, for the past two decades at least, Canadians have maintained a rather simplified and even naive view of housing markets. The upper third in the distribution of total family incomes on a national, regional or local scale were considered able to meet their housing requirements with their own resources and arrangements with the lending institutions. The middle third were judged to be those for whom the mortgage insurance and home ownership provisions of the National Housing Act (NHA) were intended. The lower third of families and individuals in the income distribution were the obvious beneficiaries of socially assisted, or "public," housing. In fact, their clear disadvantage in income and social functioning were considered by many to be the sole justification for state intervention in the field of social housing.

In the 1970s this tri-partite conception has little or no meaning. A large proportion of families in the total distribution are eligible for governmental assistance in obtaining housing. As far as social housing is concerned there are notable changes in progress which cast doubt upon most previous assumptions. These changes involve primarily a shift from principal attention on the family, towards the elderly and other special groups of disadvantaged persons; a shift from rental accommodation to home ownership involving a government investment in continued high rates of price inflation; a shift from centralized authority to decentralization in the administration and management of socially assisted housing; and, inevitably, a return to deep concern with expanding levels of housing subsidy, not merely in the current time period, but looking ahead to the end of the century and beyond.

BACKGROUND TO CHANGE

Social housing policy in Canada may be dated from 1949, when the National Housing Act was amended to permit the government of Canada to make agreements with the governments of the provinces to provide houses for sale or for rent with consequent potential financial losses. Both the capital expenditures and the anticipated losses (that is, subsidies) were to be shared on a 75-25 per cent basis between the two senior levels of government.

The federal-provincial partnership remained from 1950 until the major amendments to the legislation passed in 1964. Despite a great deal of attention to the needs of residents in so-called "blighted" or slum areas, and to the problems inherent in what was first called "housing redevelopment", then later "urban redevelopment" and finally "urban renewal" in the new National Housing Act 1954, relatively little was produced in fifteen years of joint government endeavour. It has been estimated that little more than 10,000 dwelling units were built in Canada as a consequence of the 1949 amendments and changes in the legislation over the next ten years.

There was thus great anticipation in 1963-64 when it was known that long-awaited amendments to the 1954 Act would be introduced in the federal parliament. The year 1964 was auspicious for many reasons: Canada appeared to be emerging from a severe economic recession which began some six years earlier. There was a new spirit within the country as a new government assumed responsibility with a majority in parliament after several years of minority government. Moreover, the 1964 amendments to the National Housing Act appeared to represent a degree of decentralization never before experienced in Canadian housing history.

The national government and its agency, Central Mortgage and Housing Corporation (CMHC), appeared ready to loosen the controls which had been exercised for nearly twenty years and which encompassed every detail of social housing administration from site selection through architectural design to the awarding of contracts and supervision of the process of construction until takeover. Tenant selection and occupancy required the federal authorities to turn over the completed housing to the administration and management of federal-provincial housing authorities. It was assumed that the entire process in a specific project could scarcely be achieved in less than five years.

The 1964 amendments led directly to the formation of the Ontario Housing Corporation (OHC) and within four years to the incorporation of several additional provincial housing corporations. The provinces were beginning to assume responsibilities which had been assigned to them by interpretation of the British North America Act, responsibilities which they had substantially neglected prior to 1950, and which they had scarcely been encouraged to assume in the ensuing fifteen years. The new legislation promised the largest proportion of capital advances for social housing ever offered by the federal agency, and although the federal share of the ultimate subsidies was reduced to 50 per cent, the provinces were encouraged to proceed with an expansion of public activity in the housing market on behalf of the most disadvantaged individuals and families in their community, specifically the so-called "low-income groups ".

While there was no hysterical rush during the next four years to build vast quantities of housing accommodation for those unable to provide decent, adequate and safe accommodation for themselves and their families, most provincial administrations were being organized for a substantial expansion of housing starts to be financed under the new arrangements. In Ontario, by 1967, the Ontario Housing Corporation had reached a state of organization and development whereby its role in the market for land and for construction was beginning to be felt. Moreover, it had evolved new techniques of direct purchase and acceptance of builders' proposals which enabled it to expand the quantity of public housing rapidly within a relatively short time.

Nevertheless, the federal authorities seemed uneasy about the capacity of federal-provincial co-operation to meet the enormous backlog of housing accommodation required by families and individuals throughout the income distribution. In 1968 the new Prime Minister, Pierre Trudeau, appointed the Honourable Paul Hellyer to chair a Task Force on Housing and Urban Development which reported within five months of its initiation. The Task Force questioned every facet of Canadian housing policy but was particularly harsh in its condemnation of two aspects which directly concerned social housing: the public housing program and the urban renewal program.

As far as public housing was concerned (that is, direct governmental intervention in the housing market to provide accommodation for low-income persons and families through direct construction, outright purchase or renovation of existing housing), the Task Force deplored the numerous and unmistakable multiple dwellings, often in high-rise form. In its wisdom the Task Force had re-discovered the basic desire of most North American families to "own their own home". It called for the creation of public housing accommodation in low-rise structures with every family having its front door on the street and its own living space in a private rear garden.

In the case of urban renewal the Task Force accepted, without serious question, the argument that the redevelopment of deteriorated areas adjacent to the central business districts in many Canadian cities could only be accomplished through the destruction of a significant portion of the existing housing stock. It recognized that urban renewal did result in the dislocation of some individuals and families and presented a problem in relocation which most local communities found it impossible to solve. The Chairman of the Task Force, who had been designated as "Minister Responsible for Housing", ordered a "freeze" on urban renewal projects and halted their progress for the better part of the ensuing six years.

Although Mr. Hellyer resigned when the report of the Task Force was not accepted by the federal cabinet, the recommendations of his group have had a profound influence to this very day. The Task Force recommended the creation of a Department of Housing and Urban Affairs within the governmental structure of Canada and urged that urban development be recognized as a matter of urgent priority by the government. This objective would be realized in part with the creation in 1971 of a Ministry of State for Urban Affairs, to be headed by a member of the cabinet to whom Central Mortgage and Housing Corporation would be responsible.

It has not been widely recognized that the decade since the appointment of the federal Task Force on Housing and Urban Development has been the occasion for deliberate and very significant shifts in national and provincial social housing policies. Most of these contradict the basic assumptions of the quarter century since the passage of the National Housing Act 1944 and the creation of Central Mortgage and Housing Corporation in 1945. They do represent the quiet implementation of several of the most significant recommendations of the Task Force of 1968-69. Despite the major studies and initiatives launched by the new Ministry of State from 1971 through 1975, almost every substantial change in policy can be found within the Task Force Report.

THE FALL OF THE FAMILY FROM FAVOUR

During the four decades from the early 1930s through the late 1960s the notion of "family" appeared to assume a position of centrality within both public (governmental) and private (market) housing policies. There was little or no doubt that the beneficiary of housing policies and programs ought to be the family, defined as two parents with one or more dependent children and perhaps one or more persons related by blood or marriage, living together in the same household. These arrangements were considered both the normal and the desirable state of social development within the society. Since the proportion of persons over age 65 was less than 7 per cent in the 1930s and 1940s, the housing requirements of the elderly were not considered to have the same priority. Similarly, since there was little or no sympathy for the unmarried mother who wished to retain her child, or for the separated or divorced person with responsibility for dependent children, little or no thought was given to the housing requirements of these groups. Rather, the twin thrusts of economic benefit consequent upon the re-housing of disadvantaged families from the most inadequate housing were considered the top, if not the only, policy priorities.

Within the last decade, these emphases have been altered. The reasons for a shift away from the centrality of the family within housing policy towards other priorities are once again both economic and social in origin. Economic problems of the 1970s in North America — unemployment and inflation proceeding simultaneously — are very different from those of the pre-war period. Moreover, the social circumstances in which a great many family units or households now find themselves are quite different from those which were the norm in the pre-war period. Whatever the explanation, there can be little doubt that the family as such, and particularly the low-income family, has lost its position of highest priority within public and private housing policies.

A "family of low income" is defined in the National Housing Act as a family that receives a total family income that, in the opinion of the Corporation (CMHC), is insufficient to permit it to rent housing accommodation adequate for its needs at the current rental market in the area in which the family lives. In several of the major legislative acts passed by the governments of the provinces in recent years, this definition has been expanded to include the possibility of purchase of housing rather than simply rental within their jurisdictions. It is significant that the federal definition does not include this concept, partly because it seems to imply that families of low income are expected to be tenants rather than home owners. Paradoxically, a good many of the federal-provincial housing programs initiated in the 1970s are intended to enable families with quite modest incomes to assume the responsibilities of home ownership.

A significant proportion of so-called "low income" families are in receipt of social assistance payments made available through federal-provincial or provincial-municipal social welfare programs. In fact, for the poorest 20 per cent of families in 1971, about one-third of total income was earned as wages and salaries and almost half was received as payments by governments, either through universal transfer programs such as family allowances and old age security allowances, or through direct social assistance payments.[1] While it is true that an important proportion of such families in the lowest income levels do occupy satisfactory housing, particularly elderly persons and couples, the evidence in both urban and rural areas points conclusively to the fact that the condition of housing and income levels are directly related. The poorest housing in every community is occupied by the poorest families; since the poorest families often include larger numbers of children than the average, they tend to be crowded and their needs for the basic physical amenities are often unmet. It is these families to whom, in the years 1945-64, most attention was paid when the concepts of slum clearance, urban redevelopment and urban renewal were under consideration, both for purposes of program definition and for purposes of program implementation.

The housing conditions of Canada's native peoples are generally the most unsatisfactory and indeed deplorable within the nation. When substantial numbers of members of such groups migrate to urban centres, as in the case of Winnipeg, Regina and Toronto, they move almost immediately to the bottom of the socio-economic distribution, exist for the most part with income provided through public social welfare programs, and occupy some of the poorest housing in the nation. This is not so evident in Toronto where a group of native people, Wigwamen Incorporated, formed a non-profit housing company which, with federal and provincial funds, has purchased accomodation which it rents to families within its community (Ontario, Ministry of Housing, 1976: 15).

It can readily be understood, therefore, that Canadian families of lowest income, of largest size, or where one of the two parents is deceased or has left the family unit, constitute the majority of applicants for public housing accomodation throughout the ten provinces. If, as seems desirable, the housing management organization created under federal-provincial-municipal or provincial auspices considers the need for housing as the prime determinant in selecting families for accommodation in relatively scarce public housing, the social situation in such housing projects becomes a deterrent to normal family life on the one hand, and an obstacle to further public participation in housing programs on the other.

There are, depending upon the definition used, perhaps 150,000 publicly provided non-institutional dwelling units available for "low-income families" throughout this country. At the same time, there are approximately one-half million one-parent families (Canada, Ministry of State for Urban Affairs, 1976: 5), most of whom have relatively little income and would score highly on any point rating system designed to determine priority for public housing accomodation. It is thus entirely conceivable that every public housing dwelling unit in Canada could be occupied by a one-parent family, if need were the sole criterion.

Alternatively, the needs of the elderly in Canada for decent and adequate housing accommodation are substantial, when one considers that more than half of all Canadian individuals over the age of 65 are in receipt of some guaranteed income supplement determined on a means test, over and above the basic old age security allowance. Elderly couples and individuals might well occupy a great deal more of the available public housing accommodation if need were the only criterion. In both cases, however, need is not the only criterion because the desirability of social viability (community) within the housing project itself is central in the thinking of every intelligent public housing administrator and because the size of the available accommodation is a factor which must be taken into consideration.

More important perhaps than these observations is the fact that the nature and distribution of poverty in Canada is such that antagonism has developed towards the nuclear family, particularly in its role as applicant for public housing. Not only have many municipalities who must initiate the requests for intergovernmental housing activity throughout the country been overly cautious, but often entirely discriminatory in their choice of housing programs so as to exclude poor families, whether headed by one or two parents. The reasons for such discrimination are entirely clear from a management standpoint, but from a policy point of view are entirely unacceptable.

HOUSING DEMAND: CHANGING SOCIAL PATTERNS

In addition to these factors there are other personal social innovations which affect strongly the relationship between supply and demand in the housing market. There are a great many more non-family households than ever before and they are of unusual composition. Twenty or thirty years ago, a non-family household might consist of two sisters, one sibling taking care of another sibling of the opposite sex in their old age, a son or daughter living with an elderly parent and providing care and support. The household compositions now so prevalent were relatively unknown.

Today, a unit of demand for housing may come forward from households composed of two, three or four persons of the same sex who are unrelated; they may come from common-law partners without children; they may come from single persons who in the affluence of the 1960s or early 1970s would have been able to accumulate the capital required for a downpayment on a single-detached or condominium home, certainly sufficient resources to rent a privately marketed apartment. Whatever the nature of the households which constitute the demand for housing units, the facts are that first, the nuclear family is no longer the pre-eminent source of demand for housing for sale or for rent,[2] and second, the newly constituted households of the 1970s demand a somewhat different type of housing accommodation. Their requirement is usually a set of spaces and facilities which would not meet the requirements of the traditional family of parents and children.

It cannot be argued, with the exception of the situation in certain housing markets at certain times within certain communities, that the housing demands of these new types of social arrangements have made it impossible for families to acquire housing accommodation. But it is certainly worth arguing that these new demands have induced investors in housing development to concentrate their energies in meeting the requirements of these new markets, rather than to continue building accommodation that might be more adequate for traditional family requirements. Moreover it is possible that this shift, which became evident in the early 1960s, did reduce the push towards innovation in housing construction which might have reduced the cost of traditional family housing. These tentative arguments will never be settled because it is a fact that the entire Canadian housing demand-supply situation changed relatively suddenly and very strongly in the early 1960s in the direction of multiple housing, primarily for rental, rather than single-detached housing, primarily for sale.

It is worth while, then, to separate out the private market from the public or assisted housing sector. In the private market, the housing industry responded very quickly after 1960 to the changing demands of the newly formed family or household types by shifting the kind of construction in which it was engaged. It would not have done this if it were not a fact that multiple housing in high-rise form in the large urban centre was far more profitable than the building of four or five single-family detached homes on an acre of ground in the typical suburban municipality. High-rise apartment buildings, which became particularly evident by the mid-1960s throughout Canada's twenty-three census metropolitan areas, were both an economic and a social response to changing family conditions.

In the public sector, however, which combines a mixture of self-interest and charitable impluses on the part of local politicians, local community groups and elected representatives in higher levels of governments, the changes in the family were not so welcome. Fewer and fewer intact families consisting of two parents and one or more dependent children presented themselves as candidates for public housing accommodation. By the mid-1970s, in Ontario at least, applications from one-parent families headed by a woman constituted from one-half to two-thirds of all applications received by public housing registries in the medium-sized and larger urban centres. In 1971, 80 percent of all single-parent families were headed by a woman but in the crucial area of publicly provided accommodation for low income families the proportion of applicants from one-parent families includes fewer than five families per hundred headed by a male. These facts, together with the point rating systems which have been developed to evaluate the needs of applicants for housing accommodation, could lead directly to a form of social segregation which the community would not countenance, even if there were not strong tendencies towards discrimination at work.

Although elected and appointed officials have been assured again and again that only a very small proportion of families in social housing are troublesome (perhaps 2 to 3 per cent), they have toured housing projects in various provinces, particularly in Ontario, and they do not like what they see. What they like to see is well-maintained, well-trimmed, beautifully painted apartment buildings such as those inhabited by families in the upper 15 per cent of the Canadian income distribution. What they do see is some of the evidence of poverty; the difficulties of maintaining property in its "spanking new" condition, the well-used outdoor spaces and facilities, the occasional evidence of vandalism, and the kinds of pressures on physical structures which come about as a result of densities per dwelling unit of five or six or more persons. Moreover, the decision-makers, primarily the elected and appointed officials of local government, have discovered a much safer group upon which to devote their energies and their charitable instincts; specifically, our increasingly large elderly population.

The evidence is now clearly at hand and some figures may be of interest. Table 1 illustrates the declining numbers and proportions of family housing and the increasing share of senior citizens' accommodation within the public housing programs initiated in Ontario, the province in which the greatest activity has occurred since 1951. It is clearly evident that the construction of new accommodation for low-income families in Canada's most populous province has almost dried up. The situation may be more noticeable outside the municipality of Metropolitan Toronto in terms of numbers but within Metro itself the situation is quite clear. In a word, family accommodation within public housing is out of favour with local initiating bodies and little or no pressure is being exerted by provincial governments in the late 1970s to reverse this trend.

On the other hand, almost everyone is pleased that elderly couples and single elderly individuals are attracting the bulk of attention and that most new housing accommodation is provided for them. Such persons are uniformly grateful, do not have children, cause very few problems of operation and management, pay their rent on time, and are rarely engaged in vandalism or other anathemas to public housing management.

HOME OWNERSHIP OR RENTAL HOUSING FOR LOW-INCOME AND MODERATE-INCOME FAMILIES

The response of governments, both the government of Canada and the governments of several provinces, to this situation has not been to create additional public rental housing for families whose incomes would be judged to be in the lower middle or the upper segment of the lowest third of the income distribution. Such programs as the Assisted Home Ownership (AHOP), launched in 1973, and the provincial equivalents were designed to push the capacity for home ownership down the income distribution to the lower portions of the middle third or even below.

The reasoning of the federal government was clearly stated in its written presentation to Habitat:

> Throughout most of the country, home ownership has been viewed as a social good, conferring stability on both communities and families. When, suddenly, it is no longer possible for many persons of average and even well-above average incomes to become home owners it is natural to conclude that something is seriously awry (Canada, Ministry of State for Urban Affairs, 1976: 15).

TABLE 1

Public housing provided for families and senior citizens — Ontario, 1951-76[a]

	1951-71	1972	1973	1974	1975	1976
Completions under federal-provincial and OHC programs						
Metro Toronto						
Family	13,300	2,370	4,785[c]	1,994	776	57
Senior citizen[b]	–	–	–	–	–	–
Balance Ontario						
Family	14,540	1,267	1,321	1,198	521	331
Senior citizen	8,370	3,537	3,343	3,167	5,515	3,555
Acquired by purchase of take-over						
Metro Toronto						
Family	5,885	141	–	28	24	132
Senior citizen	–	–	–	–	–	–
Balance Ontario						
Family	252	24	48	242	224	108
Senior citizen	283	–	–	–	–	–
Sub-total	42,630	7,339	9,497	6,429	7,060	4,183

SOURCE: Ontario Housing Corporation

a Excludes dwelling units acquired through Rent Supplement and Accelerated Family Rental Housing Programs

b Municipality of Metropolitan Toronto is responsible for Senior Citizens in Metro Toronto. Housing stock approximates 9,000 units.

Canada was primarily a nation of home owners when the National Housing Act was first amended in 1949 to permit intergovernmental arrangements in the public provision of housing accommodation at rentals below the amortized economic cost. It is a major paradox of Canadian housing history that low-income families and individuals were destined to become tenants in social housing accommodation at a time when most tenants were in the middle and upper income groups. Perhaps it was believed that most occupants of "blighted" or "slum" areas who would have priority for re-housing, were tenants. Perhaps it was judged that Canadians in the lower third of the income distribution could not possibly meet the payments or assume the responsibilities of home ownership, despite the fact that many were already home owners.

The major consequence of these assumptions, specifically the need to develop entirely new administrative arrangements and procedures for housing management, was not fully considered or perhaps not understood. The problems inherent in managing thousands of publicly provided dwelling units for families and elderly persons in the 1970s could not be visualized in the early 1950s, nor in 1964 when the legislation was amended to encourage the provinces to exercise their constitutional and social responsibilities.

By the late 1950s, three major socio-economic considerations began to play interrelated roles in the Canadian housing market which ultimately led to fundamental changes in national social housing policies. The first of these was the fact that the apartment building boom, which started about 1959, was beginning to run its course. Appropriate land sites were more difficult to acquire as urbanization proceeded rapidly in most large Canadian centres.

Citizen resistance in the form of neighbourhood opposition to the building of high-rise multiple dwellings was a second and strong factor in increasing the difficulty developers faced in building rental accommodation. Citizen opposition was matched within the elected local councils by legislators who were beginning to espouse the philosophy of "no growth" or a "steady state" within the development of Canadian cities. These twin pressures, from without and within elected councils, forced planning boards and their appointed officials to examine more carefully applications for building permits for multiple dwellings and to insist upon demanding physical and social requirements if such plans were to be acceptable.

The third factor of substantial importance was the aforementioned Report of the Task Force on Housing and Urban Development which recommended, in January 1969, that most Canadians should be enabled to own their own homes. This would be accomplished through the development of innovative techniques whereby working-class families would acquire an equity in their own housing accommodation.

The combination of these three factors, apparently relatively weak before

1970, became almost irresistible within a very few years. AHOP, as with almost all Canadian housing programs, had both economic and social objectives. The house building industry was depressed in the early 1970s since most builders were unable to find sufficient land and financing for more than a few detached and semi-detached homes for sale each year. Moreover, the price of houses for purchase was increasing rapidly throughout most Canadian urban centres. These facts meant that families in the lower middle income group and, indeed, in the lower half of the distribution of Canadian family incomes were increasingly unable to finance the purchase of housing accommodation.

In these circumstances AHOP made sense both in the economic and social spheres. It gave the house building industry a substantial boost which carried it forward for approximately three years until the supply of houses for sale began to exceed the demand to a substantial degree in 1976. In socio-economic terms AHOP provided an opportunity for many families to enter the housing market because it required maximum prices which varied from locality to locality and could be raised or lowered from time to time depending on changes in the cost of labour, materials and, above all, money. Moreover, these maximum prices were about 20-25 per cent below the average sale prices indicated by Multiple Listing Services in most Canadian cities

AHOP is a program with a considerable social impact, not merely because it enabled some families in the lower middle income group and in the working class (upper third of the lower third in the income distribution) to purchase houses but because it provides subsidies which, at least in theory, enable home ownership to be possible for families with as little as one-half to two-thirds of the average family income in specific localities. This was accomplished by the device of a repayable interest reduction loan offered by the Central Mortgage and Housing Corporation on behalf of the government of Canada, and "piggy backing" on the part of several Canadian provinces. This system of a double layer of subsidies, in which certain provinces such as Nova Scotia and Saskatchewan were involved as early as 1974, was a serious attempt to offer modest-income and low-income Canadian families (the working poor) a choice between assisted social housing for families on a rent-geared-to-income basis, and home ownership, with the opportunity of living in a neighbourhood of their choice in many communities, rather than in areas developed by local housing authorities with the assistance of provincial housing corporations.

At the time AHOP was launched, first mortgage rates in Canada were 12 per cent or slightly more per annum. The interest reduction provision offered a loan to qualified home purchasers, at a reduced interest rate of 8 per cent for the first five years of the mortgage. During the sixth year of the mortgage there would be no repayment of this loan. Beginning with the seventh year of amortization the home purchaser is required to meet mortgage payments at the market rate for first

mortgages then prevailing, together with a monthly payment for five years to re-
pay the interest reduction loan.

At the same time the government of Canada offered, in the first period of the
plan, an outright subsidy or grant of $300 per annum to reduce further the monthly
shelter cost of these home purchases and thus permit families with lower incomes
to enter the market. As inflation proceeded, this annual subsidy was raised to
$600 and is currently $750. In the various provinces additional grants were made
available to AHOP purchasers and in Ontario, in 1976-77, the Ministry of Housing
announced that it would match the federal subsidy. In making the announcement
the Minister expressed the conviction that families with a little less than $7,000 per
annum in total family income might conceivably become home purchasers in
certain communities.

This program is significant as an expression of public-private co-operation in the
development of housing accommodation for families who would normally be part
of a rental market in which, after 1972, there has been little or no accommodation to
rent, and certainly little accommodation – at any price – adequate for families with
more than three children.

Social housing policy has now changed dramatically from rental accommodation in
large apartments for low-income families to an emphasis upon home ownership for
a relatively wide band of families with incomes ranging from one-third to two-thirds
of the average family income in major urban centres. Since it is clearly dependent
upon the continuance of inflation, this changing social emphasis has built-in difficulties which make it a very dangerous program for families in the lowest income
group. It is unfortunate that a national social housing policy is in effect "betting on"
inflation. Repayment of the interest reduction loan without hardship is dependent
upon an increase in the income of the home purchaser over the first five years of
mortgage repayment. Moreover, such increase in income must be sufficient to enable
the purchaser to continue to pay back the mortgage at a higher rate, plus an additional repayment of the interest reduction loan from the seventh to the eleventh
year.

Perhaps the government is facing reality and recognizes that it does not have the
capacity to contain inflationary increases in the price level. Nevertheless, those
families in the lowest income group of AHOP purchasers cannot count upon a com-
mensurate increase in their income, either because they lack the skills required in an
industrial society or lack stability in their work record to enable them to predict a
steadily rising annual income. It is not a prospect without worry for all partners in
the process – the purchaser, the governmental authority and the taxpayer at large who
may ultimately be required to "bail out" those faced with default.

The shift from rental accommodation to home ownership for the lowest 40 per
cent of families classified by total family income has a further significant economic
impact in the housing market. It has already been noted that major construction

firms were moving away from multiple dwellings to investment in non-residential op-oportunities including shopping centres and the purchase of commercial buildings both within Canada and the United States. The AHOP program has had some effect in shifting the house building industry from apartment building to home building and to continued investment in home ownership residential accommodation. It would be naive to suggest that the largest apartment builders of the period 1959-72 have become builders of small groups of AHOP-financed homes for purchase. It cannot be denied, however, that many small and moderate-size house building organizations have been able to continue in existence by virtue of the AHOP program; and some new building organizations have entered the field to take advantage of these financial o$_{\text{f}}$ portunities and to meet the requirements of one sector of the infinitely complex housing market.

FROM CENTRALIZATION TO DECENTRALIZATION

It was previously asserted that, in practice, the federal-provincial partnership in social housing (1950-64) involved strong centralization by virtue of the assumed roles of the Central Mortgage and Housing Corporation. This was true despite the affirmation that local or regional governments must accept responsibility for initiation, and local (federal-provincial) housing authorities (LHAs) must administer and manage the completed housing. In reality the LHAs accepted the buildings and were forced to accommodate themselves to the structures, the locations, the site plans, the families who had applied for tenancy and all the rules for management that were laid down by the senior levels of government.

The period of hegemony of the provincial housing corporations, commencing in 1965 and by no means ended, meant decentralization from the federal to provincial political and administrative structures. Within the provinces, however, a further process of centralization became evident as the provincial governments, through their housing corporations, sought to standardize local policies, procedures and managerial techniques. In British Columbia the local housing authorities were eliminated; in Ontario, the Metropolitan Toronto Housing Authority was absorbed by the Ontario Housing Corporation and field manuals governing local authority participation in the process of development and management were revised and tightened.

In Ontario, moreover, direct management from OHC head office was instituted in areas where social housing was built but in which no local housing authority existed. This process was further strengthened after 1972 when branches (district offices) were opened in six key urban centres (Ottawa, London and Sudbury, for example) to assist and to monitor the operations of local housing authorities as well as to advise local and regional governments.

Within the past three years the government of Ontario, through its Ministry of Housing, has announced its determination to decentralize responsibility for the development, operation and management of social housing. Local governments have been advised that they may elect to assume the provincial role, seek a 90 per cent loan from the federal Corporation, provide the remaining 10 per cent capital contribution, choose sites, award contracts, operate and manage the completed housing and ultimately own the buildings. If they choose to pursue this course they may engage the OHC as operational and management consultant. On the other hand, local governments may elect to continue the process in effect since 1965 whereby the OHC receives and implements the local request for social housing.

At the same time direct management from Corporation headquarters or through the branches is to be discontinued in favour of operation and management by new housing authorities where required or by extended responsibility of existing LHAs. This decision was taken by the Ministry as early as 1974 and a Housing Authorities Expansion Program was initiated. The program encompasses a variety of possibilities: housing authorities covering an entire regional government area or an entire municipality where no authority existed previously; new authorities covering all or part of a municipal jurisdiction and superseding existing housing authorities; expanded existing authorities covering larger geographical responsibilities with or without existing bodies to be superseded; new authorities covering entire counties while absorbing several existing housing authorities; and other permutations and combinations. Fifty-one housing authorities were in operation by October 1, 1977. This was a substantial increase in number despite the fact that more than twenty older authorities were superseded by new organizations. The number of housing authorities in Ontario is expected to reach sixty-five by 1979.

Creation of new authorities and expansion of established bodies has been accompanied by a delegation of financial and administrative responsibilities not previously undertaken by local housing authorities in existence for one or two decades. Apparently the Ministry means business but the impacts of these important policy changes in Ontario remain a matter for conjecture. Past experience throughout Canada provides a basis for one worrisome observation: local housing authorities with significant power and capacity to implement decisions can and often do ignore federal-provincial social housing policies, particularly in the field of human rights, and operate their portfolios like miniature principalities buttressed by punitive value judgments. In the years of the federal-provincial partnership both Halifax and Windsor, for example, with a significant proportion of black people in the population, recorded very few black tenants for whatever reason.

The danger is that decentralization of major authority to the local level will reinforce tendencies in the tenant selection process which are negative towards poor intact families, one-parent families, deviant individuals and, indeed, children. There is little doubt that antagonism towards the family and emphasis upon housing for senior citizens reflect the views of men and women in the upper middle socio-economic group who are most likely to be appointed to board membership on local housing authorities by elected officials representing the three levels of government.

RENEWED CONCERN RESPECTING FINANCIAL SUBSIDIES

In the early years of public housing activity the federal Corporation was greatly concerned with the per unit per month subsidy required to operate and maintain social housing. By virtue of CMHC's control of the process of development it could reject or modify architectural designs and construction specifications to maintain the difference between estimated costs and projected revenues (rentals) within specified limits. There has never been a satisfactory explanation of the fact that for several years the specified maximum per unit per month subsidy was $25.00. Perhaps this was a nice round figure but it was no mere target or guideline. Projects were approved and constructed, or severely redesigned and even rejected, on the matter of acceptable or excessive subsidy. By the late 1950s the limit was raised to $42.00 per unit per month, in recognition of the increase in construction costs and the difficulty of projecting subsidies years ahead of actual building construction and completion.

When the OHC and other provincial housing corporations expanded the quantity of social housing rapidly in the late 1960s and early 1970s, the issue of total dollar losses to be met by the several levels of government seemed of little concern. Price inflation throughout the economy and within the construction industry during the last five years has caused a significant change in attitude. On the one hand, the costs of operation and maintenance in social housing are moving inexorably upward as the costs of mortgage money, utilities, municipal taxes (paid in full) and wages of operational and maintenance staff have risen from 100 per cent to 300 per cent since 1971 in Ontario. On the other hand, the rental revenues gained from public housing tenants move much more slowly upward because their incomes are quite low and, in the case of those in receipt of social assistance, relatively fixed.

As a consequence of these disparate relationships it is now impossible in Ontario to project construction of either senior citizen or family housing at less than $225-$250 per unit per month subsidy.[3] The Deputy Minister of the Ministry of State for Urban Affairs expressed concern recently that total subsidies in Canadian social housing were in excess of $500 million. In Ontario subsidies have now reached $200 million. The Nova Scotia Housing Commission referred to the matter of subsidies in its annual reports for fiscal 1973 and fiscal 1974 and noted that the government of Nova Scotia had imposed a moratorium upon the building of family housing because of its projection of the subsidies over the fifty-year amortization period.

In the years of substantial economic growth and moderate price inflation neither total nor average subsidies attracted much attention. In the years of economic constraint and relatively rapid inflation financial subsidies in social housing are becoming a deterrent. Many of the eleven senior governments in Canada have projected ahead, based on current losses, and visualize vast amounts of money for subsidies within a quarter century. Proponents of expanded social housing programs can insist correctly that such sums are, and will be, quite small proportions of annual budgets of all governments. These years are, unfortunately, a very poor time to "market" such arguments.

CONCLUDING COMMENTS

It is important to emphasize the interrelated nature of the factors affecting social housing policies and the policy changes apparent in the middle and late 1970s. The shift from public housing for families to senior citizens' housing, the shift from rental housing for low-income groups to home ownership opportunities for moderate-income persons and families, the movement to decentralize responsibility for social housing to local and regional governments, and the renewed concern about financial subsidies in social housing; these are all constituent elements of changing social housing policies which reinforce each other.

In an affluent society encountering economic distress, high unemployment and high inflation simultaneously, there is less and less tolerance of "poor people", low-income groups or whatever terminology is used. A working definition might be "those persons and families with annual incomes one-half or less than the median personal and family incomes within the jurisdiction" or, if you prefer, the lowest quartile in the population. Attitudes towards social housing are mixed with attitudes towards so-called "welfare bums", attitudes towards so-called "unemployment insurance cheats" and attitudes towards sole-support mothers with dependent children for whom love of household and children is not enough.

In these circumstances the view is that we "owe" less to broken or never-created families and more to the elderly "who built this country". We should encourage more families to assume the responsibilities of home ownership which implies "good citizenship" and attention to community development. We should encourage local governments which, in most provinces, provide little or no capital and only a modest share of subsidies in social housing, but which know and understand local requirements, to assume much greater responsibility in the development, management and financing of such housing. And, if we are to curb governmental expenditures, we must no longer neglect the projected data for absolute and average subsidies in social housing.

The total picture is not entirely bleak. Neither is it promising or pretty. Programs of social housing in Canada face further changes consequent upon restrictive policies.

NOTES

1 Nevertheless, nearly 600,000 households of the one million considered to be below the poverty line in 1972 owned their own homes, and 85 per cent of these were free from mortgage debt (Canada, Ministry of State for Urban Affairs, 1976: 5, 21).

2 This is closely related to greatly increased costs of home purchase and rental housing. It has been estimated that only 30 per cent of Ontario families in 1974 could carry the costs of home purchase with less than 25 per cent of their gross family income. The comparable figure for 1967 was 70 per cent of families (see Ontario Economic Council, 1976: table 4).

3 In Ontario new construction for senior citizens in the first half of 1977, the average subsidy exceeded $245 per unit per month.

REFERENCES

Canada. Ministry of State for Urban Affairs. 1976. *Human Settlement in Canada.* Ottawa: [distributed at U.N. Habitat Conference].

Ontario. Ministry of Housing. 1976. "Housing Programs in Ontario". Special edition of *Housing Ontario,* 20, 1: 15.

Ontario Economic Council. 1976. *Issues and Alternatives 1976: Housing.* Toronto: The Council.

6.2 DISTRIBUTIONAL AND SOCIAL IMPACTS OF CANADIAN NATIONAL HOUSING POLICY: LEAVING IT TO THE MARKET

Jeffrey Patterson[1]

In the Canadian context a discussion of the social and distributional impacts of housing policy cannot possibly take place without reference to housing markets and the operation of housing markets. A non-market sector is practically non-existent. Less than 3 per cent of the Canadian housing stock is owned by government or other agents outside the private market. Moreover, federal and provincial governments in Canada have in recent years begun relying on incentives to the private market as the primary vehicle for delivery of housing subsidies.

The Canadian state has considerable impact, both direct and indirect, on the private housing market. A wide range of policies influence the availability of mortgage funds. Currently, a very large proportion of the new housing stock being brought on the private market is either financed directly by federal or provincial housing agencies, or jointly between them and the commercial lending institutions. Tax policies influence the rate of returns to various housing producers and consumers, and hence the kinds, types and amounts of housing produced and consumed. A large proportion of government expenditures takes the form of transfer payments, often to those with no other source of income, and the recipient of these transfer payments will usually allocate a very large proportion of them to housing. The level of transfer payments, and any conditions that may be attached to their use, influence housing consumption levels and patterns. In addition both the federal and provincial governments provide mortgage funding for "public" housing owned and/or managed by provincial or local housing agencies and for dwellings owned by co-operative housing societies and non-profit housing companies, including those that are municipally owned, in addition to the market-oriented housing which they finance.

Local governments influence the amount of housing available and its allocation to different groups through their control of land use and development standards.

The fact that this control has considerable influence on housing markets and the allocation of housing is currently the subject of public discussion and attention. Local governments are often also required to take the first step in requesting the two senior levels of government to develop or acquire subsidized housing.

An enquiry into the social and distributional impacts of Canadian housing policy must therefore encompass a rather comprehensive view of the ways in which housing markets are influenced.

By distributional impact is meant the allocation of housing and housing opportunities to different sectors of the Canadian population; we are most concerned with different income groups or social strata, but various types of households and families or age levels are also involved. By social impact is meant any results which influence the way different Canadians relate to one another.

The subject matter is difficult to treat. Very few data exist. The distributional and social impact of any government policy area seems to be habitually neglected. It is an area neglected in many academic fields as well. Of course, the neglect of social and distributional impacts of policies reveals, I think, a societal bias within Canada as a whole. The literature and available data merely reflect this. For instance, the "Orange Paper" on Social Security (Canada, Department of National Health and Welfare, 1973), probably the most far-reaching document on the subject since the Marsh report (Canada, Advisory Committee on Reconstruction, 1944), focused almost entirely on issues of equity and work incentives, and barely mentioned the distribution of income as a social security concern. This paper will serve to illustrate that point in the case of housing. It will be shown below that policies that would have possibly redistributed opportunities for adequate housing, or that would have made it possible for more low- and moderate-income households to own housing, have deliberately been forsaken in favour of policies that would generate a number of new housing starts in the 1970s. It will also be shown that those policies which have been oriented towards redistributing housing opportunities have done so only to the extent necessary to enable households penalized by recent market trends to catch up to where they were a few years ago. Housing policy, then, reflects the relative power and interests of various groups and classes in society, and has not attempted, to any large degree, to redistribute housing opportunities among them.

I will start with a discussion of the impact of Canadian housing markets on access to housing of various costs and quality over the past ten to fifteen years, focusing on what indicators we possess of the social and distributional impact of changes in incomes and housing costs in recent years. I will then come back to government housing policy and the ways in which it has responded to these trends.

DISTRIBUTIONAL IMPACT OF CHANGES IN INCOME AND HOUSING COSTS

Of interest are two aspects of recent housing market trends. On the one hand there are the longer-term social implications of recent housing market trends. As will be documented below, the price and carrying costs of housing have generally increased at a faster rate than wages. What does this mean? Second, and also of interest, is the experience and expectations of various sectors of the population.

General Trends in the Affordability of Housing

Whether or not Canadians are becoming more or less able to afford housing now than a few years ago is a matter about which there is still considerable discussion and disagreement. In some part it depends on which indicators are used. This question is examined here in terms of the possible social implications of trends in affordability.

Table 1 shows trends in housing prices and incomes from 1961 to 1975. Over this term personal disposable income per capita has generally increased at a faster pace than house prices, as indicated by the change in cost of a single-family house financed under the National Housing Act (NHA). Does this mean that housing is becoming easier for Canadians to obtain? Not necessarily!

Table 1 also indicates that the costs of carrying a mortgage have risen faster than personal disposable income.[2] They have been at higher levels (using 1961 as a base) since 1973. Previously, the index for monthly payments exceeded that for personal disposable income per capita from 1967 through 1970. A lull in this increase occurred in the 1971-73 period as a result of stabilizing prices in the NHA housing sector, and reduced interest rates.

These data reveal only part of the picture. Table 2 enables one to enquire further into trends over the past five years. From 1971 to 1976 the cost of a single-family house financed under the National Housing Act increased at a more rapid rate than per capita personal disposable income. That is, prices accelerated considerably over the past few years over and above the longer fifteen-year trend. Since the approach of higher interest rates in late 1974, the costs of carrying a mortgage have outpaced both housing prices and per capita disposable income.

More profound phenomena are also indicated in table 2. First, increases in per capita personal disposable income have exceeded increases in average weekly industrial earnings by a substantial amount. This likely reflects both decreasing household size and increased female participation in the labour force. That is, family incomes have increased more rapidly than the average worker's earnings. The capability of purchasing a home on the part of a one-earner family is therefore reduced. The price of entry into the housing market may dictate that female earners in households of two or more earners should no longer be considered members of the "secondary" labour market as they have often been characterized. In fact, this change may be the single most important social impact of trends in housing markets and prices. There is a case to be made for the assertion that the advent of the two- or multi-earner family has increased "what the market can bear", the residual over and above development and construction costs being reflected in higher land prices. As will be shown below, this

TABLE 1

Trends in house prices and incomes, 1961-76

	Personal disposable income per capita	NHA single-family dwelling cost (including land)	NHA single-family land cost	Monthly principal and interest payment
1961	$1,475	$14,463	$2,453	$87.52
62	1,579	14,614	2,535	91.37
63	1,646	15,068	2,692	92.51
64	1,713	15,807	2,813	95.68
65	1,846	16,572	2,816	100.26
66	1,994	18,059	3,006	115.30
67	2,116	18,529	3,155	126.90
68	2,262	18,922	3,350	146.90
69	2,424	20,315	3,623	164.80
70	2,536	19,894	3,666	169.70
71	2,779	20,528	3,944	161.80
72	3,121	22,168	4,333	174.80
73	3,585	28,683	4,571	194.29
74	4,121	33,356	6,279	247.70
75	4,734	35,492	7,246	324.85
76	5,278	39,881	9,226	388.81
	Indexes (1961 = 100)			
1961	100	100	100	100
62	107	102	103	104
63	112	104	110	106
64	116	109	115	109
65	125	114	115	114
66	135	125	122	132
67	143	128	129	145
68	153	131	136	168
69	164	141	148	188
70	172	138	149	194
71	188	142	161	185
72	211	153	177	200
73	243	168	174	222
74	279	198	186	283
75	321	245	295	371
76	358	275	376	444

SOURCE: CMHC, *Canadian Housing Statistics*

has resulted in shifting housing policy objectives away from satisfying those with basic needs towards satisfying those whose earning power has been reduced by events of the past few years.

Also of note are movements on the price side. Upward pressures on housing prices in general on the part of land are evident. Land price increases have been occasioned by increases in the long-term returns to urban land owners. In addition, there appear to be qualitative changes in the housing product. The index for construction cost per square foot has increased at a faster pace than for either building materials or construction wage rates. This may reflect an increased preference for richer mixes of material and/or labour — more built-ins, more plastics, and so forth. It could also reflect increased construction overhead costs.

Also to be borne in mind in this discussion is the fact that the single-family house financed under the National Housing Act has a price tag that generally places it at the bottom end of the market. Furthermore, price increases have been less than in the non-NHA sector. However, as is shown in table 3, these differences are not necessarily great

TABLE 2

Selected indicators of housing sector performance, 1971-76
(1971 = 100)

	Consumer price index	Personal disposable income per capita	Total cost, single-detached housing financed under the NHA	Land prices for single-detached houses financed under the NHA
1971	100.0	100.0	100.0	100.0
1972	104.8	112.3	107.7	109.9
1973	112.7	129.0	118.3	108.1
1974	125.0	148.3	139.4	115.5
1975	138.5	170.3	172.5	183.2
1976	148.9	189.9	193.7	233.5

	Building materials (residential)	Wage rates of construction workers	Construction cost per square foot, NHA single-detached dwellings	All weekly earnings industrial composite	Carrying costs, new NHA home
1971	100.0	100.0	100.0	100.0	100.0
1972	109.8	110.4	106.7	108.4	108.1
1973	124.0	121.2	122.2	116.2	120.0
1974	135.2	132.8	149.5	129.1	152.6
1975	139.7	151.4	167.1	147.4	200.5
1976	153.7	172.7	180.6		240.0

SOURCE: CMHC, *Canadian Housing Statistics*

TABLE 3

Selected indicators, new and existing house prices, selected cities, 1971-76

	1971	1972	1973	1974	1975	1976
Montreal						
1. New house prices	100.0	107.6	125.6	177.7	190.3	200.9
2. New NHA prices	100.0	104.2	115.9	144.9	165.8	180.4
2. Dollar value, MLS trans-actions	100.0	105.6	111.3	140.8	149.6	167.9
4. Average monthly rental	100.0	–	–	136.0	–	–
Toronto						
1. New house prices	100.0	110.6	137.6	171.6	170.8	180.7
2. New NHA prices	100.0	98.1	110.9	190.6	174.9	175.8
3. Dollar value, MLS trans-actions	100.0	107.0	138.5	176.3	182.8	197.3
4. Average monthly rental	100.0	–	–	126.0	–	–
Ottawa-Hull						
1. New house prices	100.0	112.7	138.2	171.2	178.3	192.5
2. New NHA prices	100.0	103.2	118.9	159.8	169.2	192.0
3. Dollar value, MLS trans-actions	100.0	109.0	132.7	159.4	166.7	185.4
4. Average monthly rental	100.0	–	–	129.0	–	–
Winnipeg						
1. New house prices	100.0	105.2	128.4	163.5	177.5	199.8
2. New NHA prices	100.0	109.7	125.9	169.2	199.3	237.9
3. Dollar value, MLS trans-actions	100.0	106.1	116.9	149.6	181.5	214.9
4. Average monthly rental	100.0	–	–	131.0	–	–
Calgary						
1. New house prices	100.0	110.0	126.4	162.3	195.0	243.1
2. New NHA prices	100.0	104.2	122.6	157.4	194.5	251.1
3. Dollar value, MLS trans-actions	100.0	107.3	123.2	196.7	217.6	297.1
4. Average monthly rental	100.0	–	–	130.0	–	–
Edmonton						
1. New house prices	100.0	109.1	132.6	172.8	205.3	245.8
2. New NHA prices	100.0	106.6	120.2	151.2	118.6	238.9
3. Dollar value, MLS trans-actions	100.0	104.2	121.2	147.8	187.0	248.7
4. Average monthly rental	100.0	–	–	133.0	–	–
Vancouver						
2. New NHA prices	100.0	111.3	131.8	167.2	174.6	176.3
3. Dollar value, MLS trans-actions	100.0	118.9	156.8	218.6	243.5	259.5
4. Average monthly rental	100.0	–	–	138.0	–	–

TABLE 3 (Continued)

Selected indicators, new and existing house prices, selected cities, 1971-76

	1971	1972	1973	1974	1975	1976
Victoria						
2. New NHA prices	100.0	102.5	117.9	180.5	208.5	237.3
3. Dollar value, MLS trans-actions	100.0	108.4	137.1	194.3	221.4	254.3
4. Average monthly rental	100.0	–	–	134.0	–	–
Saskatoon						
2. New NHA prices	100.0	106.6	121.0	143.6	183.1	227.1
3. Dollar value, MLS trans-actions	100.0	104.3	120.3	151.7	210.3	271.5
Regina						
1. New NHA prices	100.0	113.2	135.6	163.3	198.2	241.3
3. Dollar value, MLS trans-actions	100.0	103.9	122.5	159.9	206.9	253.1
Hamilton						
2. New NHA prices	100.0	109.7	124.4	146.2	179.2	179.8
3. Dollar value, MLS trans-actions	100.0	110.8	135.7	171.4	183.8	202.8
Kingston						
2. New NHA prices	100.0	109.9	125.5	170.5	167.4	178.0
3. Dollar value, MLS trans-actions	100.0	104.1	128.0	161.9	171.8	187.2
Halifax						
2. New NHA prices	100.0	101.8	105.2	110.2	129.0	130.5
3. Dollar value, MLS trans-actions	100.0	104.5	111.2	130.2	151.3	173.3
4. Average monthly rental	100.0	–	–	137.0	–	–
Saint John						
2. New NHA prices	100.0	122.0	120.4	140.6	143.7	172.8
3. Dollar value, MLS trans-actions	100.0	107.7	124.7	159.3	181.7	202.7
4. Average monthly rental	100.0	–	–	184.0	–	–

SOURCES:

1,2 CMHC, *Canadian Housing Statistics*
3 Canadian Real Estate Association
4 Runge, *et al.*, 1975; CMHC, *Canadian Housing Statistics*

MLS Multiple Listing Service

TABLE 4

Decile income levels, 1961-71

Decile	Families				Non-family			
	1961 income interval	1971 income interval	1971 income interval (1961$)	% change (1961$)	1961 income interval	1971 income interval	1971 income interval (1961$)	% change (1961$)
1st	$1,768	$3,059	$2,123	20.1	–	–	–	–
2nd	2,931	5,056	3,509	19.7	–	$1,168	$ 811	–
3rd	3,734	6,731	4,671	25.1	–	1,550	1,076	–
4th	4,398	8,022	5,567	26.6	$1,268	1,931	1,340	5.7
5th	5,000	9,157	6,355	27.1	1,756	2,766	1,920	9.3
6th	5,662	10,417	7,229	27.7	2,360	3,806	2,641	11.9
7th	6,422	11,806	8,193	27.6	3,074	4,988	3,462	12.6
8th	7,429	13,883	9,635	29.7	3,745	6,469	4,489	19.9
9th	8,700	17,692	12,278	41.1	4,785	8,432	5,852	22.3

SOURCE: Runge, et al., 1975 (computed from 1961 and 1971 Census)

1961 refers to 1960 income; 1971 refers to 1970 income

or even in the direction indicated. For instance, new house price increases in the NHA sector have been greater than in the non-NHA sector over the past six years in such cities as Montreal, Winnipeg and Calgary. Price increases in existing houses have almost always been greater than in the case of new house prices in the cities included. Rental increases have in almost all cases been less than house price increases, and they have approximated wage rate increases.

TABLE 5

Rent (or value) per room as a percentage of total household income, by socio-economic characteristic, major urban areas — Canada, 1961 and 1971

	1961	1971
Average	3.7	4.2
Total household income		
Lowest quintile	2.4	7.5
Second quintile	3.4	5.0
Middle quintile	3.9	4.4
Fourth quintile	3.9	4.0
Highest quintile	3.1	3.2
Rent (or value) per month (1961)		
$50 or less	0.9	3.2
$51 to $100	3.8	4.2
$101 to $200	4.3	4.3
$201 or more	2.8	3.7
Persons per household		
2 or less	2.1	6.2
2.1 to 3.0	3.8	4.5
3.1 to 4.0	3.7	4.0
4.1 to 6.0	3.7	3.4
6.1 or more	2.6	NA
Age of dwelling		
Built before 1920 (1946)	3.3	4.3
Built during 1921-45 (1946-60)	3.6	4.1
Built during 1946-59 (1961-68)	3.9	4.2
Built during 1960-61 (1969-71)	3.9	4.2
Age of head of household		
65 or over	3.7	4.3
Under 65	3.7	4.2

SOURCE: Economic Council of Canada, 1974

TABLE 6

Comparative indicators of housing need by the poor and non-poor – Canada, 1972

General	Childless Single Persons			Childless Couples		Families With Children			
	Aged 20-24	Aged 25-64	Aged 65 And Over	Head Aged 20-64	Head Aged 65 and Over	1 and 2 Children	3 or 4 Children	5 or more Children	All Households
Per Cent Household Type Poor[1]	16.1	20.7	57.6	10.3	39.0	12.3	16.5	23.7	18.9
Per Cent of All Poor Households	1.3	10.0	18.9	10.1	16.4	23.3	14.2	5.8	100.0
Per Cent Poor Renting	98.4	60.2	42.4	39.8	23.4	47.2	32.6	32.3	40.7
Per Cent Non-Poor Renting	97.1	71.5	48.0	48.7	20.2	32.4	21.1	19.1	37.5
Per Cent of Poor With Main Source of Income Government Transfers	8.0	39.2	96.3	23.9	90.9	36.8	36.5	51.0	56.2
Per Cent Homes of Poor Home Owners with Mortgages	nil	10.8	4.3	15.0	6.2	24.7	26.8	16.8	14.9
Per Cent Homes of Non-Poor Home Owners with Mortgages	32.8	18.1	8.8	44.1	10.9	62.2	66.0	54.4	52.4
Shelter-to-income ratios									
Per Cent of Poor, Unsubsidized Renters with Rent-Income Ratio > 25 p.c.	91.3	81.9	87.5	79.5	73.9	76.4	67.5	51.0	77.9
Per Cent Poor Home Owners with P.I.T. Ratio > 25 p.c.[2]	nil	82.7	94.2	87.4	93.1	83.6	80.6	49.3	81.5
Per Cent of Non-Poor, Unsubsidized Renters with Rent-Income Ratio > 25 p.c.	51.3	27.9	59.8	7.5	31.5	10.5	9.8	4.5	17.0
Per Cent of Non-Poor, Home Owners with P.I.T. Ratio > 25 p.c.	nil	33.2	56.2	10.4	42.2	10.8	10.1	6.5	11.3

Indicators of crowding and condition	Childless Single Persons			Childless Couples		Families With Children			All Households
	Aged 20-24	Aged 25-64	Aged 65 And Over	Head Aged 20-64	Head Aged 65 and Over	1 and 2 Children	3 or 4 Children	5 or more Children	
Poor Renters with 1.01 more Persons Per Room	nil	nil	nil	2.2	3.4	5.3	19.8	82.5	7.9
Poor Renters with No or Only Cold Running Water	2.5	12.1	13.8	14.6	6.3	8.7	8.2	15.1	10.6
Poor Home Owners With 1.01 or more Persons per Room	nil	nil	nil	0.8	nil	3.7	26.5	78.6	10.3
Poor Renters with No or Only Cold Running Water	2.5	12.1	13.8	14.6	6.3	8.7	8.2	15.1	10.6
Poor Home Owners with No or Only Cold Running Water	100.0	30.3	21.4	21.8	16.0	19.8	23.2	33.4	21.7

SOURCE: Statistics Canada, *Urban Family Expenditure on Shelter Household Durables*, 1972 (CMHC tabulations)

1 Statistics Canada, Unrevised Poverty Lines. This level is generally three-fourths of level advocated by the Canadian Council on Social Development

2 P.I.T. Principal, interest and taxes

TABLE 7

Distribution of Shelter-to-income ratios by tenure and income line, by city, 1974[1]

Shelter-to-income ratio by population group	City				
	Halifax	Montreal	Toronto	Regina	Vancouver
Owners:					
Below low-income line					
Less than 20%	11	21	18	30	23
20-30%	17	23	13	26	18
30-40%	15	12	16	15	17
Above 40%	58	44	53	28	43
Above low-income line					
Less than 20%	75	85	76	84	80
20-30%	18	12	15	13	12
30-40%	5	1	6	2	5
Above 40%	3	1	3	1	4
Renters:					
Below low-income line					
Less than 20%	10	11	8	5	7
20-30%	12	20	21	19	10
30-40%	17	22	12	16	12
Above 40%	61	47	58	60	71
Above low-income line					
Less than 20%	59	80	61	63	53
20-30%	28	16	28	26	30
30-40%	9	3	8	7	13
Above 40%	4	1	3	4	4

SOURCE: CMHC, *Survey of Housing Units*, 1974 (unpublished tabulations)

1 Low-income line adjusted for family size according to specifications by Statistics Canada

Changes in the Affordability of Housing for Different Groups

It has been shown above that housing prices, and certainly the costs of carrying a mortgage, have exceeded income increases and to a greater extent wage increases over the past ten to fifteen years.

What has been the distributional impact of this phenomenon? There is very little conclusive data on this subject. It follows from the above that one-earner families are relatively more disadvantaged than a few years ago. Renters may be slighly better off vis-à-vis home owners, although rents appear to have kept pace with wage increases, placing at a disadvantage those renters on fixed incomes and those whose incomes have generally not increased faster than the overall consumer price index.

Table 4 shows that the distribution of income has changed little, and as well that from 1961 to 1971 the income of those in the lower income groups increased less rapidly than for those in the upper income groups. It follows that the burden of paying a higher proportion of income for housing has fallen most heavily on those of low income.

Table 5 depicts the incidence of changes in rent (or imputed value in the case of home owners) per room as a percentage of total household income from 1961 to 1971. It has been argued by others that this particular indicator distorts the picture for the worse as a result of decreasing household sizes and an excessive imputed rent for home owners. However, a close inspection of these arguments reveals that they may exaggerate the extent of changes, but not the resulting conclusions or the underlying patterns.[3] These patterns indicate that from 1961 to 1971 shelter (in terms of cost per room)-to-income ratios increased most for those in the lower income groups, for units with lower rents in 1961 and for those living in older units.

Tables 6 and 7 give some measure of the extent to which housing problem burdens fell on the poor in the years 1971 and 1972. Table 6 indicates for Canada as a whole the extent to which poor families must either spend a disproportionate share of their income for housing or, as is particularly the case for large families, accept housing which is inadequate in size or condition. Table 7 shows for selected cities the proportion of owning and renting households which must pay a high proportion of their income for shelter. With some qualification for owner-occupants in Regina, it is clear that a high percentage of households below the low-income line must pay more than 40 per cent of their income for housing.

A Summary of Social and Distributional Effects of the Housing Market

Almost by definition, the price of housing cannot exceed the resources available to pay for it. In the long run the incomes of Canadians must be sufficient to pay for our basic needs, including shelter. Changes over time which require monitoring by public policy makers include the quality and quantity of housing consumed, the price and quality of housing vis-à-vis other goods and services, and the distribution of these phenomena. As incomes increase, at least in real terms, consumers must decide whether to save or spend the increase. If they decide to spend it, they must then make decisions about how to spend it. The producers of housing are only a small proportion of the entrepreneurs who will legitimately try to capture a portion of the increased spending power.

If increased demand for housing arises, a portion of it may result in an increase in the quantity and quality of housing offered to consumers. Land developers in a monopoly position with respect to housing and land may increase their monopolistic returns as incomes increase. It should be stressed that land possesses certain monopolistic tendencies irrespective of concentration in the development industry. That is, the creation of new subdivisions on the periphery of our urban area is very capital intensive, and the creation of new land for urban use is slow enough to make increases in land supply very inelastic in the short run.

In the comments above I have stopped short of making the assertion that housing prices change so as to absorb increased spending power of consumers. In the final analysis, whether or not this is ultimately the case depends on real production costs of housing vis-à-vis other elements necessary for the reproduction of labour, and to some extent on consumer preferences.

Changes in affordability, defined here as the ability to afford a constant quality and quantity of housing, occur as a result of relative housing price changes and income changes. What we appear to have been witnessing in the past ten to fifteen years is a secular increase in housing prices. Regardless of the ultimate causes, and the discussion of these resembles the classic "chicken and egg" argument more than anything else, these price changes can be associated with rapidly rising family incomes and to some extent increased female participation in the labour force and the fact that the two-earner family has become a common occurrence. Those families with only one earner find themselves less and less able to afford a constant quality of housing. Although rents have increased much less rapidly than housing prices, approximating wage level changes as opposed to family income changes, even these less rapid changes comprise a burden for those with fixed incomes, most commonly the elderly.

I referred above to the phenomenon of the two- or multiple-earner family and its possible influence on housing prices. That recent shifts in housing prices may be more an ownership than a rental phenomenon might be explained by the fact that rental units are less likely to be occupied by two-earner households. Rental price changes, therefore, may have more closely approximated wage movements. In the case of those on fixed incomes, especially the elderly and those dependent on social assistance payments, the fact that pensions and other government transfer payments are tied to the consumer price index, either explicitly or implicitly, may act as a price restraint. Aside from explaining differentials between the price of renting and the price of owning, those phenomena may also explain at least a part of the movement of entrepreneurs from the production of rental housing to the production of housing for ownership, a move that began long before the arrival of rent review in 1975. Simply, the production of ownership housing became more profitable.

It was noted earlier that the carrying costs of purchasing a home have increased much more rapidly than the price of housing, principally due to higher interest rates. One interpretation of this is that the commercial lending institutions are asserting their power to capture a larger portion of increased disposable incomes. Given that the costs of capital have increased in other sectors as well, and throughout the western world generally, the increased costs of capital are probably a more plausible explanation for rising mortgage interest rates. Other observers have noted that mortgage interest rates have not risen relative to other interest rates, including the cost of long-term borrowing to the government, or relative to inflation in consumer prices or, especially, to housing.

Because of these trends, government policy has increasingly concerned itself with ameliorating any undesirable consequences of housing price and income changes. Housing policy has increasingly concerned itself with assisting young families trying to enter the housing market for the first time, assisting the more traditional one-earner families and assisting others whose incomes have not kept up with housing prices. Alternatively, the government might have attempted to exert more downward pressure on the cost of existing housing, but the course taken is likely the most feasible politically. The number of new entrants in the housing market is always fewer than the number of existing members.

The above discussion has indicated some of the social and distributional impacts of recent trends in Canada's housing markets. The discussion is far from complete. We could focus on the effects of suburban development on isolated mothers and children, or on the housing of poor families with children in high-rise apartment buildings. We did not, although I will include more of such elements in the discussion below. Our conclusions would not have been as certain with respect to those variables.

A CONTEMPORARY PERSPECTIVE ON NATIONAL HOUSING POLICY

Some of the objectives of housing policy are to create greater security for those unable to protect themselves, to relieve burdens for those temporarily or permanently unable to assume them, and to ensure sufficient quantity and quality of housing.

By national housing policy I mean the sum total of activities of the federal and provincial governments. Provincial governments have sole constitutional jurisdiction in matters of housing, but the federal government has greater financial leverage and generally controls the finance markets which generate practically all of the capital invested in housing.

The prop beneath Canada's housing policy has traditionally been home ownership assistance for young Canadian families of modest means. The insurance of privately initiated mortgages, as well as direct mortgage initiation, was practically the sole focus of housing policy from 1945 until 1964. Involvement in creating a rental construction and management industry in the five years following World War II was the only other initiative of note. The year 1964 becomes a watershed because it was then that the National Housing Act was amended to enable the Central Mortgage and Housing Corporation to lend money to provincial and municipal housing agencies to construct or acquire rent-geared-to-income, or "public", housing. Non-profit corporations providing housing for the elderly also became eligible for loans. Most provinces subsequently modified their own enabling legislation. Partly as a result of these legislative changes, combined with the "war on poverty" initiated by Prime Minister Pearson and a desire on the part of the provinces to invest in owned residential real estate, national housing policy became almost totally oriented towards providing mortgages for social housing. Some have observed that the provision of rented housing for poor Canadians, while the overwhelming desire of practically all Canadians was an owned home, was an aberration that was destined for failure. Between 1968 and 1971 the federal government curtailed practically all of their residual market lending for home ownership or for housing not intended for the poor. Practically all of their spending was for rental housing. Provincial activities in housing expanded significantly in this period.

This commitment declined between 1971 and 1973 when the National Housing Act was amended to accommodate a host of new programs. Chief amongst these turned out to be the Assisted Home Ownership Program (AHOP) which was intended to provide shallow subsidies to those families otherwise unable to purchase housing on the market, or to those families with incomes in the upper ranges of those normally entering public housing. Modifications in provincial housing policy generally paralleled the federal ones. Some provinces have chosen to stack subsidies atop the federal ones and some have chosen to initiate their own variations of federal programs, usually better suited to local market conditions.

As will be shown below, AHOP and a counterpart in the rental sector resulting from subsequent amendments to the National Housing Act, dubbed the Assisted Rental Program (ARP), have become progressively oriented towards providing shallow subsidies to those families, primarily young, with incomes not quite sufficient to purchase (or rent, in the case of ARP) housing in the market. The public housing program has become of minor importance in CMHC's capital budget, and over two-thirds of that which is built is now intended specifically for senior citizens. National housing policy is now oriented almost entirely towards ameliorating the impact of higher housing costs on families with modest incomes, many of them one-earner families.

I will pursue briefly the above assertions with respect to national housing policy in the case of two programs: public housing and assisted home ownership.

Public Housing

We could portray the life and death of the public housing program. Annual production under the provincial program in Ontario increased steadily to over 19,000 units in 1971. Since then, it has averaged approximately 10,000 units per year, although the proportion of the total allocated to families has decreased from two-thirds to less than one-third.

TABLE 8

Income distributions of public housing tenants — Ontario, British Columbia and Manitoba, 1970 to 1974-75

Annual income	Ontario 1970[a]	Ontario 1974[b]	British Columbia 1970[a]	British Columbia 1974[c]	Manitoba 1970[a]	Manitoba 1974[d]
Under $2,000	4.6%	1.0%	17.5%	1.0%	20.3%	20.0%
2 - 2,999	10.2	4.0	38.6	32.8	19.4	14.0
3 - 3,999	17.5	12.0	22.9	6.0	25.0	17.0
4 - 4,999	18.7	13.0	11.5	14.0	24.8	18.0
5,000 - 7,999	44.0	50.0	9.4	27.0	10.1	31.0
$8,000 and over	5.0	20.0	0.1	18.8	0.4	nil
Total	100.0	100.0	100.0	100.0	100.0	100.0
Average	$4.971	$6,500	$3,124	$4,000	$3,368	$3,800
Percentage increase	30.8%		28.0%		12.8%	

SOURCES:

a   CMHC Survey, 1970

b   Imputed from Ontario Housing Corporation Sample Survey; sample of 1,848 at the end of 1974

c   Survey of Tenants, BCHMC, Summer 1975, quoted in Runge, et al., 1975

d   Moore and Giesinger, 1974

The public housing program, including its growing rural and native component, remains the only one serving a purely low-income clientele. Approximately 85 per cent of the current residents are from the lower third of the income distribution. As can be seen in table 8, average incomes ranged in 1974-75 from $4,000 to $6,000. Increases in rent from 1970 to 1974-75 were generally less than wage increases. Many public housing tenants rely for all or most of their needs on government transfer programs that have increased less rapidly than wages or per capita personal disposable income.

While the public housing program is the only housing supply program to serve almost solely those of low income, it has increasingly become associated with undesirable social consequences that have lost it support from municipal governments, rate-payer groups and, in some cases, tenants themselves. In most large cities at least half of new residents are single-parent, usually mother-led, families.[4] They have incomes of approximately half those of their neighbours. The concentration of large numbers of children of low-income families in spaces and areas not capable of absorbing them is certainly one problem, especially in older projects which were larger and more deficient in amenities. Characterization of public housing as tenanted by "welfare bums" has militated against community acceptance as well. Finally, all three levels of government have reacted against rising subsidies.

The only currently acceptable arrangement for most provincial and municipal governments is to provide rent-to-income subsidies comparable to those in public housing in a portion of the dwellings provided by private developers or by non-profit corporations or co-operative societies, usually up to 25 per cent of the units. Of course, this mechanism requires that four times as many units must be financed to provide subsidized housing to the same number of households.

Assisted Home Ownership

Table 9 shows the income distribution and trends for beneficiaries of federal AHOP from 1970-71 through 1976. Of note is that average family incomes of borrowers have increased significantly more rapidly than either per capita personal disposable income or the price of new dwellings. The program has served a relatively higher income group in each year since 1973. It is significant that from 1971 to 1973 it did serve a significant number of households whose incomes and housing situations might have made them candidates for tenancy in

TABLE 9

Income trends, assisted home ownership borrowers, 1970-76

Income	1970-71	1972	1973	1974	1975	1976
$0-7,999	90.8%	68.7%[a]	62.0%	2.8%	6.4%	1.5%
$8,000-9,999	9.2	19.4[a]	38.0	39.6	23.0	7.2
$10,000-12,499	–	–	–	45.0	44.0	25.5
$12,500-14,999	–	–	–	12.6	18.6	26.4
$15,000 and over	–	–	–	–	8.0	39.1
Median or average income	$6,112	$6,916	$7,632	$10,672	$11,312	$14,985
Index (1971 = 100)	100.0	113.2	124.9	174.6	185.1	245.2
Personal disposable income per capita index (1971 = 100)	100.0	112.3	129.0	148.3	170.3	189.0
Consumer price index (1971 = 100)	100.0	104.8	112.7	125.7	138.5	148.9
Total new dwelling cost index (1971 = 100)	100.0	106.2	119.4	143.0	160.5	194.3

SOURCES: Canadian Council on Social Development, 1977; CMHC, *Canadian Housing Statistics*

a Percentages incomplete because of missing data

public housing. That is, it provided many families with an option that they would otherwise not have had. From 1971 to 1973, assisted home ownership was an experimental program, not officially sanctioned by the National Housing Act. Its full implementation in 1974 coincided with a serious decline in the availability of mortgage funds. Thereafter, the program became almost totally oriented towards the modest-income home purchasers. Its purpose became the supplementation of the market-place. In 1975, for instance, not one applicant had previously resided in public housing, and the average rent-to-income ratio at time of application was approximately 16 per cent, well below the national average. In other words, those renters benefiting under AHOP were not those with high rent-to-income ratios. They were, for the most part, renters who could have continued renting with no great hardship.

Table 10 shows average income trends by province. The experience from province to province is relatively consistent with that of the nation, although it has not always been so.

A number of queries could be launched with respect to the satisfaction of the occupants of AHOP projects. However, the result of such an enquiry would not differ significantly from one focused on suburban projects, which are often characterized by poor availability and co-ordination of human and other services, or from one that focused on the nature of housing developments in peripheral locations offering a product near the bottom end of the current price range. The results would be the same. We could do better.

TABLE 10

Income trends, assisted home ownership borrowers, by province, 1970-71 to 1976 Index Index (1970-71 = 100)

	1970-1971	1972	1973	1974	1975	1976
Newfoundland	100.0	96.7	123.5	169.2	210.5	228.2
Prince Edward Island	–	100.0	113.1	161.9	216.5	217.8
Nova Scotia	100.0	99.1	106.1	159.6	193.8	204.5
New Brunswick	100.0	104.9	106.4	222.3	249.0	234.4
Quebec	100.0	113.7	124.3	172.2	220.5	228.2
Ontario	100.0	111.0	123.5	157.0	192.5	232.2
Manitoba	100.0	98.4	115.9	155.5	205.0	222.8
Saskatchewan	100.0	119.6	125.6	107.1	160.9	238.0
Alberta	100.0	111.4	122.6	177.1	219.1	240.6
British Columbia	100.0	110.8	116.8	190.4	218.8	256.1

SOURCE: CMHC, *Canadian Housing Statistics*

CONCLUSION

In the first part of this paper we examined the current situation and trends with respect to the distribution of access to affordable housing. The most significant conclusion in this respect is that housing price changes have tended to approximate changes in average family incomes more closely than changes in average wages. This may reflect to a large extent increased participation in the labour force on the part of women. If one examines the rental sector alone one finds that changes in rents have on the whole approximated changes in wages. The implication of this is that those with fixed incomes which have not even kept pace with wages — primarily those dependent on government transfer payments such as welfare, old age security and government pensions — are finding it harder to rent housing within their means.

Those presumably experiencing increasing difficulty with respect to renting and purchasing housing within their means are young families, families with only one earner, and the elderly. It was asserted at the conclusion of the first part of the paper that the primary objective of housing policy on the part of the two senior levels of government has been to soften the impact of these trends on those who, until recently, have been adequately housed within their means. New policies adopted by government have tended to support this objective. Providing or assuring better quality housing within the capability of those with inadequate means has been at most a secondary objective. Likewise, increasing the overall livability of new communities and the suburban fringe has been a subsidiary objective or one not much in evidence at all.

In the second part of this paper we have examined the validity of this assertion. We focused on the assisted home ownership and public housing programs which have absorbed the vast majority of government housing capital and subsidies in the past ten to fifteen years.

Figure 1 depicts the total picture in this respect. The public housing program serves a low-income clientele. There is a significant overlap of AHOP borrowers and other borrowers of the NHA, the AHOP program serving a slightly lower income range on the whole. There is little or no overlap between the incomes of public housing tenants and AHOP borrowers.

The assisted home ownership program reflects the two-fold objective of recent housing policy: (1) to assist those made worse off by the juxtaposition of recent housing price and income trends and their distribution; and (2) to assist the private housing production market. Even the public housing program has been oriented towards ameliorating the problems of those whose affordability position has deteriorated most, to the extent that it has been transformed from a family housing program to a senior citizen housing program.

While it has not been a major subject of this paper, increasing doubt has been

FIGURE 1: Distribution of family incomes of public housing tenants, NHA borrowers and AHOP borrowers

Source: CMHC, *Canadian Housing Statistics*, 1975; CMHC Tabulations, AHOP

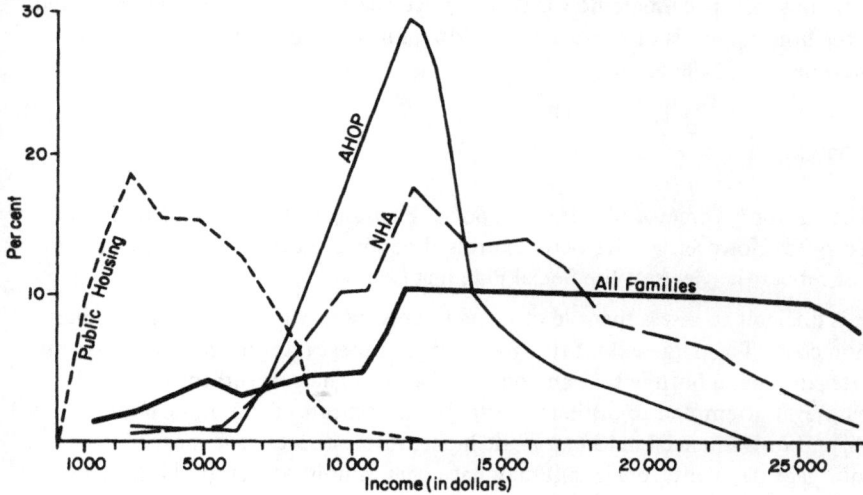

raised regarding the social consequences of the kinds of projects and developments that have been built on the periphery of Canadian cities. Much of what
might be wrong with our suburbs cannot necessarily be attributed to housing
policy. Municipal financing and social development policies are involved as well.
Nevertheless, housing policy is involved. Neither space nor time have permitted
an exploration of this theme. It is therefore encouraging to know that the Canada
Council has recently awarded a major grant to *l'Institut national de la recherche
scientifique, Université du Québec*, to pursue this subject in the suburbs of Montreal and Quebec.

Canadian housing supply policy has tended, especially in recent years, to focus
subsidies on production of new units directed to supplement the market-place.
The innovation in recent housing policy has been the tailoring of mortgage payments to incomes of young families. National housing policy is very little concerned with the housing of those with basic needs; it appears to have been in
the 1968-71 period but that period now seems like ancient history. A question
for the future is whether or not this should be rectified, or whether it is sufficient for those of low income to obtain housing through the "filtering" process,
or whether corrective action can be taken in the areas of tax and transfer payment
policies.

Up to now, the one common characteristic of shelter supplements in Canadian
income transfer programs has been that they are insufficient to purchase or rent

adequate housing on the market (Social Planning Council, 1977). Some households relying on these income transfer programs are lucky enough to have other
housing subsidies available. Most, however, must add to their shelter supplement
and/or consume inadequate housing. One must, therefore, question the likelihood
that the housing needs of those with the lowest incomes can be met through income transfer policies alone.

NOTES

1 The author is Director of Research, Social Planning Council of Metropolitan
   Toronto. However, all the views expressed herein are the author's own and do
   not reflect the views of the Social Planning Council.
2 It is difficult to assess the role of rising interest rates vis-à-vis housing production costs. To a large extent rising mortgage interest rates reflect rising interest
   rates in general both within and outside Canada. The government of Canada
   has never attempted to insulate mortgage interest rates from other trends in
   the nation's financial markets. While higher interest rates have meant higher
   mortgage payments, one result may have been simply to restrain housing production costs. That is, housing production costs, including the land component, might have been higher had interest rates not risen to the extent which
   they did. Most important to the consumer, however, is the final monthly
   cost and not necessarily the components that comprise it.
3 Cf. Walker (1975). For instance, an inspection of the relevant data reveals
   that incomes rose by 62 per cent in the 1961 to 1971 period, while rents
   (or value) per room increased by 82 per cent. Rents for rental units increased by 73 per cent, still well above the increase in incomes for the same
   period. Lack of access to the Statistics Canada tapes prevented further enquiry into differentials between rented and owned properties.
4 Cf., for instance, Moore and Giesinger (1974).

REFERENCES

Canada. Advisory Committee on Reconstruction. 1944. *Report on Social
   Security for Canada*, prepared by L.C. Marsh. Ottawa: King's Printer.
Canada. Department of National Health and Welfare. 1973. *Background Paper
   on Income Support and Supplementation*. Ottawa.
Canadian Council on Social Development. 1977. *A Review of Social Housing
   Policy*. Ottawa: CCSD.

Economic Council of Canada. 1974. *Eleventh Annual Review: Economic Targets and Social Indicators.* Ottawa: Information Canada.

Moore, L., and C. Giesinger. 1974. *Winnipeg Public Housing Tenancy Agreements.* Winnipeg: Manitoba Housing and Renewal Corporation.

Runge, D., *et al.* 1975. *A Comprehensive Social Housing Policy for British Columbia.* Victoria: Attorney General's Department.

Social Planning Council of Metropolitan Toronto. 1977. *Social Allowances in Ontario: An Historical Analysis of General Welfare Assistance and Family Benefits, 1961-1976.* Toronto: The Council.

Walker, M., ed. 1975. *Rent Control: A Popular Paradox.* Vancouver: Fraser Institute.

VII

Perspectives on the Housing Debate:
Plenary Discussion

7. PERSPECTIVES ON THE HOUSING DEBATE: PLENARY DISCUSSION

The following is an edited transcript of the final session of the conference. This session was originally scheduled as a discussion among six panelists, but the accumulation of unanswered questions during the earlier part of the conference generated pressures for a more open and unstructured debate from the floor. The resulting record is of interest both for the substantive information it provides and for the sequence and juxtaposition of ideas. Although the tapes of this session were originally intended only for our own internal reference, we have been persuaded that a vital element of the debate would be missing if we did not make some effort to capture the nature of this final session.

Rather than reprint the complete transcript, we have attempted to reconstruct the flow of ideas around the major themes which emerged. We have dealt with these themes as if they occurred in separate sessions. This disturbs the strict chronological sequence of discussion but it enhances the logical sequence. Frequently a commentator has directed his remarks, not to those of an immediate predecessor, but to an issue raised earlier. We have deleted comments which, while valuable in themselves, do not naturally fit into this structure.

The three main themes which emerged were: (1) What is a housing market? How is it perceived by different types of analyst and what implications follow from each particular definition? (2) What kind of housing research is needed for policy purposes, what should its objectives be and who should undertake it? (3) In light of current knowledge, what is the most enlightened way of introducing housing subsidies designed to assist people of low income?

WHAT IS A HOUSING MARKET?

It became evident during the discussion that different people were using the term housing "market" in several different ways. The same issue was addressed in more theoretical terms in the introductory essay in this volume. Perhaps the basic distinction in this session was between those who used the term to refer to the outcomes of the private housing sector, considered apart from government intervention, and those who were concerned with the *operation* of that private sector. In the former usage the market was seen to be "working" if it was meeting social needs without government assistance. In its second meaning the market refers to the behaviour of the private sector, taking into account various public incentives and policies. The test of whether the market was working in this sense was whether the private sector behaved in an economically rational manner, given the environment as modified by public action.

We shall introduce the discussion with comments from Jeffrey Patterson and Lloyd Axworthy which clearly reflect the first definition given above.

Patterson I do not think that the market works all that well. The federal government perceived back in 1945 that the market might not respond in the way that they wanted, that in concert with giving people money, such as through family allowances (however insufficient they may have been at the time), they had to make some sort of a thrust to remodel the whole mortgage industry. If the market worked so well, why would a major part of federal government policy in the subsequent thirty years have been focused on that industry?

I think that the market for rental housing, for instance, has never worked in the way economists would have it. From 1946 until 1951, when rent controls were lifted, the federal government initiated rental guarantees, allowances for depreciation, and all sorts of other subsidies to make the rental market work. After they lifted rent controls in 1951, and every time the rental market was in trouble, they resurrected the limited dividend program. So in my view the market has not worked that well.

We now have a federal task force on supply and price of residential land. Bringing land on the market has not always been easy, and I do not think that the market works in quite the easy fashion that some people maintain. Once housing is built it is true that bidders come into the market and bid against each other over a given piece of property or housing – and that may work. But bringing new housing on line in this country has never worked all that well, and the quality of a lot of what we have brought on line is being questioned.

Axworthy When we talk about the market, no one has talked about the fact that in the last five or six years the private rental market has almost ceased to exist and is only maintained by a heavy infusion of government funds. From what Patterson said this joint enterprise operation is not joint enterprise, it really is a major transfusion of public funds. And when you find in the province of Manitoba that of 2,500 rental units built so far this year, only ninety-three are being funded through private financing that is not subsidized in one shape or form or another, that begins to tell you something about how well the market is working.

The second definition is illustrated in the discussion below. (The remark by Smith is in response to an extended statement by Axworthy, of which the excerpt above is only a brief part.)

Smith Clearly there is the notion that the market does not seem to be working, in particular the rental market. I submit to you that the market is working extremely well, in the sense of responding to incentives that are provided to it. When government, or a series of governments, makes changes in tax legislation, as it did in 1971 with the changes in the Income Tax Act which eliminated rental housing as a tax shelter, which imposed taxes on recaptured depreciation, and which reduced the use of real estate as a tax planning or estate planning device, it is going to reduce the desirability of investment in housing. When you impose rent controls you are going to reduce the desirability of investing in rental housing; when you discourage foreign investment, especially in housing, you are going to discourage the amount of new construction. When in Ontario you introduce a land speculation tax that treats investment in apartment buildings differently from investment in commercial property, you are going to affect the amount of new rental housing that is built. And then when the government goes in directly, in competition with the private sector, through a series of other programs, you are going to do something to the response of the private sector which does not get these subsidies. So what does it do? It stops producing. And that is not evidence that the market is not working. It is confirmation that the market *is* working. It is responding to the incentives being given. Now, it may not be doing what you want it to do, but that is because you have introduced a series of policies that were not thought out in the first place; and then when you get the responses, you go around saying this shows the market is not working. But I would submit quite the contrary: it shows that what we need to do is introduce policies which let the market adjust to give the desired result, and not to be throttled.

Struyk We are coming up with the same situation in the U.S., that to get construction back up, market rents are going to have to rise. And that is unacceptable if you want to keep rents down to the former relative level. Instead, the government will have to come in with formal subsidies, which is exactly what you have done. The arguments for subsidies are that it is really much more efficient, because at least there are not tax expenditures involved that nobody sees, and that you are making the decision on subsidies very consciously.

I agree completely with Larry Smith's point: the market is working. We in the U.S. are suffering the same kind of phenomenon: we tampered a bit, through the Tax Reform Act of 1976, with the tax advantages to multi-family housing. Now the market is tight; we have the lowest vacancy rate in multi-family housing since the War (5 per cent), despite a high rate of national new starts. The hue and cry now is that we need more subsidies, but to me it is just exactly what you would have forecast. If you reduce the subsidies, rents are going to have to rise to a level where they make that up. And if you want to take away the tax advantage, that's fine, but you ought to realise that you should not be surprised when you have to come back with a subsidy to offset that tax advantage, to keep rents at the same level.

Bossons I want to make a slightly different comment from Larry Smith's, but on much the same theme. Total housing starts have not gone way down. Ignoring the current year [1977], when there is considerable unemployment in the construction industry because of the general recession, over the last five years housing starts have been at a high level. So the point is not that total housing starts have dried up, but that rental housing which is *unsubsidized* has dried up. So when Larry talks about the market working, what he is really saying is that the market is allocating housing construction in the direction that is most profitable.

A further point: not only is it true that a lot of subsidies on the tax side were withdrawn from the rental market in 1971 — subsidies that were never "costed-in" so that we have ended up substituting subsidies which we cost and which therefore politicians and provincial treasurers worry about — we have also substituted them for tax subsidies which in fact were larger but not noticed. Another point is that we put in a new subsidy, because we introduced a capital gains tax that applied to all assets except owner-occupied homes. We then went into a fiscal policy, at the same time, which has generated the highest continued inflation rate that we have had in history, over a protracted period. What that has meant is that since the capital gains on other assets rose with inflation and were taxed, the combined effect of the tax exemption on capital gains from owner-occupied houses and inflation provided a considerable subsidy for home ownership. So we have had a fantastic coalescence of many things, mainly in the early 1970s, all of which have resulted in a big shift in supply from producing rental units to producing housing units. It is very clear why this has happened, because all those things have occurred at the same time, and the market, as

Larry says, worked perfectly well. It has done exactly what you would expect, in reacting to these changes in subsidies, such that the only rental housing being constructed is in effect what is being subsidized.

It seems to me that the big lesson from this is that we had better make sure that our provincial treasurers, ministers of finance and so forth, recognize the effects of these policy changes and not be surprised that subsidies are growing. They are going to go on growing as long as inflation continues and as long as these policies remain unchanged.

Up to this point the exchanges have centred around two alternate interpretations of what the "market" is. While they differ in terms of their precise definition, they share a common perspective: the existence of a semi-autonomous private sector in which the public sector intervenes with varying results. This "model" is made more complicated by the following comments which introduce an explicit political component into the definition.

Axworthy It comes back to what you are calling a market. If you are simply saying that it is a bunch of private builders who are going to respond to incentives, that is not really the way it works. Private builders also have a very strong political effect, and it is not just a matter of the rental market. AHOP [Assisted Home Ownership Program] props up the single-family market again in that price range. Because if you took out all of those public dollars, and said OK, market, go and allocate according to your own resources, we would be building houses only for 10 per cent, maybe 15 per cent, of the population. Thus the government's response has been in part to say that the market can no longer supply a large percentage of housing needs and that this is why the subsidies are introduced. We cannot assume that it is an abstract market because the actors in that market also have substantial political influence to change its management; that is the political economy part.

Burkus I would like to take issue with some of what Lloyd [Axworthy] has been saying about the power of particular lobbies. My own personal experience has been that sure, they are a relevant factor and they happen to be a key element in how goods and services in this area are delivered. However, I would venture to say that in a sense, the builders, developers and the industry were dragged kicking and screaming into the AHOP program because their whole cost structure was based on delivering a product worth several thousand dollars more than what the AHOP ceilings permitted. And my own personal experience on the ARP [Assisted Rental] program has been that, in that particular area, we did a lot of arm-twisting to get that particular group to participate and deliver the goods. Quite frankly we felt that if the industry was not prepared to respond it was political disaster to put up a program that said we're going to provide rental housing units, when nothing might come out of the market. So we in government did a lot of market research and in a sense we became developers in order to understand that industry.

Axworthy What I am saying is that the housing market is becoming a quasi-public market, and that the construction-development-building industry is falling into the classic public trap. That is, developers know who is feeding them, and the structure of their industry and their investment strategies are now being geared for these public programs. You only had to see the kind of massive lemming-like approach on the ARP program. The form and institutional nature of that market have gone through some very major transformations in the last three or four years. Those things should be analyzed because they have long-term implications as to who is going to deliver housing and how you handle such programs.

Dear One of the lessons from this discussion is that there is an economic argument, a social argument, a geographical argument, etc., about what we call the housing market. One can separate specific technical problems, such as worrying about the elasticities of demand and so on, and what is good basic research — whatever that means — in each of these relevant areas. My point is that the housing market is a structure in itself; a structure which is embedded in the general structure of society. If we are going to talk about similar themes in housing, it is necessary to abstract from our own individual concerns like elasticities and begin to talk about this social structure, and the way urbanization is related to urban planning, to the housing problem and to the whole urban nexus. If we can do that we will have a perfectly adequate alternative model for examining some of the issues that have been raised here, one which does not separate technical and political issues, which is not a naive position, and which concentrates more on the political economy or institutional dimensions of the housing issue. It is when we begin to abstract from our own individual preconceptions and concerns that we can begin to approach an overall discussion of the housing problem.

It becomes evident from the last set of comments in this section that the definition of a housing market is inseparable from one's framework of evaluation. How you define the market determines the grounds on which you decide whether it is working properly. The following remarks illustrate some of the different criteria which might be employed to identify a "healthy market". Michelson initiates the exchange by developing a metaphor for the conflicts between supply-side and demand-side subsidies, which were discussed previously, in order to pose a question concerning the nature of the distortions in preferences which they may bring about. This comment is followed by an interesting attempt to distinguish the state of the housing market as a whole from the experience of particular groups within it, making it possible to visualize how different evaluative creieria might be reconciled with each other.

Michelson I sit here thinking of the Canadian housing problems and I have a vision of a train starting away from the station. Someone who has not quite made it to the train is running after it. The train is picking up speed and the person obviously is not going to catch it. This is the situation so commonly faced these days regarding housing for increasing numbers of the Canadian public. The normal response is to give the person a little injection so he or she can run a little faster. At the same time the train is pulling ahead even faster and the question comes, when thinking of a policy that might be effective, is it one of making the person go a little faster, but not quite fast enough, or of slowing the train down, but in such a way that the train itself will not go out of business.

The problem really revolves around a market, and we have had considerable discussion on whether the market is working or not. Why do we not go and measure it and find out? But we also have to ask, *what is a healthy market?* What is it responding to? Which kinds of interests are dominant? Is it government acting as a proxy for people (though not necessarily bringing about what people want)? Is it a healthy, efficient activity in itself (an invisible hand)? Or is it in effect the producer catching on to the product that the consumer is placing the demand for, which is my old idea of what a healthy market is? If this latter conception is the case, then is not the idea that we want to encourage producers to make a healthy profit making something that people want and can afford to pay for, rather than having producers merely respond to the availability of subsidies considered necessary because the system does not now take controlling action to prevent the unearned profits and escalating prices of everything available — its increasing speeds. The question really depends on the relative speed of two bodies and what various forms of intervention or non-intervention do to speed, slow, or ignore both bodies.

Ozanne The problem that you are raising, as I see it, is one of low-income people paying exorbitant amounts for housing in a very tight housing market. I would try and separate the question of why the market is tight, and the tightness of supply, from the fact that these people have to pay very high prices for housing, and not try to churn the whole market around so that these people can get lower priced housing.

Michelson But the problem is also that middle-income people are currently paying too much for something that by and large they do not want, simply because they need it and find little else on the market they can possibly afford. This is not regarded here as a problem, but I think it is also a problem.

Smith When we talk about the affordability of housing, everybody says that people are paying too much for housing in Canadian urban centres. But too much in what way? If you would talk about the rental market for a moment, people have said, well, the market is not going to adjust, you are not going to get any increase in supply if you do certain things. It seems to me a strange statement to say that if you generate more demand and prices start to rise, you will not get more supply unless you have a model in which prices are already so low that even a slight increase is not going to be sufficient. But if that is right, then how is housing too expensive? Housing cannot be too expensive in a resource allocation sense. In that sense, prices are not too high if they are not sufficiently high to bring more resources into the housing sector. If prices are so low that resources are not coming into the housing market, then that seems to me reasonable evidence that the price is not "too high". The evidence is that prices are too low. If you look at rents in Toronto, you will find that they are a real bargain compared to the opportunity costs of almost anything else.

Bossons Surely the point is that prices in Toronto are now too low from the point of view of the prices required by the market to bring in a new supply of housing for low-income people. They are too high from the political point of view that reflects the position of low-income households who have found that those prices have been rising at a rate faster than the rate of increase in their income.

POLICY-ORIENTED RESEARCH

A second major theme in the panel discussion concerned the need for research which is directed toward meeting currently identified social needs. Questions of what kind of research is "relevant", who should do the research, with what objectives and under whose direction, are obviously considerably more complicated than might at first appear.

The issue was first raised explicitly in a preceding session of the conference, when Ann McAfee used a simple, perhaps overstated but nonetheless relevant, piece of imagery to convey the sense of frustration which some planners have with the apparently remote discussions of some housing analysts:

> I would like to bring a homeless, mother-led family with an income of $8,000, and dump that family into the laps of the economists in the front row here, and say, "Now you tell me what I am going to do with this family".

Although this remark was directed to economists, they are not the only intended audience.

This same theme of immediacy and urgency was picked up by Axworthy in his opening remarks at the final session:

Axworthy I want to make some comments from the political perspective. It's a very fresh one. The bruises are still healing from an election [Manitoba, 1977] in which housing was a major issue, at least in my constituency, and where I had to beat off more real estate agents than I could count who were not particularly fond of the policy positions I had advocated and pursued in the Manitoba legislature. The fact is that the "quantum leap" that one has to make from the door-by-door discussion about dealing with a woman who is paying $210 in rent out of $280 a month income, to some of the other discussions I have heard recently, requires a fair degree of what some call a "leap of faith".

The real issues that we should be asking about go back to the question posed by Robert Lynd in a book called *Knowledge for What.* Using his example, we are engaged in a lecture on navigation while the ship is going down. We have been doing a lot of navigational development but there are some very precise, specific issues that are politically strong at the present moment. Someone said that we should not get prematurely into policy discussions until we have a greater empirical base. However, that empirical base will be of little consequence because of the requirement for very immediate, superficial and at times impressionistic judgements on enormously important policies which relate to housing. For example, you now have ten provincial legislatures which in some form or other are going to have to wrestle with the issue of rent review policy. There will either be transference out or maintenance of some kind of regulatory mechanisms on rent within the next six months. If you look at the literature, there is very little to say about the Canadian experience in relation to rent. There is the Canadian Council on Social Development study on rent controls of about two years ago; some of the research done at the University of British Columbia was based almost exclusively on information derived from outside Canada. Yet here you have a major policy debate going on in the provincial legislatures which has very little relevance to what is happening here.

Smith May I make a couple of comments about Mr. Axworthy's discussion, because it seems to me that he and I read a different literature. A lot of problems he is interested in *are* addressed. It seems to me that the problem is not that there is insufficient research on which to make the policy decisions, or that a lot of people at this conference haven't talked about research (although the last step of putting them into the policy world may not have taken place) that is not relevant for policy; but that the policy-maker either chooses to ignore

it, does not pay attention to it because he is unaware of it, or else he happens
to see people who give advice that he wants to hear in the first place, and that
he doesn't listen to the other things that are being said.

Attention shifted then to try to identify the kinds of research questions which
were particularly fruitful for policy purposes:

(Unidentified) Could I suggest that the meeting conclude that the question
of whether the market is working not be decided on the basis of a yes or no.
Instead, it might be decided that perhaps there should be some qualifications
as to whether the benefits that are being provided to producers at this point
are necessary in order to make the market function, and what other level of
subsidies would be required to make it work better, or whether there is some
oversubsidization involved. I think it is the quantification of these benefits
that we researchers should be concerned with, not the general position of
whether the market is working or not.

Axworthy That is part of it; the other part is the institutional analysis of how
the market is working. Take a look at the changing investment patterns in the
mortgage markets, such as large banks which for the most part no longer lend
in older neighbourhoods. The lending pattern has changed radically because of
the fact that we have a substantially different financial system, say, than the
Americans. This creates certain patterns in our mortgage market, and therefore
in our housing market, such that you may be able to make a stronger impact
on housing by changing the institutional structure than you do by going back
to forms of public subsidy again. You may make a much stronger impact on
older neighbourhoods in our cities by simply changing the Bank Act than you
do by tripling the amount of RRAP [Residential Rehabilitation Assistance Pro-
gram] funds available.

The government's response has also been in part that the market can no longer supply a large percentage of housing needs. That is why the subsidies are
built in, not that somehow they want to change the market, but because the
market was not going to provide those needs. The question I am raising is, should
that money be used in that way? Let's examine more specifically whether you
get the best distribution and effectiveness from an ARP program or from one
that is going to relate back to a housing allowance program. If you have to spend
public dollars, and there is a limited basket, you had better decide where you
want to allocate them. Right now there is an enormous amount – $2 billion
of capital a year, plus a very large operating budget, and $250 million of rental
subsidies – going into an area which might be questioned, as opposed to expanding third-sector housing or going directly into government housing. There are
a lot of choices we can make but we seem not to be making them.

Bossons That is the right question: given that we are going to spend a certain amount of money, where will it have the greatest redistributive effect? It seems to me that the answer depends a lot on the kind of research that Ray [Struyk] and Larry [Ozanne] talked about [see Section IV] : what is the effect of cash subsidies on housing prices?

Struyk It seems to me that if you were looking for help as a policy-maker from an analyst, what you would want him to do is to tell you, quite independent of the politics of it, what is the most efficient way of achieving your objective. If your objective is maximum income redistribution, using housing as a tool, that is what you would like from him. You are perfectly aware that if this means giving out housing allowances instead of building subsidies, there is going to be a big, unhappy lobby. That is your problem to cope with as a politician. And it seems to me that the trick is to get people to give the advice that they know how to give you. What I see frequently is a total confusion of the technical and the political, so people do not really understand what point is being made. When you are unable to sort that out, you get both qualities discounted.

Burkus One part that I think is horrendously difficult to come to grips with is that in a constrained environment you cannot easily shift expenditures from A to B. Historically, governments have tended to do A and B, with A withering at some point in the far distant future when it becomes no longer relevant or becomes a very small part of the pie. And one of our major problems in this area, in policy development, is how do you turn off A (particularly in a minority government situation) without telegraphing an undesirable political message that you are taking something away from somebody, whether it be the builders, the recipients or whomever. A large part of our activity is wrestling with substituting B for A without making it appear that we have closed down the shop, for reasons of the type that Lloyd Axworthy mentioned. And that adds an incredibly different dimension to policy and program development that in some sense was not there when budgets tended to expand at rates of 25 or 30 per cent a year.

Goldberg I think that the only people who have a vested interest (if anybody does) in the total system, are politicians. They are the ones we are paying to worry about technical issues, not just sociological technical issues, or engineering technical issues, or economic technical issues, but a merging of these, dealing with the various alternatives, picking out that set of alternatives which does not give credence to any one discipline but does somehow give the system some rights of survival — someone said that politics is the art of the possible — and I think that is a very important job. I think politicians have become much more questioning of the technical information that they are getting; I think they have a responsibility to the public to sort out the technical wheat and chaff and then come up with some synthetic solution that they need not apologize for; neither good economics nor good sociology nor good engineering, but which does make good sense from a political point of view. I think it is absolute nonsense to try to separate technical issues from political issues, because ultimately all the choices that society makes are political.

Axworthy An essay which everyone, whichever side of the fence you work on, should read, is Weber's "Politics as a Vocation and Science as a Vocation". We are beginning to see the very different attributes and requirements of these two roles that people play. Part of the problem now is that people say that it is up to the politician to do it; yet there are a lot of political people, among whom I include the senior administrative policy-makers in the corporations, who are wrestling with those questions. What John Burkus says about the incrementalism in housing policy is not quite true. We have been going through some substantial zig-zags at the federal level: every four years (and now) we re-write the National Housing Act [NHA], with substantial impact, much of which we do not understand. In the last two years, Central Mortgage and Housing Corporation [CMHC] has made a major change in direction in terms of how it uses its own public money to try to lever private capital into the housing market. All I am asking is that the group with the technical skills here should be examining these fundamental issues, as opposed to some of the things talked about previously. That is what you really want to know because they are going to be changing it again in six months, changing it without knowing what the impact was originally.

Struyk You obviously cannot keep these things separate all the way. My point was very simple: if people with the backgrounds of those in this room wanted to be best used in a policy framework, they should be used in terms of their strengths. Obviously when we get to the decision point you hear from the group which merges those points of view and comes up with some sensible policy.

The previous comments have largely neglected the question of which institutions should be responsible for policy research. Smith suggests the hazards of relying on any single group and indicates the resources for policy analysis which already exist. The starting point for his comments was the statement that CMHC was now actively considering amendments to the National Housing Act.

Smith If there are going to be significant policy decisions made in rewriting the NHA, unless all this is so confidential that getting feedback from the private sector was going to destroy part of it in advance, then it would seem to me, from the point of view of efficient policy-making, that the discussion should be thrown open. Let the private sector and researchers in the universities and elsewhere have a chance to comment on it. And at the same time it seems to me that a lot of the research that has been going on in the private sector, either directly on policy, or theoretical work that can be applied, could help in reaching the conclusions. We keep hearing criticisms of private research, and of estimates of elasticities and so on that suggest the research is unimportant. *The latter are very important;* they tell you what the outcomes are going to be, and not just picayune things like it is going to be 2 per cent or 3 per cent different. They have enormous implications, depending on what the elasticities are of some of the other variables. Why not draw on people who have done this work, both technical and policy-oriented, and integrate it with the work that is coming in, so at least there is some airing of the problems before dramatic changes in policy direction are made.

And a final comment in that regard: somebody said earlier that we look too much at the U.S. But that is the only work we have; we do not have specific work on Canada. These markets are also so similar that there are enormous lessons to be learned from the U.S. experience and from that of some other countries. We should also try to draw on that and not just plug in new policies and then be surprised when they work the way you should have anticipated they work, but don't give you the results you wanted in the first place.

Axworthy How about that critical fact that the financial, institutional arrangements in Canada are fundamentally different from the American ones? This creates very strong differences in the development industry to the point where we have a much higher degree of concentration in the industry than the Americans have. And that is simply a reflection of a very big difference in banking and financial systems and in the way that moneys are allocated.

Smith Well, if you look at capital flows and the responsiveness of the market to differences, there is more intermediation in the U.S. because of the rigidities in the Savings and Loan system. But if you look at the sensitivity in interest rates and availability effects from work that I have done on Canadian markets and compare them to those in the U.S., they are very similar. If you look at econometric models of housing markets in Canada and at the models in the U.S., they are responding to the same variables in the same way, with the same elasticities. There are structural differences. You do have to modify the results according to these structures, and there can be major local differences — I agree with all that, but there are still enough similarities that you can learn a lot from looking at them.

A number of commentators noted the complexity of housing issues and the fact that housing markets were affected by policies normally considered to have no housing content. Some interesting points were raised concerning how housing policy analysts might overcome this difficulty.

Struyk The question is, how do you keep your oar in when other decisions are being made? We have just had something nice happen, something that has not happened much in the American experience. In the recent discussion of tax reform a number of changes hit housing directly, and there are other provisions which are going to affect the relative position of city versus suburbs. We in HUD [U.S. Department of Housing and Urban Development] were asked for the first time by the White House to develop an urban impact statement on a number of pieces of tax reform policy that we would not have seen in the past. And our comments were taken seriously, apparently. But it is only when whoever is directing these other agencies will let you, that you can have something to say in the discussions. There is something called the Economic Policy Group in the U.S. which, in concept, makes the basic economic policies of the country. HUD now gets to be a full member of that committee. That is wonderful, because you can get your oar in, trying to broaden the perspective of these conversations. My guess is that those kinds of effects are much more important than any single housing program you can put out, given all the dollars involved. So the trick is to have some mechanisms for participation, and very recently we seemed to have started some. Whether that works is something else.

Burkus I venture to say that the establishment of the Ministry of Housing in Ontario had much the greatest impact, if it has had any impact at all, exactly in the area that Struyk was mentioning. This means that we have essentially ended up as a lobby group that is forcing housing considerations in areas of taxation and in areas of servicing. Let me give you one example: the Ministry of the Environment made decisions on servicing that, intriguingly enough, had no reference to the need for providing servicing for growth. Here is a province which is growing in all directions, all kinds of new growth taking place, but the services needed were largely ignored in the weighting system used at the staff level. The thing that saved it was the political input, which said we don't care what the staff says, Whitby is growing, or somewhere else is growing, therefore we will put the sewer there. One of our greatest impacts was that we managed to get a weighting factor of 20 per cent (or whatever it was) which meant that when the staff made those decisions, they gave 20 per cent or 20 value points to the areas of growth rather than to improving the environmental quality of the water and sewer systems that were already there. That is astounding. From our point of view that is a virtually cost-free decision. But in the great scheme of things, nobody out on the street would ever recognize that as a factor and yet these are the kinds of areas where, if we have had any impact at all, it has been substantial. Essentially, you institutionalize an interest or lobby group that forces trade-offs on things such as land speculation, land transfer, etc. Unfortunately, what it means is that you have to set up, within your policy group, an enormous amount of expertise totally unrelated to housing, and that is very difficult. What you have done is to try to set up virtually a mini-government within a government to force those kinds of trade-offs. If you do not have that kind of talent on board, you really cannot say anything about anything because you are so easily discredited. But that is one of the things that governs how decisions are made and why some of our research activity and interests are totally unrelated to planning or housing: there are incredible nuances in the system of how decisions are made.

Finally, Patterson returns to the theme of agency secrecy, alluded to earlier by Smith, and its consequences for policy-related research.

Patterson A representative from CMHC made a couple of references to research going on there, evaluations that are being done and to the 1973 NHA amendments. A very important question is the fact that to arrive at the 1973 amendments to the National Housing Act, for instance, a very extensive consultation process was undertaken with professionals, with researchers and with provincial governments. But the process was very secretive. The federal government tried to squelch our own report, the Low Income Housing Task Force Report. The same secretive process is going on now. People mention the fact that the Part Five research funds under the NHA are larger than they have ever been but very little of it is being spent externally with professional researchers.

We have talked about the issue of shelter allowances. In a recent meeting the CMHC executive committee said that they would like to go the shelter allowance route; I think that bears credence to what some people have said about the federal government wanting to transfer funds to individuals and wanting to get out of the shared cost programs. But our problem is the administrative vehicle for doing this. A couple of weeks ago a proposal call went out from CMHC asking for proposals to do research on the administrative mechanisms for setting up shelter allowances. Now, some discussion here suggests that market conditions might be a factor which could determine whether or not you go that route. As far as I know, a similar proposal call did *not* go out for market research on the outcomes of shelter allowances, and we know from the American experiments that you have to pay a great deal of attention to those outcomes.

Returning to my point, the process is very secretive. Nine researchers received this one proposal call; probably nobody else knows that it went out. I am not blaming anyone *here;* I think everyone here would like to see what is done published and debated openly. But the research is not published; most of it is even done under secrecy oaths. And of course now we have a Green Paper on secrecy from the federal government which actually is a Green Paper on how to keep things secret. That is really a basic part of the problem. As researchers interested in how the market operates and in how people gain access to adequate housing, I think we all have to ask ourselves, in addition to what we need to know about the market, how are we going to organize our research capability in order to do the right things in terms of policy?

HOUSING ALLOWANCES

The last major theme of this session concerned the current state of our knowledge about the appropriateness of using housing allowances to subsidize consumers, rather than subsidies for housing production. The exchanges clearly reveal the importance of knowledge about regional housing markets. The discussion starts with a question from Anne Golden, who, in effect, was challenging the researchers in the audience to state the policy significance of their work.

Golden An important issue, raised by Professor Rose and Jeff Patterson, concerned what we should do about the low-income segment of society which is being left out by programs such as AHOP, particularly families that are single-parent led. A number of related questions were raised concerning assumptions as to the social benefits of home ownership, the problem of political realities and the fact that we use housing as an economic tool. We talk about the cost of subsidies, we talk about the fact that there are many variables involved in determining the kind of housing that people want and why, and especially we asked the question of whether or not we should be using housing to deal with poverty. I guess I am disappointed with the answers.

Is there any advice from people in the room who have done a lot of research? Jeff Patterson made one comment this morning which tended to favour an approach including more shelter allowances. I suspect that there is also an opinion that maybe we should take the constraints off developers and the building industry so that hopefully the market will be able to function the way it should function — filtering down, and so on. Now these are two opinions — two different opinions — but is there a consensus among experts such that we do not have to wait for the research again?

Struyk Some research has been done on this question. We have a very serious experiment under way in the U.S. on the use of housing allowances or simple cash grants or alternative mix of those things. John Quigley could speak to this in great detail since he has mined data on the demand experiment as much as anyone. There has also been a fair amount of research on the relative benefits of using mixes of supply-side and demand-side subsidy programs. Although those are simulation model results, they seem to have some validity.

Quigley The point that you are raising is the absolutely fundamental point about the operation of what we call housing markets. One view is that there is no particular moral reason why housing is more important to human beings than food or anything else which they happen to prefer doing with their money. The implications of this are straightforward: if one is willing to take consumers' own views as paramount, then fiddling around with very complicated subsidy policies to redistribute income is likely to be inefficient. By inefficient I mean that if you gave them an equivalent amount of money they would be better off. One problem, in taking this view seriously, is the question raised yesterday — do you presume, for one reason or another, that you know better about what is good for people than they do themselves? If you do, I suppose the implications are clear. That is, instead of giving individuals unrestricted cash, you put them in a dwelling unit or you give them particular kinds of transfers which force an outcome that you want because you "know better" than they do.

Golden We are going back again to the academic debate on moral issues. But Lloyd Axworthy, as a politician, is saying that he does not have a choice: that he has to help low-income people with housing.

Quigley Look, a number of people here basically take the perspective, which I guess can be discredited, of scholarship about this issue, and are interested in understanding in some meaningful sense. When politicians want us to say what their policy should be, we are willing to tell them what we think are the best things for them to do. Some of our advice is based on hard science and numbers; some of it is based on guesses. We do not really "know" the answers but we are willing to tell them what we do know if they ask us. They can throw this advice away — they can say that it is wrong or that other things are more important.

Struyk Anne Golden is not asking the broad question; she's asking the question: given that society has made the decision to provide housing services rather than cash income, what is the most efficient way to do it?

Quigley OK. Every bit of empirical evidence that we have seen so far, from the demand experiment and from other studies, suggests that the cash transfer approach — that is, giving people money to spend on housing — has not significantly increased the price of housing — so far. It could, but it does not seem to have yet. Thus, if you are worried about low-income consumers, you transfer resources to them to spend on housing; that way, it doesn't become a rip-off for landlords. To a substantial extent it actually goes into the pockets of those people. Now that is what you might predict from a series of abstract models in the long run, and if you could extrapolate from today to the long run that would be a sensible response, assuming that people know how to spend their resources. In the short run, however, and in some kinds of housing markets — places with very low vacancy rates — you know those results would not come about. Aggregate results suggest that over time, and within a reasonable policy period, the benefits will go to the poor. But in places where the vacancy rates are 0.5 per cent you also know that, over a short-run period, there are going to be a lot of rip-offs.

Golden In Metro Toronto we have a very low vacancy rate. In Vancouver I think there is a 0.5 per cent vacancy rate. Given those low rates and given that we have a very high level of housing need, would you say that cash transfers would not work well? What would you recommend then?

Quigley That gets back to the question of mixed programs; and it depends very much on particular housing markets.

Bossons Surely the answer is that if you are talking about one housing market the effect is going to be different from what happens in another market, depending on conditions in that market. If you talk about conditions in Vancouver, or in Toronto, with very low vacancy rates, the general proposition that John [Quigley] made about cash transfers generally being the best will not be true in those markets.

(Unidentified) Unless you control rents.

Bossons No. Controlling rents is not going to help change the supply: it makes the situation worse.
[Loud protests]
Well, you don't make water run uphill by building a dam. Let me just make a point: if you are worried about the situation in the tight vacancy markets, if you are worried about having a policy that will work well in all parts of the country, then you need more than one program. The cash grants program can work in a number of places, but in Metro Toronto and Vancouver, areas of tight market conditions where the growth rate is high and where you are not going to have a trickle-down effect because immigration is pushing demand, then you had better have another program, a supply program such as non-profit housing, which will create some of the supply aimed at that particular part of the market.

Struyk If you look at American housing policies today, the one thing that jumps out at you is that they try to provide for diversity of markets. The Section 8 program, which is designed to provide something that looks like housing allowances to low-income households, allows for a varying mix between renting existing units or entering into long-term leases for new units or rehabilitating units, market by market. Local areas get a block of money that they can spend any way they want to, subject to some broad guidelines. If you have an enormously high vacancy rate, for example, you can't build new units.

The other major piece of housing policy — the Community Development Block Grant Program — is putting out $4 billion a year, largely in major cities. And that money is restricted in two ways: one, it has to be tied into low-income and moderate-income areas; and two, it has to be used *mainly* for bricks and mortar kinds of programs. You can pave streets with it, you can give grants for rehabilitation, you can do a lot of things, as long as it is a bricks and mortar program. Obviously, the important thing for us to do is to find out how much difference that mix makes.

Ozanne I would recommend, in the U.S. context, subsidies for these low-income people, so that instead of spending 40 per cent of their income for housing they are paying a smaller proportion. Some other policy seems to be appropriate for dealing with the whole market and with the question of why no rental housing is being built. That seems to be something different, affecting the whole market and not just low-income households, and should be dealt with itself.

Bossons There is surely a problem with Larry Ozanne's comment though: if more money is provided so that people's incomes go up and the fraction of their income represented by their current rent goes down, it is going to stay down only if landlords do not raise their prices. And landlords will refrain from raising their prices only if either that additional income does not push up the demand for housing, or the market responds by providing additional supply. And if it is the case, as I suspect it is currently, that you would not get that expansion of supply under current market conditions — with the current rate of inflation, etc. — then it is entirely possible and, I suspect, likely, that there will be no real change in the position of low-income families except through a program that actually provides the additional supply, as is done by existing non-profit housing programs.

Ozanne I have to disagree with that because it sounds as if many people at least have some housing, but the major problem is that they spend too much of their income on housing. What I am talking about is their having more money to spend on other things, so that housing is not such a large proportion of income. That sounds to me to be a big portion of the problem. And second, I am talking about redistribution, not about additional income. We are going to be taking away from some people and giving it to others so that they can afford more of the things that they need. I am not talking about increasing total demand. I do think the question of increasing the total supply is important for the whole market, but it should not be addressed with just low-income housing.

Struyk What happens if the housing you are living in now doesn't meet current standards? Somehow society sets a standard of what minimum housing ought to be and so people have double problems. You have a double objective of relieving rent burdens and improving quality. In that case, what do you do?

Ozanne If your objective is to improve housing quality, I would have to say that you need a program directed towards housing. Another problem is how much of their income people have left to spend on other things. I would build housing to address the first of these.

Bossons There is no point just increasing incomes if that increase is simply going to be represented by an increase in rents. Now once that income gets to the point of permitting an increase in rents, which brings in new supply, then you will start getting a response. But it is quite possible that a cash subsidy program would permit an increase in rents to a point that is still too low from the point of view of bringing in new supply, in which case virtually all of the cash transfer represents a transfer to property owners, with no real net change in the position of the low-income groups, the recipients of grants.

A question was raised concerning the appropriate locus for policies on housing subsidies if those policies had to be different in each regional housing market. The following comments revealed the political dimension of this question:

Axworthy I would make a guess that the federal government is going to move more into direct transfers to the individual and away from intergovernmental transfers.

Burkus I agree that the federal government is moving, and will continue to move at an accelerating rate, towards dealing with individuals. That is politically a lot more sexy than fooling around with sewage treatment plants and all the rest of it. And the new area (you heard it here first) is going to be rehabilitation. And there is no question in my mind that they will be moving directly to home owners and renters. The first signs of this were really through the RRAP program. RRAP now looks like a mouse in comparison with what it is going to become in five years. There are other indications certainly that that is the direction;

the home insulation grant program, for instance. These programs are incredibly
attractive politically: no hassles at all, marvellous stuff. That is going to leave
the other two levels of government in a bad bind, though.

Bossons And what happens when the market responds, as with the home
insulation program, by driving up the price of insulation more than the amount
of the cash grants?

Burkus [Sarcastically] It doesn't matter!

Struyk What you have got, if that really happened, is the worst possible thing:
you're giving money to the captains of industry through excess profit, knowing
that you haven't produced any more insulation than you would have in the
first place.

We feel the last word should go to Tom Gunton, whose comments near the end
of the discussion period expressed the sentiments of many, and also serve to reunite
the three themes which we have, up to now, artificially separated.

Gunton I am coming away from this conversation really quite confused. It
seems to me that this Conference started with a very neat problem: how do housing markets operate? The conclusion was that housing markets seem to operate
quite well. Thinking the problems were indeed solved, the discussion then turned
to social housing. It was argued that the proportion of the population not being
served properly by the housing market was something in the order of 80 per cent.
Then it was suggested that, well, we can deal with this problem quite easily. The
obvious solution is to set up some shelter allowances. Then it was suggested that
shelter allowances only work in certain conditions and a number of qualifications
were put on the proposal. And when John Quigley was pressed on the point of
what do we do in the current situation of tight markets, he pointed to some
other fellow and said, he has the answers over there. Then, as the conversation
evolved, it seemed that people were saying yes, indeed, there are some very serious problems here and we are going to have to have a number of supply programs. Some people suggested non-profit programs, and other sorts of things,
which are programs that people like Lawrence Smith and the Fraser Institute
seem to think are to a large extent the causes of the market imperfections in
the first place.

There seems to be a cumulative causation problem here. We started with the
market working well (in spite of what Smith says, you do not conclude that
the market is working well by saying that developers respond to various incentives). You then conclude that the market has to have some modifications —

326

interventions — which we then conclude are the causes of the market imperfections.

It seems to me that there is no really successful resolution coming out and I would like to put the onus on someone like Larry Smith to recommend a number of policies which will deal with the housing problem, starting from the point we are at in 1977.

GLOSSARY OF ABBREVIATIONS

AHOP	Assisted Home Ownership Program
ARP	Assisted Rental Program
BLS	Bureau of Labor Statistics (U.S.)
CBD	Central business district
CES	Constant Elasticity of Substitution
CINCH	Components of Inventory Change (data compiled by U.S. Bureau of the Census)
CMA	Census Metropolitan Area (Canada)
CMHC	Central Mortgage and Housing Corporation
CPI	Consumer price index
FHA	Federal Housing Administration (U.S.)
GVRD	Greater Vancouver Regional District
HUD	Dept. of Housing and Urban Development (U.S.)
IIPS	Inter-Institutional Policy Simulator
IMF	International Monetary Fund
LAC	Land absorption coefficient
LHA	Local housing authority
MLS	Multiple Listing Service
MUA	Major urban area
NBER	National Bureau of Economic Research
NHA	National Housing Act
NHI	National Housing Inventory (U.S.)
OHC	Ontario Housing Corporation
PDI	Personal disposable income
PDIC	Personal disposable income per capita
RRAP	Residential Rehabilitation Assistance Program
SHU	Survey of Housing Units (CMHC)
SMSA	Standard metropolitan statistical area (U.S.)
TSE	Toronto Stock Exchange

BIOGRAPHIES OF AUTHORS

JOHN BOSSONS is Professor of Economics at the University of Toronto and a Research Associate of the University's Centre for Urban and Community Studies. He received his Ph.D. from Harvard in 1962, and has taught at MIT, Carnegie-Mellon University, the University of Chicago and at Yale. Prior to joining the University of Toronto he was a Research Supervisor for the Carter Royal Commission on Taxation. He is currently also Vice-Chairman of the City of Toronto Planning Board.

LARRY S. BOURNE is Professor of Geography and Director of the Centre for Urban and Community Studies at the University of Toronto. He received his B.A. from the University of Western Ontario in 1961, an M.A. from Alberta in 1964 and a doctoral degree in Geography in 1966 from the University of Chicago. Following a year as a post-doctoral fellow in urban and regional development he took up a position at the University of Toronto. His current research interests include urban systems and national policy, the inner city and housing. His most recent books include *Urban Systems: Strategies for Regulation* (1976) and *Systems of Cities* (1978) a readings volume edited with J.W. Simmons.

STEWART J. CLATWORTHY is a former graduate student in the Department of Geography at Queen's University. After graduating from the University of Western Ontario, he wrote his master's thesis at Queen's on the land development process in London, Ontario. Subsequent work has focused on changing consumption of housing by low-income households in Wichita, Kansas.

GORDON W. DAVIES received his B.A. from the University of Western Ontario in 1968 and his Ph.D. in economics from the University of Michigan in 1972, since when he has taught urban economics at the University of Western Ontario. He is the author of several articles on the economic effects of population change, and on urban housing and land markets. His book for the Ontario Economic Council, on housing markets and government policy in Ontario, is to be published late in 1979.

MICHAEL A. GOLDBERG received his B.A. from Brooklyn College and his M.A. and Ph.D. from the University of California at Berkeley, all in economics. He joined the Faculty of Commerce and Business Administration at the University of British Columbia in 1968, where he is now Professor and Chairman of the Urban Land Economics Division. His research interests include transportation and land use,

328

location economics, urban housing and land markets, and strategies for planning and intervening in complex systems such as cities. He has been involved in urban simulation modelling since his association with the Bay Area Simulation Study in 1965. Most recently he has begun to explore more general questions about Canadian urban and housing policy and the related questions surrounding land use and development controls.

WILLIAM G. GRIGSBY received his Ph.D. in economics from Columbia University. He has been associated with the Department of City Planning at the University of Pennsylvania since 1959 and since 1975 has been Chairman of that Department. He has written numerous books and articles on housing markets, including *Housing Markets and Public Policy* (1963) and *Urban Housing Policy* (1974). He is currently president of the American Real Estate and Urban Economics Association.

JOHN R. HITCHCOCK received his Ph.D. in urban planning from the University of North Carolina. He is an Associate Professor in the Department of Urban and Regional Planning, and Associate Director of the Centre for Urban and Community Studies at the University of Toronto. His teaching and research interests are concerned with the planning of residential areas.

ROBERT J. HOBART was born in Lloydminster, Saskatchewan in 1950. He received his B.Comm. degree from the University of Alberta in 1972, where he held Queen Elizabeth and Francis Reeve fellowships. He received his M.B.A. degree in 1973, also from the University of Alberta. He is currently on educational leave at the Faculty of Commerce and Business Administration, University of British Columbia, from his position at the Ministry of State for Urban Affairs.

STUART M. McFADYEN received his B.Sc. degree from the University of Manitoba in 1959, majoring in mathematics and statistics, and became a chartered accountant in 1963; he is now a member of the Institute of Chartered Accountants of Alberta. He received his M.A. in economics from the University of British Columbia in 1967 and his Ph.D. from the University of California at Berkeley in 1969. He is now Associate Professor in the Faculty of Business Administration and Commerce at the University of Alberta. Among his publications are "Control of Foreign Ownership of Canadian Real Estate" (1976) and, with Robert Hobart, "An Alternative Measurement of Housing Costs and the Consumer Price Index" (1978).

ERIC G. MOORE is Professor of Geography at Queen's University. He received his Ph.D. from the University of Queensland in 1967 and taught at Northwestern University for seven years before coming to Queen's in 1973. He has written widely on the nature of residential mobility in urban areas and its role in neighbourhood change: more recently, this research has been focused on the development of information systems for monitoring neighbourhood change particularly as this relates to the demand for public services. The bulk of this work has focused on the city of Wichita, Kansas under funding from the National Science Foundation. In Canada, his primary research has been on developing systems for monitoring change in student enrollments at the local level, this work being funded by the Ontario Ministry of Education.

LARRY OZANNE received his Ph.D. in economics from Stanford University in 1975. Since 1972 he has been a member of the research staff of the Urban Institute in Washington, D.C., where he has contributed several papers to the Institute's publications series: "Market Effects of Housing Policies" with F. de Leeuw and others (1974); two papers on housing allowances in 1975; *Housing from the Existing Stock,* with R.J. Struyk (1976); and "Calculating Benefit/Cost Ratios with the UI Model" (1977).

JEFFREY PATTERSON is currently Director of Research at the Social Planning Council of Metropolitan Toronto. He served from 1973 to 1977 as Program Director, Housing, at the Canadian Council on Social Development in Ottawa. While there, he co-authored *Rent Stabilization: A Review of Current Policies in Canada* (1976) and directed the *Social Housing Policy Review,* from which many of the ideas contained in the paper herein were drawn. He took his first degree in geography and a master's degree in city and regional planning.

JOHN M. QUIGLEY is Associate Professor of Economics and a member of the interdisciplinary Institution for Social and Policy Studies at Yale University. He has co-authored three books on problems in urban economics and public finance. His papers have appeared in leading economics journals. He currently serves as a consultant to the U.S. Department of Housing and Urban Development and to the Urban Institute.

ALBERT ROSE is Professor of Social Work at the University of Toronto. He holds a doctorate in economics and political science, and during the past thirty years has devoted his research to the study of social and economic implications of housing policies and urban planning in Canada. He is the author of two major books in this field: *Regent Park, A Study in Slum Clearance,* (1958) and *Governing Metropolitan Toronto: A Social and Political Analysis 1953-1971* (1973). Dr. Rose was a founding member of the Centre for Urban and Community Studies at the University of Toronto.

DAVID SCHEFFMAN received his Ph.D. in economics from MIT in 1971; since then, he has held an appointment at the University of Western Ontario, where he is now Associate Professor of Economics. He has also acted as a consultant to the Ontario Economic Council and to the Joint Federal-Provincial Task Force on the Supply and Price of Serviced Land. His major area of research is in economic theory, concentrating in recent years on urban economics. His publications include (with J. Markusen) *Speculation and Monopoly in Urban Development* (1977). He is currently engaged in building an econometric model of the Canadian housing market.

LAWRENCE B. SMITH is Professor of Economics and Associate Chairman of the Department of Political Economy of the University of Toronto. After receiving his B.Com. from the University of Toronto in 1962 he obtained a Ph.D. in economics from Harvard University. Since coming to the University of Toronto in the same year he has been a leading researcher in housing and land economics and in Canadian economic problems. Among his recent books are *The Postwar Canadian Housing and Residential Mortgage Markets* (1974) and *Anatomy of a Crisis: Canadian Housing Policy in the Seventies* (1977).

RAYMOND J. STRUYK was appointed Deputy Assistant Secretary for Research, Office of Policy Development and Research, U.S. Department of Housing and Urban Development in April 1977. Previously he had been involved (1972-77) in the Urban Institute's Housing Studies Group, latterly as Manager of the Housing Market Behavior Project. He has also been a member of the Urban Studies Group, National Bureau of Economic Research (1968-72), and has taught economics at Rutgers and at Rice University. His recent publications include *Should Government Encourage Homeownership?* (1977); *Urban Homeownership: The Economic Determinants* (1976) with S. Marshall; *The Web of Urban Housing* (1975) with F. de Leeuw; *Housing from the Existing Stock* (1976) with L. Ozanne.

CONFERENCE PARTICIPANTS

Dominique Achour, Institut d'urbanisme, Université de Montréal

Donald Altman, Ryerson Polytechnical Institute, Toronto

Howard Andrews, Social Sciences, University of Toronto (Erindale)

John Auld, Dept. of Consumer Studies, University of Guelph

Lloyd Axworthy, Institute of Urban Studies, University of Winnipeg

Alan Baker, Dept. of Geography, University of Toronto

Bruce Becker, Centre for Urban and Community Studies, University of Toronto

Conrad Biernacki, Dept. of Geography, University of Toronto

Hans Blumenfeld, Urban and Regional Planning, University of Toronto

John Bossons, Institute for Policy Analysis, University of Toronto

Larry Bourne, Centre for Urban and Community Studies and Department of
    Geography, University of Toronto

Helen Breslauer, Centre for Urban and Community Studies, University of Toronto

Philip Brown, Central Mortgage and Housing Corporation, Ottawa

A.C. Brummel, Dept. of Geography, Lakehead University, Thunder Bay

Pamela Bryant, Bureau of Municipal Research, Toronto

John Burkus, Policy Program Development Secretariat, Ontario Ministry of Housing

John Carline, City of Toronto Planning Board

Peter Cave, Social Sciences, University of Toronto (Scarborough)

J.H. Chung, Université du Québec à Montréal

Frank Clayton, Clayton Research Associates, Scarborough, Ontario

Denise Coderre, University of Guelph

Diana Collins, City of Toronto Housing Department

Eli Comay, Environmental Studies, York University

Barry Crump, Centre for Urban and Community Studies, University of Toronto

Barry Cullingworth, Urban and Regional Planning, University of Toronto

Gordon Davies, Dept. of Economics, University of Western Ontario, London

Michael Dear, Dept. of Geography, McMaster University, Hamilton

Michael Denny, Institute for Policy Analysis, University of Toronto

Gérard Divay, INRS – Urbanisation, Montréal

George Fallis, Division of Social Science, York University

Susan Fish, Alderman, City of Toronto

Douglas Flowers, Urban and Regional Planning, University of Waterloo

Suzanne Fraser, Dept. of Geography, Simon Fraser University, Burnaby, B.C.

Len Gertler, Urban and Regional Planning, University of Waterloo

Stephen Glogowski, Cadillac Fairview Corporation, Toronto

Michael Goldberg, Faculty of Commerce and Business Administration, University
    of British Columbia
Anne Golden, Bureau of Municipal Research, Toronto
Jacob Goldschmidt, Ontario Ministry of Housing
William Grigsby, Dept. of City Planning, University of Pennsylvania
Patricia Gunning, Urban Development Institute, Don Mills
Tom Gunton, Urban and Regional Planning, University of British Columbia
Karen Hansen, University of Guelph
Elizabeth Hay, Central Mortgage and Housing Corporation, Ottawa
John Hitchcock, Urban and Regional Planning, University of Toronto
David Hulchanski, Urban and Regional Planning, University of Toronto
Jay Jones, Dept. of Economics, University of Western Ontario, London
S.F. Kassam, Ontario Ministry of Housing
David Kennedy, Ontario Welfare Council, Toronto
Leslie King, McMaster University, Hamilton
Judith Kjellberg, Centre for Urban and Community Studies University of Toronto
Morry Koperwas, Ontario Ministry of Housing
Larry Kurtz, Dept. of Political Economy, University of Toronto
Vernon Lang, Canadian Council on Urban and Regional Research, Ottawa
P.T. Laverty, Ontario Ministry of Housing
Diane Lees, University of Guelph
James Lemon, Dept. of Geography, University of Toronto
Linda LeSueur, Urban and Regional Planning, University of Toronto
Larry Martin, Urban and Regional Planning, University of Waterloo
Georg Mathews, INRS — Urbanisation, Montreal
Mary Matusoff, University of Toronto
Ann McAfee, City of Vancouver Planning Department
Stuart McFadyen, Dept. of Commerce and Business Administration, University
    of Alberta
Steve McGill, Dept. of Geography, University of Toronto
Christine McKee, Institute of Urban Studies, University of Winnipeg
John Mercer, Dept. of Geography, University of British Columbia
William Michelson, Dept. of Sociology, University of Toronto
Simon Miles, Centre for Urban and Community Studies, University of Toronto
Beth Milroy, Community and Regional Planning, University of British Columbia
John Miron, Social Sciences, University of Toronto (Scarborough)
Eric Moore, Dept. of Geography, Queen's University, Kingston
Peter Moore, Dept. of Geography, University of Toronto
Philip Morrison, Dept. of Geography, University of Toronto
Robert Murdie, Dept. of Geography, York University

Alex Murray, Environmental Studies, York University
G.A. Nader, Dept. of Geography, Trent University, Peterborough
Edwin Neave, School of Business, Queen's University, Kingston
David Nowlan, Dept. of Political Economy, University of Toronto
Larry Ozanne, Urban Institute, Washington, D.C.
George Papageorgiou, Dept. of Geography, McMaster University, Hamilton
Jeffrey Patterson, Social Planning Council of Metropolitan Toronto
Richard Peddie, Central Mortgage and Housing Corporation, Ottawa
Peter Penz, Environmental Studies, York University
J.V. Poapst, Faculty of Management Studies, University of Toronto
John Quigley, Institute for Social and Policy Studies, Yale University
Gerald Romsa, Dept. of Geography, University of Windsor
Rizwan Rana, Ontario Ministry of Housing
John Riffel, York University
Albert Rose, Faculty of Social Work, University of Toronto
Jeremy Rudin, Centre for Urban and Community Studies, University of Toronto
Eva Samery, Urban Planning, Ryerson Polytechnical Institute, Toronto
Barbara Sanford, Urban and Regional Planning, University of Toronto
David Scheffman, Dept. of Economics, University of Western Ontario, London
Jack Scheu, Central Mortgage and Housing Corporation, Ottawa
Nalla Senathirajah, Metropolitan Toronto Social Services Department
Christopher Sharpe, Dept. of Geography, Memorial University, St. John's
Adrian Shaw, Dept. of Geography, University of Toronto
Warner Shippee, Center for Urban and Regional Affairs, University of Minnesota
James Simmons, Dept. of Geography, University of Toronto
Joan Simon, Dept. of Consumer Studies, University of Guelph
Mary Lynne Simpson, Dept. of Consumer Studies, University of Guelph
Ray Simpson, Peter Barnard Associates, Toronto
Larry Smith, Dept. of Political Economy, University of Toronto
Godfrey Spragge, Queen's University, Kingston
Peter Spurr, Central Mortgage and Housing Corporation, Ottawa
Edward Starr, Region of Peel Housing Task Force, Bramalea, Ontario
Rudolph Stocking, Ontario Ministry of Housing
Ray Struyk, Dept. of Housing and Urban Development, Washington, D.C.
Jeffrey Stutz, City of Toronto Housing Department
Beverly Thompson, Centre for Urban and Community Studies University of Toronto
Peter Tomlinson, City of Toronto Planning Board
Keith Ward, City of Toronto Housing Department
Robert Warne, Central Mortgage and Housing Corporation, Ottawa
Barry Wellman, Dept. of Sociology, University of Toronto

334

Michael Wheeler, School of Social Work, McMaster University, Hamilton
Marilyn Whitaker, Central Mortgage and Housing Corporation, Ottawa
Rodney White, Dept. of Geography, University of Toronto
Katherine Willson, Dept. of Geography, University of Toronto
Jeanne Wolfe, School of Urban Planning, McGill University, Montreal
Elizabeth Wong, Urban and Regional Planning, University of Toronto
Fred Wyers, Metropolitan Toronto Planning Department